Louisa May Alcott

Also by Martha Saxton

Jayne Mansfield and the American Fifties

Louisa May Alcott

A Modern Biography

Martha Saxton

Illustrated with photographs

The Noonday Press

Farrar, Straus and Giroux

New York

LIBRARY OF CONGRESS CATALOGING-IN-PUBLICATION DATA
Saxton, Martha.
[Louisa May]
Louisa May Alcott: a modern biography / Martha Saxton.
p.   cm.
Originally published: Louisa May. Boston: Houghton Mifflin, 1977.
Includes bibliographical references and index.
1. Alcott, Louisa May, 1832–1888—Biography. 2. Women authors,
American—19th century—Biography.   I. Title.
PS1018.S2   1995
813′.4—dc20   [B]
95–13114   CIP

To my father, Mark Saxton,

with my love

Contents

INTRODUCTION   xi

1. *Little Women*   1
2. The Lovers   18
3. A Victorian Courtship   35
4. Boston and Bronson   50
5. A New England Marriage   63
6. The Temple School   81
7. Eccentric Circles   101
8. Concordia   114
9. Fruitlands   134
10. Hillside   153
11. Midcentury   172
12. Beth   202
13. "Love and Self-Love"   218
14. *Hospital Sketches*   251
15. *Moods*   269
16. Europe and *Little Women*   285
17. *Work*   301
18. Abba   326
19. Duty's Faithful Child   345
20. Father and Daughter   363

Contents

ACKNOWLEDGMENTS AND
A NOTE ON SOURCES   381

NOTES   383

BIBLIOGRAPHY   407

INDEX   417

Illustrations

following page 208

Louisa May Alcott
Boston, 1841, from Dorchester
The Water Celebration on Boston Common, 1848
Amos Bronson Alcott
Louisa May Alcott
The young Theodore Parker
Henry David Thoreau, 1856
Ralph Waldo Emerson
Emerson's house, Concord, Massachusetts
Center of Concord, Massachusetts, about 1865
Orchard House, Concord
Bronson Alcott's Sketch of Hillside, 1845
Abigail May Alcott
Amos Bronson Alcott
John Brown
Nathaniel Hawthorne, 1841, oil by Charles Osgood
Thomas Carlyle
Sophia Peabody Hawthorne
Henry James, Sr.
Margaret Fuller
Jones Very
Colonel Joseph May
William Lloyd Garrison

Introduction

LOUISA MAY ALCOTT's work continues to wield its gentle power over our imaginations. *Little Women*'s presence on the *New York Times* best-seller list at this writing testifies to the lively engagement between Alcott's ongoing influence and charm and our ongoing hunger for identity and moral direction. Her plain story of the adolescence of four girls, but particularly the trials of Jo, the strong-willed writer who battles temper and unwonted outbreaks of self-assertion to become acceptably female, resounds still. This story goes on speaking to many American girls who discover in adolescence that this continues to be, after all, a man's world, a place in which girls are expected to shape themselves and their desires to fit molds not of their own making: to confront what Carol Gilligan has called the "wall of western culture." In adjusting to the abrupt shock of that encounter, readers find coherence and reassurance in the March girls' lives, in Marmee's loving encouragement of her daughters, the efficacy and humanity of her discipline, the clarity of her view of right and wrong, the salubrious effects of hard work, and, above all, the unquestioned value of female self-sacrifice and self-suppression.

As a new feminist reevaluating old icons in the 1970s, I found that the most compelling aspect of Alcott's life was the disjuncture between *Little Women* and the real events from which she drew her tale. *Louisa May Alcott* explores the wasteland between what the novel had led me to expect from the author's experience and what it really had been. I came to believe (and still do) that Alcott wrote *Little Women* for her parents, obeying the expressed wishes of her father by writing a tale which would provide moral lessons for children, and the unexpressed wishes of her mother in making her the heroine of a story which, in reality, had been both complex and painful. The book represents an artistic and emotional retreat from the morally and emotionally slippery world of adult fiction with which Alcott had experimented. So powerful were her needs to do her parents' bidding that even today the story, pervaded as it is by her nostalgia for an illusory past, remains fluent, convincing, and seductive. In writing *Little Women* she transmuted the pain of rejection, emotional diminution, and correction into a wise acceptance of the existing order. Jo achieved contentment in coming to share in her parents' moral identity. The story's cheer and charm obscure the truth that Alcott did not tame herself without great cost, nor did she adjust to feminized selflessness so gracefully. The uplifting picture Alcott paints of her own evolution tells us about the ways that many women must consent to reproduce both themselves and the social values by which they were raised.

In her childhood, Alcott had derived much pleasure from writing lusty dramas for her sisters to produce, but as she grew, her freedom to create diminished. When trying to establish herself as a fiction writer in the mid-nineteenth century, she found her ambition thwarted by a deep sensitivity to criticism and an alacrity to abandon the risks of an adult voice for the artistically safer tones of a moralistic older sister. Self-doubt contributed to the unexpected and, to her, somewhat unwelcome direction her creative life took. Not only did she realize her greatest success with children's books, which she did not respect, but she also had to relinquish the secret enjoyment she had once felt in writing, under a pseudonym, unabashedly melodramatic stories of revenge, deceit, disguise, and drugs, tales akin to those she had composed as a girl dramatist. In *Little Women*, the vigilant Professor Bhaer dissuades Jo from pursuing this clandestine vice as an adult, and she must learn to renounce it before marrying him. In real life, the tremendous success of *Little Women* relieved Alcott of financial worries while establishing her as a children's exemplar, a role which required some prudent sacrifices to maintain. The degree to which she found the success of *Little Women* and its sequels burdensome may have had something to do with the associated loss of an old, reliable source of erotic and aesthetic pleasure in writing.

The moral world to which Alcott was indentured growing up seemed a uniquely punishing one to me as I was rediscovering it in writing this book. It appeared, as the nineteenth century does in so many ways, simultaneously foreign and all too familiar. More than a century could not diminish the moment-by-moment intensity of life in a morally wakeful family, self-consciously engaged in turning out submissive, self-denying females. Nor could it balance the grotesquely disproportionate shares of liberty allotted to antebellum males and females according to gender and race. It seemed to me an urgent task to bring these experiences and disparities into focus, and what better lens for doing so than the most important moral primer for growing girls in the last two centuries? Framing her novel within the real picture of Louisa's life seemed a way to post caution signs around *Little Women*, a way to suggest that the journey Jo had made was far more problematic than it seemed; that Jo's task was to dwarf herself cheerfully; that this was a book written for the guards, not the inmates. *Little Women*, when read against Alcott's real life, as I believe it should be, comes across as the story of a young female learning to accept the loss of her voice, learning to drive her thoughts, wishes, and sexuality underground.

Louisa May Alcott was animated and inspired by the anger I shared with many other women, that the lessons we had learned about growing up female, including the lessons of submission, inferiority, repression, and self-deformation, had not changed so dramatically in the century since *Little Women* was published. I wrote the book at a particularly confident and combative moment in women's history, when outrage at the discovery and revelation of oppression was still fresh and appeared transformative. Now many years have passed; the focus of women's history has shifted. Meanwhile, feminist thinking has grown more sophisticated, investigating the interplay of gender-related behavior and thought with politics, breaking literary codes to explore and question notions of self and sexuality. Ambiguity and nuance are edging out blame and outrage. In the current intellectual atmosphere, my biography strikes me as youthful, highly partisan and brash; yet *Louisa May Alcott* still provides a context for reading

Little Women, whose renewed popularity just now—in the era of "family values"—has a sinister side. To read Alcott's story without caution—to read it as an inspiring depiction of reality, historical or contemporary, is dangerous, but to read it in the context of her embattled, even heroic, life can be a reminder of our unfinished struggle to make womanhood a bit less little.

MARTHA SAXTON
New York City, 1995

Louisa May Alcott

1

Little Women

LOUISA MAY ALCOTT WAS THIRTY-FIVE in the spring of 1868 when she began work on *Little Women*. She was tall and broad-shouldered, with dark eyes and dark hair thinned and grayed by disease. She looked older than her age. She had never had much of a childhood and her young womanhood had been truncated by illness. She was suffering from the degenerative effects of mercury poisoning caused by massive doses of calomel, which she had received as an army nurse during the Civil War. Since the war she had been troubled with increasingly painful aches in her arms and legs. Often she would stand up from her writing table and walk around, trying to stretch the discomfort from her limbs.

She was a pale, serious woman with strong features and deep-set eyes, and she always dressed in black or dark brown. If a draft came through the walls of the old frame house Louisa would throw a shawl over her shoulders. She worked steadily over her desk, turning out a chapter of neat backhand every day. She bore down hard, holding a steel pen tightly. Later, when her right hand became too cramped from overuse, she would learn to write with both hands.

Louisa had returned to the family's Orchard House in Concord, Massachusetts. It was a three-story clapboard home with a gabled roof and a center dormer above the arched entrance. The main house was rectangular, with a kitchen and studio growing out from the back. From her window upstairs, Louisa could see the green yard sloping down to the main road below. Behind the house, the yard continued its climb, terminating in a stand of locusts, maples, and oaks a hundred yards up the hill. Adjacent to the house stood a two-story barn where Louisa and her sisters had produced plays not so many years before.

Louisa's corner room was a light and airy square with windows on two sides. The wide plank floors of the low-ceilinged chamber were covered with oval braided rugs, and on the mantel stood pictures of the family. Hanging on the walls were black panels on which Louisa's youngest sister, May, had painted stylized birds and flowers in extravagant colors. Louisa's small writing table was under the front windows, where the soft spring light filtered into the room through the trees outside.

May occupied the downstairs studio near the kitchen, which the girls' father had built to catch the light for his artist daughter. At twenty-five, May was a strong blonde woman with blue eyes and a noticeable chin. She wasn't pretty, but her manner was so agreeable that she was more attractive than her handsomer older sister. And unlike Louisa, she trusted and enjoyed people. May worked in charcoal, ink, and oils. She sketched nature and portraits. Her real skill as a still-life painter and copyist didn't emerge for some years. In the meantime, her work had a freshness and energy that kept it from being merely sentimental.

Downstairs, in the front parlor, directly beneath Louisa's room, sat Louisa's mother, Abigail May "Abba" Alcott, or "Marmee." Abba had been an energetic woman, but at sixty-seven she was glad to let her daughter take on the burden of supporting the family. She sat on the horsehair sofa, working on her sewing or writing in her journals, straining her already weak eyes. Abba was the descendant of an aristocratic Boston family. She had always been proud of her forebears, but age and inactivity had made them something of an obsession with her. Her favorite story concerned Lafayette's visit to Boston in 1820 and her Aunt Dorothy Sewall Quincy's meeting with him at a ball in his honor. Abba ruminated on past glories of the May family in the homey room, furnished with some plain wooden tables, a small spinet, and decorated with May's work.

Louisa's father, Bronson Alcott, had his study across the hall. The room was lined with books. The light came from the front windows and a green-shaded brass student lamp that sat on his table in the center of the room. The pine floor was painted green and covered with braided rugs. Bronson, whose tastes were classical, had created archways from doorways and pillars from beams. He set busts in alcoves in the parlor and study. Deeply influenced by Plato and Pythagoras, he dealt in ideals and symbols more readily than in realities. The touches he added to Orchard House reflected his effort to lead an exemplary rather than an exigent life.

At sixty-eight, Bronson was a tall, thin man with shoulder-length silver hair, a high forehead, and blue eyes. He spoke softly and never raised his voice. His demeanor was calm and his words plenteous. In the winter he wore black and in the summer white and also affected a silver-tipped cane. He ate no meat.

Bronson had not earned money regularly since 1839, when his experimental school in Boston failed. Since then he had been writing in his journals, holding "conversations" on transcendental topics for interested auditors, and waiting for the world to accept his progressive ideas on education. He led a life that included no compromises with the venal world. Consequently, he turned to his wife and daughters for his support. The difficulties among the Alcotts stemmed from the chafing between Bronson's ideals and daily realities.

Louisa was reluctant to write the book that was to bring her so much fame and money. The project was something of an assignment. For years her father had discussed the need for plain stories for boys and girls about childish victories over selfishness and anger. And Louisa's publisher wanted a "girl's book." Louisa didn't have much respect for the genre but was willing to write anything to earn money, so she took the opportunity to try something her father had so long recommended.

Louisa had always used writing to get away from herself and her unhappiness, but *Little Women* forced her to relive the most difficult years of her life. Instead of a retreat into a heady, imaginary world, Louisa sat day after day, re-creating her past into shapes and pictures of what it should have been. She summoned up her adolescence and put it into an ethical order. *Little Women* was a demanding job, requiring hard work and regular hours. It didn't tap that part of Louisa's mind where fantasy generated exhilaration and optimism, sending her into a temporary euphoria. It was only rarely a labor of love.

* * *

Little Women, the story of Meg, Jo, Beth, and Amy March, has a place in American culture along with taffy pulling and Flag Day. It's nearly un-American not to have read this monument to family life. Four girls grow up under their mother's loving tutelage to become what their father wants them to be: "little women." On their way to achieving complete diminution, they struggle with selfishness, greed, vanity, and temper.

Louisa's publisher, Little, Brown and Company, lost its records at the turn of the century and cannot estimate the number of copies of *Little Women* in existence, but in 1929, for example, three million books were sold. There have been plays, movies, condensations, and countless translations. The popularity of the novel is an enduring phenomenon. Boys as well as girls respond to Jo's (or Louisa's) struggle to be good. She personifies the battle to channel raw energy into acceptable conduits. Girls find in Jo their own fight to repress their aggressive, humorous, spontaneous instincts and turn them into ladylike submission. No one wants to be Meg, old and placid before her time, or Beth, too good to live, or selfish and vain Amy. But Jo is tender and loving, brusque and abrupt, awkward and poignant. Everything she does is understandable, forgivable, and touching, and it is with regret that we see her leave her childish frankness behind her.

Little Women seduces everyone who wants to believe in a sensible universe. Louisa's world works with clocklike moral regularity. Every sorrow and act of abnegation brings an unexpected reward in love and self-esteem. In the terms of Louisa's father's best friend and her adolescent idol, Ralph Waldo Emerson, Jo is compensated for every disappointment by spiritual growth. Jo's development is a sweetly sentimental version of the journey everyone has expected to make. She leads us through the traps of selfishness, temptation, and anger and comes out the other end wiser and rewarded for her sufferings. Seemingly intractable Jo learns to be the ideal woman: patient, forgiving, soothing, undemanding, unselfish, and uncapricious.

Jo's mother, Marmee, is the mother everyone needs: selfless, available, with no life of her own beyond her family. She is the woman Jo tries to be. She is deeply sympathetic and strong, and her aims for her girls are, finally, always in concert with their own. She is the model mother, patient and loving, who has learned to derive her satisfactions solely from the satisfactions of others. She has no conflicts or desires of her own to separate her from her family. And Jo is on her way to achieving her mother's perfection.

Little Women provides a vision of the struggle to achieve ideal womanliness, with its rewards of moral satisfaction, cessation of interior discord, and the discovery of a species of Zen peace in self-sacrifice. It details a girl's conflicts with her family on the road to transcendent integration. Just as Louisa's father regarded *The Pilgrim's Progress* as a guide to personal contentment, so *Little Women* became a handbook for girls desiring wisdom about becoming good women. It defines the dream of American family life.

Meg, the oldest sister, battles to subdue her desire for finery. Otherwise, she is almost passive and expressionless enough to qualify for little womanhood. Her reward is the penniless but honorable John Brooke, a man quite as boring as herself.

Beth, the third sister, was born the littlest woman of them all. She is patient, undemanding, quiet, docile, timid, and unassuming. She doesn't even assume her life for very long. She teaches the lesson of self-sacrifice, demonstrating how the quintessential little woman fades away behind other people's needs and desires until, in a display of ultimate good manners, she disappears forever. Beth dies of a wasting disease, so popular with sentimental Victorians.

The youngest, Amy, is a sunny girl, too self-centered for the author's complete approval, lacking a taste for self-denial. Her femininity is defined by her graceful manners and pretty appearance. Louisa is never entirely comfortable with Amy's moral progress and tries to make the case that Amy grows to womanliness through good luck and happiness.

In contrast Jo, Louisa's alter ego, has an impossible time becoming a little woman. Jo's growth is lengthy and uncertain. Like Christiana in *The Pilgrim's Progress,* on whose passage Louisa modeled Jo's journey, she seems to take as many steps backward as forward. She is a lively girl whose aggressive "male" characteristics give her dimension and charm. But she must overcome her temper and her active, impulsive nature. These are the qualities that she must wrestle to the mat if she is to become a little woman.

Little Women has four values, good and bad, male and female. Good and bad differ for each sex, which is the source of Jo's confusion. Louisa needed to stamp out the ambiguity this circumstance engendered, and gave the book a highly rigid ethic.

Jo March, blunt, energetic, and ambitious, full of a desire to do rather than be done for, must tame herself not to be "rough and wild; but do my duty here instead of wanting to be somewhere else . . ." Jo discusses her temper problems with her mother, who, to Jo's astonishment, tells her, "I am angry nearly every day of my life, Jo; but I have learned not to show it; and I still hope to learn not to feel it, though it may take me another forty years to do so." Her husband, she explains, has helped her control herself all these years: "He never loses patience, — never doubts or complains, — but always hopes, and works and waits so cheerfully that one is ashamed to do otherwise before him." This lesson teaches Jo "not only the bitterness of remorse and despair, but the sweetness of self-denial and self-control . . ." For Jo, the idea of controlling her anger is a harder task than "facing a rebel or two down South."

Louisa wrote about her anger in a vocabulary sufficiently mild that it seemed as if she were discussing a quick, sparking temper that flared up and went out. Instead, she suffered from a sullen, vaporous rage that smoked from a pit of disappointment, long-cherished grievances, sorrow, and loneliness. The anger carried with it tremendous guilt and frequently was inverted into depression. It was a defensive arrangement that prevented Louisa from looking to its causes. The anger remained in place, the guilty center of her life. So Louisa examined surfaces: jealousies, fears, and frivolities. She didn't pose psychological questions or look for causes. She needed a cosmic legality, just as a child wants things to be "fair." *Little Women*'s great appeal is this tidy justice. Every good action is etched in gold leaf and hung in the museum of God's memory. Every bad action requires expiation and repentence and will, if faced, understood, and absorbed, lead to future good.

* * *

It is ironic that Bronson Alcott, whom Louisa could so little understand that he barely appears in *Little Women*, should have set the terms for the book. It was the father who wanted his girls to be "little women." It was her father who wanted Louisa to write what became her most popular book. It was also her father who never liked Louisa, who found her too aggressive, willful, and fierce for his definition of feminine. Bronson kept Louisa at a critical distance from him throughout her life. He was never comfortable with her expressive temperament. He and Louisa did years of battle over what kind of girl she should be. He let her know that he desired a variety different from what she was. She couldn't repress her whole spirit, but she absorbed enough criticism to become depressed and sullen. She was divided between the impulsive, outgoing, opinionated, large-spirited woman she was meant to be and the withdrawn, hostile introvert who kept that vital woman locked up.

The strenuous Victorian distinctions between boy and girl forced Louisa to wish to change sexes so she could run free and raise her voice. Bronson further complicated Louisa's problems by demonstrating all the "feminine" virtues himself. Being passive came naturally to him, just as activity and anxiety came naturally to Louisa and her mother. Bronson, with his wife's concurrence, considered himself a saint. He was a constitutionally cold man who displayed little or no temper. He seemed to have achieved a female docility, and Louisa, born to the gender, couldn't match it. There were no two ways in the Alcott home. Bronson was good and therefore right. Louisa's models were reversed. She was like her mother, and that was unacceptable to both her parents and society.

It seems, from exaggerated nineteenth-century sex definitions, that Victorians were afraid men and women might not be able to distinguish gender. So women were trussed, corseted, and bustled into immobility while men posed in musclebound attitudes of emotionless strength. This suppression of tenderness, warmth, and most expressions of feeling produced the male equivalent of the vapors. Louisa's teacher and secret love, Henry David Thoreau, decamped to Walden Pond rather than confront social demands that he be conventionally "male." Louisa's father's friend Ralph Waldo Emerson retired into his study and ruminated on his female nature. Bronson Alcott renounced his role as provider, allowing his wife to perform that male function. So Louisa was familiar with people who crossed the sex barriers, but for women the tariff was very high.

Abba suffered interminably both in health and spirits. She felt obliged to think and do like a man while behaving "feminine."

Abba's struggles with Bronson and life were too great for her to bear alone, so she shared them with Louisa. The depressed, overwrought mother poured her bitterness, grief, and disappointment into her daughter. Abba, a passionate, intense woman, needed her girl desperately. This need, so valuable to Louisa, grew to be a burden, as attached to it were obligations, demands, and restrictions that kept Louisa in chains all her life.

Out of this complex of emotions and roles, Louisa learned to fear and distrust men. She needed warmth and found it in women, but it frightened her and she expected to be trapped as she had been with her mother. So she alternately approached and retreated. It was this struggle to stabilize, to balance her needs and fears and to subdue her guilt and anger, that motivated her to transform her experience into prose. *Little Women* derives its vitality from Louisa's efforts to dominate her indomitable self. She tries to make Jo into Beth, willing, submissive, and dutiful.

Even the act of writing *Little Women* was Louisa's attempt to transform herself. *Moods,* her first novel, had been a stormy, triangular love story based on her long-term, secret infatuation with Henry Thoreau. It was a story from the heart, lingering over passionate possibilities and displaying Louisa's desire for an absorbing, erotic love. The book was indifferently concluded but had genuine life and promised more mature work to come. Louisa had intelligent, romantic, and piquant ideas about the relations between men and women, but she grew frightened of pursuing them. The book's mixed reception caused her great anguish, and she took the opportunity of *Little Women* to denounce *Moods* and blame its failure on her efforts to please her family and publisher.

In writing *Moods* and her pseudonymous gothics, Louisa fell into what she called a "vortex." It was her term for indulging in writing as if it were a carnal act. She would lock herself up for days at a time and give herself over to her vice. She lived with her characters, losing consciousness of the real world. These periods of prolonged mania were food, love, and sex to her. They provided her with oblivion: an absence of fear, worry, tension, and, best of all, neither guilt nor anger. This intense, violent productivity was fueled by the energies of repressed sexuality, loneliness, rage, and a great craving for love and attention. She felt unified and could stop watching herself. Work was an acceptable passion, a receptacle for her fantasies and desires. She literally emptied herself into her books.

In writing *Little Women* Louisa abandoned the vortex. To the extent that she had renounced her dreams of love, she found her work on *Little Women* unexciting. She worked steadily but with none of the joy and manic abandon she had derived from her earlier material. The voice in which she wrote was that of her parents and Mr. Emerson.

The book outlines the adolescence of American morality. It has an ethical structure with no gray areas, no grown-up dilemmas, no confusions, no sensuality or ambiguity. It parallels Charles Dickens's universe, in which everyone is a caricature of some virtue or vice. The possibilities of such a world are only comic or tragic, good or bad.

Little Women was a regression for Louisa as an artist and a woman. She had abandoned the struggle for multifaceted truth and replaced it with a programmatic morality. Instead of considering carefully the possibilities of character, she stuffed people and circumstances into Emerson's framework, in which every event and action has a meaning, and from all evil come lessons of goodness. Louisa made her childhood into a pilgrim's progress, with each trial and sacrifice leading her toward the Celestial City. Presumably, each time Jo was rebuffed, she learned something more about herself and became better. The lesson to be learned was acceptance, cessation of conflict, relinquishment of will.

At thirty-five Louisa was a chastened, ill woman, ready to make her peace with the forces that she had fought all her life. She had been through a near-fatal illness, had seen one sister die and another marry. Her experiences during the Civil War had been brief but traumatic, bringing her in intimate contact with ghastly suffering and her own deep fear of men. She hungered to come to some kind of terms with her past, to lay to rest the devils of guilt that leaped out at her from behind all her memories. She tried to add meaning to every pain she had felt. She tried to confess her worst faults and find forgiveness. She tried to write her anger away.

For even at thirty-five her childhood and adolescent feelings still dominated her emotional life. Instead of expanding her existence, adding new experiences and relations, she burrowed deeper into her world of obligations, taking on new family burdens, giving herself tighter restrictions. Similarly, she limited her imagination, retreating into her past, refusing to consider emotional problems broader than whether a woman should indulge in an occasional vanity. She was intent on rearranging the pieces of her history until a just pattern emerged.

Louisa reverted to an adolescent morality after experiencing and rejecting new and complicated involvements. The criticism she garnered for her efforts to write adult fiction, the uncertainty of her grasp of grownup emotional concerns and conflicts and her willingness to believe negative assessments of her work facilitated her turn away from ambiguity and toward simplicity. With *Little Women*, she gave up the tiring effort to hold conflicting ideas at the same time. She wanted everything to fall into moral pleats: good, bad, good, bad. She had to find a meaning in the death of her sister, in her own miserable and lonely girlhood, in her permanently damaged health, in her spinsterhood. She had to understand her inability to fit the Victorian definition of woman as her fault.

Louisa no longer had the strength to be defiant. Her struggle was to learn to stop struggling, not to add another guilty fight to her willful history. She had to accept that her sister Anna, or "Meg," was her parents' favorite, that she deserved her husband and two children. She must accept the fact that May (Amy) got everything she wanted simply by asking. Louisa's faults must be greater than her sisters' or she, too, would be happy.

Little Women is the story of the childhood Louisa would have had if her parents had described it. She wrote the book to sanctify them, since she couldn't blame them. She gracefully lets them off the hook for everything she suffered. In the case of Beth's death — which resulted from Abba's relentless philanthropy, for she brought home an infection from a poor family — Louisa gives Jo the responsibility for carrying disease to her sister. The guilt in Louisa's world was undifferentiated. She accepted responsibility for everything in an effort to pay for sins she had never understood.

Louisa recast her adolescent troubles with sexuality as a struggle with vanity. When Jo's father becomes ill in Washington, Jo, in a moment redolent with significance, steps in to take his place. She has her hair cut off to pay for her mother's trip to the capital. Cropped and boyish, Jo sacrifices her femininity to her duty. Her mother wails with a distinct lack of tact, "Your one beauty," but Jo counters by remarking that "I was getting too proud of my wig." Like Louisa, Jo knows nothing of moderation or compromise, and therein lie both her charm and her downfall. To be female is to sacrifice, but, ironically, for Louisa/Jo the sacrifice is so great that it is no longer a passive giving up but an active, male assertion.

Jo makes friends with a neighbor, Laurie, a charming, high-spirited, attractive youth who grows to love Jo. They get into trouble together, sharing pranks and good times. Laurie goes away to college and comes home wanting Jo to marry him. She refuses, thinking they are too much alike, too male. The fact that they enjoy each other and share interests and honesty argues against Jo's decision. But Louisa declares inexorably that Jo must not have fun. Instead, and with characteristic perversity, she gives Laurie to Amy, Jo's youngest sister. She always resented Amy for getting everything, and engineers it so that she has the only male prize in the book. For Amy is sweet, hypocritical, and manipulative — in short, female.

Between the publication of Volume 1, in which Jo and Laurie are close friends, and Volume 2, in which Laurie and Amy marry, Louisa's readers wrote, hoping to see Jo and Laurie wed. Bronson on his conversation tours spoke of his disappointment with Jo's thwarted romance. But Louisa insisted on punishing the fictional Louisa. Feeling caught in the clutches of her life, not in control of it, she struck out at circumstances, usually hurting only herself. Since she had built her identity on doing what others expected of her, her only power, she felt, was in reversing the process. So she behaved spitefully toward both her literary self and her readers.

Instead of Laurie, Jo gets a big, middle-aged German professor for a husband. Professor Bhaer is a man indistinguishable in temperament and philosophy from Bronson. He provides moralisms and control, telling Jo to stop writing lurid stories. The professor is sufficiently old so that Jo's interest in him cannot be construed as sexual. Louisa offers him as a sop to her readers, for her preference was to leave Jo single. Her guilt and depression made her unable to contemplate intimacy for either herself or Jo.

Love appeared to Louisa like a painful, dangerous trap into

which her mother had dragged her and from which she had never quite escaped. Her love for Laurie was real, based on comradeship. It would become hurtful, she reasoned, the moment sexuality was introduced. Jo and Laurie are two asexual adolescents and feel comfortable in this relation. The minute Laurie wants to intrude male-female definitions, Jo must run away. The demands of romance and sexuality make friendship impossible, partly because they stir up primitive fears of the prison that intimacy implies, and partly because they make relations between men and women stylized and unnatural. Jo cannot convert her love for Laurie into a stable association. She suddenly panics, feeling that she cannot control the exhausting and insatiable demands that love connotes to her, nor can she avoid the depths of anger, guilt, and misery that her redoubled attempts at passivity will prompt. So Louisa gives Jo a husband who will stay separate, cool, and detached, an older philosopher like Bronson, who will leave her hotter feelings untouched.

One of the misleading aspects of *Little Women* is that many emotions get transformed into pathos. Louisa had referred to the Alcotts as "the pathetic family" since adolescence, prefiguring their sentimental aspect in *Little Women*. Rather than look too closely at the dynamics of their relations, she chose to feel sorry for all of them. It was a trick she had learned from her mother, who supplied pathos wherever she saw a questionable situation. Bronson, for example, was the victim of a cruel and selfish world. The Alcotts were a forlorn, forgotten lot who worked valiantly and without praise for their tiny portion. Abba's constant theme was how sorry she was for her girls and how hard she was working to make them happy. Abba drew Louisa close to her, and the two formed a kind of mutual protection society, each shielding the other from the grief and loss inflicted by the outside world. Louisa stepped easily into her mother's hand-me-down feelings of abuse. She saw herself as the world's victim, with only her heroic mother between herself and oblivion. She came to see the family as an embattled huddle of women hanging on to each other for dear life. Bronson was frequently part of the alien foe. He floats around this configuration sometimes as part of the problem and sometimes as part of the solution. This us-them division dictated all of Louisa's actions. She felt the world to be an ungrateful, unrewarding, and unsafe place. Her only refuge was with her mother.

Louisa sanctifies Abba as "Marmee," the most lovable, understanding character in American literature, sympathetic, responsible, honorable, fun-loving, dear, and warm. Louisa took over whole her mother's vocabulary of emotions and tried to become her whole life-support system to justify her existence. Marmee tells Jo that she is a "great comfort . . . I always feel strong when you are at home . . . when the tug comes you are always ready."

Jo replies, "Why, you know I don't mind hard jobs much, and there must always be one scrub in a family. Amy is splendid in fine works, and I'm not; but I feel in my element when all the carpets are to be taken up, or half the family fall sick at once. Amy is distinguishing herself abroad; but if anything is amiss at home, I'm your man."

Abba, who always needed something — security, love, money, or comfort — was Louisa's personal mission. Louisa tried to satisfy the unhappy woman but grew angry and tired in the effort. Rather than recognize her anger as the cause of her anguish, Louisa canonized the woman and castigated herself for her failure to provide more.

Louisa had more difficulty with her father's hagiography, for Bronson was complicated for his second daughter. "The girls gave their hearts into their mother's keeping, their souls into their father's," wrote Louisa in *Little Women*. He regarded himself, and Abba supported him in this, as the human being most nearly resembling Christ. Abba, whose self-distaste was acquired very early, found compatible Bronson's view of himself as godly. And he confirmed her opinion of her own sinfulness. He referred to his wife and Louisa as his two demons.

Alcott controlled his world by wanting very little. He left voids of activity and feeling for his wife and children to fill. He supplied the guilt for motivation by quiet disapproval. Louisa was completely unsure of herself with her father and could never make sense out of what appeared to be his superhuman self-control. Since he defined quiescence and withdrawal as good, and exertion, expression, and aggression as bad, Louisa could only conclude that he was saintly and she, like her mother, was damned.

In *Little Women*, Louisa puts Bronson in his study and leaves him there. The truth was not much different: "To outsiders, the five energetic women seemed to rule the house, and so they did in many things; but the quiet scholar, sitting among his books, was still the head of the family, the household conscience, anchor, and comforter; for to him the busy, anxious women always turned in troubled times, finding him, in the truest sense of those sacred words, husband and father."

Bronson's distance and disapproval frightened and angered Louisa. As she grew up she came to understand his virtues better and appreciate his tranquility and his dedication to philosophy. But she could never accept and judge him as she did other human beings. In her effort to put her life and family in clear perspective, she had to leave Bronson out of the reckoning except for his definitional contributions. For Bronson set the terms of Louisa's life and her work. Bronson wanted little women, and although he disappears during their endeavors to achieve that state, he has supplied the nomenclature, and it is for him that the women work to remain small.

Louisa's oldest sister Anna is as difficult for her to understand as Bronson. For her sister had her father's calm, undemanding personality. Meg is boring because she is so lifeless. Her virtues are passive ones and her faults no greater than a twinge of greed or self-love. She is a little woman almost before the book begins.

Louisa, who had been taught that her own desires should count for nothing, got along with Anna by managing her. In Anna's dependence, Louisa found the kind of satisfaction she could allow herself. In *Little Women,* Jo's most trying time comes when Meg gets married. Louisa treats the matter as a natural fact of growing up, making sixteen-year-old Jo sad at the loss of her sister. In fact, Louisa was twenty-nine when Anna defected, and her great depression was triggered by the realization that even dependence wasn't an assurance of permanence. Anna found a man on whom to depend, and Louisa was left unneeded and shorn of her belief in her own indispensability.

May, eight years younger than Louisa, was favored by parental neglect. She had missed out on the worst years of poverty and, as the baby, was fussed over more than her sisters. And, by the time she was born, Bronson had lost some of his messianic fervor to make his children models of transcendental perfection.

May had had a childhood without responsibilities, unlike Louisa. Louisa worked for the family, telling herself that her own needs must be sacrificed to the general Alcott good. But May enjoyed herself and believed, quite accurately, that if she didn't fight for herself no one else would. She did not identify herself through her duties toward others. She went after her own pursuits, pestered her parents for drawing lessons that they could ill afford, and studied and painted and drew despite her family's judgment that she had "talent" but not "genius." She learned social graces and made herself agreeable to people. Louisa found these characteristics deeply disturbing.

Louisa disapproved of what she saw as her sister's frivolity and irresponsibility. Her resentment runs deep throughout her journals. Her references to May's good fortune are always juxtaposed against lamentations of her own. She concludes that she must be more degraded than her sister and in need of more trials. But beneath that theme runs a current of anger against the one sister who prevailed in a worldly way. May did what Louisa claimed she wanted to do but couldn't allow herself. She didn't curl up and die like Beth, or retreat into brusque defensiveness like Louisa, or hide herself in a frightened, unexciting marriage like Anna. She stepped into the world and tried to find out what it could do for her. She asked people for things and often got them — art lessons, trips to Europe, flowers, clothes, and a prosperous husband. May baffled Louisa, challenging her vision of the dangers of life beyond the Alcott preserve.

Louisa saw May's expression of her desires as power. In *Little Women* she gives Amy everything. She surrenders to Amy her own first trip to Europe and dwells on Jo's disappointment. In fact, Louisa went to Europe before May and took her sister along only on her second voyage. Louisa gives Amy Jo's lover for a husband. Louisa tried to quell her resentment for her sister by making her a personal charity ward, but the anger remained. She made herself suffer from her own self-inflicted spite, refusing to see that she could have behaved as May did.

Little Women is accessible because of the rigidity of its ethical structure and the limited range of human feeling it encompasses. Louisa lets her characters feel jealousy, anger, admiration, affection, love, and pity. They feel in limited rations, and there are no difficult passions, sexual or otherwise, to confuse things. No one harbors more than one feeling at a time. Louisa stunned complicated emotions into submission and packaged them in easy-to-understand moral lessons.

The popularity of *Little Women,* which articulated the wishes of hundreds of thousands of American girls, astonished Louisa, who had been bored by the labor. Its success convinced her that her father's philosophy and a plain domestic narrative were morally superior to her gothics and *Moods.* She continued to write in the voice she had used to describe the March family saga and turned out sequels populated by batallions of little women.

The book, which had been written as a kind of expiation of her sins toward her parents, grew, ironically, to be Louisa's greatest burden. She discovered that she loathed popularity. She reacted to the public accolade the same way she reacted to any kind of love — she thought it an act of persecution. She considered the wishes of her audience a positive affliction that had to be coped with. She didn't feel she could write what she wished, only what others told her to express. In this spirit she resisted "lionization" with the fervor of one who truly desires attention and can't accept it. She was abrupt and feisty with those who came to admire. She insisted she only wrote for money and doggedly wrote stories she didn't enjoy long after her financial needs were satisfied. She called them "moral pap" and had contempt for her readers. In this, as in the rest of her life, Louisa never did become the little woman her father had ordered.

Little Women is Louisa's summation of her emotional existence. It contains all the material that, using her father's standards, she thought fit and important to reveal about herself. She tried to let nothing remain in her journals and letters that did not conform to Bronson's pastel version of a Victorian girlhood.

By the time Louisa wrote *Little Women* she had stopped growing. Poor health demanded energy that she might have used trying to shake her old, painful habits of feeling. She held on to early patterns with more tenacity after her thirtieth year. *Little Women* marks the first petrifaction of her emotional and moral posture. Its charm lies in the sweetness of the wishful writing. But as the hopes so often and tragically held out remained unfulfilled, they turned to bitterness. This gives her later books their obligatory quality.

Like everyone, Louisa was the product of her experience and heredity. But, unlike everyone, she was unable to become more than that, and couldn't relinquish the events that had affected her. Throughout her life she felt the same feelings and held on to the same pain. *Little Women* represents the fullest and most poignant example of Louisa Alcott's perpetual effort to transform her history.

2

The Lovers

LOUISA'S FATHER, Amos Bronson Alcott, was born on November 29, 1799, in a tiny Connecticut farming community about twenty-five miles north of New Haven. Spindle Hill, in Litchfield County, now part of the town of Wolcott, lies just west of Mad River, which turns there and flows into the Naugatuck. The terrain is hilly, with stony soil. White birch, chestnuts, oaks, and swamp maples grow on the hills dotted with gray rocks.

The center of town, hardly more than a crossroads, was marked by a whipping post last used in 1817, when Bronson was seventeen. Two cow thieves each received seven lashes over which rum was poured, a treatment that was reported to be worse than the whipping.

Bronson was the first child of Joseph and Anna Alcox, whose surname Bronson later refined. His father was a descendant of the first settlers of Wolcott. Shy and melancholy, he was, according to his son, "the most diffident man I have ever known." He ran a self-sustaining farm and supplied his neighbors with tools. Like most eighteenth-century farmers, Alcox was a carpenter, cooper, lumberman, mechanic, and blacksmith. He could tan leather, fashion shoes, and shear sheep. He grew rye and wheat, oats and corn. His orchards produced apples and pears. The vegetable gardens supplied the family with potatoes, beets, cucumbers, pumpkins, squash, tomatoes, parsnips, cabbages, and turnips. Alcox had cows, sheep, swine, and fowl. He worked seven days a week, fourteen hours a day. After a day's labor outdoors, he would eat and nap and begin again. "On winter evenings," his son recalled, "he made boxes and baskets, and never lost a moment."

Alcox commanded his son's respect, but did not invoke much warmth in him. With his mother, on the other hand, a "gentlewoman," Bronson shared a rare closeness. "Her sweet and placid disposition nourished and was the source of the finest qualities of my own, and her sympathies were the best education I knew." Anna Bronson Alcox loved and protected her oldest son, giving him the benefit of her limited education and suggesting to him an alternative to the demanding and harsh life of a farmer. Bronson recalled his mother's two prominent traits as being "benignity and trust." When he was wooing Louisa's mother, he was reminded of his deeply satisfying relation with Anna. "A Mother!" he apostrophized in his journal. "When is woman more like herself like what her Author disposed her to be. I could not love a woman destitute of maternal qualities."

Anna Alcox, who could read and write only a little herself, had put her brother Tillotson through Yale by taking in sewing. She gave Bronson lessons in reading and writing, and the boy practiced on the floor with chalk on washing days. He wrote in the snow and, at his mother's suggestion, began keeping little diaries. He would transcribe dictionary definitions into his journal and practice spelling. He attended the district school for a few months every winter until he was twelve but found that he learned little or nothing there. His spotty education "left me shamefaced, ignorant and awkward; and fair game for city youths and collegians." The school was a flexible institution. The parish members voted each year on the length of the school term and paid according to the number of children they sent. The school itself, which Bronson attended with his cousin William Andrus Alcox, a stuffy little boy a year older than Bronson, who was later to become a doctor and the author of books of advice, was small, cramped, icy in winter, and hot in summer. Students read uncomprehendingly, Alcott recalled, from *Webster's Spelling Book, The American Preceptor,* and the New Testament. The schoolmaster would write "Avoid Alluring company" at the top of a page in his copybook and Bronson would practice his penmanship. So he acquired the rudiments of what was to become his genteel, flowing script, often more ornamental than legible.

At thirteen Bronson went to spend some months with his uncle, the Reverend Tillotson Bronson, who ran the Cheshire Academy. But the boy was homesick "and soon returned to my father, oppressed by the show of learning and the demeanor of the students and the company I there encountered." The next year Bronson and his cousin William went to study with the Pastor John Keys at Wolcott Hill, where they specialized in grammar and composition. They began corresponding with each other to improve their rhetorical skills. Bronson wrote to his cousin:

> Sir:
>
> In commencing the present correspondence our motives, it is believed, are mutually understood; and in its continuance the exercise of candor to each other's opinions, it is hoped, will be scrupulously regarded. We write to benefit each other. Let us then be plain and familiar.

Disregarding utterly his own injunction, Bronson went on to be fussy and formal:

> This period is perspicuous: the collocation and choice of words is judicious, and exhibited to the best advantage. It is distinguished by clearness, unity and strength. The synonyms are properly applied. The style is nervous, and approaches to neatness . . . The remainder of the paragraph is objectionable. The first period is verbose; the ideas might have been expressed in fewer words, and the sentence would have been clearer had the affirmation been direct. The commencement of the third sentence is obscure. "To follow a road" and to "dare the laws," are common, but elliptical and inadequate expressions. The next sentence is harsh, and the turn in the sentence is abrupt. The style is loose and feeble . . .

It's easy to see why neither Bronson nor William ever benefited from this early and confusing scrutiny. Bronson remained all his life a puffy, inexact writer given to pretentious classicisms and the passive voice.

The Reverend Keys, with whom Bronson studied, had been installed by the famous and fiery Reverend Lyman Beecher on September 21, 1814. Beecher had impressed Bronson with his sermon on the decline in piety and the duty of giving children a thorough religious education. Keys was a conscientious preacher and a good scholar but inclined toward a dark and unpopular Calvinism. His congregation deserted him to form an Episcopal society, unusual in Congregational Connecticut. Bronson's uncle, the Reverend Tillotson Bronson, often preached to this society, and they hired occasional ministers for six dollars a sermon. On October 18, 1816, after William and Bronson had been reading prayers at the Episcopal Society for some months, both were confirmed in the Episcopal church in Waterbury, a few miles away.

In the spring of 1814, Alcott had gone to work at the Seth Thomas clock factory in Plymouth, Connecticut, two miles from Spindle Hill. "I was permitted to come home in 1815," Bronson wrote, having been miserable assembling clocks. Farm life didn't make him happy either. Since there was no money for the boy to go to Yale, he left, in 1815, on a short peddling trip to Weston, Massachusetts. He and his cousin Thomas Alcox went from house to house selling small trinkets supplied by a Bristol, Connecticut, merchant. These short peddling trips into Massachusetts and New York made him curious about the United States, and he was anxious to go south. The War of 1812 had opened up a large southern market for northern goods, and the Yankee peddler had emerged as a contender in the American sweepstakes. Bronson's parents wouldn't let him go until he was eighteen, so he spent the intervening months working on his grandfather's farm in Plymouth, a few miles north of Wolcott on the Naugatuck River. In his leisure Bronson began drawing, kept his diaries, and carved himself a violin. He sold the instrument to pay for his first tailor-sewn suit of clothes, made out of his mother's homespun.

Bronson enjoyed indulging a limited and idiosyncratic vanity. He wore clothes to suit his idea of himself. He could be shabby, but he took great pains to be genteel. He was aware of the impression he created and grew to affect a certain musty elegance.

On October 13, 1818 Bronson sailed on the sloop *Three Sisters* from New Haven to Norfolk, Virginia. He set about looking for a teaching position, but finding that "difficult, if not quite ridiculous," he began selling trinkets and almanacs in the area of Norfolk.

Yankee peddling had its beginning in 1740, in Berlin, Connecticut, where the brothers Edward and William Pattison, two Irish tinsmiths, had begun importing sheet tin from which they made pots lighter than iron and cheaper than brass. The Pattisons needed a market for their products, so they hired salesmen and outfitted them with tin trunks full of plates, reflectors, nutmeg graters, and whistles. Each salesman would trail a vine of pots around his neck and go off to sell his materials. The trade grew to include Terry and Seth Thomas's clocks, buttons from the Naugatuck Valley, ivory combs and tableware from Essex, and coffee mills, pins, thimbles, and hooks and eyes from Waterbury and Meriden. The peddlers stocked themselves with whatever they thought they could sell, including sheet music, knives, knitting needles, cookbooks, almanacs, and songsters. "Yankee notions" from roguish Connecticut peddlers had become a staple in the South, and Bronson found the trip entertaining and productive.

Bronson returned home in May of 1819 with an $80 profit and a new suit of clothes, this time tailored in New York from broadcloth. He made quite a snappy reentry into quiet Connecticut life. The dandified outfit made him "a little conspicuous among my mates at the time," who thought he was putting on airs.

Bronson picked up some polish on his southern travels. He found that he liked southern graciousness and the charming manners with which he was greeted. He liked more fat on the bones of life, and Southerners appeared more congenial than the pinched, hard-working, tight-fisted people he was used to. He developed a new set of manners to go with his suit and changed his speech so that it lost its nasal New England flatness.

On his return Bronson donated the $80 to his father, who was building a new house. There were now nine Alcoxes and money was extremely scarce.

In November of 1819, Bronson sailed back to Virginia, this time with his brother Chatfield. The two of them peddled in and around Norfolk until May, when Chatfield returned to Connecticut with $65. Bronson stayed on till July, by which time he had accumulated $100. It was the last profit he made for decades.

Cousin William considered accompanying Bronson to look for teaching jobs in Charleston, South Carolina, in October 1820. The boys had heard that there was yellow fever in Charleston and William debated the trip: "Should the prospect of doing good, improving my mind, and bettering my condition in many other respects, weigh against the danger of disease . . . ?" Despite his worries and the deplorable ethics of peddling ("to sell tin lanterns, worth fifty cents each, for silver, at forty dollars, and tin toddy sticks, worth a New York shilling, for twelve dollars, did not in the final result redound much to our New England credit"), William decided to accompany his cousin. They sailed from New Haven, making the voyage to Charleston in seventeen days.

Failing to find teaching positions, they set off on foot for Columbia, one hundred and twenty miles away. There were still no jobs, so they separated, Bronson proceeding from Columbia to Norfolk, another six hundred miles. In his journal Bronson recorded that he was "dangerously sick from Feb. 16 till March 12, 1821 of typhus fever." He lay unattended in a Norfolk boarding house for many days before William found him. William cared for his cousin and tried to protect him from the gigantic cathartic doses of a local doctor, whose ministrations, William was convinced, greatly prolonged Bronson's illness. During Bronson's convalescence, William heard that his sister and brother-in-law had died of "Connecticut River fever," a variety of typhoid, and he returned home, having found his calling in medicine. Bronson remained, met his cousin Thomas, and stayed on till July.

When Bronson returned to Spindle Hill with yet another suit of clothes and a debt of $270 to a Norfolk merchant, he was dethroned as the favorite Alcox.

It was then that he and his cousin William officially changed Alcox to Alcott. They hoped, according to Alcott's biographer Odell Shepard, to prevent obscene jokes. Along with his new elegant ways, Alcott had also picked up a measure of gentility that was to help him gain entrance into the middle-class circles he desired to join. Although proud of his family's self-sufficiency and their grim virtues, he wanted to separate himself from them, their mean, rural poverty and the coarseness that even their name betrayed.

Bronson tried peddling again in October of 1821. He borrowed a horse, wagon, and money from his father and set off for Virginia with Chatfield and his cousin Thomas. Alcott's self-consciousness had waxed with his majority, and he wrote to his parents:

> Father and mother, how do you think we look? Like two awkward, poor, unpolished, dissipated, homespun, begging, tugging, Yankee peddlers, think you? No, — this is not the case with your sons. By people of breeding and respectability, they are treated with politeness and gentility; and if they are sometimes treated with contempt by the low, vulgar class of the community, it is then not worth minding. For my part, I can make peddling in Virginia as respectable

as any other business. I take much pleasure in travelling, and in conversing with the Virginians, — observing their different habits, manners, customs, etc.; and I am conscious that it is of great advantage to me in many points of view.

Whatever the advantageous points of view, it was a fiscal disaster. In March 1822, Bronson sold everything at a loss and took a two-month job teaching penmanship. That June he walked the five hundred miles to Spindle Hill, arriving with sixpence in his pocket and a debt of $600 to his father. He worked on the farm that summer "assisting him in his agricultural affairs."

Cousin William was worried about Bronson's erratic behavior and profligate ways. In October 1822 he wrote a letter exhorting him to devote himself to some moral occupation. William's advice only galvanized his cousin to organize a final peddling trip to recoup his — or rather, by now, his father's — losses.

When Alcott returned to Connecticut in July 1823, he was still $600 in debt to his father, but he had done some heavy thinking. His travels had taken him to Albemarle Sound in North Carolina, where he had met many Quakers. They had given him George Fox's *Journal,* William Penn's *No Cross, No Crown,* and John Woolman's *Journal* to read. During an illness in May, Bronson had had time to reflect on these books and integrate them with his adolescent favorite, *The Pilgrim's Progress,* a volume he later said kept him out of factories and in philosophy. Alcott began to conceptualize life as a moral progression "from this world to that which is to come." This conceit provided Bronson with a rationale for extracting optimism from the direst circumstances and a method for incorporating tragedy and catastrophe into life, which became for him God's teaching process. This outlook forms the moral superstructure for Louisa's life and work. The Quakers provided a formal structure for some of Alcott's religious and emotional instincts. God, he concluded, he could only experience directly; the only real religious moment occurs in a personal moment with God, and no ritual or observance can substitute for that communication. These Quaker tenets were, of course, subversive in even the most liberal Protestant churches, where ministers accrued power by interpreting dogma, delivering sermons, and making religious policy. For Alcott, no religion ever again was as good as his own.

Alcott began looking for a teaching position in Connecticut. William, the good example, was teaching in Wolcott. Bronson felt comfortable with children. They didn't make him defensive about his social and educational gaps. And he wanted to feel out his exciting new ideas about the divinity of mankind and especially of children. He believed with Wordsworth that they were just arrived from heaven "trailing clouds of glory." He wanted to combat the prevailing theory, as expressed by Jonathan Edwards, who said that children were "young vipers . . . infinitely more hateful than vipers in the sight of God."

It wasn't until November 1825, after several false starts and temporary jobs, that Bronson took over his own school in Cheshire, Connecticut. In describing the students' progress when he allowed them to think for themselves, he also described his own evolution when given the opportunity to work on his own: "I found that whatever children do themselves is theirs; and besides the advancement of intellectual progress, this gives also an increase of intellectual power. Originality, at the same time that it marks the progress, tends to produce strength, and ability to encounter more severe trials."

Bronson began by outfitting his pupils with physical comforts — large desks, chairs, slates, and pictures. He provided a library of more than texts, including, of course, *The Pilgrim's Progress*, Adam Smith, Locke, and Maria Edgeworth's extremely *Moral Tales*. He and his scholars agreed to add some physical exercise to the curriculum.

But Bronson's major, in fact, revolutionary, innovations were theoretical and stemmed from an assumption, which he articulated in 1829, that "infant education . . . is founded on the great principle that every infant is already in possession of the faculties and apparatus required for his instruction, and, that, by a law of his constitution, he uses those to a great extent himself; that the office of instruction is chiefly to facilitate this process, and to accompany the child in his progress, rather than to drive or even lead him . . ."

From this it followed that the teacher "should be, what to the apprehension of the children they ought to become." He should be tolerant, patient, and kind, appealing to the child's conscience, not his fear. The teacher's manner and lessons should be a constant reminder of virtue, and his motive should be to improve and bless.

To effect good behavior, Alcott believed that kindness worked best: "I found that the system which does not cultivate the affections is very imperfect, for no permanent results could be had otherwise. Once gain the affection of children, and they may be led at your inclination; no compulsory measures will be necessary; they will obey, not from fear of punishment, but because it is a pleasure to obey." This stood in stark contrast to the rule of all other schools, where corporal punishment was customary and the medium of exchange between teacher and pupil was humiliation and fear.

Although Alcott's methods were extraordinarily, even, some thought, alarmingly progressive for the period, he was by no means permissive. In his mild way he was an arch disciplinarian. He set up a jury system in his school, and the students selected jurors to try infractions of classroom rules. "It lessens the labors of the Instructor," wrote Alcott, "and prepares the young minds for a proper discharge of official duty. The younger members are much pleased with the office . . . As the superintendent overlooks and marks down the violations of rule, so does the Great Superintendent overlook and mark down the deviations of duty."

Education was redemptive, Alcott thought, and should focus on promoting self-awareness in the pupils. They were to question and understand themselves. "An unrelaxing attention should, therefore, be given in all instruction that affects motive, since it is this which lays the permanent foundations of character, and constitutes the true glory of the soul."

To achieve this end, Alcott helped his students develop their analytic skills by defining, discussion, and reading. He was concerned that there was not adequate reading matter: "Well written biography carries with it to the young mind, the simplicity and the force of truth and certainty; and conveys instruction in the happiest form . . . It is much to be regretted that so few have been written; and that those few have chiefly embodied the lives of children remarkable for some great excellence, or great defect; while the simple, the beautiful, and at the same time, the elevated character of genuine childhood, has been left almost entirely untouched." This was a theme to which Bronson often returned.

Louisa, saturated with her father's concerns, put his thoughts into words with *Little Women,* made to order for his moral designs.

The main object of teaching, Bronson believed, was not the instillation of knowledge but the activation of the child's conscience. The child was morally perfect, and the teacher had to extract this perfection. Education was only justified by its moral productivity.

Alcott's model was Jesus Christ, whom he classified along with Socrates as one of the great teachers. He did not regard Jesus as any more divine than, for example, himself, a belief that caused him a good deal of trouble in the community. He called the son of God "Jesus" and referred to him frequently in conversation in what people considered a dangerously casual tone. It was Bronson's opinion that "the Christian religion is the best yet promulgated, but do not thence infer that it is not susceptible of improvement; nor do I wish to confound its doctrines with its founder, and to worship one of my fellow beings."

There was always a direct relation between the oracular quality of Bronson's prose in his journals and his worldly difficulties. As two years passed in Cheshire, Bronson's rhetoric grew more orotund and resonant. The community mistrusted his methods and assumptions. They wanted their children taught and disciplined in the traditional ways, in the ways they themselves had been taught and disciplined. They recoiled from Bronson's enthusiasm and his unshakable conviction that he was God's spokesman and Jesus' equal. When asked, essentially, just exactly who he thought he was, Bronson replied, in his journal, falling into the messianic third person: "He has listened to the instructions of *Him who spake as never man spake,* who saw as man never saw before, who did as man never before did. And making due allowances for the imperfections of human nature, *he is going to do likewise."* But a rival school had been founded and Alcott was losing his students.

Alcott's financial position was precarious. His earnings of $18 a month hardly helped to pay off the $600 he owed his father, especially as he usually spent what he had on equipment for the school.

These troubles propelled Alcott into his first major martyr phase, a recurrent state that prompted him to great biblical rhetoric: "Virtue sleeps confined, benevolence is doomed a beggar,

— unclothed, unshod, without a friend, without a home." He raged against the weakness of men who wouldn't think for themselves. He fulminated against his critics: "To think for oneself is denominated pride and arrogance. And millions of human minds are in this state of slavery and tyranny. How shall they escape? Rebel. Think for themselves; let others grumble. Dare to be singular; let others deride. Follow reason; let others dwell in the land of enchantment. Be men; let others prattle. Practise; let others profess. Do good; let others define goodness. Act; let others sleep. Whatsoever thy hand findeth to do, that do with all they might, and let a gainsaying, calumniating world speculate on thy proceedings; let them go from house to house and hear some new things; let them spend their money for that which is not bread, and their labor for that which satisfieth not."

Bronson closed his school in June of 1827, saddened by his failure to excite local imaginations and inspire philanthropy. He reasoned that while he could keep thirty students at three dollars a head, it wasn't worth it. "The common sentiment is not sufficiently elevated there to give my efforts the greatest efficiency, nor my feelings the most sincere sympathy." The community he judged greedy and prideful, and too inflexible to learn from his simplicity and goodness. "With sentiments like these I do not feel called on to wage war. I leave them, though urged to say, — having spent the labor of eighteen months upon them, with the expenditure of $125."

In July Bronson received a letter from the Reverend Samuel J. May, an earnest, liberal young preacher in Brooklyn, Connecticut. May had heard about Bronson's educational experiments and wanted to discuss school reform with the innovative teacher. Bronson made the sixty-mile trip northeast across Connecticut by a great, swaying coach to Brooklyn, a pretty, tidy farming town of forty some houses set among low hills. Coming into the village Bronson saw the Unitarian church, with a high spire and a simple gabled roof, standing at a fork in the dirt road across from the square, frame courthouse. This was the Reverend May's church, abandoned by the Society of Calvinists, who had broken off from the liberals in 1817 and built their own church in 1820. Bronson saw the wide fields along the road where cows grazed beside the Quinnebaug River. Dairy farming produced most of Brooklyn's revenue. The town's only industry was a cotton mill on the Quinnebaug.

On August 8, Bronson arrived at the Reverend May's house, on the elm-lined main street of Brooklyn on the town green. There he met the preacher, his beautiful, timid wife, Lucretia, and the reverend's sister, Abigail May.

Bronson was twenty-seven years old, a slender, six-foot blond with blue eyes and a significant nose. He dressed in black and exuded moral fervor. His enthusiasm was rescued from vulgarity by the elegance of his speech. He was a persuasive talker with a genteel, Latinate vocabulary, and decorated his sentences with the abandon of a berserk pastry chef. He talked excitedly and at prodigious length about his plans for an experimental school in Boston, the question of women's education, his own theories, the inflexibility of old-line Calvinism, and New Harmony, a cooperative community founded by the Scottish philanthropist Robert Dale Owen. Abba May, who couldn't resist the taste of self-improvement, was drawn to the lean teacher.

Sturdy and big-boned, with dark hair and eyes, Abba found herself indulging in a little lofty flirtation. She used her expressive, dramatic manner and her responsive eyes to encourage the young theorist. She glowed in his company, followed his speculations enthusiastically, and agreed with his plans. Bronson, who had come to commune with Samuel May, stayed to improve with the reverend's sister.

When Alcott returned to Cheshire, he wrote in his journal that he had finally met "the interesting woman" whom he had "often portrayed in his imagination." But being of infinite, indeed, unwholesome patience and inclined to passivity, he concluded that "the results of this interview must be determined by time."

The young man had made conquests of both Mays. Samuel wrote later: "I have never, but in one other instance, been so immediately taken possession of by any man I ever met. He seemed to me like a born sage and saint. He was radical in all matters of reform: went to the root of all things, especially the subjects of education, mental and moral culture."

Abba was disposed to like Bronson because of her favorite brother's partiality. And Alcott's idealism spoke to her. "I was charmed by his modesty, his earnest desire to promote better advantages for the young. Not an educated man himself he was determined that the large fund of one million, then given by Connecticut for educational purposes should be used for higher ends than they were appropriated to at that time."

Abba May was a Boston woman from a distinguished family. Her father, Colonel Joseph May, the son of a lumber dealer, had earned his rank in the Revolution. Her mother, Dorothy Sewall, was the daughter of Deacon Sewall of the Old South Church and was related to the Quincys and Hancocks. Dorothy Sewall and Joseph May married in 1784 and had seven children. Abigail, the youngest, was born on October 8, 1800.

Abigail's birth coincided with a period of great difficulty in the May establishment. Her father had been involved with a trading concern that, through the malfeasance of one of its members, went bankrupt. The colonel, then thirty-eight, went into a deep depression and sold all his goods, as his son Samuel remembered, "even to the ring on his finger, for the benefit of his creditors." He emerged from this ordeal firmly decided never to be wealthy. He took a job for $1500 a year as secretary to the Boston Maine Insurance Company and devoted his spare time to philanthrophy. He took orphans into the family, gave charity, and went around Boston looking for people to help. In this enterprise his wife joined him, so that the May home was transformed into a kind of informal parish house. The colonel was the president of the board that established the Massachusetts General Hospital. He selected the site for the original granite building and oversaw the convicts who erected the building from 1817 to 1824. In 1801, friends of the Mays bought them a house on Federal Court, a sunny, cheerful spot in the North End in a gracious, quiet residential area.

Abigail was proud of her father, a large man with a sizable, square head. He wore eighteenth-century "small" clothes, that is, breeches, and gray stockings that outlined his muscular legs, and affected buckles at the knee and shoe. The colonel cut a dashing figure in his embroidered or brocade waistcoats with an occasional lace ruffle. At home he read some Gibbon, Pope, or Addison in the morning and the evening. He loved to talk and would sit with one leg crossed over the other, tapping his snuff box to facilitate a large pinch as he told stories about the Revolution or business on State Street.

Abigail's father was a romantic figure, very remote from her in age and in custom. The eighteenth-century family practiced no easy familiarity between generations, and children often addressed their parents as "Honored Papa" and "Honored Mama."

Colonel May was a just man but not a sentimental one. When his son Samuel graduated from Harvard, the colonel announced that he was glad he had been able to afford to give him the advantage of an education: "If you have been faithful, you must now be possessed of an education that will enable you to go any where; stand up among your fellow-men: and by serving them in one department of usefulness or another make yourself worthy of a comfortable livelihood, if no more. If you have not improved your advantages, or should be hereafter slothful, I thank God that I have not property to leave you, that will hold you up in a place among men, where you will not deserve to stand." As a philanthropist, the colonel's style was brisk and authoritarian. After he read Thomas Malthus on population he rethought his position about real charity and began to take an interest in preventing poverty rather than relieving it. As Samuel recalled, "He was therefore continually suggesting to those who were on the verge of poverty, principles of economy and kinds of labor, by which they were enabled to put themselves into a comfortable estate."

When the colonel could take time from his charities, he would discuss his favorite authors with Abba. She read Hume and Johnson, trying to please him by devoting herself to her studies. Unfortunates seemed to get her parents' deepest attention, so Abba tried to interest them with her talent for self-sacrifice. At nineteen she wrote, begging to be freed from social obligations: "I should like this winter to devote *much* of my time in study . . . I am willing to do my share in the family, and more than my share if I may be allowed to refuse visiting. This has been for a year or two one of the greatest taxes on me, and I *must* be permitted this winter to withdraw, or rather not to enter again those gay scenes where once was my delight. For visiting is altogether incompatible with study and improvement. I own that some good may be gained in some circles, but in selecting friends, you give offence; it is better to treat everybody well, and be intimate with nobody." The colonel was not disposed to love Abba for the amount of suffering she inflicted upon herself, so the gap between them remained unbridged and unexplained.

Shortchanged is the best word to describe Abba's perception of her relation with her father. She always felt he gave her too little, for she always felt empty, unappreciated, and melancholy. So she turned to her mother.

Dorothy's style was quite different from her husband's, being personal and emotional. She had no analytic interest in the economics of pauperism, but found a ready sympathy with its victims. It was to her mother that Abba turned for solace from what seemed the chilly practicality and intellectualism of her father, and it was with her mother that she studied womanhood and grew to see women crucified on the rationality of men.

Abba later wrote to Bronson that her mother's "most striking characteristic was her affectionate disposition — she adored her husband and children — she loved the whole human family — and went about doing good — Her attachments were strong — her sufferings proportionately severe — She was constantly solicitous that her daughters should be educated as fit companions for man — " Abba might have been describing herself.

Dorothy May, an intermittent invalid, had borne twelve children, of whom only half survived infancy. Abba, with psychological and poetical justice, adopted both her mother's philanthropy and personal semi-invalidism as well. She aped her mother's passionate style. Her father remained at the periphery of her grasp. He was not drawn into her emotional orbit, but her sisters and female friends were. Abba learned from her mother a kind of Victorian seduction technique in which she appeared to be giving herself almost sacrificially, and the enormity of her commitment bound women to her in chains of loyalty and gratitude.

Abba had an intense, confiding relation with her sister Louisa, who was eight years older than she and who, in 1823, had married Samuel Greele, a deacon in Dr. Channing's Federal Street Church. She was also intimate with her sister-in-law Lucretia, who read French and Italian and who shared with Abba a deep respect and love for her brother Sam. Abba's closest friend was Lydia Maria Francis, sister of the minister and transcendentalist Convers Francis. Lydia later became a significant leader of the abolitionist movement, sacrificing her popularity as a journalist when she wrote a tract deploring slavery. But Abba's tightest bond was with her mother. When Dorothy May died after a long illness on November 5, 1825, the blow was a grievous one to Abba, whose world was suddenly shaken into new insecurity. Eleven months later her father married Mrs. Mary Ann Cary, the widow of the assistant minister of King's Chapel, where the Mays belonged. Abba regarded this marriage as a betrayal of both her mother and herself. Mourning for them both, she made the eighty-mile, two-day stage trip from Boston, through Providence, to Brooklyn, Connecticut, where she moved in with Sam and his wife.

Sam's reform activities interested her. In May 1826 he took the temperance pledge; Abba teased him about it but admired the gesture. Through him she made friends with a neighbor, Helen Benson, who later married William Lloyd Garrison. But she was lonely in the center of herself, ached for her mother, was daily tantalized by Sam and Lucretia's intimacy, and was subject to prolonged periods of sorrow and gloom. Abba was ready when Bronson appeared. She pretended to learn to love him, but she was smitten instantly and the rest was logistics.

*   *   *

The courtship of Amos Bronson Alcott and Abigail May was high-minded, sentimental, and lengthy — in short, Victorian. After Bronson's departure from Brooklyn, Abba pursued her friend by letter. On September 16, she made an innocent-sounding proposal: "Should you go to Boston . . . in the Spring, and should you require a female assistant, and will in the interim consider me your pupil, instructing me in reference to this object, I should be pleased to associate myself with you for that purpose . . . It would give me much happiness to form an arc in your social circle wherever you may be."

In the fall of 1827 Abba returned to Boston, where she lobbied busily among her friends and family on Bronson's behalf. She managed to convince her father, her sister, and a number of Boston's substantial citizens that an infant school was necessary and that Bronson was the man for the job.

In November 1827, while Abba was whipping up support for a Boston school, Bronson left Cheshire for a teaching position in Bristol, Connecticut. He remained there until March, when the antipathy of the Congregational community forced him to close his establishment. The parents of his students objected particularly to Bronson's assertion that children were not only not evil, as Calvin taught, but that they were divine and deserved to be treated and taught as such. Alcott wrote of his trials in Bristol: "Our plans having been misunderstood and prejudice having been busy in attempts to injure us, the minds of some are at this time in doubt respecting the success and correctness of our plans." (In those days he employed the royal we. He later dropped the appellation, but not the state of mind it supposed.)

Bronson's troubles in Cheshire and Bristol cried out irresistibly to Abba, who began to see in Bronson a potential saint and martyr. If Bronson were the victim of a selfish and sinful world, then Abba could become his loving exhortation to keep his purpose. As much as she wanted a lover, she also wanted a cause. In the spring of 1828 she wrote to him: "I fervently hope your labors will be appreciated in Bristol, and your success commensurate with your exertions. If prejudice tinctures opinion there as it does here, you may toil seven years — yea, seventy times seven — and not establish the truth." She complained that Samuel's efforts to better his Brooklyn congregation had been in vain: "My brother would persuade me I lack charity. I confess my cloak is not so large as his, nor so well lined."

Abba's efforts finally resulted in an invitation to Bronson from a group of progressive parents to come to Boston and set up a school.

In May, Bronson visited Boston for the first time. It was love. He wrote: "There is a city in our world upon which the light of the sun of righteousness has risen. There is a sun which beams in its full meridian splendor upon it. Its influences are quickening and envigorating the souls that dwell within it. It is the same from which every pure stream of thought and purpose and performance emanates. It is the city that is set on high. It cannot be hid. It is Boston!"

3

A Victorian Courtship

THE MAY FAMILY stymied Abba's plan of assisting Alcott in his school. Her father and brother judged the prospective proximity too compromising. Sam wrote to her from Brooklyn: "I will frankly say that I see no other objection than the remarks and opinions of the world. A man may bid defiance to these. A woman cannot, without incurring the greatest danger."

Abba was loath to give up the opportunity of being in daily contact with Bronson. His calls at her father's home on Federal Court were too infrequent to satisfy her, and she felt shy about lurking near his school. She protested Sam's decision, but he prevailed, arguing propriety and reputation. In a letter to his sister Sam reiterated his position: "The circumstances of our acquaintance with Mr. Alcott, and his having gone to Boston at my suggestion and with my recommendation, would lead a censorious world to ascribe selfish views both to myself and you, if you were now to unite with him in his school." Sam advised her to direct her charity toward another recipient and suggested that she not worry herself too much about Bronson's trials. "I am rejoiced to hear that he continues to gain favor, he may gain a handsome compensation too. But don't distress yourself about his poverty. His mind and heart are so much occupied with other things that poverty and riches do not seem to concern him much." Indeed, they concerned him not at all, but they were of great concern to Abba. She hadn't admitted it to herself, but she was nurturing nuptial fantasies for the impoverished pedagogue. It was to be her cross to bear, throughout her long life with Bronson, that while she distressed herself continually about his poverty, he never concerned himself about riches or even wages.

Abba, prevented from assisting him, proposed a substitute. The woman in question was forty and, according to Abba, "she is sedate without austerity, cheerful without levity, and has perfect control of her temper and feelings." Alcott was gracious about the sedate understudy, but pressed Abba, ever so slightly, about her own plans. "But must I relinquish," he wrote, "the pleasing anticipation awakened a year since, while visiting Brooklyn, of *your* assistance? I must acquiesce if your decision is irrevocable. But I shall hope that you will sometimes visit my little circle in Salem Street. I thought I caught a glimpse of you in that vicinity the other day. Shall I add that only my diffidence prevented me from accosting you there?"

Alcott's diffidence was a hindrance to courting and a trial to the courtee. Abba's rendition of this period was laconic and misleading. She wrote later: "Mr. Alcott was sent for to organize . . . a school; this brought him to Boston — and I had still further opportunities of becoming acquainted with him. I found," she concluded, "I loved him." The passivity implied was foreign to Abba's voice and gait. To be womanly, she tried to appear that way, but, in fact, she had decided on Bronson in Brooklyn and had devoted herself to strategy ever after.

Alcott had no designs, but spent his time crocheting spidery fantasies about "the interesting female" and pulling them all out. At the end of May 1828 he was wishing he were more worthy of her confidence and respect: "There is no female on earth for whom we have a higher respect . . ." In his reformer's imagination, and in his journal, Alcott was already including Abba in the moral progress he intended to make: "Let us . . . indulge the pleasing anticipation — will it ever be realized? — of enjoying her friendship and her confidence, her affection, also — and engage with her in the good work of doing good." By the next day, the first of June, he was employing euphemisms for marriage: "We are unwilling she should engage in this school — for we are desirous — and are becoming more and more interested in her — that she should assist in the more desirable situation which we propose for ourselves in a school of a higher order. And we have reason to think that she herself is more interested in the latter situation. Perhaps we are indulging in a pleasing hope which we can never realize. Let us pay regard to the sage lessons that have been taught us by our eventful life, and prepare for every disappointment — "

One step forward, one step back. Alcott executed a hesitation step while Abba made herself as accessible as she could manage tastefully. In the middle of June, after a visit with Abba, Alcott berated himself for having any hope whatever and noted, not for the last time, that he was morally alone in a corrupt world, "a world of beings where so few are found to sympathize with us." Ten days later his confusion about his feelings and Abba's probable response had not been dispelled. He had spent a perplexing evening at Colonel May's, and planned to wait out his indecisiveness in silence.

On July 15, Abba took matters upon herself again and addressed Bronson. Writing on infant education, Abba slipped in enough personal encouragement to give Bronson her message. She came close to succeeding. Her warmth and open admiration made him feel some confidence in his own attraction to her: "We cannot," he wrote, again thinking of himself in the plural, "but feel an affection and esteem for this interesting female — whose moral goodness is everyday becoming more and more, a trait on which we love to contemplate — Would that we were worthy of her personal society and attention — " He continued in a rhapsodic vein about the holiness of women: "How great is the influence of female direction and sentiment on our sex — What intellectual power may they exert upon the interests of man — when we think of it, we shrink in insignificance . . . How long must we be obliged to be ignorant of the high intellectual and moral pleasures which grow out of this relation — How long shall we exist but to know, that we but *half* exist."

After this unusual burst of eloquence and passion, Alcott lapsed into gloom again. He was unwilling to take any initiative until he was absolutely sure of his reception. "July 19: But one thing depresses our mind — the ambiguous nature of our acquaintance with *Miss M.* We must endure this state of painful suspense until, in the progress of things, her views and feelings in regard to us shall be disclosed."

Unable to cope with this doubt anymore, Bronson devised a simple and deliciously nineteenth-century solution to his dilemma.

He spent an evening with Abba and left pages 33 to 94 of his journal with her, to explain, in case she had missed it, his moral stance and to elaborate on his feelings for her. "We will now wait, but with great anxiety, for the subjects to which this step may lead — a step which we have taken *with much fear and trembling.*" Alcott continued, his anxiety dispelling his vagaries: "We know we *love her* — we *almost* believe that she *loves us*. Let us enjoy the pleasing idea."

Feelings were never easy for Alcott, who was only comfortable with abstractions. Details, facts, and specifics eluded him and he preferred to see general trends, first causes, governing principles. Emotions mystified him, and he regarded as awesome, puzzling, or silly Abba's easy conversance with her sentiments. In this case, Abba's display of her postponed passion thrilled Bronson. She wrote: "The thoughts of your Journal handed me this evening are so in accordance with my own heart that I cannot quench the spirit you have lighted up . . . I love your mind and heart the more they are revealed to me; they are a citadel in which I feel a security and find rest. How my beloved mother would have valued this companion of her daughter . . ."

When Alcott received Abba's note he arranged a meeting with her. On August 2, 1828, they exchanged pledges. Alcott recorded that "a mutual disclosure took place of our feelings — purposes and hopes — " The couple vowed their love for each other and discussed in flowering moral paragraphs their mutual esteem and dedication to improving each other.

It is recorded that Alcott once lost control of himself to the extent of drawing Abba into an embrace. It seems likely that this momentous clinch occurred on the seventh of August, when he and Abba took a walk through Roxbury, where Abba's brother-in-law, Dr. Warren Windship, lived. In his journal Alcott waxed ecstatic about Boston scenery, "and particularly at Roxbury is very fine of a romantic, moral character — We enjoyed it much." Bronson and Abba were engaged and strolled through the small village south of Boston, along dirt roads, past cow pastures and large frame houses. Their three-hour ramble and affectionate, optimistic exchanges left them exhilarated and eager for more of each other.

Abba immediately sat down to write her brother a typically impassioned, scattershot, breathless description of her altered circumstances and to make what was to become a standard plea for assistance: "I am engaged to Mr. Alcott not in a school, but in the solemn — the momentous capacity of friend and wife — He has been attached to me from the evening of our conversation in Brooklyn . . . I do think him in every respect qualified to make me happy — he is moderate, I am impetuous — He is prudent and honorable — I am formal and arbitrary — He is poor — but we are both industrious — why may we not be happy . . . I am afraid he is embarrassed a little in his circumstances — I do think the ladies ought to remunerate him generously — Is there not some indirect way that you could manage it for him — . . . Depend on it this is the way people are got into notice — by some exertions of friends; my hands are tied — and my tongue too . . . I feel anxious for his means — . . . I never felt so happy in my life — I feel already an increase in moral energy — I have something to love — to live for. I have felt a loneliness in this world that was making a misanthrope of me in spite of everything I could do to overcome it . . . My heart is as boundless as eternity in its loves and charities . . ." Bronson had become an excuse for Abba's existence. She would perform feats in his name that she couldn't imagine doing for herself. "Moral energy" is a precise definition of the current running through her. He provided her with a reason to struggle.

Immediately after the journal-lending episode, Abba repaired to Hingham, about twenty miles from Boston, on the South Shore. The night after their decisive conversation, she couldn't sleep. She relived the evening before, savoring the intensity of yearning occasioned by their separation. She commenced a mail watch and alerted her journal of its results: "Rather impatient for some intelligence from Boston. I shall write tomorrow, if nothing arrives. How much I already enjoy this connection! I hope I am grateful." On the next day she was disappointed: "Nothing from Boston." But everything righted itself the following morning: "Have a letter from my friend. I exhibited more pleasure than was consistent with my worldly stoicism."

Abba was sure of her feelings, but to Bronson she was still in the proving stage. And there, in his quiet way, he kept her forever. Bronson's uncertainties about his own emotions caused Abba pain she could only relieve by doubling her demonstrations of devotion. She wrote from Hingham: "I am leading you, I know not where. I cannot help being impressed by the idea which your letters and conversation invariably leave on my mind, that you are a *trembling believer* . . . Now this is a spirit you must exorcise. I realize, and am in the full enjoyment of all which such a reality can afford me. I close by quoting Montaigne, who in trying to describe the affection he left for his friend said: 'When I ask myself whence it is that I feel this joy, this ease, this serenity when I see him, it is because it is he, it is because it is I; and this is all I can say.' "

While Abba was certain of her regard for Bronson, she was uncertain of her own value. Her own imperfections appeared so large to her that she could never take Bronson's affection for granted. It made her uneasy when he idealized her, as he was wont to do. She worried that he only saw her as she should be and avoided recognizing her as she was. But this idealism, she thought, might prompt her to try to live up to his hopes for her.

Alcott turned his own doubts, which were identical to hers, over to Abba and asked her to be convincing enough for both of them. "I sometimes wonder," he wrote, "what claim I have for the possession of her affection — and think her affection is placed on what I would like *to be;* what she would love to have me *be,* rather than on what I really *am.* "

When Bronson took this up with Abba he found himself stunned by the dense and fibrous strength of her adoration: "The *female heart* what do I know of it? — How can I measure its fervor and devotion by the feelings of my own? — I have yet to learn its character. I am unacquainted with its attributes. I know not how to estimate its affections." In what was to become a routine of reassurance, Abba exhausted herself in the rhetorical extravagance of her outpourings. This was her heaviest artillery, this crushing cannonade of devotional verbiage with which she blasted Bronson's doubts and reassured him that not only had she enough love for him, but she also could make up for any lack of love on his part. After her passionate expressions, they could both relax in her heated love. Alcott needed reverence, not just acceptance, for his equanimity.

Their Boston reunion after three weeks was joyful. He visited her at her father's and, reassured, wrote significantly: "I do love this good woman, and I love her because she is good — I love her because she loves me."

They saw each other as often as possible, sometimes at the comfortable house at 1 Federal Court, where Colonel May sat in his armchair by the fireside and held forth. Often people would drop by to seek the colonel's help or advice, or just his witty, outspoken company. Abba's tense relationship with her stepmother, Mary Ann Cary May, made her prefer evenings at her sister Louisa Greele's, where the talk was often of Dr. Channing and religious reform.

Bronson had plans for Abba. He saw her as an underdeveloped country, rich in moral minerals that he intended to mine. Moral extraction was Bronson's idea of love, whereas Abba's always had an emotional base that supported the moral superstructure. Abba insisted on the human in her striving for righteousness; Bronson never lost sight of the principle and bumped into the human infrequently.

He tried, for example, to think up the circumstances under which he would give her up. "Nothing," he concluded, "but a *total* failure of your character — and entire destitution of moral excellence — and abandonment of your affection for *me,* can alter my design and frustrate my hope of enjoying with *you,* those intimate delights which living with pure hearts finally — gives vitality to life — soul to body — sense to flesh."

Abba looked upon her impending marriage as an escape from the temptations of frivolity and as a guaranteed life of hard work. She congratulated herself on her victory over worldliness: "I despise fashion and have known many instances of fine girls who would have become fine women and exemplary mothers had they been directed in the choice of friends. But they were immersed in the vortex of fashion and folly before they knew it, and then, with susceptible hearts, strong impulses, feeble principles, perfect innocence but not firmly rooted virtue, they attach themselves to some object who strikes them agreeably." She toasted her engagement in the fervent, hyperbolic language that characterized her: "How happy, how grateful I am, how good I ought to be that I have been saved from this greatest of trials , worst of evils and have been conquered by moral power."

She loved Alcott very much, and the vocabulary of her love was flowery and courageous, at times ridiculous and at times deeply moving. The overblown words derived from an oversensitive nature that experienced in extremes, and therefore had to experience very cautiously.

Abba intended to feel the world through Bronson, although he would reveal himself to be singularly lacking as a buffer. Yet Abba always held on to the myth she elaborated that September, that he was responsible for her, particularly for whatever goodness she might achieve: "He shall be my moral mentor, my intellectual guide. He analyses my mind with care and judgment, my character with discrimination and charity, my heart with love and confidence. He is my benefactor, he shall see that he does me good, that I am not only his lover, his mistress, but his pupil, his companion." She went on prophetically: "It shall be my business to secure his respect and affection, not my boast that he loves me."

Living through Bronson demanded that Abba study the art of self-denial. She contemplated the activity with much satisfaction, since she was tempted by self-sacrifice as others are by dessert. Pursuing pleasure could easily turn into sin, but indulging in the unpleasant was beyond reproach. "I must be scrupulously careful," she enjoined herself in her journal, "not to disturb his plans by doubts when I find him intent on an object that is magnanimous in design and agreeable in pursuit. I can cheerfully make sacrifices of feeling and opinions for one whose every action is masked by benevolence and justice.

"As the Master gives his most hopeful scholars the hardest lessons," she continued, really getting her teeth into it, "so does God deal with the most generous spirits, and the encounters of fortune we are to look upon not as cruelty but as a contest." She expanded on the relation of virtue and happiness and concluded with words that she would have years to ponder, and even regret, as their fortunes declined and went on declining: "Let us do what seemeth to us right *now,* we may be poor we cannot be miserable with such an income as virtuous action will afford us. I shall therefore encourage Mr. A. to do what seems right in his own eyes."

The death of Abba's dearest sister, Louisa May Greele, in November 1828, caused the first real rift between Abba and Bronson. Abba was shocked by the death of her confidante, and she was doubly grieved when Sam's infant son died a few weeks later. She wrote of her sister that she was ethical, humble, and devout. She thought little of herself and well of others "who had any redeeming virtue be it ever so little. She loved virtue for its own sake, and practiced its precepts as a being responsible to God and society for the minutest action. I love to contemplate her character — I will try to imitate her example by my life and conversation. I look upon her absence as the greatest affliction of my life. But I will trust in the Lord at all times; when every other support fails me, when the fountains of worldly comfort are dried up, and will refresh my drooping spirits from those living waters which flow from the throne of God."

Bronson was most certainly not to be counted among the fountains of worldly comfort. He himself acknowledged this failure and felt it came from a coldness in his nature. He saw Abba and was helpless to cheer her, and he resented her preoccupation: "I doubt my power of reaching the hidden springs of comfort and consolation in seasons of sorrow. I feel the want of resource. I am but coldly sympathetic. I speculate upon sorrow, when I ought to be relieving it. I fear I have been and still am, but a philosophical friend in the time of affliction."

A month later things were worse. Abba was depressed by Louisa's death, and further so by Bronson's inability to help. When she asked for sympathy, Bronson responded that the fault was hers for thinking so much of her problems and so little of him. He recorded his efforts at moral therapy in his journal: "I have led her mind to thoughts regarding *herself* — regarding *me.*" He tried to distract her by turning her attention to himself, thinking that her grief was debilitating her. He thought he might appear ungenerous, but that finally she could see his moral purpose and respect him for his effort: "I suggested a few slight incidences of conduct, in which there might have been *immorality* of intention. This was sufficient to excite doubt — doubt, it seemed to me, would elicit thought upon a subject which would lead her from the more immediate causes of her grief and despondence . . ."

He knew that he was taking a risk, and possibly alienating her confidence, but he believed his new position of authority of "advising, suggesting, directing" was to make Abba better even if it made her unhappy. He accused her of selfishness not "to impair confidence, but to *increase* and *strengthen* it. If I am loved for what I *am*, the basis of our affection will be permanent. If I am loved for what I *should be*, rather than what I am, it is time that my true character were known . . . I hope I may never cease to be a subject of observation — of reproof, and contrition. Gladly would I receive, and gratefully would I acknowledge, the kindness of a friend, exhibited in the mention of my errors. This is friendship's true office."

Alcott's regard for Abba was saturated in narcissism. As he wrote, he loved her partly because she loved him. He loved her attention and her willing subordination. He did not love her distracted by other worries. He sincerely believed that he would be open to the kind of critique with which he served Abba, because he put himself through lengthy and continual catechising sessions about his motives and methods. In fact, however, he did not tolerate the kind of moral improvement that he dished out, and criticism of any kind made him retreat into a cold silence.

Bronson ruminated on his dissatisfactions with Abba's behavior: "I have been impatient for exclusive conversations with her, when circumstances presented and have, for a moment, indulged in feelings of unkindness to those who were . . . preventing such interviews." He confessed that on occasion he even felt angry at her for not arranging to see him: "In one or two instances I have even doubted the sincerity of her affections, and the motives which led to our connexion."

Abba, deep in her grieving, found this hard to bear when what she needed was uncomplicated love and understanding. But, as always, she decided that Bronson was right, that she was overly emotional, unstable, and probably selfish. They discussed her plan to go to Sam's, in Brooklyn, to recover her equilibrium. Her family thought the idea sensible. Bronson, a little relieved himself to have the emotional factory shut down for a while, acquiesced with a little martyred sigh at his sacrifice: "Circumstances suggest the propriety of her leaving me for a while to improve her health — restore her cheerfulness — and discharge her duties to others . . . I will not urge her to stay, from the selfish consideration that I *alone* am to be made happy by her society."

Colonel May wanted his daughter out of the way. If he could ship her to Sam's, he thought, there was some chance that she would forget the penniless educator and either turn up something better or devote herself to good works other than Bronson Alcott. The colonel had married above his station, and he didn't relish the prospect of his daughter reversing the trend. He didn't think highly of Alcott's financial abilities, nor did he sympathize with his philosophical vagaries or his proclivity for an abstraction when May thought a fact would be in order. Bronson needed a hothouse atmosphere of total acceptance to flower. The colonel felt no obligation to supply him with this, so the two men regarded each other with mutual dismay.

Alcott remarked that the colonel was "rather too old-fashioned in his views to be entirely congenial. His mind has been forged by circumstances very different from those which have influenced mine . . . He is contemplating the physical fluctuations of things. I am observing the moral and intellectual changes. He is recollecting and relating the *past* — I am looking upon the present and anticipating the *future.*"

By Alcott's standards, Colonel May was a secular man. He was certainly far more practical than Alcott, although everyone, including Thoreau, fell into that category. But May was an idealist as well. He had renounced moneymaking years before and frequently observed that "life was not given to be all used up in the pursuit of what we must leave behind us when we die."

In Bronson's estimate, May was a religious conservative, but he urged abandoning the most rigid aspects of Calvinism and had come to worship an essentially Unitarian God. He found the Old South Church congregation too illiberal and had joined a group of twenty reformist communicants at King's Chapel. A hymnal, published in 1799, was the work of the colonel.

James Freeman Clarke, a transcendentalist and a contemporary of Bronson's and Abba's, recalled his boyhood impressions of May: "He was one of those striking figures not easily forgotten. As a boy attending King's Chapel, I recollect him passing our pew every Sunday morning on his way from the vestry to his own seat, his sharp clear eye, firm step, knee breaches, and shoe buckles giving the impression of a noticeable character . . ."

* * *

As soon as Abba arrived at Sam's, her health collapsed. Bronson worried, the more so because he heard the news from her family.

Abba was too self-effacing to wish to concern Bronson with her difficulties, and her experience with Louisa's death made her even less willing to risk a complaint.

Bronson was finding Abba's absence very unsatisfactory. To ease his loneliness he wrote to her, suggesting that they correspond for purposes of "mutual improvement" on subjects of benefit to both of them. The first topic was "Woman." Abba reflected in her journal that she was eager to improve mutually but doubtful of her ability to offer Bronson anything of intellectual use. He knew more about "Woman" than she did, she figured, but she would try because he wished her to: "Not that I can give him any light on the subject, but in the hope that it will be beneficial to myself. I am gratified by this expression of his interest in the cultivation of my mind and heart. Oh, may I ever be watchful to increase this interest by that attention to his wishes, however, slightly indicated. My success may not meet his expectation but my wish to please him by a prompt and cheerful acquiescence will at least convince him that my want of ability is amply made up in my exertion to oblige."

Abba had predictable views of womanhood, with which Bronson agreed. A woman's definition and rewards came from her family; she lived for and through her husband and offspring. This made her family responsible for her happiness or despondency, and gave them the power of approving or disapproving of her. "A woman's home," wrote Abba, "knows no location but the bosom of her husband, and the hearts of her children. Let man cherish her affections, enlighten her mind, encourage her powers and he possess the inhabitant of heaven, an angel. The social institution of Christianity has done much to repress the morbid energy of the passions, and reason and religion are emancipating woman from that intellectual thraldom that has so long held her captive. She is finding her place by the side and in the heart of man, thus compelling him by the irresistible force of merit to accept her as an intellectual companion, and by this means rescuing from the captivity of his disregard, and what is worse, conscious and almost contented inferiority, one half of the world and refining and escalating the other half. If man's best happiness begins at home, and home is what the wife makes it, would it not be policy (to use no higher argument) to cultivate the mind of his companion in some proportion to his own? If marriage be for the mental improvement of the moral and intellectual natures of the sexes what must we think of the husband who requires of his wife an unquestionable obedience instead of a sympathy of thought taste and feeling?"

Abba was even more revealing about the question of woman when she was talking directly about herself. She related a dream to Bronson that reflected on her specifically female vulnerability to emotion, a vulnerability implied in her locating all of woman's satisfactions in the heart of her husband and children.

She wrote that she was sitting at her work table with him by her side, "rather dejected. I burst into tears, and in a subdued tone broke a silence I could no longer endure." She asked him if he would always be pointing out her faults and begged him to be patient with her. She told him that if he loved her for her "perfections" he was loving an imaginary woman: "You spoke not, looked not. I ran upstairs, fell on my knees and thanked God with as true a fervor as I ever did in waking hours, that I had a feeling heart, if not a knowing head. In a moment I was by your side: my tears were smiles. You rose, embraced me most tenderly — 'My dear, these transports of feeling are amiable, but unmeaning.' 'What,' said I, 'is nothing wise but what can be proved to a demonstration.' You laugh, I cried and melted into life . . . It is too true that love is a mere episode in the life of a man. It is a whole history in the life of a woman . . . my fear is that I may cease to please . . . I fear lest absence and adverse occurrences may convince you how important the presence of a mere woman is to you."

Bronson set her mind to rest by explaining that the place of a woman in a man's life was as a moral example. This definition made emotional sense to Abba and suited her inclinations. She saw a woman's role as setting a moral table and making a moral bed. Women didn't need to join societies for reform, like temperance committees, but rather "adopt those measures which promote temperance in everything. Spread their tables with delicate and wholesome food, pleasant but harmless drinks; cultivate their minds and purify their hearts that they may make intelligent and agreeable companions." The obligation of woman was to be the household's chief of righteousness, which would win her appreciation, love, and the affirmation of her family's conscience. If she did things right enough, there would be no sin or violence in the world.

Abba's supremely Victorian assumption that the purpose of

marriage was for the moral and intellectual improvement of men and women sustained her through many a crisis that she couldn't have tolerated any other way. This idea of reciprocal moral progress, the most attractive of nineteenth-century tenets, gave coherence to what otherwise appeared as random suffering and meaningless sacrifice. It also provided Abba with support when Bronson seemed remote or disapproving.

Bronson and Abba were agreed on the piety that held women to be emotional, spiritual, and good, while men were intellectual, carnal, and capable of being bad. So Abba could take some satisfaction in being a "feeling heart if not a knowing head." But even this satisfaction was in jeopardy since they were also agreed that Bronson did not sin. He, not Abba, became the angel at the center of his household heaven. They gave him the halo and left Abba with all her good deeds as her only reward.

For both Bronson and Abba the separation was a trial. Abba noted how similar her views were to Bronson's, how they agreed without consulting each other on books and opinions. This seemed a favorable omen for their wedded future, but even more encouraging was her belief that they would make each other happy: "I did not realize till my separation how happy I was in those daily reciprocities of affection and kindness which after all make up the charm of life."

For Bronson it was a time of growing affection. "I wish the good girl would write to me. But she is busy and will favor me with one of her letters ere long. I am already deeply in debt to her — when I shall be able to repay all her love and kindness — the intellectual pleasure which she has given me my heart only knows," Bronson wrote, typically confusing his mind and heart.

While Abba was away, Bronson could honestly admit that it was not her inconstancy that bothered him, but his own that troubled her. He called himself, with some self-deception, unworthy of her love and trust: "Good girl, I have too often pained her sensibilities by allusions to doubts and fears — one of those habits of mind, which . . . is perhaps of too questionable a character in the delicate expressions of love, when the language of confidence and trust are invariably demanded by the mind and heart: . . . Perhaps a woman must *trust,* and find her happiness in this habit of mind, more than our sex . . ."

In January 1830 Alcott, as was his habit at the beginning of a new year, was engaged in examining his life to find out what was on his mind. An inveterate list maker, he liked to know, on a sliding scale, what was important to him. He listed, that January, the following concerns:

1. Means of becoming acquainted with some of the best minds of the present day; and of influencing public opinions on some important subjects.
2. Self-improvement, by reflection, from reading and writing.
3. An elementary book, embodying the principles of moral, intellectual culture, in the form of a tale, simplified to the capacity of children.
4. My school — its progress — and claims upon parents and guardians.
5. My marriage and domestic affairs.
6. My pecuniary affairs.

The arrangement of Alcott's list is both funny and prophetic. Abba came after Bronson's philosophical ideas and his plans for his own moral regeneration. He attended to her after he had attended to everything else, except making a living. Although it was sentimentally correct that she preceded money, Abba, had she been clairvoyant, might have preferred to come last.

In April, Bronson considered the marriage he was about to contract: "In a few weeks now I am proposing a union with her which the termination of life is alone to dissolve. I am about to take upon me the character of *husband* — perhaps that still more responsible one of father. I am about to identify my dearest and holiest interests with those of another . . . Truly it is no inconsiderable step in the path of life. It is one of deep responsiblity — of calm, dispassionate reflection. I enter upon it with confidence and hope — with fear and trembling. But with the desire to learn, and the sincere purpose of performing the duties which will fall upon me . . ."

On May 23, 1830, Abba and Bronson were married at King's Chapel in Boston by the Reverend Francis Greenwood. Bronson was very laconic about the proceedings: "Passed the evening at Col. May's: and came to M. Newall's my place of board, with my friend, Miss May after the civilities of the evening." Fortunately for the sensibilities of all, Miss May had become Mrs. Alcott.

4

Boston and Bronson

THE CITY ON THE HILL returned Bronson's love. The only good review the Cheshire school had received was in the Boston *Recorder and Telegraph*, which read, "There is one school of a superior or improved kind, viz., Mr. A. B. Alcott's school in Cheshire, — the best common school in this state, perhaps in the United States."

The 1820s and '30s were a period of great change and expansion for the nation, and Boston was no exception. Boston had been a town until 1822, when the 7000 eligible voters of its 58,277 residents decided at Faneuil Hall to incorporate it under its first city charter. John Phillips was elected Boston's premier mayor. He was succeeded shortly by the energetic Josiah Quincy, who reorganized the fire department, set up a "House of Industry" to separate the honest poor from the "rogues and vagabonds," established a House of Correction and a House of Reformation for young delinquents, and presided over road construction and building.

The Boston of 1830 was a peninsula. On the west was the Back Bay, formed by the Charles River, which bordered the city along what is now Beacon Street and continued on north around Beacon Hill to meet the Mystic River, where the docks began. They ringed the peninsula in spiny projections south into Boston Harbor.

The Mill Dam, across the Back Bay (which would be the midcentury site of Louisa's suicidal longings), was built in 1819 in an effort to promote the building of gristmills. It failed in its original purpose but succeeded in changing Boston's topographical possibilities, connecting the peninsula with the western mainland and giving easy access to Cambridge. Ultimately, the unsavory and stagnant bay was filled in, and Boston began growing into its surrounding waters.

Surrounded on the west and north by water, Beacon Hill was sparsely populated. Louisburg Square wasn't planned until 1826 or completed till 1844. The Hancock family, Abba's relatives, were responsible for turning the City on a Hill into the City on a Slight Rise when they had the peak of Beacon Hill cut down to make way for housing.

The northern slope of Beacon Hill, bordered by Mount Vernon Street, was called Mount Whoredom. The Reverend James Davis told the Boston Female Society for Missionary Purposes in 1817 that this was "the place where *Satan's seat* is . . . Here, week after week, whole nights are spent in drinking and carousing; and as the morning light begins to appear, when others arise from their beds, these close their doors . . . Here in one compact section of the town, it is confidently affirmed and fully believed, there are *three hundred* females wholly devoid of shame and modesty . . . Multitudes of coloured people, by these examples, are influenced into habits of indolence."

Boston's centerpiece, then as now, was the Common, a large, more or less five-sided pasture where cows grazed. It was topped by the capitol, Charles Bulfinch's arresting new brick edifice with its splendid golden dome. The Common spilled away, down a long hill ideal for sledding, toward the Frog Pond, where children sailed boats and shied stones at hapless frogs. The Common was where celebrations and elections took place. On the Fourth of July merchants opened booths, selling rum from hogsheads, ginger and spruce beer, tamarinds, dates, oysters, and candy. The General Election of state officers occurred on the last Wednesday in May, and vendors set themselves up in rows arranged by products — candy outside, cake and buns in the middle, and inside for "ancient election beverages." This election was also known as the "Nigger 'Lection," because it was the only time of the year when blacks were allowed on the Common. The two malls adjacent to the cobbled streets bordering the Common, Beacon and Tremont, were used for promenading, Punch and Judy shows, the annual militia muster in October, and informal entertainments, such as an amateur scientist's demonstration of astronomical wonders. Daniel Webster, Edward Everett, Ralph Waldo Emerson, Colonel Joseph May, and other citizens made it a habit to take a brisk morning walk along the footpaths, which were lined with all varieties of trees — elms, lindens, tulip trees, arbor vitae, sycamores, oaks, maples, hemlocks, buttonwoods, slipper elms, and black aspens.

At the southwest end of the Common, where it bordered the Back Bay, were Braman's hot and cold baths. They were housed in a large square building that also served as a swimming school. The whipping post and pillory stood near the West Street entrance to the Common after their removal from State Street, in the northeast, where business and banking were carried on.

Boston had narrow dirt or cobbled streets laid out in comic disorder, taking their logic from the rhythms and convenience of cattle. An unwieldy, tilting yellow coach, or accommodation, would lumber through streets edged with three- and four-story brick and granite houses with steep gables, dormers, and perilously high, skinny brick chimneys. The exteriors were Georgian or classical Greek, a style that Bulfinch helped to make popular. The wealthy lived along the Common, or to its east, in townhouses punctuated by Boston's seventy churches rising to seventy white steeples. In the North End, the architecture was similar but the congestion was much greater, and the stone and brick houses were divided up, with rooms let to couples and families.

If the Common was the social and civic center of Boston, its commercial focus was the harbor. Mayor Josiah Quincy took a special interest in the dock area. He encouraged the building of Alexander Parrish's long, spacious, granite market buildings, which opened in August 1826. These markets, between the eastern wharves and Faneuil Hall, were a conduit for goods going to and coming from the sea. Traders drove livestock along the streets from the Common to the market, avoiding pranksters who enjoyed throwing passing pigs into nearby shops or at passersby. Mayor Quincy also facilitated the construction of half a dozen new streets connecting the docks with the market.

The harbor itself was a vibrant confusion of all kinds of ships, riggings, cargoes, smells, and sounds. Nathaniel Hawthorne, watching the activity one day, saw "vessels flitting past; great ships, with intricacy of rigging and various sails; schooners, sloops with their one or two broad sheets of canvas: going on different tacks, so that the spectators might think there was a different wind for each vessel . . ." In 1830 the Boston–Liverpool packet was instituted and sailed on the first and twentieth of the month. The steamer was not yet taken seriously, and wouldn't threaten the packet until the 1840s.

Seals played among the fifty islands and rocks scattered throughout Boston's seventy-five square-mile harbor. In the packet season, Wednesdays and Saturdays were sailing days. They were also the days, in the summer, when cargoes of lemons, oranges, figs, and raisins arrived. Commercial Street, leading to the wharves, was impassable at those times. Fishing excursions departed from Long Wharf; fish were unloaded at T Wharf, a pungent landing that housed the city's largest dry fish packing establishment.

The economic turmoil of Boston was far less interesting to Alcott than its spiritual ferment. He took lodgings in a rooming house on Franklin Street, northeast of the Common, and, on June 23, 1828, opened a small school on Salem Street, near the Haymarket. His curiosity and the novelty of his educational experiment immediately propelled him into Boston's reform circles, and he began a thorough exploration of the religious and intellectual reaches of the city.

The temper of Boston at the time was decidedly Federalist, conservative, moneymaking, and placid. It did not so much welcome reformers, eccentrics, and crackpots as it absorbed them. Richard Hildreth, a historian who was sympathetic to the principles of Jacksonian democracy and transcendentalism, wrote in the *Boston Atlas:* "The truth is that so stern, severe, active and influential was the authority which the allied hierarchy exercised, that few men who had property, standing, character, friends to lose, cared to risk the consequences of those bills of excommunication which were fulminated from the pulpit and the press, and those torrents of calumny, denunciation, and abuse poured forth by a thousand fluent tongues, against whomsoever deserted the ark of the covenant and allied himself to the uncircumcised Philistines." It was precisely toward these "uncircumcised Philistines" that Bronson directed his steps.

On Hanover Street, in the North End (now the Italian district), was the Second Church, where Ralph Waldo Emerson was pastor from 1829 to 1831. And on Federal Street, in the South End, was the Federal Street Church, designed in 1809 by Bulfinch; it was the first Gothic building in Massachusetts and, from 1803 till 1842, the home of Unitarianism's reigning king, William Ellery Channing.

Channing delivered the first sermon Alcott attended in Boston. Emerson called him "the star of the American Church. And we then thought," he continued, "if we do not still think, that he left no successor in the pulpit. He could never be reported, for his eye and voice could not be printed, and his discourses lose their best in losing him. He was made for the public; his cold temperament made him the most unprofitable private companion; but all America would have been impoverished in wanting him."

Alcott was impressed with Channing and recorded in his journal: "Amongst the list of divines here of the liberal character, Dr. Channing ranks pre-eminent, both in originality of thought and felicity of expression." Channing, a small, shy man, let a breath of mysticism into the closed rooms of dogmatic and rational Protestantism. He argued for the superiority of intuition over the rationalism of Locke. Although not a transcendentalist, Channing provided them with a platform on which to perform their metaphysics. He also provided them with a benign father-figure against whom they benignly revolted.

Alcott visited Channing and came away feeling disappointed, as many of his friends did. Frederick Hedge, who became a renowned German scholar, remembered gatherings at "our bishop's," as Emerson called him: "There was no gossip at Dr. Channing's; the conversation, if you could call it conversation, was always on some high theme. But in truth it was not conversation; it was simply a monologue by Dr. Channing himself. This, or something about it, led you to feel very much dissatisfied with yourself when you came away. He did not pay the slightest attention to anything you said. If you asked a question, he very probably did not answer it; he went on talking on the thing which interested him."

Unitarianism was as acceptable in Boston as it had been heretical in Connecticut. Bronson found the climate a relief but not an answer. "Unitarianism now looks a little pale and puny," he wrote after only a few months in Boston. "Does it lack love, knowledge and faith?" Bronson was asking these questions to himself and to his Sunday school classes on Berry Street, where he was holding discourses on Jesus. There he elaborated his denial of the special divinity of Jesus, portraying him as a great educator. More and more, Christianity was becoming for Bronson a "system of education." And Bronson was not alone in his religious dissatisfaction. He had arrived in Boston at the precise moment when a uniquely American romanticism was infecting the Protestant community. Its carriers had emerged largely from the Harvard Divinity School.

The prevailing Unitarianism, representing the best, most liberal efforts of Boston's ruling generation, was a rational religion, based on the verities of logic and Locke. Octavius Brooks Frothingham, a latter-day transcendentalist and historian of the movement, described these early Unitarians as "good scholars, careful reasoners, clear and exact thinkers, accomplished men of letters, humane in sentiment, sincere in moral intention . . ." They belonged, he said, "to the class which looked without for knowledge, rather than within for inspiration. The Unitarian in religion was a Whig in politics, a conservative in literature, art and social ethics . . . The Unitarian was disquieted by mysticism, enthusiasm and rapture."

Unitarianism seems so bland that it is hard to understand the necessity the young transcendentalists felt to revile it. Yet they mobilized their most creative energies to attack its mild, sensible dogma. The worst kind of Unitarian thinking, transcendentalists avowed, resulted in disgraceful sensuality, of which the French were, naturally, most guilty. In the United States, sensualism had never been quite the danger it was abroad, but any association with Voltaire or the other Enlightenment philosophers was likely to produce the theological equivalent of venereal disease. "The results of such teaching," wrote Frothingham, "appeared in a morality of selfishness, tending by self-indulgence — a morality destitute of nobleness and sweetness, summing up its lessons in the maxims that good is good to eat; that the pleasurable thing is right, the painful thing is wrong; that success is the measure of rectitude; that the aim of life is the attainment of happiness, and that happiness means physical enjoyment; that virtue and vice are names for prudence and for folly, — Virtue being conformity with the ways of the world, Vice being non-conformity with the ways of the world; no ideal standard being recognized for the one, no law of rectitude being confessed for the other."

Unitarianism at its most degraded oozed with smug, self-righteous unconcern. Alcott witnessed the worst of Unitarian materialism. In 1829, Joseph Buckminster, minister of the Brattle Street Church, preached the virtues of being rich: "We look around for the poor, and we meet with here and there the infirm, the diseased, the aged, the imprudent, and the profligate foreigner, but for the native, irremediable want, we search in vain . . . Our common prosperity is indeed unexampled, but it is not out of the reach of injury. While it lasts, it is the duty of every man to contribute what he can to preserve it."

It is not surprising that young men at Harvard in the 1820s — men like Emerson, George Ripley, James Freeman Clarke, Theodore Parker, Convers Francis, and Frederick Henry Hedge — needed something a little better than this. They got help from the Reverend Edward Everett, a Greek professor at Harvard who was the first American to receive a doctorate from Göttingen, and who brought from Germany firsthand knowledge of Immanuel Kant and his followers. Kant opened the epistemological debate at the heart of transcendentalism by providing an alternative to the plodding realism of Locke. Kant offered the route of immediate, mystical knowledge and experience, and he called such knowledge "transcendent." Suddenly, the polite young men of Harvard turned on their bewildered mentors. Andrews Norton, dean of the Harvard Divinity School, became the "pope" and the school the "ice house." Theodore Parker, who was something of an anomaly, being a transcendentalist with wit, called the school an "embalming institution" and referred to Norton's three beautiful daughters as "Norton's evidences of Christianity."

The controversies ranged all over, but they began and ended in a dispute over the nature of man. The Unitarians argued a variant on the "you are what you eat" doctrine, and the transcendentalists, finding this unspeakably prosaic, claimed that man partook of the divine. Transcendental man had a certain a priori wisdom that gave him access to spiritual truths and directed his unique genius.

The transcendentalists were romantic idealists, concerned with things as they should be rather than things as they were. Henry David Thoreau was Alcott's friend and a great studier of things as they were, in order to evoke things as they should be. He expressed this duality: "I, standing twenty miles off, see a crimson cloud in the horizon. You tell me it is a mass of vapor which absorbs all other rays and reflects the red, but that is nothing to the purpose, for this red vision excites me, stirs my blood, makes my thoughts flow, and I have new and indescribable fancies, and you have not touched the secret of that influence. If there is not something mystical in your explanation, some unexplainable to the understanding, some elements of mystery, it is quite insufficient. If there is nothing in it which speaks to my imagination, what boots it? What sort of science is that which enriches the understanding, but robs the imagination?"

Alcott voiced his awe and reverence and the wondering mood of his contemporaries in the "Orphic Saying" on "Sensualism": "He who marvels at nothing, who feels nothing to be mysterious, but must needs bare all things to sense, lacks both wisdom and piety. Miracle is the mantle in which these venerable natures wrap themselves, and he, who seeks curiously to rend this asunder, profanes their sacred countenance to enter by stealth into the Divine presence. Sanctity, like God, is ever mysterious, and all devout souls reverence her. A wonderless age is godless; an age of reverence, an age of piety and wisdom."

The aim of all this wondering was, as Emerson and Margaret Fuller put it in the opening issue of the transcendental magazine *Dial,* to "give expression to that spirit which lifts men to a higher platform, restores to them the religious sentiment, brings them worthy aims and pure pleasures, purges the inward eye, makes life less desultory, and, through raising man to the level of nature, takes away its melancholy from the landscape, and reconciles the practical with the speculative powers."

This kind of rhetoric and thinking opened itself to the often justifiable criticism of murkiness and obscurantism. The transcendentalists were guilty of inexactitude and fuzzy thinking to the degree that they tried to be specific about subjective experience: zeal, rapture, mysticism, and rarefied spirituality. Nathaniel Hawthorne, Bronson's friend and neighbor in later years, parodied an earnest transcendental thinker in *The Celestial Railroad,* itself a parody of Alcott's favorite *Pilgrim's Progress:* "He is German by birth, and is called Giant Transcendentalist; but as to his form, his features, his substance, and his nature generally, it is the peculiarity of this huge miscreant that neither he for himself, nor anybody for him, has ever been able to describe them. As we rushed by the cavern's mouth we caught a hasty glimpse of him, looking somewhat to be an ill-proportioned figure, but considerably more like a heap of fog and duskiness. He shouted after us, but in so strange a phraseology that we knew not what he meant, nor whether to be encouraged or affrighted."

Alcott's place in this controversy was, it emerged, to be a living example of idealism. He never wrote well but was, as Frothingham put it years later, "a thinker, interior, solitary, deeply conversant with the secrets of his own mind, like thinkers of his order, clear, earnest, but not otherwise than monotonous from the reiteration of his primitive ideas." The movement needed an exemplar, and Alcott, Christ's equal, set about living life as it should be rather than as it was. It was this that made him the most transcendental of all — and doubtless the hardest to live with. Emerson characterized him as a "pure idealist, not at all a man of letters, nor of any practical talent, nor a writer of books; a man quite too cold and contemplative for the alliances of friendship, with rare simplicity and grandeur of perception, who read Plato as an equal . . ."

Alcott agreed with the British journalist Harriet Martineau when she wrote about Boston: "I am certainly not aware of so large a number of peculiarly interesting and valuable persons, living in any near neighborhood, anywhere else but London." There were societies for everything — from ending flogging in the Navy to distributing Bibles to criminals, from abandoning corsets to eating whole wheat. Alcott found Boston a smorgasbord of reformers and divines. He sampled Lyman Beecher again, having admired him in Connecticut, and found him wanting. "We need no further proof," he concluded, "than we here see, that our professing teachers are mostly intent to build up their own peculiar form of faith . . . Our hopes must rest on the rational instruction of the young."

William Lloyd Garrison, who became a friend of Alcott's, was also disappointed in Beecher, who differed with him over immediate emancipation. Garrison had come to Boston to edit a paper called the *National Philanthropist,* the motto of which was: "Moderate Drinking is the Downhill Road to Intemperance and Drunkenness." Garrison fulminated against Sabbath mail deliveries, tobacco, war, and religious infidelity. In 1828, Garrison met a Quaker named Benjamin Lundy, who preached abolition and transportation of former slaves. In Boston he converted only Garrison, but in Garrison he had found not a follower but an army.

Beecher found Garrison's enthusiasm "commendable" but "misguided." Bronson found it irresistible. Alcott heard Garrison in the company of his brother-in-law, Sam, and Ellis Gray Loring, who donated the money for the *Liberator*. Sam May recalled the event: "Presently the young man rose, modestly, but with an air of calm determination, and delivered such a lecture as he only, I believe, at that time, could have written; for he only had had his eyes so anointed that he could see that outrages perpetrated upon Africans were wrongs done to our common humanity; he only, I believe, had had his ears so completely unstopped of 'prejudice against color' that the cries of enslaved black men and black women sounded to him as if they came from brothers and sisters." When Garrison had finished, May said to Alcott and Samuel Sewall, May's cousin, "This is a providential man; we ought to go and give him our hands." They went to Garrison and May said, "Mr. Garrison, I am not sure that I can indorse all you have said this evening. Much of it requires careful consideration. But I am prepared to embrace *you*. I am sure you are called to do a great work, and I mean to help you."

Alcott invited them all back to his house, where they talked until well after midnight. Garrison plainly demonstrated to them that "immediate unconditional emancipation with expatriation, was the right of every slave, and could not be withheld by his master an hour without sin."

In response to Garrison's lectures, Beecher urged his congregation to shun "the few foolish whites" who were stirring up trouble over slavery. Garrison was advised by May to cool down: "Oh, my friend, do try to moderate your indignation . . . Why you are all on fire!" To which Garrison replied: "Brother May, I have need to be all on fire, for I have mountains of ice about me to melt." He believed in the justice of his cause and his methods: "My language is exactly as suits me; it will displease many, I know — to displease them is my intention. There shall be no neutrals, men shall either like or dislike me."

Beecher and the clergy took out after Garrison. After an issue of the *Liberator* reached the South, Senator Robert Hayne of South Carolina wrote to Boston's very conservative mayor, Harrison Gray Otis, to complain of the indignities he found therein. The aristocratic mayor replied that he had never heard of William

Lloyd Garrison, but that the paper was supported "by a very few insignificant persons of all colors . . . edited by an individual who formerly lived at Baltimore," and that the incandescence of this individual "had not made, nor was likely to make proselytes among the respectable classes of our people."

Alcott supported Garrison, but not with the zeal of his brother-in-law. He was somewhat put off by Garrison's style, which he attributed to Garrison's working-class background: "The spirit and grain of this class is essentially discourteous." Like Emerson, who said he could "never speak handsomely in the presence of persons of Garrison's class," Alcott was something of a snob. He preferred his reformers with some polish, like the Scots immigrant William Russell, founder of the *American Journal of Education,* and Dr. Charles Follen, a Harvard professor and German émigré who had arrived in Boston in 1824 to escape the oppressive conditions in Prussia. In addition to teaching German law and language, Follen introduced gymnastics to Harvard. He and Russell and Alcott discussed their educational theories at Alcott's rooms on Franklin Street.

Elizabeth Palmer Peabody was another ardent educational reformer who, when Bronson first knew her, was an acolyte of Channing's. She worked in his study every evening, taking down entire sermons and supplying him with ideas for others. She volunteered her services and her devotion, noting on his return from a trip "how much more *immortal* I found him than ever before — and how I felt my mind serene under the all annealing influence of his mind and feelings." She was not serene enough, however, for the doctor judged her disorderly and hired young Dorothea Dix, who later reformed mental institutions and the nursing profession, to replace her. Right-thinking though she was, Miss Peabody could never find it in herself to like Miss Dix.

Elizabeth was a dizzy, convinced woman, the oldest of three sisters. The middle sister, Mary, married Horace Mann, and young Sophia eventually wed Nathaniel Hawthorne. Elizabeth never married but, like Henry James's characterization of her as Miss Birdseye in *The Bostonians,* devoted her life to all manner of good works.

Alcott didn't take to her at first, finding her unwomanly: "She may perhaps aim at being 'original' and fail in her attempt by becoming offensively assertive. On the whole there is, we think, too much of the man and too little of the woman in her familiarity and freedom, her affected indifference of manner. Yet, after all, she is interesting." Miss Peabody did not share Alcott's concern with refinement, and her indifference caused her to wear blouses inside out, collars backward, and to fall asleep on lecture platforms. Her manner was as disheveled as her dress. She startled Longfellow when they were first introduced by asking his advice on a Chinese dictionary.

Alcott's main problem with Elizabeth was her garrulity. Sophia remembered one occasion, shortly after Bronson and Abba's marriage, when "Mr. and Mrs. Alcott spent the evening, but Betty talked all the time and I did not have a chance to hear a word from the interesting and contemplative man." It was rare for anyone to outtalk Bronson and, as he came to know Elizabeth better, he came to talk more. And when he found her in agreement with him, he admired her very much.

Alcott was drawn in a more unequivocal way to the beautiful Frances Wright, who visited his school in 1829. The Scots advocate of free love, like the young teacher, saw change and moral regeneration everywhere: "The most dull can perceive that a moral excitement, new in its nature and rapid in its progress, pervades the world."

Walt Whitman, later to be Alcott's friend, expressed some of what Alcott felt when the lovely young woman asked Bronson to teach in New Harmony, Robert Dale Owen's collective venture. Whitman wrote: "She has always been to me one of the sweetest of sweet memories, we all loved her: fell down before her: her very appearance seemed to enthrall us . . . graceful, deer-like . . . she was beautiful in bodily shape and gifts of soul. I never felt so glowingly towards any other woman . . . she possessed herself of my body and soul."

Bronson was perhaps more attracted to the woman than to the $1200 a year she was offering. He couldn't bring himself to teach what the Owenites required, that is, Lockean facts and truths verifiable by the senses. But more than that he was nervous about the application of theories like free love in an imperfect society. "I have very little confidence in the character and intentions of this Society," he wrote. "Mrs. Wright, whose cause they nominally represent, may be, and *is* right in many of her views, but their party are not wise enough to understand her, or good enough to apply her precepts. I shall have nothing to do with them."

Still, Mrs. Wright had raised a question on which Bronson, with Abba nearby, was disposed to speculate. Having turned his back with tense haste on the fact of free love, he wondered, in the safety of his journal, "whether *the intercourse of the sexes in a reasonable state of society* will be wholly promiscuous or whether each man will select for himself a partner to whom he will adhere, as long as that adherence shall continue to be the choice of both parties . . . Friendship, therefore may be expected to come in *aid* of the sexual *intercourse* — to refine its grossness, and to increase its delight . . . It is by no means necessary that the female with whom each man has sexual intercourse, should appear to each the most deserving and excellent of her sex."

Bronson had never had so much excitement to metabolize. For him nothing was banned in Boston.

A New England Marriage

BRONSON AND ABBA BEGAN MARRIED LIFE at Mrs. Newall's on Franklin Street, not far from Bronson's school. Mrs. Newall provided meals, so Abba had only to care for their rooms while Bronson taught.

In marrying Bronson, Abba had suddenly stepped into a role rigid with conventions; they were bolstered on the one hand by popular culture and on the other by transcendentalist doctrine. Bronson's cousin William, who had become a husband and doctor since nursing Alcott in the South, turned out what was considered liberal advice to young husbands. "If your wife be such a woman as she ought to be," he intoned, "a decision which does not exactly please her will hardly be more painful than suspense, and will, at any rate, be submitted to in the fear of God." He suggested that a wife's advice be sought, "and highly valued; but her native diffidence, or at least her modesty, will render her backward to take the lead. Accordingly, I have seldom observed a woman to go before her husband in these matters; though whenever her attention becomes drawn to the work of reform, I have usually found her more persevering than our own sex." If women were bad, corrupt, power-hungry, silly, and lazy, even that wasn't their own business: "If woman is vile — and vile indeed she sometimes is — she is so because she has been corrupted by others; and that corruption may always be traced, by a longer or a shorter course, to the other sex."

An accurate reporter, if not a maker of mores, *Godey's Lady's Book,* published from 1830 throughout the century, featured fashions, fiction, and advice. A middle-class, genteel publication, it offered the services of a well-intentioned busybody, passing out praise and tongue cluckings where needed. It listed seven steps to a happy marriage for the total Victorian woman:

I. A good wife receives her husband with smiles — leaving nothing undone to render her home agreeable — and gratefully reciprocating his kindness and attention.

II. She studies to discover means to gratify his inclinations, in regard to food and cookery; in the management of her family; in her dress, manners, and deportment.

III. She never attempts to rule or appear to rule her husband. Such conduct degrades husbands — and wives always partake largely in the degradation of their husbands.

IV. She is in everything reasonable, complies with his wishes — as far as possible anticipates them.

V. She avoids all altercations or arguments leading to ill humor — and more especially before company.

VI. She never attempts to interfere in his business, unless he ask her advice or counsel, and never attempts to control him in the management of it.

VII. She never confides to her gossips any of the failings or imperfections of her husband — nor any of those little differences that occasionally arise in the married state. If she do, she may rest assured that however strong the injunctions of secrecy be on the one hand, or the pledge on the other, they will in a day or two become the common talk of the neighborhood.

One of the most serious threats to serenity in Victorian love was the possibility of exposure. Men worried that women would talk about them to other women. By idealizing women so assiduously, men isolated them from normal contact with members of the opposite sex and drove them into conspiracy with members of their own. A woman couldn't relax while being holier and purer than all the males she knew, but with her women friends she could loosen her stays, admit her shortcomings, discuss her depressions and confusions. She looked for support, compared notes, and formed passionate attachments based on the intimacy of a shared secret with women. Female attachments were often supercharged with misplaced resentments, jealousies, and anger that could not be expressed between a Victorian husband and his ideal wife. So Abba's relations with females, especially the relation she was to have with her daughter Louisa, were characterized by an intensity that was denied in her marriage. She wrote to her sister-in-law that "love is with us a principle not a passion — and I have already seen the good effects operating in our lives and conversation — I already feel the influence of moral and intellectual society constantly and exclusively enjoyed — "

Because the thought of women confiding in each other, revealing secret weaknesses about their men, was so disturbing, women's talk was ridiculed. Thomas Wentworth Higginson, later a friend of Bronson's and editor of the *Atlantic Monthly,* expressed a typical sentiment when he described the conversation of his recently married niece: "The gossip of her young lady acquaintances fills me with renewed dismay at the contemplation of young ladies' lives, especially those who have had what are called 'advantages.' Girls talk folly enough to young men, but nothing to what they talk to each other."

Godey's advised men to:

> Be to her faults a little blind;
> Be to her virtues very kind;
> Let all her ways be unconfin'd,
> And place your padlock on her mind.

Beyond this, a good husband allowed a sensible wife free reign in domestic matters. He consulted her when he had problems and treated her with courtesy whenever possible.

Harriet Martineau, who was all but deaf and a foreigner as well, could hear troubling cries from American women that local observers missed: "While women's intellect is confined, her morals crushed, her health ruined, her weaknesses encouraged, and her strength punished, she is told that her lot is cast in the paradise of women: and there is no country in the world where there is so much boasting of the 'chivalrous' treatment she enjoys."

She attributed this dismaying situation to the division of men and women into separate moral races, or the "persuasion that there are virtues which are peculiarly masculine, and others which are peculiarly feminine. It is amazing that a society which makes a most emphatic profession of its Christianity, should almost universally entertain such a fallacy: and not see that, in the case they suppose, instead of the character of Christ being the meeting point of all virtues, there would have been a separate gospel for women, and a second company of agents for its diffusion . . . But it is actually supposed that what are called the hardy virtues are more appropriate to men, and the gentler to women."

Martineau was witnessing the results of the transcendental version of women. Octavius Brooks Frothingham, who noted that a transcendental tenet was the "spiritual eminence of woman," defined theirs as an "interior, poetic, emotional" nature. Theodore Parker refined this, explaining: "The feminine characteristic being affection, which is spontaneous, and the masculine being intellect, which is not, the feminine was set above the masculine — love above light, pity above justice, sympathy above rectitude, compassion above equity." Alcott and Emerson repeatedly used the word "womanly" to describe traits such as intuitive understanding, diffidence, receptivity, warmth — in short, qualities that made the men feel welcome.

Frothingham argued in favor of the uplifting consequences of idealization: "The only criticism that can fairly be made on the Transcendentalist's idea of woman, is that it has more regard for essential capacities and possibilities, than for incidental circumstances, more respect for the ideal than for the actual woman. However grave a sin this may be against common sense, it is none against purity, nobleness, or the laws of private or public virtue. The dream, if it be no more than a dream, is beautiful and pure."

But, as Martineau saw so clearly, the dream both denied women full development and also divided them unnaturally from men. For Abba, marriage meant improvement, and improvement meant working on her submission, docility, and gentleness. It meant denying her emotionalism and her temper. An aggressive woman, she wrestled wretchedly for years with characteristics that she couldn't accept and that the dream informed her were bad *and* unfeminine. The exaggerated respect for the ideal woman implied a commensurate distaste for the real one. The gap between the real and the ideal could produce exhilaration and challenge, but also despair, as Abba tried to shroud her lively nature in passivity.

A common result of the oppressive demands of delicate virtue was illness. Neurasthenia, which covered everything from itching to writer's cramp, from dyspepsia to hopelessness, became women's most popular pastime. So, deprived of most avenues of expression, women frequently adopted invalidism as a way of life. Ailing women were regarded with approbation, particularly if their illnesses caused them to become frail and interesting. Pulmonary tuberculosis, which killed Emerson's first wife, was especially romantic because the patient remained optimistic and alert while wasting away.

Historians of the period document an alarmingly high proportion of sickly women, and Abba was no exception. Between her frequent pregnancies and various neurasthenic complaints, she was often unwell.

* * *

Alcott's school had thirty pupils until the summer of 1830, when the season took its toll on the student body size and, consequently, on Bronson's take. Abba wrote to her sister-in-law, Lucretia, hoping that "some good salary offer will be made him ere long. It is important to him, for all financial concerns are very . . . embarrassing to him — a salary would relieve his mind from all those anxieties which are incident to the fluctuations of a private school."

Roberts Vaux and Reuben Haines, wealthy Quakers from Philadelphia, had admired Alcott's methods and offered to sponsor him if he would move to Philadelphia. Vaux was a handsome, middle-aged merchant whose main achievement was in prison reform. Haines, one of the city's richest men, helped finance Philadelphia's first railroad. The two men wanted Bronson to bring his radical teaching ideas to enliven the stodgy Germantown Academy, established in 1759 about six miles north of Philadelphia.

Alcott's friends paid up his Boston debts, and he and Abba, who was pregnant, made the long trip to Philadelphia. The best way to get there was by steam packet, or "water-stage." The coach trip was arduous, taking two days from New York to Philadelphia over perilous roads. Accidents were the rule. The roads were booby-trapped with logs and potholes into which horses fell, spraining and breaking legs. Frequently the overloaded coaches broke wheels or an axle. The steamboat, a side-paddler, had been making the trip to and from Boston at a leisurely six miles an hour since

1817. At Philadelphia's Spruce Street Wharf, where the packet docked, passengers were swamped with porters, black and Irish men with their names stamped on the tin badges they wore on their hats or chests.

Philadelphia in 1830 was a beautiful city lying in two long grassy flanks along the Schuylkill River. It had lost its commercial preeminence to New York after the opening of the Erie Canal in 1825, and Jackson's victory over Nicholas Biddle and his bank finished Philadelphia's financial monopoly of the young country in 1836. But these are historical judgments. Philadelphia was a lively, thriving port, showing no signs of its imminent decline. The port was full of clipper ships, and in the northern section of the city were plants that produced white lead, drugs, paint, chemicals, and all varieties of textiles, lace, cloth, carpets, and woolens. The hosiery and knits produced near what would be Alcott's school were known all over as "Germantown goods."

Germantown, a suburb for rich Philadelphians who wanted to retreat above the stale air of the city, was known for its limestone houses flecked with gray and black mica. Streams ran through the hilly fields and estates were separated from each other by stone fences. Germantown was renowned for its gardens. Everyone had hyacinths and tulips and went on to compete with each other, importing gardening ideas and exotic flowers from Europe. Reuben Haines lived in a baronial Germantown mansion called "Wyck," which he had remodeled in 1824, joining two stone houses into one gigantic rectangle, 24 feet by 79 feet, covered with a slate roof. Surrounding the house were a woodshed, granary, and smokehouse and, spreading in all directions, glorious gardens and orchards.

Haines wanted Alcott to open a lower school that would be part of the Germantown Academy. He made Alcott the principal, leased the school to him, and collected the tuition himself. He guaranteed the financial security of both the school and the Alcotts. Further, he bought "Pine Place," a cottage on Germantown's Main Street, where Alcott could live and run his school.

The Alcotts' house was fitted out with new furniture and busts of Locke and Isaac Newton, courtesy of Mr. Haines. They had large Venetian windows and a garden, Abba wrote to Sam, "lined with raspberries, currants, gooseberry bushes, a large ground with a beautiful serpentine walk shaded with pines, firs, cedars, apple, pear, peach and plum trees, a long cedar hedge from the back to the front fence, with good health, clear head, grateful heart, and ready hand, — what can I do when surrounded by influences like these?" Abba asked rhetorically. They had more than an acre of land, on which they planted flowers and vegetables. The house was freshly painted inside and out, and Abba was comfortably settled for the first and last time in years.

Bronson was to teach the younger students, and William Russell, another Bostonian and fellow educator, was to run the "female department." Russell, a Scotsman who had come to the United States in 1819, had been teaching elocution in Boston when he attracted Haines's attention. The two men formed a tight friendship, sharing their notion of "Human Culture," which implied the development of all the human powers, moral, intellectual, and physical, but with spiritual growth as the theme. Culture was a key word in Bronson's lexicon, a shorthand way, in certain circles, for identifying himself with the forces of liberalism and reform. (A Vermont cousin of Thomas Higginson's remarked once that "the greatest objection I have to Boston is that there is always some word which everybody uses. When I was there last, the word was *culture*. Every chit of a girl . . . talked about *culture*. I got so tired of it I forbade . . . it in my presence.")

Alcott formed strong attachments with men who seemed to him to approach his idea of a lofty moral and intellectual companion. Of Russell he said, "There is no living individual residing in this country with whom a connexion would in any sense be desirable beside him — none whose influence on my mind would be equally happy and improving — none with whose thoughts I could so entirely sympathize and whose plans I could so beautifully espouse . . ." Alcott's appraisal of Russell endured. At seventy-three, Bronson wrote of his colleague's profound influence: "My friend was the first of my contemporaries to appreciate any gifts of mine that later friends and acquaintances have since recognized and acknowledged. My debt to him is greater than I know for suggestions literary and religious . . . Nor have I known among American teachers anyone who more completely filled my idea of an educator."

Alcott's transactions with Russell took place in the intellectual market, where each displayed his ideas and examined the other's. Their partnership was untainted by the messy details of intimacy, but Abba was quick to sniff out unpleasantness. Elizabeth Peabody and Abba corresponded, and from Abba Elizabeth passed on to her sister the information that "Mrs. Russell's sufferings from Mr. Russell's selfishness are all that we might imagine they would come to — an absolute destitution of every comfort at home, in order that *his* taste, *his* wardrobe, *his* whims might be satisfied." Thanks to Abba's information service, Elizabeth soon reported to her sister Mary that "he had now gone into Philadelphia, taking a house of 600 dollars rent, furnished two parlors magnificently on borrowed money, made so many engagements as to be irregular in the discharge of them all and losing the little business that he got. The sooner he dies and his wife and children are in the almshouse the better for all, I should say." Miss Peabody harbored these uncharitable feelings toward Russell because she believed he had absconded with a sizable sum of her money when they had run a school together in Boston. Whether it was carelessness or feloniousness is an unresolved question.

Whatever the case, the Alcotts imitated the Russells in spending, and soon Abba was writing Sam a letter at once cavalier and sheepish to explain her latest loan application: "I thought my dear Sam you would be surprised at our application for the 50 dollars — But I ought to have told you both for my own and my husband's reputation, that tho' we belong to Genus Generous . . . Class Spendthrift — yet we are not quite so bad as that — we have property now about us worth 7 or 8 hundred dollars — We do not look upon our money as spent — it is deposited in furniture, Books — and those things without which we could not live — the bump of acquisitiveness is nowhere on my cranium . . . but we have stood in awe of debt — previous to my receiving your letter I had written to Father — made a simple statement of our immediate want of money to render our establishment sufficiently comfortable for 10 boarders — and wishing to obtain the loan from him or someone else of 300 hundred dollars for one year."

Alcott begain teaching in January 1831. To defray expenses, he and Abba boarded some students. Bronson developed unique relations with them. He carried on a correspondence with eight-year-old Elizabeth Lewis on religion, self-improvement, and the development of the soul. Elizabeth wrote in her perfect script: "I read your letter with great pleasure. I think there are many good thoughts in it. By the mind; and by *outward nature,* I get knowledge; but I do not think that I or you, from what I have seen of you, get much knowledge from the Bible, for I do not understand it. I think that it is a beautiful allegory with a deep meaning." Alcott replied, characteristically: "But it is not, as you are doubtless aware, even the frequent reading of this Book, that can make us wiser and better. Our benefit will be equivalent only to our precious knowledge of self — unless the inward eye be opened, we shall look in vain in the *Divine Page.*" Elizabeth with common sense and uncommon frankness tried to keep Bronson honest. "I think that our letters will be better," she wrote, "if we write them when it is pleasant to us, and not just for the sake of saying 'I have done it' . . ."

Some of Bronson's students were less willing to cooperate, and one, Charles Godfrey Leland, a writer and historian, remembered him as "the most eccentric man who ever took on himself to train and form the youthful mind. He did not really teach any practical study; there was indeed some pretence at geography and arithmetic, but these we were allowed to neglect at our own sweet will. His forte was 'moral influence' and 'sympathetic intellectual communion' by talking; and, oh, heaven! what a talker he was! . . . The word *ideal* was ever in his mouth. All of the new theories, speculations or fads which were beginning to be ventillated among the Unitarian liberal clergy found ready welcome in his dreamy brain and he retailed them all to his pupils, among whom I was certainly the only one who took them in and seriously thought them over. Yet I cannot say that I *really* liked the man himself. He was not to me exactly sympathetic — human. Such training as his would develop in anybody certain weaknesses — and I had mine — which were very repulsive to my father, who carried plain commonsense to extremes, and sometimes to its opposite of unconscious eccentricity, though there was no word which he so much hated."

Bronson also failed to comprehend his student and later complained, "His imagination, fed by tales of romance and adventure, has got the mastery of his intellect, and thus wrong-headed impulse sweeps all before it. Of moral truth and beauty I have tried in vain to give him an insight. He cannot understand them."

* * *

Into the house of children came the Alcott's first girl. On March 16, 1831, at 11:00 P.M., Abba delivered Anna Bronson Alcott. Her father wrote ecstatically: "How delightful were the emotions produced by the first sounds of the infant's cry — making it sure that I was, indeed, a father! Joy, gratitude, hope, and affection, were all mingled in our feelings . . . May the *father* feel the sublime dignity of his relation; becoming both to mother and child, a friend and teacher, drawing his wisdom from on high."

Abba suddenly had a focus for her fervid, purposeful energy and she took to motherhood with a vengeance. A few days after Anna's birth she wrote to Sam and Lucretia: "I am so well and happy that I cannot resist the wish any longer to give you your actual demonstration of my strength and enjoyment . . . Lucretia I suppose is ready with her condolence that it is a girl — I don't need it — My happiness is in its existence . . . and should she be taken away we shall be glad that her early infancy was recorded — and had she not lived an hour after the pangs of birth, I still should rejoice that she had been born — the joy of the moment was sufficient compensation for the anguish of 36 hours — But she has lived long enough to open all the fountains of my higher and better nature — she has given love to life — and life to love."

Seven weeks later Abba reported to her father that Anna was well. "She is blessed with her father's mild and gentle spirit, and gives me no anxiety or trouble. Mr. Alcott has kept a record," continued Abba, "of her physical and intellectual progress which is truly interesting. It seems as if she were conscious of his observations, and were desirous of furnishing him daily with an item for his record."

On Anna's birthday Bronson had begun his "Observations on the Life" of his child, a record he kept for his first three children. He intended to record all the physical facts he observed and relate them to the moral and spiritual development of the baby. He hoped in this way to isolate and define the soul when it first made its appearance. The work was to be a history of the human mind, which Anna would continue as her journal when she was old enough. From his meticulous observations, Bronson was after nothing less than the secret of life. If he had just enough information, he thought, enough facts. To these facts he would apply the transcendentalists' favorite reasoning tool, analogy. He was con-

vinced, watching Anna, that ideas had physical or emotional coun-
terparts, and that only the connective tissue of metaphor was miss-
ing to explain life's relation to ideals: "The powerful influence of
analogy on the human mind had not been duly adverted to the
writers and teachers of mental philosophy. The outward world of
things and the inward world of ideas, have not been connected.
The relations existing between them, have not been pointed out.
The human mind has been regarded as a mysterious agent, discon-
nected from all other things. Its ideas have been supposed to be
innate, by one sect of philosophers, and by another, to be drawn
from external things. Analogy as the connecting medium has not
been recognized."

Bronson attempted various experiments on Anna to produce
emotions whose nature and physiology he hoped to explore. He
recorded even those that backfired. He made faces at her to represent anger, love, and fear, then wrote: "She seemed impressed by
them all, and especially by that which embodied the emotion of
fear, so much so that terror was manifested by loud cries, and the
desire of seeking protection in the presence of her mother; and it
was with difficulty that she could erase this form from her mind,
and restore herself to her accustomed tranquility.

"This experiment," concluded the research metaphysician,
"must not be repeated. The influence of fear, even in its milder
forms, upon the mind of infancy, must be unfavorable to its improvement and happiness."

Occasionally Bronson derived conclusions that were startlingly
illogical. "The motion of the cradle," he opined, "is deemed inju-
rious to the intellect."

Being an idealist, Bronson did not think much of corporeal pain.
But he grew to understand that events like teething do produce a
real manifestation known as bodily pain. He decided that although
it seems stronger than mental pain, "it is no more so, and in our
greater ability to deal with matter soon relieve it, than when *ailing*
from the mind itself." Because Bronson didn't consider physical
pain very important, his disciplines were emotional and cerebral.
He was extremely successful with Anna in communicating disapproval and displeasure. Anna, he recorded, liked to play with his
head, an activity he did not enjoy. He made some of his faces
indicating dislike and gently pulled her hair. He recorded: "She

seemed . . . to understand his purpose, and to connect the idea of pain with the act in which she was engaged; she immediately desisted; looked very significantly at her father; and could not be induced afterwards to repeat the act; though the means were still in her power. Repeated tries have since been made: she only pats the head . . ."

Bronson was, of course, developing theories on motherhood with tropical lavishness. He objected to mothers' tendencies to leave their children alone, which, he said, spoiled a child's disposition. Abba had been left without household help for a few days "and," continued the pitiless reporter, "has been occupied more than usual in household cares, sometimes leaving her upon the bed, to employ herself alone. This neglect she has deeply felt." A mother had a double duty, Bronson felt, to be both caretaker and moral example: "It is their duty to give the mind its true bias, or rather to permit it by sure care and attention, to follow that which is impressed upon it by the hand of nature: to keep the mind pure, the body pure, that . . . the good itself may be reflected in its modes of expression, and, like a mirror, give back the image of itself in its original purity and beauty . . ."

Alcott's first child was his favorite. Anna was a sweet, placid baby who was easy to tend and welcomed love. She had, as Bronson said, a "peculiarly amiable disposition," one that was, everyone agreed, identical to his. He wrote with approbation: "I have seen no indication of anger, or of any of the malevolent passions." Calm, nonviolent Anna, who watched her father to see how to please him, confirmed his revolutionary, transcendental belief that children were born righteous: "Infant nature has been wronged by the erroneous and imperfect views which have been entertained regarding it. The parents, conceiving the first movements of the infant's nature to be the dawnings of evil, they anticipating their appearance, mistake the innocent expressions of the child's desires, for the workings of evil . . . In this way man is prepared to doubt his fellow man: beginning with infancy to doubt himself, his doubts are gradually transformed to others; until the bonds of confidence are broken . . . Education can never accomplish its whole work, when guided by principles like these."

So Anna and Bronson became fast friends, and he encouraged in the real baby the ideal he was after. He treated her with affection, tolerance, and consideration, writing: "It is by respecting the will, by kind and rational means of influencing it from the beginning, that the dawning of conscience is called forth, connected with parental desires and becomes an agent in the work of progress." Anna was a child who took Alcott's direction.

Subtly, an alliance emerged: Anna and Bronson on one side and Abba on the other. "The Will," Bronson observed with some satisfaction, "is becoming more and more individual. She begins to choose between two things. The mother has held her in her arms during the forenoon, and exhausted her means of interest. She wanted something new and exciting. While in this state of feeling her father offered to take her at which she seemed much pleased; extending her arms to be received: and expressing her pleasure by her most intelligible means of expression. Soon after her mother made her understand that she would again take her; but she refused to go; looking . . . at her mother, then at her father, as if deciding within her mind, and at last turning from her mother. These movements were repeated, but with the same result; she chose to remain with her father . . . The higher faculties of her mind are beginning to act, and exert an influence upon her actions."

The Alcotts had a few peaceful months until, on October 19, 1831, Reuben Haines abruptly died. He had been overseeing the construction that summer of Philadelphia's first railroad, a five-mile track set on great stone blocks three feet apart. One thousand men attached iron rails to wooden ties on which four-wheeled cars, with their bodies suspended on leather braces, would ride for the first time in June 1832. Twenty passengers in each car, sitting on wooden benches around the sides, would be drawn by a horse, thus traveling the six miles from Philadelphia to Germantown in forty minutes. Haines didn't see the result of his stock-selling venture, or the first steam locomotive, showering the countryside with sparks, which would traverse the tracks on November 26, 1832.

Bronson found that several of his pupils were withdrawn after Haines's sudden death. He and Abba struggled along, but their confidence was shaken and things grew harder. Abba took her worries to her husband, expecting that he would allay them. But Bronson would shrug. "What would you have me do, my dear?"

he would ask. "Can I hunt or trap in Germantown?" In the Victorian code, Bronson was to provide and Abba was to soothe. But both failed in their prescribed tasks.

Into the middle of these anxieties came Louisa May on November 29, 1832. She was born on her father's thirty-third birthday and was, he wrote to his mother, "a very fine, fat little creature, much larger than Anna was at birth, with a firm constitution for building up a fine character, which, I trust, we shall do our part to accomplish." In his own journal, he wrote that Louisa's birth was "a most interesting event. From the great experience of domestic life which has been mine, I have derived much enjoyment, finding in the ties there originated the necessary connexions with sympathetic existence from which my abstract habits incline me too strongly, perhaps, to escape."

The tone of this entry, compared with Bronson's effusions about Anna, indicate his retreat within himself occasioned by Haines's death, his troubles, and Abba's insistent demands on him. Louisa arrived inauspiciously when her parents were at odds, and Bronson retreated from her as he had from her mother. The little girl was dark-eyed and dark-complected, like Abba and unlike Anna. Bronson considered blond complexions like his own a sign of grace, and Louisa's coloring indicated to him that she was lower on the spiritual ladder than her sister and father.

Louisa, unlike Anna, was an abstraction to her father. She was demanding and ruffled. She cried frequently and was hard to pacify. Bronson blamed it at first on the environment of the nursery: "The young heart is often filled by opposition; the young fancy filled with dark and gloomy fears."

Bronson coped with his fretful child, who did not inspire him with sentiments about the divinity of children, by retreating into philosophy or blaming Abba. He opened his record of observations on Louisa with: "That was a beautiful idea of Plato's, that mundane experience was but the recollection of the divine." He quotes Coleridge, rhapsodizes with abandon ("How wonderful, how mysterious is the origin and mechanism of life!"), and discusses phrenology, education, maternal duties, but not Louisa. He censures mothers for allowing neglect to spoil the dispositions of children: "How almost universal are the complaints of mothers that their children are troublesome, wearing away their very health and cheerfulness, by fretful cries and unknown wants; And yet the very office of the mother consists in preventing or relieving these pains, in ascertaining the causes of tears, and preserving the whole being in that state of purity . . ."

Louisa's frequent squalls were all the more puzzling to Bronson, who had thought that all preparations had been made for the birth of a truly transcendental child. Abba's health was good as was her environment. Bronson remarked wonderingly on how Abba had spent much time in conversation with the remarkable Elizabeth Lewis and "the character of the subjects too, upon which the thoughts chiefly fastened, was favorable to the forming offspring. The mind dwelt upon topics of an intellectual and moral nature — both reading and conversation were restricted to these — the remarkable power of the little girl, capable of discussing deep questions on these subjects, and the predilection of the husband for ethical enquiries, and particularly, early education, seemed to raise the mind during this period of physical depression and inertia, above the consideration of ungenial circumstances . . ."

Abba, however, remained impervious to all edification. She remembered that period as one of unusual depression and later blamed Louisa's moody character on her own dreary humor. Abba recovered her health rapidly, however, and soon Bronson was telling his father-in-law that she was about to be "restored to the discharge of those domestic and maternal duties in which she takes so much delight, and in the performance of which she furnishes so excellent a model for imitation." He wrote to his mother at great length about Abba's devotion to her family, for whom "she lives and moves and breathes."

Abba could see the affinity between Bronson and their first-born. And she agreed when he wrote to his mother that the girl's "heart and mind develop beautifully — she is full of affection and intelligence — of freshness and activity, and begins to talk a few words intelligibly. We think she has the *mother's heart* and the *father's mind* . . ."

She and Bronson carefully observed Anna's reaction to Louisa. They could see her jealousy, although Bronson recorded that Anna only struck Louisa or her mother when Abba was inattentive to her. But Anna's jealousy was quickly dispelled. "She is," Bronson noted, "generally quite docile, gentle, and happy." One day

Anna smacked her sister and ran immediately toward her father's room, saying, "Father punish . . ." Bronson explained her transgression to her and Anna expressed regret. Even in matters of discipline Bronson and Anna were of a mind.

The Alcotts' financial difficulties worsened in the early months of 1833. Bronson's school dwindled to almost nothing. He considered returning to Boston, but after what he called "mature deliberation" he decided to remain in Philadelphia. He told Roberts Vaux that he didn't wish to "return to New England without expressing my desire to make trial of my views on the minds of a few children in your city — fraught as I deem them to be, with genial influence on the juvenile being."

Bronson and Abba auctioned off much of the furniture they had recently bought. Abba and the girls stayed on in Germantown while Bronson moved into the city and took rooms near the library. He spent his early mornings reading, studying, and absorbing Coleridge, Carlyle, Plato, and the thoughts of the Swiss educator and reformer Henry Pestalozzi.

On April 22, 1833, Bronson opened a school with fifteen students. He doubted Philadelphia's ability to support and appreciate him. He had no "great faith in the people. They are not deeply interested in intellectual and moral subjects. Their objects are chiefly outward and the arrangements and associations of society are predicated on material forms." Philadelphia wasn't as receptive to Bronson's notions of education of the soul as Boston. But for a year the school struggled on, providing the Alcotts with a modest living.

In April 1834, Abba was pregnant again and Louisa and Anna were not in excellent health. Bronson continued his study program in Philadelphia, walking the six miles to Germantown on weekends.

In May parents began withdrawing their students from his school. Alcott stewed about his dilemma. He was feeling very sorry for himself, thinking of "the noble work upon which I had been called to enter — the loneliness of life to which it would subject me — the want to sympathy — the misunderstanding and false estimate which I must have . . . As I returned to my room no little prattlers welcomed my presence. It was tenantless and unswept . . ." Finally he called on the parents of his pupils and explained himself, telling them that they should have confidence in his ends and respect his methods. "I felt relieved by this act," he noted, although it did nothing to prevent the diminution of his school. The meager size of his remaining class dispirited him, and he was obsessed with the negative reports that were circulating about him.

On the weekends, Abba and Bronson went over and over what a family meant, what responsibilities it entailed from whom. She found him thoughtless and heartless. He understood that his wife and children suffered from his clinging "too closely to the *ideal.*" He justified himself by saying that he had set out to find the truth about himself, to live and to teach an exemplary life: "Sacrifices must be made to the spirit of the age . . . My family must feel the evil of this in some degree, but this should not deter me from striving to effect what has been attempted in conception of duty and right."

Abba agreed that sacrifices had to be made, but she found Alcott "unkind, indifferent, improvident" and wondered why *she* had to make all the sacrifices. Alcott explained again that she couldn't understand his inner, spiritual exploration, mired as she was in her temporal problems of child-rearing and her own infirm health: "During the period of life, when the woman is chiefly absorbed in the duties of the mother, such must be the case. And it is doubtless mysterious and irritating in the highest degree, to feel but the colder abstractions of intellect influencing the spirit . . ."

For Abba, this period of separation operated on a symbolic as well as a physical level, and it began to work a real division between her and her husband. She told Bronson that she was unhappy, that his absences "keep her mind in a state of excitement, between expectation and doubt . . . They . . . fill the heart with the sense of injustice, disquiet, vexing comparisons, and all the train of sensations which belong to absence." She drew closer to her girls and shunned society more and more. She told her sister-in-law that the world was so full of "selfishness" and had so little "brotherly love that I am very much disposed to revolve in as small a circle as possible." She had joined the Philadelphia Female Anti-Slavery Society, founded in 1833 by Mrs. Lucretia Mott. It was the first significant political organization for women, but Abba was too busy to attend its meetings: "I cannot smile or engage very much in anything apart from my children while they are so young."

Bronson had written to Colonel May that only the people who

had seen Abba in her domestic relations, "much as there is in her general character to admire and esteem, can form a true estimate of her personal worth and uncommon devotion of heart. She was formed for domestic sentiment rather than the gaze and heartlessness of what is falsely called 'society.' " Abba had to blame something for her troubles, so she wrathfully blamed society and removed herself from it. "Society" would not support Bronson, so he could not support her. Since it was impossible to think that Bronson might be at fault, she could only castigate the world at large with impunity.

Her girls became her only resource. They received her tense surveillance. She followed their developments with breathless, unnatural anxiety. "I live in constant fear," she wrote to her sister-in-law Lucretia, "that I may mistake the motive which instigates many of her [Anna's] actions. Mr. A. aids me in general principles but nobody can aid me in the detail and it is a theme of constant thought . . . If I neglect everything else I must be forgiven." Abba clutched Louisa to her. Anna was already aligned with Bronson, but Louisa, who resembled her mother physically and temperamentally, was an ally. Abba could give her all the worried love she couldn't express to Bronson. The allegiances grew more polarized. Anna was old enough to look forward to her father's visits. Louisa, at eighteen months, accepted a female society as normal and even desirable, since she got more attention when her father wasn't there.

Bronson was enjoying his solitude. "Delightful morning," he wrote; "I have a few hours before school for thought, but am too much inclined to indulge in bed, particularly when I have sat up later on the preceding evening." Suddenly, on May 18, he was called to the cottage, where Abba was recovering from a premature birth. She was not strong, but she was comfortable. Bronson later wrote: "Had she fallen into the hands of an ignorant or even timid physician, her *life* would have been sacrifice."

Abba's doctor prescribed a visit to the shore. Instead, Bronson closed his school, and on July 10, the destitute family arrived back in Boston.

6

The Temple School

THE ALCOTTS TOOK LODGINGS on Bedford Street, which ran into West Street, perpendicular to the north end of the Common. Elizabeth Peabody had taken samples of Bronson's correspondence with Elizabeth Lewis and had found four students whose parents were interested in his methods. Abba, Bronson, and Elizabeth found twenty-six more students from Boston's most distinguished families. On Temple Place, a twelve-foot passageway, was the Masonic Temple, which had been completed only in 1832. And in its hammered granite basement Bronson opened the Temple School on September 22, 1834. From there it was a short walk southeast to the docks, two blocks northwest to the Common. Bronson couldn't afford a full-time assistant, so Miss Peabody volunteered to teach two and a half hours a day "for such compensation as he could afford to pay. When Mrs. Alcott found I was really in earnest she was in a *rapture* — and Mr. A., too . . . ."

Boston was in a boom period. The economy was expanding along with the city. Boston's first railroads were completed in 1835, their development encouraged by the city's Federalist mayor, Harrison Gray Otis. The neo-Grecian court house, with four tall ionic columns flanking wide steps up from the cobbled court square, was finished in 1832. In 1834 the city streets were illuminated by gas, and the Common was ringed in by a large, menacing iron and stone fence. There was money to buy and build, and to encourage liberal experiments like Bronson's.

The airy schoolrooms were decorated with busts of Plato, Jesus, Socrates, Milton, and Shakespeare, and Alcott hung engravings, biblical scenes, landscapes, and a portrait of Dr. Channing. The master was pleased to find that half his students were girls, who, he was sure, would exercise a moral influence on the boys. He found his pupils "free from the usual entailment of school habits. They seem to have been well taught, having few vicious tendencies either of spirit or body." Bronson hoped to teach no more than five hours a day and to have a steady income of $1800 a year.

Things went well for several months, and in July 1835 Alcott and Miss Peabody published "The Record of a School," an account of their first months in the Temple School and its aims and methods. Miss Peabody enthusiastically described Bronson's attempts to engage his students in self-analysis. Through examining their spiritual qualities they would, through analogy, reach the Oversoul. Traditional subjects were neglected in favor of long discussions designed to extract the moral lesson from every action, feeling, and word. These strange discourses delighted transcendentalist visitors, who thought they were witnessing the emergence of a holy generation undefiled by rationalism and secular education. The liberals nodded approval and Alcott began to enjoy a minor celebrity.

In 1835 the Alcotts took rooms on Somerset Court, two blocks north of the State House. Elizabeth Peabody took a full room with them in lieu of the promised salary of $100 a quarter, which she hadn't seen. Abba was pleased with the company, and wrote to her sister-in-law that Elizabeth was poor "but hopeful and resolute — she is not the first genius that has craved bread and received a stone. Her death would be celebrated in Marble and Eulogy — that her life is almost forgotten and her peculiarities vilified and chastized." Miss Peabody often cared for Louisa and Anna, and when Abba gave birth to her third daughter, in June 1835, she and Bronson named her Elizabeth Peabody Alcott. (The girl's name was later changed to Elizabeth Sewall when relations among the friends cooled down.)

Elizabeth confided to her journal that she liked Mrs. Alcott very much, "but I admire parts of her character — still more than I do her . . . I look upon her faults also as phenomena . . . and also as necessities . . . They seem the growth of the Eternal Fall of Man rather than of her own." This rumination came to her when she was brooding over the egregious Dorothea Dix and trying to reconcile her loathing for the woman with her principles ("I particularly detest such a character as Miss Dix — I don't detest Miss Dix herself however. I think she is rather better than her character — if such a discrimination can be made — and this discrimination can be made." Elizabeth's jealousy forced her into tortuous metaphysics.

Dinnertime soon grew to be a trial for Miss Peabody, for she found Alcott a tyrant and a bore. He forbade her to speak to the students boarding with them about anything controversial, because he felt that any views but his own must be harmful to them. At one point he argued that by eating a certain diet men and women could live to be one hundred and fifty or two hundred years old. Miss Peabody suggested that she would prefer not to live that long, nor would she wish herself on her friends for two centuries. Alcott accused her of suicidal impulses, selfishness, and " 'asked what claim a friend had on us?' A question I did not understand in the connection and could not answer.' "

Miss Peabody found Bronson intolerant and closed-minded. He never wanted to hear an opinion different from his own and "only seems to look in books for what agrees with his own thoughts — ." She felt tainted by Bronson's negativity and inhospitality to the positions of others. She listened with increasing disapproval to Bronson's critiques of educators, ministers, reformers, philosophers, and writers. He made her, she wrote, "think less well of many persons, himself included and myself also."

In 1835 Alcott began conversing with his students on the New Testament. He would read from the Bible and ask questions designed to increase their understanding of the text and make Jesus accessible to the children as a model of behavior. Starting from the Gospel stories, Bronson used analogy to discuss all kinds of human behavior. Frequently he brought in his own family to illustrate morals. Three-year-old Louisa was an example of the struggle with selfishness: "Two little girls were standing in the parlor with their mother; and their father, looking over his papers, found a beautiful picture, and gave it to the oldest girl; and her sister, who was younger, in a moment of jealousy, said, 'I don't like father.' And her father said, 'I will give you a picture'; and he found another and gave it to her. And she said that it was not so pretty — that she did not like her sister. And their father said to the oldest, 'Will you give your beautiful picture to your little sister?' and she gave it to her immediately; but the younger sister did not look pleased. She held her head down, and looked unhappy. Bye and bye her father said to her, 'Which is the best girl, the one who gives away her picture, or the one who takes it?' She replied, 'the one who gives it away.' Soon the father went out of the room; and the little girl followed him, and said, 'Father, I am going to give this picture back again'; and so she went and gave it back to the sister."

Alcott's method was the dialogue. He tried to create a climate in which the truth would spontaneously emerge from his class. He believed that through argument and discussion they would naturally arrive at the same conclusions he had. "It is the part of the wise instructor," he told them, "to tempt forth from the minds of his pupils the facts of their inmost consciousness, and make them apprehend the gifts and faculties of their own being. Education, when rightly understood will be found to lie in the art of asking apt and fit questions, and in this leading the mind by its own light to the perception of truth."

Alcott dwelled on the theme of birth, the mystery that intrigued him most profoundly, because it was the moment of intersection between the spiritual and material worlds. So, after reading about Jesus' birth, he would ask his students questions like: "What does conceive mean?" "How do you think a mother would feel, when she knew she was to have a child?" "What does love make?" and so on. The ensuing conversations were metaphorical and delicate in the extreme, although occasionally a child would make a remark like the body was formed "out of the naughtiness of other people."

It was these innocent conversations that were Bronson's downfall. However genteel the intent and vocabulary, the subject was sex. Boston, on reading these talks, expressed its shock and horror at Bronson's unconscionable frankness. In discussing birth, its pain and its causes, Bronson had done something obscene and degrading.

Miss Peabody, who was transcribing these conversations, began to have qualms about the direction Alcott was taking his school. She felt he encouraged his students to confess their sins in class. One of his methods of discipline was to have the offender hit him, a penalty steeped in unnatural guilt and depriving the child of the right to be angry. These measures troubled Miss Peabody, who in

October 1835 wrote to Alcott, mentioning that she was afraid for the "modesty" of the students. She objected to the great publicity the school was getting, the number of visitors disrupting classes: "This I do merely that you may understand me, and not because I have the least expectation or intention of influencing you . . ."

She concluded with a paragraph that reiterated how hopeless trying to convince him of anything was: "I do not think that Evil should be clothed in *forms* by the imagination. I think every effort should be made to strip it of all individuality, all shaping, and all coloring . . . I might specify further, and argue further; but my only object is to tell you where I differ from you, not to make good my difference, as I do not suppose you will ever change your mind through the influence of another."

Throughout 1836 the school prospered. Bronson received visitors with dignity, including Emerson, who found the school a demonstration of transcendental truths. He wrote in June 1836: "I felt strongly as I watched the gradual dawn of thought upon the minds of all, that to truth is no age or season. It appears, or it does not appear; and when the child perceives it he is no more a child. Age, sex, are nothing, we are all alike before the great whole."

Elizabeth left the school in 1836, after transcribing most of Bronson's Gospel talks. She wondered, as she went, whether the "sagacity of [Alcott's] head would compensate him for the want in his heart of that humility — and sober estimate of his own place among his fellows." Alcott tried to enlist Elizabeth's sister Mary to assist and continue recording, but she privately confessed to finding Alcott an "oversevere taskmaster." Instead Sophia, the youngest sister, volunteered, having recently returned from Cuba, where she had gone to cure her paralyzing migraines. Sophia was a timid neurasthenic who disliked Elizabeth's aggressive spirit. She preferred Bronson's gentle domination to that of her sister's, but she suffered from nerves and only lasted long enough on the job to warn Elizabeth that people were already speculating on the scandalous nature of the conversations and wondering what Elizabeth's part in them was.

Rumors suggested that Elizabeth had had to leave the school for reasons of delicacy, and she was not anxious to dispel that fiction. She wrote to Alcott on August 7, 1836, feeling both sheepish and squeamish, asking her name to be taken off every remark she had recorded that seemed of questionable decency: "In the first place, in all these conversations where I have spoken, I should like to have that part of the conversation omitted, so that it may be felt that I was entirely passive . . . I should like, too, to have the remarks I made on the Circumcision omitted. I do not wish to appear as an interlocutor in that conversation either. Besides this, I must desire you to put a preface of your own before mine, and express in it, in so many words, that on you rests all the responsibility of introducing the subjects, and that your Recorder did not entirely sympathize or agree with you with respect to the course taken, adding (for I have not the slightest objection), that this disagreement or want of sympathy often prevented your views from being done full justice to, and she herself freely acknowledges."

Elizabeth goes on rhetorically, feeling guilty and confused about her desertion: "Why did the prophets and apostles veil this subject in fables and emblems if there was not a reason for avoiding physiological inquiries et.? This is worth thinking of. However, you as a man can say anything; but I am a woman, and have feelings that I dare not distrust however little I can *understand them* or give any account of them."

Elizabeth, who had disagreed with Alcott most of the way, panicked at the thought of the censure she would endure if she didn't dissociate herself completely from what now looked like an experiment in sex education. So progressive Miss Peabody had to fall back on the Victorian woman's "I don't know anything about sex, but I know what I don't like."

Sophia's assistance had been sporadic and, in December 1836, a month before the publication of the first volume of *Conversations on the Gospels,* Bronson hired Sarah Margaret Fuller to help him. Margaret, whom Alcott had met at Emerson's, was an intense, short woman with brown hair and a long neck. She was nearsighted, had a tendency to squint, and affected Grecian costumes. Margaret's education was both wide and deep, transcending the parochialism of most of her contemporaries. She had a romantic disposition and a probing manner that appealed to Alcott: "She is more given to free and bold speculation, and has a more unity of mind than most of her sex, with whom I have become acquainted." Margaret was a closet sensualist, which led her finally to Europe to escape the New World puritanism. She carried on the transcription of Bronson's conversations without a qualm. Bronson was right when he said, "Miss Fuller seems more inclined to take large and generous views of subjects than any woman of my acquaintance. I think her more liberal than almost any other mind among us." As for Margaret, she professed some enthusiasm for Alcott, at least in the beginning of their association. She wrote to him later, from another school, that "there were details in which I thought your plans imperfect, but it only needs to compare pupils who have been treated as many of these have with those who have been under your care to sympathize with your creed that those who would reform the world should begin with the beginning of life . . . In *your* children I found an impatience of labor but a liveliness of mind . . ."

*　*　*

Louisa spent these critical years largely with her mother. Bronson's success kept him out of the house. It also made him more and more didactic. He found fault quickly and, recognizing no weaknesses in his own thinking, he dismissed the opinions and feelings of others. He loved his oldest girl as a reflection of himself, and often took her to school with him. Louisa was too young, so she remained with her mother and Elizabeth Peabody. The new baby, Elizabeth, a placid creature like Anna, took up most of Abba's time. Louisa found herself in the least desirable location in the family grouping. Neither her father's favorite nor her mother's baby, she got most of her attention by making trouble. This alienated Bronson further and exasperated her mother, making her not so much an ally as an irritable protectress. Abba was more forgiving than Bronson, but she too found Louisa's behavior difficult. Elizabeth Peabody spent many hours with the little girls and found Louisa, as her father did, too violent for her taste. The intensity of Louisa's feelings, especially her anger, grew as her problems remained static — her need for attention and reassurance. Her parents treated her three-year-old outbursts with fully the gravity of adult crimes. Louisa fell into an unfortunate gap between her sisters' needs and her parents' desires, and the attention she received was usually critical. She quickly came to feel that whatever she did was likely to be wrong and that, in some unfathomable way, her very existence was wrong.

There was a spillover from Bronson's missionary zeal in school to his home life. He wrote that the task was to "redeem infancy from the slavery of false discipline — to assume the untarnished glory of its being — ." Periodically he applied his messianic enthusiasm to his girls: "I have hitherto perhaps been negligent in this respect — contenting myself, or rather not venturing to interfere with the maternal dispensation further than to make statements of general principles to the mother, without personal example, as practical illustrations on my own children." He worried about the effects on their natures of spending too much time alone with Abba: "I believe that I understand their peculiar dispositions, tempers, the predominating associations of their minds, better than their mother, and that it behooves me, from a sense of duty, to devote every moment, not appropriated to the necessary duties of my profession, to their supervision and culture. More *life* has been quickened into action, than they can guide, and harmlessly enjoy; a skillful *touch* is requisite to conduct it into the channels intended and prevent its wasteful overflow, or obstructed passage. They are *alive* with the *infinite.*" When he neglected his duties as a father the results were "disastrous. *Without* me, they soon lose their tranquility: they irritate each other — Anna, unconsciously, Louisa intentionally."

Bronson felt that Anna needed protection from Louisa, who "from the mere love of action, often assaults her sister and looks on to see what will be the results of her temerity. Instances are not infrequent when the eldest flies to her mother for protection from the wild and querulous vexations of the younger." Anna's serenity and enjoyment, he thought, were often fractured by Louisa's "impetuosity of temper." Anna was actively afraid of her sister, Bronson noted, and "some discipline will be necessary to reduce Louisa to tenderness . . . Anna suffers a good deal from this temper of her sister's. She bears the mark of her sister's hand, at present, on her cheek."

Bronson worried that Abba did not understand Anna's delicate nature: "The mother does not comprehend Anna's *wants* — neither does she seize the happiest *moment,* or the best means of allaying them." He went on to say that Abba had lost her early enthusiasm for motherhood and no longer entered "into the simple wants of childhood." Anna asked her lots of childish questions and Abba ignored them, reducing Anna to tears or sullen silence. Anna would repeat the questions, and Abba would answer with vagueness or annoyance, causing Anna pain.

"With *Louisa* the mother has more sympathy, she comprehends her mind more fully, and is, of course, more fully master of its associations. They are more alike: the elements of their beings are similar: the *will* is the predominating power, whereas in *Anna* the *intellect* and *sentiment* are most apparent," their father noted.

Bronson remarked that "Louisa and Anna have separate claims upon my affections, but I have rather more sympathy with Anna's nature. Louisa has a noble heart. The right love and look penetrate her, but her *force* makes me retreat sometimes from an encounter."

After Bronson had concentrated on his children for a week he noted Anna's great improvement in docility, obedience, and a desire to obey out of love, not fear. He saw her self-indulgence disappear to be replaced by self-control. "Could I have her under my influence continually," he noted, "and provide suitable aid for her mother in the performance of domestic duty, I could shape her into the image of my desires." These results did not apply to her sister: "Not so Louisa. There is a self-corroding nature — a spirit not yet conformed to the conditions of enjoyment . . . There is a morbid action of the spirit, induced by indulgence. The *will* has gathered around itself a breastwork of *Inclinations* and bids defiance to every attack . . . She does not, I think, fully comprehend the object of punishment: she is awed into obedience by the fear of results not *love* of yielding."

Anna, in an effort to please her father, was often to be found greeting him at the door with an account of her faults so that he would discipline her. She would then say, "Father, I love you for punishing me," or "Father, you are good," which he would record in his journal, remarking: "Early is the sense of the good unfolded from the young spirit."

Louisa had no such understanding with her father. And he recorded a relentless effort to make her accept his terms: "Louisa required authoritative measures in a few instances. She yields with less reluctance than yesterday; but her deep seated obstinacy of temper is far from being conquered. She is by no means docile." On another occasion he remarked that she "refuses and that obstinately, whatever opposes her inclinations: her violence is at times alarming — father, mother, sister, objects, all are equally defied, and not infrequently, the menace terminates in blows." He struggled with her: "I *punished* Louisa once or twice, and her mother found an occasion to do the same . . . Louisa seems more fond of *destroying*, than of *preserving* . . . I have punished her for it — and she has improved." Alcott persisted in believing that penalties would subdue the angry, upset child. "Louisa gave signs of impending evil yesterday . . . On returning from school today, I found she had caused her mother some trouble; had been discontented and required discipline . . . At supper she threw away her food, expressed great dissatisfaction at her sister, and seemed determined to yield up her spirit to the domination of passion. I took her from the table, undressed her, and put her to bed, shutting the door of the bed-chamber, and leaving her to self-isolation, without the usual story or parting caress . . . I shall anticipate a suppleness of will to result from this; if not the same punishment, or similar, must be repeated till her obstinacy is effectually checked."

Bronson was fond of moral experiments, and the girls were fond of apples, so he combined the two and performed a series of apple tests designed to measure the girls' self-control. One day he catechized Anna and Louisa:

"Anna, should little girls take things that do not belong to them without asking their fathers or mothers — things to eat or drink — things they may like?"

"No they should not," responded Anna.

"Do you think you shall ever do so — take an apple or such thing if you should see one — without asking for it?"

"No."

"And shall you, Louisa?"

Louisa from her small chair allowed as how she wouldn't.

Bronson then left an apple on a wardrobe, in a place where they would notice it, and left them to their struggle. When he returned the apple was only a core sitting next to Louisa's place at the table, where she was waiting for her dinner. After dinner Bronson asked Louisa what was lying beside her plate.

"Apple" came the obvious truth.

"Where did you get it?"

"By the fire," Louisa answered, watching her sister.

Anna elaborated that she had put it there: "Louisa and I took it

before I could get it — I told her she must not — but she did, and
then we ate some of it, and then I threw the rest into the grate
— but Louisa took it from the grate, and bit some more from it.
I was naughty — I *stole,* didn't I. I didn't ask you, as I ought to
— shall you punish me father, for it?"

Bronson said that he wouldn't punish her and explained that he
put the apple there "on purpose to try you, and I rather thought
that you *would* take it; but I hoped you would think of what I had
said, and that you *would not* take it. Did you think you were doing
right when you took it?"

"No," said Anna, "my *conscience* told me I was not."

"And shall you mind it next time," pursued her father.

"Yes, I think I shall."

"Well, Anna, always *mind* that, and then you will do right,
whether father or mother be by, or not."

Louisa came over and sat on Bronson's knee. He asked her if she
had eaten some of the apple.

"Yes, I did."

"Why did you take it before father said you might have it?"

"I wanted it," she answered with a big smile. As soon as she saw
Bronson's serious mien she threw in, "But I was naughty."

"A little," he agreed, "but you will try to be good again."

Louisa almost thought her father was joking, but Anna knew
better. She had come to understand and even enjoy this kind of
attention. The notion of goodness was intoxicating to her, and she
and Bronson flirted in the vocabulary of good and evil. One day,
very daringly, Anna said, "Father I don't love you as well as I do
mother."

"Ah," said her father, "I should like to be loved as much as
mother. I suppose when I am as good as mother, you will love me
as much, don't you think you shall?"

"Yes, father, I think I shall."

"But Anna, *why* am I not as good as mother — what have I done?
I wish you would tell me, so that I may try to make you love me
as much as you love her. Do you think you can tell me?"

"You punish me and mother does not."

"Aye that is the reason then. Well should not naughty girls
— naughty children be punished to make them better?"

"Yes father."

"And is not Anna naughty, sometimes, and does her father punish her then to make her better, and make her *love* to be good."

"Yes father."

"Well then, cannot you love father, though he does punish you sometimes for he punishes you to make you love him; and to *dislike* your naughtiness, that makes you feel so bad."

Anna bought this kind of reasoning and felt uplifted by it and by her ensuing closeness to her father. She had tasted the security and peace of her father's approval and never wanted anything else quite so much. But Louisa, who had never basked in his complete acceptance, always had to struggle with choice. She had to incorporate the logic of craving into her world. Anna accepted her father's terms without a struggle.

Bronson performed a second apple experiment on Louisa, with results that gave her trouble but satisfied him. He left another apple *"in sight."* Louisa took it, played with it, almost ate it several times, but heroically denied herself, saying, "No, no — father's — me not take father's apple — naughty! naughty!" Later Abba went out, and when she returned the apple was largely consumed. Louisa, repentant, explained, "Me could not help it — me *must* have it." Bronson congratulated himself on producing the *"spiritual principle,"* and he said nothing more to the little girl: "She has withstood the temptations of the appetites through a whole morning, and although they *triumphed,* at last — the triumph was not without a struggle." Louisa did not share her father's satisfaction since she knew she had failed, and she could not calculate the dimensions of her sin. While her father saw her as a battlefield where good was eventually to subdue evil, Louisa's potent imagination and the silence about the forbidden fruit could only magnify the distance of her fall from grace.

Bronson distinguished Louisa and Anna by their transcendental qualities. Anna was ideal, sentimental, intellectual, and imagined things but couldn't carry them out. Louisa was decidedly untranscendental in her practicality and executive skills. Her reference points were thoroughly rational and earthbound. One day she wanted a piece of her father's gingerbread, having already finished her own. He said she must be patient and wait until the afternoon. "Do you know what patience is?" he asked. "It means wait for gingerbread," she replied with irrefutable logic.

Bronson took Louisa to the Temple School for their birthday celebration, his thirty-sixth and her third. Louisa got to wear a crown of flowers, and listen to the students present Bronson with a copy of *Paradise Lost.* One girl recited an ode, another gave an address, and Bronson returned the compliment by delivering an "account of my life." After that came the refreshments, which Louisa handed out from her position at the teacher's desk. As she later recalled, "By some oversight the cakes fell short, and I saw that if I gave away the last one *I* should have none. As I was queen of the revel, I felt that I ought to have it, and held on to it tightly till my mother said, " 'It is always better to give away than to keep the nice things; so I know my Louy will not let the little friend go without.'

"The little friend received that dear plummy cake, and I a kiss and my first lesson in the sweetness of self-denial, — a lesson which my dear mother beautifully illustrated all her long and noble life."

It wasn't easy being Louisa, a rebellious little girl banging her head against the hard reality of too much demand and not enough supply, whether it was love, attention, or food. Unlike Anna, she never felt at rest, peaceful in the easy acceptance of herself and her father's love. Bronson found her a fierce little carnivore; he once speculated that her violent temper came from her preference for meat, while his sweet Anna opted for vegetables like her pacific papa. As a second child, Louisa could never take anyone's love for granted. Every wish entailed a new battle. She viewed her father as a disciplinarian and her own personal torment. She turned to her sympathetic mother but often found her distracted and depressed. Louisa, not understanding depression, thought she herself was to blame and felt hurt, angry, and confused.

Abba's troubles with her father made her angry, contributing to her depression and therefore to Louisa's unhappiness. Bronson and Abba tried once too often to borrow from the colonel, and he smoked with self-righteous indignation. He wrote, asking them to reread a letter on economy he had sent them two weeks before their wedding. He asked them to read it twice "deliberately, for I am fearful you are indulging in a habit of thoughtless expenditure, the consequences of which should alarm you." He quotes Alcott, telling him that they were glad to sacrifice their "animal" wants.

"This correct sentiment it would delight me to see influence your conduct but I cannot discover it . . . Why not *'cut your coat according to your cloth?'* " The colonel listed their faults, beginning with marrying without adequate means of support, Bronson's incompetence, moving, furnishing a large house in Germantown, auctioning their furniture, moving to Philadelphia, and finding themselves two years later $1000 in debt.

Abba replied in a fury with an and-another-thing letter that revealed the size of the hurt and anger she had dammed up for so long: "And let me add here, that ever since this excellent man was connected with my *family,* discouraging prediction, questionable civilities, and querulous surmises have been made to and about him and me, which, had our connexion not been founded on the most disinterested affection, and devoted principle, it would have been dissolved into *annihilation.*" She continued bitterly, telling her rosary of wrongs: "But the admonition is more directly for *me.* Let me then enlarge a little on my own merits; they are few, and be more briefly enumerated . . . I am barely decent. I am this moment (as I showed my brother) wearing the clothing of my mother . . . We took lodgings . . . at $15 per week. Where could I place my family in decent circumstances for less? . . . I keep a girl, why? Because there are times when I must have help independent of the family, my children are too young to go to the table [at the boarding house] and too young to be left alone at meal times. I want water, wood, and other attentions from the house help which I could not have without paying for them just what I pay now, short of one dollar . . . Would you have me take in washing?"

This interchange resulted in a breach between Abba and her father that lasted until only three years before his death. It was another of those events that confirmed Abba's theory, which she expressed to Mary Peabody, that "as our virtues susceptibilities and capabilities are developed and educated — are we tortured and crucified — we *suffer* because we *feel;* and *die* because we *know.*" She worried for the future of her "incipient women," dreading "the contamination the conflict with the world."

*　*　*

Boston turned against Bronson with the publication of his *Conversations on the Gospels.* Miss Peabody's objections turned out to be

prophetic. Channing felt that Alcott held too powerful a magnify-
ing glass over the human soul, which, he thought, was "jealous of
being watched . . . The strong passion of the young for the outward
is an indication of Nature to be respected. Spirituality may be too
exclusive for its own good." Alcott gathered in criticism from all
directions, especially unexpected ones. Harriet Martineau, friend
of reformers everywhere, abused the Temple School in her *Society
in America,* calling Alcott to task for doing mischief to his pupils by
"relaxing their bodies, pampering their imaginations, over-
stimulating the consciences of some, and hardening those of others; and by his extraordinary management, offering them every
inducement to falsehood and hypocrisy. His system can be beneficial to none and must be ruinous to many." It was Abba's conviction that Martineau had "taken the bread from the mouths of my
family." Margaret Fuller wrote to the British journalist, condemn-
ing her abuse: "Would your heart, could you but investigate the
matter, approve such overstatement, such a crude, intemperate
tirade as you have been guilty of about Mr. Alcott; a true and noble
man; a philanthropist, whom a true and noble woman, also a philanthropist, should have delighted to honor; whose disinterested
and resolute efforts for the redemption of poor humanity, all independent and faithful minds should sustain . . ."

It was welcome to have a supporter, and Emerson offered his
sympathy as well, but the Boston *Courier* expressed the city's sentiment: " 'Conversations' " was "a more indecent and obscene book
(we can say nothing of its absurdity) than any other we ever saw
exposed for sale on a bookseller's counter."

The school dwindled and the Alcotts moved to Cottage Place in
the South End. Abba gave up her domestic help. Bronson had
about ten pupils. He took this dismantling of his high reputation
quietly, but he screamed to his journal: "The hour is coming when
I shall have some other home than that of the poor man's. Yet if
I do not, the poor man's residence is honorable . . . Society owes
me a debt, which she will not pay today. I live for posterity, not less
than the present.

"The clergy eye me with suspicion; teachers are jealous; parents
lack faith in my views; and there prevails, beside all these hin-
drances, a very general misapprehension of my purposes; and not
a few rumors are afloat to my injury."

Abba watched Bronson's behavior, marveling at his stoicism. She wrote to Sam that while she complained, *Bronson* comforted *her:* "I do not know a more exemplary hero under trials than this same 'visionary.' He has much more philosophy than half the persons who are afraid of thinking too much." Abba's main worry was her children: "But oh, my girls! What exposure they may be subjected to. I do not doubt, but I wed sorrow and I surely do not need that alliance to promote either my faith or my hope."

Bronson fell sick in the spring of 1837 and went to recuperate with Sam and Lucretia in South Scituate. On his way home he stopped off in Concord to spend some days with Emerson before returning to Abba, whose "courage began to fail her."

They instituted a spartan regime, eating mainly vegetables, little butter, cheese or honey, and no coffee or tea. Abba did all the housework and cooking. They rose at five, and Abba served bread, cakes, pies, potatoes, fruit, and nuts. Alcott got the children dressed and took them to the Temple School, where he still retained a basement room. They came home for dinner at one-thirty and ate breakfast leftovers, as they did at supper at five-thirty. Alcott spent the afternoons in his study and the children did chores and played. After supper the girls went immediately to bed. Abba held out till nine o'clock, when she retired, and Bronson stayed up working till eleven. For him it was an exhilarating experience: "Amidst the hours of need, or rather of dubious dependence on goodwill of friends, I have been richer than at any former period. I have never been more busy. Never have I written more pages; never felt the free independent exercise of my talents in more delightful consciousness."

Abba's health declined in concert with the family fortunes. Throughout 1838 and 1839, the little girls' journals are dotted with references to their mother's ill health. In February 1838, Abba was bedridden for five weeks in the aftermath of a premature birth. Her next pregnancy followed almost immediately and went to full term. She almost lost her life in giving birth in April 1839 to a dead boy. "Mysterious little being!!" she wrote. "Oh for the quickening power to breathe into its nostrils the breath of life to make it mine, even for a short lease — Oh for one vital spark of that heavenly flame to rekindle to reanimate its cold and quiet clay!!! . . . I shall yet be permitted to read this hidden secret — Why after nine months of toil; a severe and tedious labour, a yearning panting hope of a living son; my soul should be pierced with this sharp sorrow. I do not *ask* for a revelation, I know I *must have* it, or the needful dsicipline cannot be complete which my soul needs."

Abba did not receive a revelation, and she began to suspect a random, nonsensical universe. She wrote to Sam when she had somewhat recovered from her despair and near death, describing how seductive death had appeared: "I care less for this world than ever — and when for 24 hours I was balancing into another — I feel a . . . satisfaction which I may never know again — and which I could not account for — what is it? a satisfaction in the past, a hope in the future, indifference in the present, no!! it was none of these . . . — what then could have produced that calm and serene sensation at the almost inevitable prospect of leaving all . . .?"

Abba suffered greatly from "the cruel neglect" of her father. Her stepmother, who was dying in 1838, made an effort to reunite father and daughter. A tentative reconciliation took place in June 1838, and the families visited each other. But even after Mrs. May's death in February 1839, Abba was still struggling with her father to get his approval and support. "This new attitude," she wrote to him after the death of her stepmother, "in which this death places me both in regard to yourself and the world embarrasses me exceedingly but it shall be my continual effort to do what is right. If I can live acceptably to *you,* circumspectly to the world, and in a holy and sacred deference to the claims of mother's memory, it will be all I can do or you can desire. I am confident that the remnant of your days cannot be embittered by a reunion with me, my husband and children."

Colonel May and Abba never got over their differences. Her life was too haphazard for him and she took his criticisms to heart and brooded over them. But he made an effort to help out and stopped by in June of 1838 to talk money with Bronson. Alcott "stated my willingness to labour with my hands and earn the bread of independence." May listened politely and went home to decide how much he could afford.

Visits became more frequent, and soon Bronson was sending the girls off with warnings that Grandfather liked quiet as much as Father did. And when the colonel came for dinner, Bronson saw for himself the need for quiet. He described the colonel as "one of those persons with whom you are to sit in silent acquiescence and become a lie, for the sake of peace and courtesy, or speak frankly, and find yourself engaged in disputation, as unprofitable as interminable. The good old man is in his dotage, garrulous, tells his stories with graces, and is a comical companion withal — a man of some note in his day."

With Abba so often indisposed, Bronson and the girls did many of the household chores. Cooking was simple since Bronson and Abba had adopted the principles of Sylvester Graham, a reformer and nutritionist whom Bronson had invited to lecture at the Temple School. Graham, for whom the cracker was named, prescribed a meatless diet that included rye meal, unbolted coarsely ground wheat, and Graham flour. He advised against meat, coffee, tea, and butter. He recommended cold showers, hard mattresses, fresh air, and cheerfulness at meals. He advocated homemade bread eaten after it was at least twelve hours old. So great was his influence that once a mob of Boston bakers and butchers, frightened by falling profits, attacked him.

Occasionally Abba wanted meat for herself or the girls. Once she lapsed from Grahamite principles and sent Bronson to the butcher. Alcott, who had developed passive resistance to a high art, allowed himself to be sold the wrong piece of meat. Abba called him out of his schoolroom to account. He replied, "I knew this marketing to be a fool's errand for me, and could only plead guilty to the sin of not knowing one piece of flesh from another, and to beg that I might not be used in this service more.

"What have I to do with butchers?" wrote Alcott, getting quite wild-eyed and hot under the collar. "Am I to go smelling about markets. Both are an offence to me. Death yawns at me as I walk up and down in this abode of skulls. Murder and blood are written on its stalls. Cruelty stares at me from the butcher's face. I tread amidst carcases. I am in the presence of slain. The deathset eyes of beasts peer at me, and accuse me of belonging to the race of murderers. Quartered, disemboweled creatures on suspended hooks plead with me. I feel myself dispossessed of the divinity . . ." Abba never asked him to go the butcher's again, and she remarked later that if she sent Bronson out to get milk he was as likely as not to come home with a cow.

Bronson spent as much time as he could with his children, or, as he referred to them, "living manifestations of my intellect." He expected to become better for this experience — "the better shall I be fitted to discharge my duties at the schoolroom as well as at home — the more useful will be my life to others in every relation of duty."

Anna, who thought "Father is the best man in the world," didn't think he needed much improvement, but worried about her own: "I make resolutions sometimes, but do not always keep them. I cannot keep good without resolutions." Anna noted that she "felt best when I have been useful," so she tried to be as helpful as she could. "I put Mother's chamber in fine order before I went to bed," reads one entry; "I helped mother get supper ready," reads another. "I expect to wait on people who come to his Conversation this evening," she noted.

Bronson tantalized her with the good little girl she might be. On her eighth birthday he gave her her own copy of *The Pilgrim's Progress* and a note to encourage her pilgrimage: "Your father knows how much you love him and your Mother and sisters and wants to have you love him and them still more dearly, so that you can never give them pain by anything you wish or say, or do, but bear pain rather for them, and disappointment without complaining or impatience. He wants to see his little girl kind and gentle and sweet tempered: as fragrant as the flowers in springtime, and as beautiful as they are when the dew glitters on them in the morning dawn." He asked if she knew how to be so sweet, and answered that she need only try and listen to her conscience. He added: "A birthday is a good time to begin to live anew: to throw off all old habits that are not good, like old clothes, and never putting them on again. Resolution clothes all anew. It makes you a new girl. It makes you beautiful and lovely. Resolve, my daughter, on this your birthday, to be as good as you know how to be through the year which you now begin, so that when the next birthday comes, you may have the pleasure, and give us all the joy, of finding yourself a good and happy little girl, loved by all who know you, and making all happy by your goodness."

The underside of this inspirational work was the message that Anna in her present state wasn't good enough. She was found wanting in sweetness and gentleness and it would be another year before she might achieve goodness. Incessant exhortation to be better left Anna without the confidence to be herself or to do anything on her own. When Bronson asked her to draw a picture, she was so afraid of failing that she couldn't put much of anything on paper and cried copiously, while the baby Elizabeth "dashed off hers with great boldness and freedom, enjoying the sense of success."

Louisa rolled her hoop on the Common. Anna came along, but noted fussily that Louisa got her feet wet in the grass. Through her experiments in opposition, Louisa had developed enough self-reliance to act in spite of the possibility of failure. Louisa, unlike Anna, had the courage to follow through, even if she was taking an unfamiliar path.

One day, when she was six, she ran away from home. She fell in with a group of Irish children, with whom she ate cold potatoes and shellfish. She wandered around the Common until twilight, when she got quite lost and fell asleep on a doorstep six blocks east of the Common. The sound of the town crier calling "Lost little girl" and describing her outfit woke her up. She ate bread and molasses with the crier's family and was taken home. There Abba tied her to the arm of the sofa with a string, knowing that, for Louisa, the loss of freedom punished her more thoroughly than any criticism could. In this, too, Louisa was not like Anna, who could hardly bear a cross word and who rarely volunteered to leave the house.

7

Eccentric Circles

THE YEARS OF ANDREW JACKSON'S administration were marked by frequent, random violence occasioned by economic dislocations and the intense scrutiny of social means and ends. Boston was fractured and knit and fractured again over women's rights, Graham's dietary innovations, the organization of the fire department, Sunday mail delivery, and, always, slavery. Harriet Martineau called the era America's Martyr Age, and when a Boston clergyman protested, saying, "We don't burn people in Smithfield here," her response was that while "Boston refinement" recoiled at the stench of burning flesh, "you rock their consciences and wring their souls."

Slavery forced Boston's moral hand as nothing ever had or would again. Bostonians had to examine their consciences and decide on what terms they would live with themselves and their country. The question was ethically simple, and the abolitionists knew they were secularly and divinely right. Their opponents were therefore not only wrong but wicked. The rhetoric of this moral war engendered a conflict of epic bitterness.

The simplicity of the issue helped shape what became a characteristic American view of all struggle as between right and wrong, good and bad. The battle over slavery defined the moral and evaluative terms of the century, reducing issues more complex than slavery to either-or possibilities. The abolitionists did not have to incorporate moral ambiguity into their thinking, and the vocabulary of this just crusade came to dominate all nineteenth-century thinking. Louisa was trained to judge by duality — if *a*, then not *b*. She never learned to try to hold two judgments or feelings simultaneously.

Louisa later said, "I became an Abolitionist at a very early age, but have never been able to decide whether I was made so by seeing the portrait of George Thompson hidden under a bed in our house during the Garrison riot, and going to comfort the 'poor man who had been good to the slaves,' or because I was saved from drowning in the Frog Pond some years later by a colored boy." This is literary hindsight, as no single event was required to convert Louisa.

She rarely encountered anyone lower than a general in the abolitionist army. Her Uncle Sam had quit his pulpit in Brooklyn, Connecticut, to work full time to free the slaves. He was mobbed five times in his travels around New England, once being stoned in Concord, where he was trying to speak with the Quaker poet John Greenleaf Whittier. Abba wrote to her brother of how saddened the colonel was that Sam was "going to leave the dignified and *respectable* office of minister of the everlasting gospel and become an itinerant fanatic."

When Abba had been a member of Philadelphia's Female Anti-Slavery Society, she had met Angelina and Sarah Grimké, converted Quakers and abolitionists from South Carolina, who later made a revolutionary speaking tour in New England. George Thompson, the handsome British abolitionist, had arrived in the United States in 1834 and began a circuit of lectures in October. He was mobbed everywhere and called a "foreign incendiary."

Nat Turner's uprising in 1831 had frightened the South into a state of hysteria over abolitionist activity. They accused Thompson of saying "that every slave-holder ought to have his throat cut." Thompson denied it. In the late summer of 1835, William Lloyd Garrison published in the *Liberator* (two dollars a year, "always payable *In Advance*") an appeal to Boston to let Thompson speak. On August 21, Mayor Theodore Lyman permitted a gathering of fifteen hundred pro-slavery citizens at Faneuil Hall to discuss the agitation of the abolitionists. On October 21, 1835, Thompson was expected to appear in Boston, but he stayed away from the city. That night, a crowd of angry anti-abolitionists, looking for Thompson, met and broke up a meeting of the Boston Female Anti-Slavery Society. They had to be content with dragging Garrison from the meeting, tying him up with a rope, and hauling him through Boston's narrow streets. Mayor Lyman rescued Garrison and put him in the Leverett Street Jail to protect him from the mob. He left town the next day to sit out the wrath he had incited.

The abolitionists counted over three hundred riots in the years 1835 and 1836, a figure they were not a little proud of. But most meetings were peaceful, where Bronson and Abba could meet with young Parker Pillsbury, a theological student who wanted Boston's churches to join in the abolition struggle, or with Abba's girlhood friend Lydia Maria Child and her husband, David Lee Child. Lydia, a fragile, pretty woman, had been a popular writer until the publication of her abolitionist *Appeal in Favor of that Class of Americans Called Africans* in 1833, when the public stopped buying her books. Beautiful, resourceful Maria Weston Chapman, head of the Female Anti-Slavery Society, and her prosperous husband, Henry, met the Alcotts at these gatherings. And, of course, always there was mild-mannered, affable Garrison, with his rimless glasses and his ailments. In the thirties he was plagued with mysterious skin irritations that sometimes required him to be hospitalized.

Abba and Garrison were especially fond of each other. They shared a taste for the florid and saw abolition in the same emotional, moral, hellfire-and-brimstone terms. Abba wrote to Mary Peabody after the Garrison riot that "we shall shake hands over the victories of abolition before long. The dawn is obvious in the dark horizon depend on it — dearest Mary we shall live to see the perfect day. Then how those *mistaken patriots* will exhort the hills to cover them — and the mountains to fall upon them — and the oblivious shades of forgetfulness to hide them from the scorn and contempt of posterity. I mean in particular those men who desecrated Faneuil Hall — and who have tried to make the cradle of liberty the Coffin of Freedom — What they intended for a stumbling block, will prove a stepping stone to this righteous cause — "

Bronson, on the other hand, was not so fond of Garrison's excesses, thought him "far from catholicism and comprehension of the whole truth . . . The most intolerant of men, as trenchant as Ajax, he has not yet won self-victories . . . Mercy is no attribute to his justice. He knows all the manners of the snake, and, were he self-freed, might crush his head; but as it is he will only scotch the hydra and play with its tail."

He preferred Angelina Grimké, known by the press as "Devilina," the lovely and powerful speaker who was the first woman to address any state legislature, a feat she performed in Boston on February 21, 1838. Bronson wrote that she "realized my conception of a woman, — intellectual force of a high order, graceful speech, elegant manners, beautiful person, tasteful dress, and deep, divine piety. She is surely a noble creature. Her sister, somewhat older and plainer of features, is distinguished chiefly by her fervent piety." Angelina and Sarah were already friends with Samuel and Lucretia May, having spent a week with them in South Scituate. Angelina spoke from five pulpits that exhausting week, and Sam wrote that "I have never heard from other lips, male or female, such eloquence as . . . her closing appeal." He continued that he had lost any remaining doubts about the capabilities of women.

Alcott heard Angelina give her famous address at the State House. He was impressed again with the regularity of her features, her simple Quaker outfit accented with a white throat scarf, her dark blue, serious eyes, and her chestnut curls. The crowd was so big, the occasion so momentous, that a member from Salem suggested that "a committee be appointed to examine the foundations of the State House of Massachusetts to see whether it will bear another lecture from Miss Grimké." She spoke again two days latter, as planned, to another standing-room-only audience. The State House survived, and Bronson found new confirmation that women could match his ideal: "Such forms of human character shed enduring glory; they give assurance of the power that woman is destined to wield when she shall be free, and cherished as she deserves. Angelina! fit name for the sex as God designed it."

The Alcotts also encountered fringe characters, whom Louisa later remembered, like Father Lawson, an old man with a beard and scythe who stood silent throughout all meetings, and Abby Folsom, a free speech advocate, who drove speakers to distraction with her continual interruptions. Once three men carried her from a meeting after one interruption too many. She was heard to say, "I'm better off than Jesus — he had one ass to carry him, but I have three." Bronson was invariably courteous to Abby and all hecklers and crazies. For transcendentalists in general, and Alcott in particular, the distinction between lunatic and saint was a tricky one.

A case in point was Jones Very, certainly the weirdest patron of the Alcott household. Very had graduated from Harvard in 1836, and became a Greek tutor there the next year. One of his students was Henry David Thoreau. Very was, at this time, receiving instructions from the Lord. When his visions were doubted, he would burst into tears. One day Very told his Greek class that they should "flee to the mountains, for the end of all things is at hand," whereupon he was incarcerated in McLean's asylum, a new institution. He spent only a month there and left to pursue his poetry and Shakespearean criticism. Elizabeth Peabody, who was on the alert for American geniuses, bagged him and brought him to Emerson for inspection. Emerson couldn't decide whether he was the most transcendental of them all or just out of his mind. He did know, however, that he didn't like him: "Grim, unmarried, insulated, accusing, yet true in itself, and speaking things in every word. The lie is in the detachment; and when he is in the room with other persons, speech stops as if there were a corpse in the apartment." Very's delivery and verse irritated Emerson. When told that Very's words came directly from the Oversoul, Emerson wanted to know "cannot the spirit parse and spell?"

Bronson found him strange and fascinating and let Very come often in 1838 and 1839 and tell his girls about reading. At one point Very was sending Alcott a sonnet every week. Bronson was spellbound by this intense, pale young man with the hot eyes and endless forehead who told Bronson seriously that he considered it an honor to wash his face. Alcott was "much impressed by the soul of the man. I reverence it. I feel myself in the presence of a superior creature. He upbraids me; he rebukes me . . . At other times he seems wild, mystical, and I rather pity than worship the presence before me. I am the insane now, and now the sane soul. What does this mean?" Very posted mysterious letters to Bronson, saying things like: "The heralds are sent forth for the marriage feast may you soon have put on the wedding garment lest we sit down without you. If you will read this letter to your class it will be my presence and for their comfort." Alcott took some pride in the fact that he was one of the few people who appeared to understand Very. Alcott had a rare fluidity that allowed him access to other people in whom he was interested. He made no a priori judgments about what was acceptable, and as long as it seemed spiritual, Bronson tried to hear it. Of Very he said, "I find it quite possible by translating his thought into my own vocabulary, mentally, and then, in turn, translating mine into his."

In Very, Bronson thought he had found someone close to heaven because he was so nearly dead: "He is a psychological phenomenon of rare occurrence. He lives out of his organs. He is dead . . . The somnambulist walks about on earth, acting and speaking, from the memory of terrestrial experience, while his soul is in the presence of spiritual realities alone . . .

"I think he will decease soon. He dies by slowly retreating from the senses, yet existing in them by memory, when men or things are obtruded upon his thought. Nature is to him a charnel house, and the voices of men, echoes of the dead who haunt its dark chamber." For anyone else, an extinct friend would have been something of a wet blanket, but Alcott hoped to learn about the soul and God from Very. Unfortunately, the poet could only speak in spasms of inchoate gloom, and, as his delusions lifted, the inspiration for his poetry abandoned him as well.

Orestes Brownson, who lived with the Alcotts for several months, had tea with Alcott and Very one extraordinary evening. Alcott was amused by the "wide polarity between these two men. They sat opposite each other at the table, but were sundered by spaces immeasurable. It was comic to behold them! They tried to speak, but Very was unintelligible to the proud Philistine."

Brownson, a slim, black-haired man over six feet tall, had deep-set gray-green eyes and a loud didactic manner. He had been known to argue with the divine Channing and pound his fists on the table. His style was too earthy and ham-fisted for the ethereal Alcott, whom he would interrupt to ask what he meant. When once asked to list the three profoundest men in America, Brownson included himself.

Orestes, like Bronson, had come from a poor farming family. He had been ordained a Universalist minister, turned to Robert Owen, turned again to found the Workingman's party, and turned yet again to join the Unitarian movement. In 1839 he founded the *Boston Quarterly Review,* a conscientious, outspoken journal of reform.

He was a stern, lonely man who retreated from his wife and family and, wearing a swallowtail coat, studied until midnight every evening. He played interminable chess games with his son and cried when he lost.

Brownson was temperamentally unfit for the rarefied company of the transcendentalists, and they objected to his aggressive manner. Emerson once complained, when badgered by Orestes, that he felt himself "to be in the company of a truth I do not comprehend, but which comprehends me."

But Brownson defended Alcott when his school was dwindling. "As a man," wrote the feisty Orestes, "he is singularly evangelical, pure minded, in love with all that is beautiful and good, devoted soul and body to what he deems truth, and the regeneration of mankind. He is conscious of being sent into this world on a high and important mission, and his great study is to discharge that mission to the acceptance of him that sent him . . ." Then came the part that Bronson probably considered damning with faint praise: "Mr. Alcott may not be sound in his philosophy, he may not be correct in all his views, and he may carry, and we believe he does carry, some of his favorite notions to extremes; but he deserves profound reverence for his determination to be a Man; to be true to Human Nature; for his fearless assertion of his own convictions, and for his deep and living faith in God and Humanity."

Brownson, with his political background, could not give himself up to the transcendental exercise of flying along on words without a serious regard for the terrain of people and facts to which they attached. He agreed with the transcendental concept that gave man the capacity for knowing truth intuitively. But he denied "that feeling is to be placed above reason, dreaming above reflection, and instinctive intimation above scientific exposition . . ." In the end, he found transcendental Unitarian thought a cold substitute for the warmth he found in the Catholic church. His conversion in 1844 appalled his associates and allowed them to discount all his criticisms, but many agreed with his parting shot: "Unitarianism has demolished Calvinism, made an end in all thinking minds of everything like dogmatic Protestantism and Unitarianism itself satisfies nobody. It is negative, cold, lifeless, and all advanced minds among Unitarians are dissatisfied with it, and are craving something higher, better, more living and life giving."

Alcott and his friends discussed the Oversoul and human culture no more frequently than they discussed each other. A man's opinions about his friends were a measure of his idealism, and Bronson always liked to converse about personality, presumably distinguished by moral intent from gossip, although from the records the two appear identical in all essential characteristics. The most interesting personality for Bronson was Ralph Waldo Emerson. He discussed Emerson with Very, Brownson, Margaret Fuller, Elizabeth Peabody, Abba — indeed, everyone he knew. He always felt that no one understood Waldo as well as he, was jealous of his inside "apprehension" of the man, and judged others by their comments on his friend. Orestes failed by being insensible to Emerson's subtleties.

Four years younger than Bronson, Emerson was to be his closest friend for the next four decades on both the human and ideal planes. Although the former usually suffered from the requirements of the latter, Emerson came as close to the perfect transcendental companion as Bronson was ever to know, and evoked from Alcott as much of human love as he was capable of giving. To observers like Louisa, this exclusive, self-conscious, and intellectual friendship was a lesson in the remoteness of idealism.

Waldo, whose parents died young, grew up poor, sharing an overcoat with his brother. His Aunt Mary Moody Emerson oversaw his education and haunted the boy with morbid Calvinist visions. Aunt Mary, who considered tact "only another name for lying," interrogated Waldo on theological matters. The pale, blond, blue-eyed boy grew tall and serious. Intense shyness and self-consciousness robbed him of spontaneity and openness. He recalled drinking wine at Harvard with his friends and growing "graver with every glass." After graduation he taught at a school for girls, but they scared, attracted, and generally upset him. His poor health gave him an excuse to quit and travel to South Carolina to restore his lungs. There he found himself "not sick . . . not well; but luke-sick."

Waldo looked to the Unitarian ministry as a likely vocation, but he was temperamentally unfit to tend to people. He visited a dying man, couldn't think of any appropriate words of comfort, and so talked of glassmaking. The invalid got mad and suggested that Emerson, if he had nothing better to offer, could leave. Another time Waldo found himself in the middle of a prayer, with no clue as how to finish the thing off. He picked up his hat and left. His own manner worried Waldo. He found himself "sluggish; my speech sometimes flippant, sometimes embarrassed and ragged; my actions (if I may say so) are of a passive kind . . . I laugh; I blush; I look ill-tempered; against my will and against my interest."

At twenty-five, Emerson married lovely, frail, seventeen-year-old Ellen Tucker. Theirs was a romantic married interlude, terminated a year and a half later by Ellen's death from tuberculosis. This crisis provoked Emerson's major religious upheaval. He left his parish at the Old North Church and went on a retreat to the White Mountains, where he read the Quaker George Fox's *Journals.* He decided to leave the church permanently.

Emerson took a trip abroad, meeting Coleridge, Wordsworth, and Carlyle. Emerson was drawn to Carlyle, a passionate, overbearing, witty, explosive talker, whose romantic, anarchistic essays appealed to the transcendentalists. The strength of Carlyle's egotistic energy and his theatrical warmth reached Emerson, who returned quiet, steady admiration.

He returned home in 1834 and successfully sued Ellen's family for her substantial inheritance, which was in dispute because she had died underage. With that money he bought a house into which he moved himself, his favorite brother, Charles, and Aunt Mary.

Emerson was married again, sensibly, not romantically, to a stately young woman from Plymouth, Massachusetts, named Lydia Jackson. "This is a very sober joy," wrote Emerson, and he communicated this sobriety so successfully to his wife that she suffered from the chill throughout their long marriage. Waldo, finding "Lydia" disagreeable, changed her name to "Lydian," after the mode, evidently feeling that a classical allusion was better than a New England fact. Elizabeth Peabody described "Queenie," as Emerson sometimes called her, as *"very refined* but neither beautiful or elegant — and very frail — & as if her mind wore out her body — she was unaffected but peculiar."

Charles died of tuberculosis on May 9, 1836, leaving Emerson without any relaxed, affectionate companionship. "When one has never had but little society, — " wrote Waldo from his despair, "and *all that society* is taken away — what is there worth living for?"

When Alcott and Emerson first met, they admired each other. Emerson said that Bronson was "a wise man, simple, superior to display, and drops the best things as quietly as the least." Alcott's intellectual shapelessness intrigued him: "The wise man who talks with you seems of no particular size but like the sun and the moon quite vague and indeterminate." Bronson's restless nonspecificity encouraged Emerson to assign him desirable traits.

Their friendship intensified suddenly in 1836 after Charles's death. Emerson needed a recipient for his love, and Alcott was ready to provide the service. In the transcendental tradition of friendship rings, the two men exchanged journals. It was a measure of the profundity of Emerson's need wholly to admire his new friend that he convinced himself he liked Alcott's prose: "He has attained at least to a perfectly simple and elegant utterance. There is no inflation and no cramp in his writing. I complained that there did not seem to be quite that facility of association which we expect in the man of genius and which is to interlace his work with all Nature by its radiating upon all. But the sincerity of his speculation is a better merit. There is no peg to hang fine things on; no sham enthusiasm; no cant; but his hearty faith and study by night and by day . . .

"And whatever defects as fine writers such men may have it is because colossal foundations are not for summer houses but for temples and cities. But come again a hundred years hence and compare Alcott and his little critics."

In 1836 Alcott took Emerson a copy of *Psyche, The Breath of Childhood,* his book of observations on his daughter Elizabeth, born the year before. The culmination of his efforts to isolate the soul, it has none of the charming details of the previous records and is instead an interminable trail of vaporous generalizations dotted with "doths" and "verilys." Alcott wanted criticism and advice on whether or not to publish. Emerson replied that "it seems to me too much of a *book of one idea,* somewhat deficient in variety of thought and illustration, and even sometimes pedantic from the wilfulness (shall I say) with which every thing is forced into the author's favorite aspects and forms of expression. The book has a strong mannerism. (Much of this might be removed and I think the fastidious eye relieved by striking out the antiquated form of the verb as *'revealeth,' 'seeth,'* etc. and writing *reveals, sees,* etc. and by a more frugal use of certain words, as 'mirror forth,' 'image,' 'shape forth' and others of that character.) But its capital fault, I think, is the want of compression . . . we are tempted to linger around the Idea, in the hope, that what cannot be sharply stated in a few words, may yet chance to be suggested by many."

Emerson, after some backing and forthing, eventually advised Bronson not to publish. Understanding better the limits of their friendship, he refused to criticize further works of Alcott's, telling his friend "that it would be as absurd to require them to conform to my way of writing and aiming, as it would be to reject Wordsworth because he was wholly unlike Campbell; that here was a new mind and it was welcome to a new style." Alcott, "well pleased," answered, "This is criticism." Anything less than praise and acceptance from Emerson made Bronson withdraw. Emerson, who needed a man to love, was not disposed to jeopardize this friendship with honesty.

Emerson was fascinated by Alcott's disregard for other people, which allowed him to be himself at all times. This ability, which Waldo felt deficient in, made him feel whole in Alcott's company: "In conversation, Alcott will meet no man who will take a superior tone. Let the other party say what he will, Alcott unerringly takes the highest moral ground and commands the other's position, and cannot be outgeneralled. And this because whilst he lives in his moral perception; his sympathies with the present company are not troublesome to him, never embarrass for a moment his perception. He is cool, bland, urbane, yet with his eye fixed on the highest fact. With me it is not so. In all companies I sympathize too much. If they are ordinary and mean, I am. If the company were great I should soar; in all mere mortal parties, I take the contagion of their views and lose my own . . . As soon as they are gone, the muse returns; I see the facts as all cultivated men always have seen them, and I am a great man alone."

Waldo saw strength of character even in rudeness and the ludicrous extremes of Bronson's idealism. When he praised a financier to Alcott, Bronson replied that he had more "austerity" than Emerson and that he would be unwilling to shake hands with "a mere merchant or banker."

Alcott frequently found fault with his friend and took no trouble to hide his disappointment. He complained that Waldo was too interested in fame, that he was proud and had devoted himself more to scholarship than to becoming "the perfect man — a great intellect, refined by elegant study, rather than a divine life, radiant with the beauty of truth and loftiness. He is an *eye* more than a *heart* — an intellect more than a *soul.* "

Emerson was inclined to agree with this appraisal as with Margaret Fuller's complaint that he "Always seemed to be on stilts." Waldo castigated himself regularly and poignantly for his detachment: "Most of the persons whom I see in my own house I see across a gulf. I cannot go to them nor they come to me. Nothing can exceed the frigidity and labor of my speech with such. You might turn a yoke of oxen between every pair of words; and the behavior is awkward and proud."

Emerson often remarked with admiration and awe that Alcott had a presence that "rebuked": "The steadiness and scope of his eye at once rebukes all before it, and we little men creep about ashamed." For Emerson, Alcott was the perfect friend. Waldo wrote that if he had a friend "I am tormented by my imperfections. The love of me accuses the other party. I wish he were nobler than to love me. Were he so, then could I love him and rise by my affection to new heights." The supremely egotistical Alcott would take whatever Emerson offered and feel that it was no more than, and possibly a good deal less than, his due. Emerson, who helped support Bronson for the next two decades, remarked on this "haughty beneficiary," but continued to give, finding confirmation of his own imperfection in Alcott's confident condescension that "rebukes and threatens and raises." Waldo could see many of Bronson's limitations: "He is, to be sure, monotonous . . . one gets tired of the uniformity — he will not be amused, he never cares for the pleasant side of things, but always truth and their origin he seeketh after." But Bronson's unshakable self-regard, which demanded nothing of Emerson but quiet admiration, quite turned Emerson's head. Wonderingly, he recorded that Bronson coldly asked "whether Milton is to continue to meet the wants of the mind? & Bacon & so all." Bronson dared to a hubris that left Emerson gasping. Like Waldo's Aunt Mary Moody Emerson, the "constant east wind" who equated tact with lying and who told young Waldo that she couldn't grieve for his dead father because he had practiced a "defective theology," Alcott took Emerson over by his ruthless pursuit of the soul at the expense of the human.

* * *

Finally, Bronson closed his school for good. He had admitted a black child, Susan Robinson, whose presence had caused the parents of his few remaining students to withdraw their children. Abba didn't know if she and the girls would survive. Anna dreamed that her father cut her to pieces (to which Bronson suggested that

God had sent her the dream to make her feel that she had been wicked). Bronson was very melancholy: "I shrink from the eyes of men. I weep over their blindness. My labors rise in magnitude before my mind's eye, and I feel aggrieved at the slight and wrong which these have received. I sigh over the weary idleness which besets me. My days and nights are void unto me. I have gifts that the age needs to have put in exercise, yet it calls me blasphemous. O! What shall I do?"

Emerson had been trying for some time to persuade Bronson to move to Concord, give up teaching, and become a writer. Bronson resisted because he felt he had a more active role to perform. But the idea of being a "philosopher" began to appeal to him, and the possibility of holding conversations in communities like Lexington was mentioned. Abba was dubious and thought they were likely to starve. Bronson conceded the possibility, but felt "that a purpose like mine must yield bread for the hungry and clothe the naked, and I wait not for the arithmetic of the matter."

They decided to auction off the Temple School accouterments and pay some of the several thousands they owed. Alcott reserved a little to buy gardening tools. Abba thought she could work, although her "constitution is more enfeebled than I am willing to realize.

"But I will not anticipate evils. The quiet, pure air, and the genial influences of the approaching season may promote a more vigorous state of health. And then we cannot materially suffer, even if the patience of the most tried friendship should weary of our dependence."

On March 31, 1840, the family left 6 Beach Street, Boston, for a small cottage belonging to Edmund Hosmer in Concord. It was near the old South Bridge and lay about a mile from Emerson's. Hosmer charged them $52 a year.

8

Concordia

CONCORDIA, AS BRONSON LIKED TO HAVE IT, was a small, quiet town west of Boston, connected to it by the new Fitchburg Railroad. It had a dusty main street bordered with elms and maples, behind which lay neat lawns occupied by square white clapboard houses, with an occasional yellow or red frame cottage to break the oppressively stately effect. Concord was as old as a town could be in America, and was quite aware of its heritage. It had a conservative character and a sober populace of English stock. The 1840s brought the first Irish from Boston. They came to work on the line and formed a small, impoverished community near the railroad tracks along Walden Pond.

Concord is one of New England's loveliest examples of collaboration between nature and man. The white homes and churches sit on flat lawns that gracefully evolve from back yards into wide meadows. These undulating fields edge the placid Concord River, which, in Hawthorne's words, "kisses the tangled grass of mowing-fields and pastures, or bathes the overhanging boughs of elder-bushes and other water loving plants." The river grows yellow water lilies, and along the shores stand silvery green reeds, bullrushes, cattails, and golden pickerel weed. Mud turtles slither from the overgrown banks into the slow brown river, where they join eels and fish. In the fall the river freezes completely. The ice doesn't break up till the first week in April, when the river floods free from its solid state.

Walden Pond is a twenty-minute walk from Concord. Thoreau's famous lake, small and clear, is set in a thick grove of firs, maples, oaks, elms, and birches. Near one particularly beautiful cove, the small community of Irish workers lived in shanties constructed of ill-assorted planks with earthen roofs from which grass would sometimes grow.

Concordia would have been just another New England town, but for the fact that it was the home of Ralph Waldo Emerson and Henry David Thoreau. Emerson attracted visitors and settlers — not just Alcott, but the poet Ellery Channing, Margaret Fuller, and Elizabeth Peabody and her sisters: Sophia Peabody, who brought along her husband, Nathaniel Hawthorne, and later Mary Peabody, who came with her husband, Horace Mann. Emerson was the town's most sustaining figure, and through him Concord became characterized by a noble, vague, romantic transcendentalism. It was the home of American idealism, and although many found it gloomy and cold, notably Henry James, who compared Concord to one of Turgenev's more dreary settings, nevertheless it was unique in the attempts of a disproportionate number of its citizens to lead exemplary lives. Their standards were not worldly or even similar. (Their eccentric interpretations of the dictates of the Oversoul may have been on Emerson's mind when he called the virtue of consistency into question.) Concord was a tight, judgmental town, but it tolerated Alcott's weirdness.

On April 1, 1840, the Alcotts moved their few possessions into the Hosmer cottage, the "Dove Cote." It was a square wooden house with a wide flight of stairs leading to a porch, which opened onto four large rooms. The river ran behind the house, which was about a half a mile from the center of town. Edmund Hosmer was an amiable, unexacting landlord, a sort of crackerbarrel transcendentalist who would trade rustic wit for Alcott's ethereal epigrams.

Alcott had little else to trade. He dug a garden beside the house and spent long hours in communion with his vegetables. The family ate what he produced, but it was not enough. In the winter the family diet was apples and squash. If Louisa had been bad she would get no dinner at all, and if she had been particularly bad, her father would deny himself food.

Concordia gave Louisa a chance to stretch her legs and work off some of the tension and energy she quickly collected. "I always thought," she said later, "I must have been a deer or a horse in some former state, because it was such a joy to run. Nobody could be my friend till I had beaten him in a race, and no girl if she refused to climb fences, and be a tomboy."

"Running over the hills just at dawn one summer morning," she wrote of her twelfth year, "and pausing to rest in the silent woods, saw through an arch of trees, the sun rise over the river, hill, and wide green meadows as I never saw it before.

"Something born of the lovely hours, a happy mood and the unfolding aspirations of a child's soul seemed to bring me very near to God; and in the hush of that morning hour I always felt that I 'got religion' . . ."

Louisa learned to love nature while padding around after her teacher, twenty-three-year-old Henry David Thoreau, whom Hawthorne described as "ugly as sin." He was a short, stocky man with large deep eyes between gray and green, an enormous nose, and a sad, down-turned mouth. He took long strides and kept his eyes on the ground, rarely taking a walk without turning up some Indian artifact. Usually he would turn down petitioners for his company, saying, "I do not know. There is nothing so important to me as my walk; I have no walk to throw away." But he sometimes made an exception for children. Louisa would trot behind obediently, watching Thoreau in his checked shirt, straw hat, and gray pants. He always carried a pencil and notebook for his observations, a spyglass, an old music book to press plants, and a jackknife and twine for all eventualities. The boy-man who could not pass a berry without picking it would wade into streams and ponds for water lilies, climb trees for birds' nests, and bring chirping frogs as a prize to his friend and mentor, Emerson. Fish would swim into Henry's hands, and snakes would coil around his short legs. He could predict the weather from the clouds and could tell within two the day of the year, according to what plants were blooming. He offered Concord's natural beauty to the little girl, and she worshiped him. In the only adult novel of love she ever wrote, she described him as a man with "much alloy and many flaws; but beneath all defects the Master's eye saw the grand lines that were to serve as models for the perfect man . . ."

Louisa and Anna went to Henry and his brother John Thoreau's school, the Concord Academy, which reminded the girls of their father's Temple School. The atmosphere was liberal, and Henry would wander off into moral monologues, as when he explained why profanity was bad: If one wished to discuss business with a man, "and he persisted in thrusting words having no connection with the subject into all parts of every sentence — Boot-jack, for instance — wouldn't you think he was taking a liberty with you, and trifling with your time, and wasting his own?" Henry then demonstrated by saying "Boot-jack" frequently and irrelevantly throughout a sentence. Henry and John offered geometry, algebra, grammar, and geography as well as field trips, when they set off with jugs of lemonade to tramp through the Concord underbrush.

Louisa and Anna's cousin, twelve-year-old Edmund Sewall, came from Boston to attend Henry's school. He arrived on March 23, 1840, in time to take early spring walks with the Alcott girls and Henry, John, and their sister Sophia. John cut strips of birch bark and fashioned a drinking vessel for the females. In April, Henry plowed up an old potato patch near the academy so his scholars could raise their own vegetables. Often he would visit the Alcotts with his mother and Edmund, and he would check with Edmund to see how his new journal habit was taking.

Louisa grieved for her friend Mr. Thoreau in the winter of 1842, when his brother John died of lockjaw. Henry shut himself up in Emerson's house, where he was living, with a sympathetic case of the disease. He never spoke of his brother afterward, but would occasionally sing in his harsh, untrained voice a lament for a kind-hearted sailor. John and Henry had been very close. John had all of Henry's strengths without his defensive pugnacity, and Henry was bereft without the sweetening influence of this older brother.

Thoreau had gone to Harvard, at Emerson's recommendation, and had returned to Concord to live with Emerson rather than at his mother's boarding house in town. He built the Emerson children an elegant doll house and made himself useful around the house in exchange for a small room at the head of the stairs and board. His relation with Emerson grew thin from Waldo's patronizing and from his own refusal to be grateful. Thoreau found himself drawn to Lydian Emerson, whose melancholy half-confidences appealed to him, for he enjoyed the fancy that he was able to supply Lydian with an understanding that failed Emerson.

Thoreau had once believed himself in love, with Edmund Sewall's lovely older sister Ellen. But the passion had been refused; she had turned him down. Thoreau blamed Ellen for wanting to say in words what should only have been a sublime understanding. Love, he believed, was "the profoundest of secrets. Divulged, even to the beloved, it is no longer love . . . I require that thou knowest everything without being told anything. I parted from my beloved because there was one thing which I had to tell her. She *questioned* me. She should have known all by sympathy. That I had to tell it her was the difference between us — the misunderstanding." Henry's obsessive, critical, and intrusive mother led him to some frigid ideas about friendship. In his journal he plotted a transcendental relationship: "Friends do not interchange their commonwealth but each puts his finger into the private coffer of the other . . . each will be to the other as admirable and as inaccessible as a star."

Thoreau didn't think well of women. Emerson's aunt, Mary Moody Emerson, was an exception, "a genius, as woman seldom is, reminding you less often of her sex than any woman whom I know." But when a woman in Concord intimated that she wanted to marry Henry, he "sent back as distinct a no as I have learned to pronounce after considerable practise, and I trust that this had succeeded. Indeed, I wished that it might burst, like a hollow shot, after it had struck and buried itself and made itself felt there. There was no other way. I really had anticipated no such foe as this in my career." The violence of Thoreau's reaction reflects the strength of his misogyny.

Truculent, surly, systematically unconventional, Thoreau was as eccentric as Alcott but angrier. He wouldn't black his boots or brush his hair. Oliver Wendell Holmes complained that he "nibbled his asparagus at the wrong end," which counted among Thoreau's mildest sins against decorum. From his sharp-tongued, officious, loquacious mother, Henry learned to take everything personally — from the government to the weather. Unconvinced that human relations could be anything but frightening and painful, he sought out tree frogs and blackberries instead of people.

He allowed himself to lavish sentiment on little boys who didn't frighten him. Thoreau developed an affection for poor little Johnny Riordan, an Irish lad who lived in a hovel near Walden. "He had on," Thoreau reported with deep feeling in his journal, "in the middle of January of the coldest winter we have had for twenty years, one thickness only of ragged cloth sewed on to his pantloons over his shirt, and shoes with large holes in the toes, into which the snow got, as he was obliged to confess, he who had trodden five winters under his feet! Thus clad he walked a mile to school every day, over the bleakest of railroad causeways, where I know by experience the grown man would frequently freeze his ears or nose if they were not well protected, — for his parents have no thermometer, — all to get learning and warmth and there sit at the head of his bench."

Louisa shared Thoreau's preference for little boys, taking as her best friend seven-year-old Cyrus Hosmer. Anna fell in love with Cyrus's older brother Henry, but Louisa attempted to subdue her friend by running faster and jumping higher. The girls also made friends with the Emerson children, Waldo, Ellen, and little Edith.

Louisa took walks by the Old Manse, where Nathaniel and Sophia Hawthorne came to spend their first married months. Emerson's grandfather had built the rambling, stone-gated home, and Emerson himself had written *Nature* in its downstairs study. The house was owned by George Ripley, who owed Hawthorne $1000. Rather than repay his friend the money when he left the experimental community of Brook Farm to be married, Ripley offered him his house rent-free.

Hawthorne, a tall, marvelously handsome man with dark hair and gray-blue eyes, took his lovely, fragile wife to the dark house, where the two of them hid out, letting almost no one into their lives. Thoreau was an exception, and he and Hawthorne became quite fond of one another, each observing the other's desire for long-distance friendship. Occasionally the Hawthornes would see the unstable poet William Ellery Channing, who had married Margaret Fuller's sister Ellen and had moved to a small red house in Concord in the fall of 1842.

The first spring in Concord, Louisa tried to express some of her wonder as she watched the ice break up on the Concord River behind the house, seeing spring come as she had never seen it in Boston. She composed her maiden poem, "To the First Robin":

> Welcome, welcome, little stranger,
> Fear no harm, and fear no danger
> We are glad to see you here,
> For you sing, "Sweet Spring is near."

Now the white snow melts away;
Now the flowers blossom gay;
Come dear bird and build your nest,
For we love our robin best.

Abba was beside herself with her daughter's promise and made much of the little girl. She was worried about Louisa: "There is at times the greatest vitality and wretchedness of spirit, no hope, no heart for anything — sad solemn and desponding. Fine generous feelings — no selfishness — great good will to all — and strong attachment to a few." She thought Louisa's moods were "rather uncommon for a child of her age — united to such firmness of purpose and resolution."

Anna spent as much time as possible with her father. She talked with him about alcohol and concluded that she was temperate. When he went away she observed that she did not like to have the days pass without lessons. She discussed her faults with Bronson and considered how to correct them: "I like conversation with father . . ." She listened to him explain how she might govern herself and his hope that she would learn obedience. She watched him with a maternal affection: "Father got breakfast this morning all himself." Anna adopted matronly ways, especially after Abigail was born on July 16, 1840. She loved looking after her tiny sister and could be punished by being denied "the pleasure of tending baby." Louisa preferred neutral chores like washing dishes and cleaning.

In her worried journal, Anna reported her father telling her and Louisa "how people had treated him, and why he came to live at Concord, and how we must give up a good many things that we like." Anna continued that she knew "it will be hard, but I mean to do it. I fear I shall complain sometimes about it." Louisa was silent and brooded. The family had given up butter and milk and were down to apples and bread.

Abba was sick and distracted by pregnancy and baby care. Bronson earned nothing, and only charity kept the family from starving. Abba wrote to Sam that "the claims of my children keep me from despair but I feel sometimes as if life was more of toil than was good for my peace of soul or health of body. — I experience at times for whole days the most exquisite sense of *weariness*. I cannot get rested — I feel like a noble horse harnassed in a yoke —

and made to drag and pull instead of trot and canter — Mr. Alcott would like a more graceful movement but an animal without spirit . . . must be commiserated for its lack of life rather than lack of grace."

In her despondency and worry over Louisa, Abba gave her moody, unhappy little girl an engraving of a sick mother and a hard-working daughter. Her accompanying note is an eerie prophecy of what was to come: "Dear Louisa, I enclose a picture for you which I always admired very much — for in my imagination I have thought you might be just such an industrious good daughter — and that I might be a sick but loving mother, looking to my daughter's labors for my daily bread — Take care of it for *my sake,* and your own, because you and *I,* have always liked to be grouped together. Mother." She made Louisa feel specially loved while simultaneously marking her for a special burden.

Bronson's notion, in moving to Concord, was that he would combine his study with manual labor. Dr. Channing, like most sedentary intellectuals, had loved Bronson's intention of getting his hands dirty with some glorious chore: "One of my dearest ideas is the union of Labor and Culture. Mr. Alcott hiring himself out for day-labor and at the same time living in a region of high thought is, perhaps, the most interesting object in our Commonwealth." Alcott loved the idea and warbled to his brother-in-law about the bliss of blisters: "Tomorrow I enter the meadows with my neighbours. Labor is, indeed sweet, nor is that a severe, but benificent decree, which sends man into the fields to earn his Bread in the sweat of his face. Labor invests man with his primeval dignity."

Alcott chopped wood for a dollar a day in the winter of 1840–1841, but there was little call for his services. The country was in the middle of a depression, which had begun with President Jackson's fight with Biddle over the bank and had ended with shutdown factories all over the East and Horace Greeley advising men to go west. There were long soup lines in Philadelphia and alarm over the hoards of beggars in Boston. Abba had sewed for money, but she could do little while the baby was so young. In the spring of 1841 she wrote to Sam that she would wait a few months to find out if Bronson could come up with anything, and if not, try to get some work herself, "and tho I may adopt some scheme of life giving me more labors if it makes me independent of the charity of my relations and friends it will give me life indeed — My girls shall have trades and their Mother with the sweat of her brow shall earn an honest subsistence for herself and them — I have no accomplishments for I never was educated for a fine lady — but I have handicraft . . . and *will* enough to feed the bodies and save the souls of myself and children."

Colonel May died on February 27, 1841. The Alcotts and their friends hoped that this would alleviate some of their difficulties, but this was not the case. The colonel left Abba $3100, which was immediately attached by the creditors of the Temple School, leaving an unpaid debt of $3400. Abba wrote that her father "has left a will, disposing of the few thousands he had to give without any . . . seeming regard to *me* . . . I had supposed that time was mellowing his severe judgment of my motives, and that my husband and children were becoming objects of care and regard to him . . . he *did* not love me."

The texture of Abba's lifelong depression was woven from the strands of dependency on her father. Theirs had always been a distant relation and was, at best, respectful. The colonel's disapproval of Abba's husband and their unsound financial ways stirred up in Abba her old feelings of defensiveness and pain. Even after his death, her father still managed to make her feel cheated and belittled. She could see that he loved Sam, and it grieved her that she never shared such relaxation and acceptance. What she could not see was that Sam didn't try to extract from the colonel more than he could provide. In her adult mind, Abba still had a child's view of her father as a giant, carelessly dispensing life-and-death critiques. She refused, in relation to him and to her husband, to see her own force and effectiveness. Women, she had been taught, were the helpless ones, dependent upon their fathers and husbands for support and identity. She had neither husband nor father who would provide these necessities. Her father was born and raised before the nineteenth century drained women of their spirit. Bronson was eccentric, narcissistic, and passive, though his affection for his wife was genuine. But Abba's disappointment was stronger than any human-scale sympathy. Her melancholy and anger were hard for her, but disastrous for her children, especially Louisa, who bore the brunt of it.

* * *

A few months after going to Concord, Bronson had decided that he did not believe in working for a wage, that it was unrighteous. He could give conversations and accept charity, however. He began traveling to surrounding communities such as Lynn, Haverhill, Marshfield, Scituate, Dedham, and as far as Providence, where he would stay with a minister or friend who would open his parlor to those interested. Bronson conversed on topics such as "Man," "Character," "Temperaments and Pursuits," "Social Life," and "Human Culture." He would usually talk for sixty minutes in a modified Socratic dialogue. Ednah Dow Cheney, a Quaker woman of reverential disposition and earnest demeanor, transcribed some of Alcott's conversations: "He read Plato's parable of Man, as a figure with a hundred heads of bird and beast, which represented the desires; then the figure of a lion, which was Anger; and then the figure of a Man; and he who loves justice gives the rule to this man over the beasts. He then gave some phrases, such as: Instincts, which desire; Understanding, which apprehends; Fancy, which images; Reason, which comprehends; Imagination, which seizes truths; Conscience, which perceives laws; Inspiration, or intuition." At this point Alcott was interrupted by the precise Reverend Theodore Parker, who wanted him to define understanding and reason. Alcott, irritated with the sudden descent to reality, replied that "God only can define; man can only confine." Parker indicated that he would be satisfied if Alcott would confine. Alcott persisted in his evasion: "All language is fluent: a word means what we will have it mean at the time; it needs the whole experience of life to explain it, and no definitions can make it convey the thought to one not in a condition to receive it."

From all reports, Alcott provided listeners with a sense of well-being and heightened spirituality, but the content of his talks was elusive, and from the foggy, insubstantial transcriptions left, it seems clear that their effect vanishes without the speaker himself. One exception was Alcott's outrageous contention that dark-skinned people were demonic, and that blue-eyed blonds were closest to God. Someone interrupted him in this discourse to say that "Swedenborg says that the Negroes are the most beloved of all the races of Heaven." Alcott paused and responded frostily, "That is very kind of Mr. Swedenborg."

Once Alcott expanded upon the demonic man. He very deliberately described a man in the audience, characterizing the demonic nature as a dark, strong logician who smoked. The logical smoker, the victim of the attack, began questioning Bronson. It became clear that he was leading Alcott into a semantic trap that would make him look foolish, but before the last question Bronson began to talk. Mrs. Cheney said, "He soared higher and higher, as if he had taken the wings of the morning, and he brought us all the glories of heaven. I believe none of us could tell what he said, but we listened with rapture. Mr. Greene sat with one finger crossed upon another, waiting for a pause to put in his question; but the time never came, his opponent was borne away in a cloud far out of sight. I always queried whether this was intentional or whether his good angel carried him away; but Louisa said, 'Oh, he knew well enough what he was doing.' "

Honest Sam May complained mildly that he did not understand Bronson and Emerson. He wished they would make themselves "more intelligible to others." This complaint was echoed when Bronson made his first contribution to the *Dial,* the transcendentalist journal that Emerson and Margaret Fuller began editing in 1840. The first number of the magazine, published by Elizabeth Peabody, contained a number of Alcott's "Orphic Sayings," epigrammatic paragraphs in which he attempted to confine some of his notions long enough for them to be examined. Under the title "Vocation," for example, Bronson made himself clear: "Engage in nothing that cripples or degrades you. Your first duty is self-culture, self-exaltation: you may not violate this high trust. Yourself is sacred, profane it not. Forge no chains wherewith to shackle your own members. Either subordinate your vocation to your life, or quit it forever: it is not for you; it is condemnation of your own soul. Your influence over others is commensurate with the strength that you have found in yourself. First cast the demons from your own bosom, and then shall your words exorcise them from the hearts of others."

At his most obscure, Bronson was most obscure. Under the heading "Gravitation" he wrote: "Love and gravity are a twofold action of one life, whose conservative instincts in man and nature preserve inviolate the harmony of the immutable and eternal law of spirit. Man and nature alike tend toward the Godhead. All seeming divergence is overruled by this omnipotent force, whose retributions restore universal order." This kind of unenlightening thought led a critic to compare the "Orphic Sayings" with fifty boxcars rattling by, containing only one passenger.

Alcott was dissatisfied with the *Dial* and wrote to Margaret Fuller about his discontent. "The *Dial* prefers a style of diction not mine; nor can I add to its popularity with its chosen readers. A fit organ for such as myself is not yet, but is to be. The times require a full speech, a wise, humane, and brave sincerity, unlike all examples of literature, of which the *Dial* is but the precursor. A few more years will give us all we desire, — the people all they ask."

Margaret came to Concord many times in those years. She stayed with the Emersons, and she and her host would from their rooms write each other long, intense letters, simmering with flirtation, and get little Waldo to deliver them. Once Margaret ambushed Emerson and forced on him some lessons in "German pronunciation never by my offer and rather against my will, each time." Margaret visited the Alcotts and observed Bronson's "model children" careening around the cottage much like any other children.

Margaret had quickly made a name for herself after leaving the Temple School. She had given several series of conversations for women, in which she displayed her extraordinary erudition and her equally extraordinary wardrobe of Grecian draperies. She was anything but an idealist, and Emerson's presence at one of her conversations "gave her opportunity and excitement to unfold and illustrate her realism and acceptance of conditions," wrote the indefatigable conversation-goer Mrs. Cheney.

Margaret, like Bronson, was inclined to take herself too seriously, and once she told Richard Henry Dana, Jr., that she often asked herself, "How came I here? How is it that I seem to be this Margaret Fuller?" Emerson related that Margaret made an unpleasant first impression, in part because she demonstrated "an overweening sense of power and slight esteem for others . . ." She was famous for her satirical tongue: "The men thought she carried too many guns, and the women did not like one who despised them."

Alcott came to visit Margaret in Boston and described to her his great difficulties. She reported to Emerson that Alcott had said he'd found himself nearly crazy, but that he'd begun to learn his limitations, and he'd gained a great deal in Emerson's friendship. "He wept a plenteous shower of gracious tears.

"He then spoke of me, how he had often distrusted me from the very first, at times, did so still. I told him that was nothing peculiar to him, it seemed the friends I loved the best and had supposed my fellow pilgrims did the same, but the fault, in his case, was he never showed distrust to me, but spoke of it to others, — now that he had spoken of it to myself, all was well.

"This interview did not increase my confidence in him, nor did I feel that I could respond to his expressions of wish for sympathy. I still saw the same man, seeing states in the intellect which he will not humbly realize in heart and life. He had been to see W. Channing, and was going to West Roxbury, and I felt that after he had talked out this new phase to a dozen people it would have done its work, and truth be left unembodied as far as depends on him. Yet I see, too, he is sincere in his own way, and that it is very hard for me to be just to him. I will try to be more gentle and reverent in my thoughts of him, if only because he has felt you at this moment."

Margaret was not alone in noting Alcott's difficulties. On his conversational circuits, friends found him bitter and complaining. His peaceful manner was disturbed. He railed against a society that made no place for him. He had expected praise for his work with children, and the unexpected censure turned his benign radicalism into a sour nihilism. He thirsted for an angry judgment day to bring his critics to their knees.

Emerson tried to help, and invited the Alcotts to live with him. He had toyed with the idea of joining his friends in West Roxbury, where George Ripley had begun an experiment in communal living, Brook Farm. There writers, reformers, and sympathizers, including Hawthorne and the musicologist John Dwight, shared their labors and produce. They farmed together so that all could indulge equally their scholarly interests. Emerson thought they were too much like a hotel in their concern for practical affairs. "I had wished to be convinced," lamented Emerson, "to be thawed, to be made nobly mad by the kindlings before my eye of a new dawn of human piety. But this scheme was arithmetic and comfort . . ." In 1835 Emerson had bought a square white clapboard house of imposing dignity, large enough for two families. The house had a sophisticated air, unlike the rusticity of the Hosmer cottage, and sat on nine acres of land that included a fresh brook behind the house. So Emerson invited the Alcotts and, in a burst of democracy, tried to persuade the maid and cook to eat with the family. Both the cook and Mrs. Alcott refused, although the maid and Bronson were willing enough. Abba wrote to Sam that he had offered "half his house and store-room free — Mr. A. to work with him in his land and I am to share the household labor with Mrs. E. — the families and tables separate."

It was undoubtedly just as well that Abba decided as she did, for relations between her and the Emersons would have deteriorated catastrophically at close quarters. Little Waldo Emerson fell sick early in 1842. Ten-year-old Louisa ran over to the Emersons to find out how he was; Ralph came to the door to say, without expression, that he had died. Louisa ran home, stricken, to tell her mother, who wrote in her journal: "I cannot offer sympathy . . . for I see so much culpable neglect of the means of *living* — great errors in education, modes of living, feeding, clothing, bathing, exercise, sleeping . . . The mind over-worked and not exercised enough."

Alcott reached a dangerously low point in the winter of 1841–1842. Abba wrote to Sam that she thought he wouldn't survive long; "if his body don't fail his mind will — he experiences at times the most dreadful nervous excitation — his mind distorting every act however simple into the most complicated and adverse form — I am terror stricken at this and feel as if I would rather lay him low than see his once sweet calm, imperturable spirit experiencing these fluctuations and all the divine aspirations of his pure nature suffering defeat and obloquy."

Alcott had been in touch with a group of English reformers who had opened a school called Alcott House, in honor of Bronson's educational theories, which were more popular abroad than at home. Emerson thought it would do him good to visit a community of admirers and, two weeks after Waldo's death, offered him the opportunity to go to England. He wrote to his friend, saying that he thought the trip could be made for four or five hundred dollars and that he would be glad "to be responsible to you for that amount; and to more, if I shall be able, and more is necessary."

Abba worried about this separation but wanted some tranquillity. To Sam she wrote that "this is to be the 'test act' of my Transcendentalism. If I do indeed believe in that intercommunication of souls that renders the body a mere incidence to this state of being, then will his absence in the flesh be of small consideration — we have in no wise been alien in affection — but our diversity of opinion has at times led us far and wide of a quiet and contented frame of mind — *I* have been looking for rest — *he* for principle and salvation — *I* have been striving for justice and peace — *he* for truth and righteousness. My *will* had always been a stumbling block to my success — and my constant prayer and effort is to subjugate *that*."

Bronson installed his nervous younger brother Junius Alcox in the cottage. Junius, born in 1818, was only twenty-four when he came to stay with his sister-in-law and nieces. He was a religious, unstable, sickly young man who died abruptly in his thirty-fourth year. He and his older brother shared their spiritual longings.

Bronson sailed on May 8, 1842, on the *Rosalind*, supplied with potatoes and applesauce and an introduction from Emerson to his good friend Thomas Carlyle. In London Bronson visited twice with the bearded Scots writer, who had become a transcendental hero. Emerson had warned his friend that if he had heard Bronson's name to "forget what you have heard. Especially if you have heard anything to which his name was attached, be sure to forget that . . ." Irascible, opinionated, and uninhibited, Carlyle tried for Emerson's sake to like his friend, but found him, according to Henry James, Sr., "a terrible old bore." Carlyle wrote to Emerson that Alcott had called "at considerable length, the second time all night." He saw the good intention in the man "bent on saving the world by a return to acorns and the golden age: he comes before one like a venerable Don Quixote, whom nobody can laugh at without loving." This was not strictly true, since Carlyle laughed at but did not love Bronson. He told James later that it was "almost impossible to be rid of him, and impossible to keep him for he would not eat what was set before him." Carlyle served potatoes for breakfast, and ordered for his guest some strawberries. Alcott put the strawberries on the same plate with his potatoes and let the juices run together, which so appalled Carlyle's sensibilities that he refused to eat himself and ranted around the room instead.

The outspoken Carlyle was as intolerant as the mild-mannered reformer, and neither could abide the other. Bronson complained that he was "impatient" of any "interruption, and faithless in all social reforms . . . His conversation is cynical, trivial, and gave no pleasure . . . I know his trouble; also his cure." After their second encounter, which, Bronson wrote, "sped not better than at first," Alcott wrote to his wife that he had "seen Carlyle once more but we quarrelled outright and I shall not see him again." Bronson did try to see Carlyle again, to convert him to what Carlyle called his "potato gospel," but his quarry was out. Carlyle wrote Bronson a gracious farewell, wishing that he didn't appear "as an incorrigible heretic and infidel." He hoped Alcott's plan for reform worked out well, adding that although "not precisely my church, I do reckon it a branch of the true church, very worthy to spread and root itself according to its power in a world so overgrown with falsity and jungle as ours is."

Alcott House and its reformers were all Bronson could find to like in England. The beer-drinking, beef-eating Britons disgusted him. The women all seemed tearful and "tragic all," and he despaired of finding an edible apple. He wished to be back "in the land of my birth."

With his two new friends, Charles Lane and Henry Wright, Alcott expanded his homeopathic horizons, discovering cold baths and different vegetables. Alcott House operated on the principles of James P. Greaves, who had written that "education can never repair the defects of Birth." Man's duty, therefore, was to purify his body for perfect procreation. An Alcott House pamphlet explained that "the elements for a superior germination consist in an innocent fertile mind, and a chaste healthful body, built up from the purest and most volatile productions of the uncontaminated earth; thus removing all hinderances to the immediate influx of Deity into the spiritual faculties and corporeal organs." Any disease must be from greed or lust and "originates in the soul — the body but reports the state of the soul: the diseased have sinned . . . Medicine of all kinds appears to be quackery." In order to marry, man and woman had to have led a "Divine Existence" up to the wedding. Consequently Lane was celibate and Wright had lied to keep his marriage a secret.

Alcott convinced Lane and Wright that in the purity of New England they would be able to establish a moral kingdom. He wrote to Abba, asking her to look for a suitable farm for such a venture. Abba and Emerson shared their doubts about the project. Emerson was "greatly apprehensive that Mr. Alcott had dipped his pencil in Rembrandt's pot of gay coloring, and that his friends would find themselves in a barren field with no sun to cheer them — and no shade to shelter them — ." Abba worried that "we are not favorably situated here for any experiment of diet — Having little or no fruit on the place — no house — room — and surrounded by those whose prejudices are intolerable."

Emerson was deeply concerned with the reports of and from Alcott. He wrote to Carlyle that Alcott was a great man, but that he was afraid "he has already touched what best he can, and through his more than prophet's egotism, and the absence of all useful reconciling talents, will bring nothing to pass, and be but a voice in the wilderness. As you do not seem to have seen him in his pure and noble intellect, I fear that it lies under some new and denser clouds."

Bronson's departure had prostrated Abba. She suffered wild bouts of weeping and lost her appetite. She prayed that she might "improve by this great, this heavy discipline." Soon, however, she found that she could appreciate Bronson in absentia as well, if not better, than in the flesh. It was easy to wax rapturous about his saintliness when she wasn't face to face with its consequences. She began sounding like her courting self: "My letters are hardly worth the expense of transportation, and are a feeble expression of the thoughts that breathe, and words that turn toward him — But the effort to gratify him has a virtue in it — and I will try to meet his wishes — ." She had to concede that "wife, children, and friends are less to him than the great ideas he is seeking to realize. How naturally man's sphere seems to be in the region of the head, and woman's in the heart and the affections." As for her: "It is your life which has been more to me than your doctrine or theories." From the dispassion of distance Abba affirmed that "I Love your fidelity to the pursuit of truth."

Anna missed her father constantly, but Louisa sensed a new freedom and liveliness in the atmosphere and an occasional burst of unexpected hilarity from her mother. She enjoyed the new flavor of liberty and her mother encouraged her to explore.

Abba and the girls expected Bronson home in August, but he postponed his departure, hoping for new subscribers to the coming Eden. Abba tried to remain unprejudiced about Bronson's lofty-sounding plans and reflected that her "powers of adaptation to circumstance have usually been sufficient to sustain me comfortably to myself and agreeably to others." She looked back over her marriage with some satisfaction, gathering her girls around her as a proof of her industry and worth: "My children may not turn out wits or beauties, but the monopoly of happiness is not engrossed by beauty nor that of virtue by genius — a docile child will seldom be found to want understanding sufficient for the purposes of a useful, a happy, and a pious life — If I do but plant and water the true seed in their hearts, God *will* give the increase . . . " She staked out her turf with one daughter at each corner of the plot, remarking that she was the only one of four sisters to have survived twelve years of marriage: "Oh may my dear daughters love to feel that it has been well for *them* that I have been spared to them yet a little longer . . . " And, instinctively, the girls drew closer to Abba's skirts, finding in her their one real security, as she found in them her definition.

As Bronson's arrival approached, Abba grew apprehensive that he might have lost interest in his family, but she hastily said, "I know it cannot — for my own experience has often taught me that duty, home, offspring are the world to a parent — This dear companion has had a weary and solitary sojourn thus far in life — perhaps he may find that truth after all dwells not in men or places, — why seek either."

On October 20, 1842, Alcott came soaring home with his two English friends, convinced that they were going to accomplish the final moral experiment and plant the heaven that would regenerate society. Bronson's reentry into Concord was marked by unassailable confidence and moral certainty, just as his departure had been by vacillation and despair.

The first two years in Concord found Louisa vibrating back and forth between her mother and Anna. With her mother she was peaceful and calm, listening to the strong, familiar voice tell her about self-sacrifice and controlling her temper. Louisa would bargain with herself and decide to be good for her mother's sake. In

Anna she found a willing friend and sergeant who would execute her commands. Twelve-year-old Anna took direction easily, looking first to her father, then to Louisa, whom she admired and feared slightly for her rebellious spirit and firm will. Unlike Anna, Louisa was never cowed by the prospect of punishment.

Louisa's years between eight and ten were a painful extension of her experience in Boston. With the addition of little Abby in 1840, her mother was constantly busy. Abba had, out of necessity, defined Louisa as her strong child, old enough to look after herself, her placid sister Beth, and even, on occasion, her mother. Abba had completed her annexation of Louisa's loyalties in her unspoken struggle with Bronson and the world. The bitterness of her complaints to Louisa about their poverty gave Louisa a lifelong sense of want — thirty years of which was imaginary. Abba assigned fault to the world, but it was Bronson who was not providing, Bronson with whom she pleaded. For Louisa the message was not to trust men, or non-Alcotts, and to barricade yourself in behind a bulwark of family obligations. Abba's dependence on Louisa for affection and an uncritical ear made the little girl proud and feel adult. It also burdened her forever with hopeless guilt and an unshakable conviction that wherever something needed fixing, it was up to her to provide the service. Her anxiety only relaxed in the service of others, but the constant pressure to sacrifice her aims and desires to the needs of her family caused her both anguish and fury.

On Anna's tenth birthday, in March 1841, Louisa spent all day virtuously keeping her temper and letting her sister know of her sacrifice. As Anna later remembered it, Louisa's concept of Anna's birthday was presenting her sister with a gift of a toothbrush and making the presentation with a triumphant flourish. Anna's birthday poignantly underscored the definition of Louisa's moment. Her parents taught her to behave as if every day were someone else's birthday. Louisa obliged but couldn't resist the attention-asking flourish.

Through her mother's instruction and her father's example, Louisa soon came to feel that their Concord neighbors either patronized them or despised them for their poverty. Abba's constant money talks caused Louisa to see her small world as an unmitigated financial disaster. She came to feel that people considered her and her family only as a trial. They were always a burden to someone, always obligated. Their own kindness and generosity could never be expressed because they were always in debt, and indebtedness breeds hypocrisy and resentment. Louisa couldn't calculate family finances, but she felt deeply the economics of misery and, with her mother's constant encouragement, the shame of dependence. Her relation to her mother and sisters took on more and more of an inappropriate if fiercely protective aspect, just as she appeared to her father and all non-family friends as either a disappointment or the enemy.

9

Fruitlands

EMERSON HAD RIGHTLY PREDICTED that the praise and admiration of Bronson's British followers would lift his spirits. Alcott came home quite unhinged by glory. Always a dreamer, he was in the throes of a vision. Adulation had been too much for his minimal appreciation of reality.

In his dream, Bronson saw himself perfected, and by his example he would implement the improvement of his family and associates. This was to be the culmination of all his theories of education, the ultimate in nineteenth-century self-culture schemes. Like all the convinced, Bronson believed that he had seized the one true answer and that all righteousness would follow if only people would listen to him.

Abba was prepared to listen and to cooperate, but, in sanctifying himself, Bronson had withdrawn completely from her. She needed companionship and help, he wanted reverence and obedience. James Greaves had preached celibacy, that human ties were all to be voluntary and impersonal, not familial and close as Abba and her girls knew them. Bronson's British friends believed that the Alcott females were going to inhibit him from living the pure life. Anna, who worshiped her father under any circumstances, didn't have to adjust to the new situation. Louisa could sense, if not articulate, that her interests and those of the strange Englishmen were discrete. She stayed away from them as much as possible.

The Alcott family enacted a grand-scale battle between heart and mind. Bronson attempted to realize perfection through the application of his intellect, while his family tried to reach him through emotional ambushes. The dilemmas occasioned by Bronson's dream produced the greatest strain Abba and Bronson's union was ever to undergo. The Fruitland experiment made their marriage an issue in a period when separation was inconceivable. Finally, Fruitlands resulted in a rearrangement of duties to allow Bronson to pursue his interests with fewer family responsibilities. And Abba undertook to support and run the family with fewer pretenses and excuses about what she was doing.

That the marriage endured in its new fashion is a testament not only to the unthinkableness of divorce in 1843, but also to the vision that Bronson and Abba shared. They both saw Bronson as righteous. And they saw their marriage as a mission to cooperate in doing good. Bronson's good was somewhat of a more ethereal cast than Abba's, whose idea of goodness was food and warm clothes for the poor. But Abba considered it her responsibility to make it possible for Bronson to continue to think good thoughts. Bronson and Abba believed that by enabling him to do this they were enriching the possibilities for mankind's improvement. This is the only context in which to understand why she persisted in a relation that, on its surface, seems to have provided her with nothing but penury, discouragement, criticism, and rebuff.

*   *   *

Abba and the girls swept and dusted the cottage and decorated it with autumn flowers to welcome home "the Lord of our house and life." Abba wanted Bronson to see that "his servants and lovers have not slept or idled during his absence from the field of labor." The homecoming was ecstatic, but overnight the smiles thinned. Abba had desired Bronson's approbation for having managed so well in his absence, but his eyes could only see their coming perfection, not their recent past.

Bronson had lost his head, if not precisely his heart, to Charles Lane. He told his friends to write to either of them and "one or the other Janus will reply." But Lane and his twelve-year-old son, William, were a somber package to the females. Lane was a grim, prim man of no small intelligence, with a rigid, humorless bearing. Unlike Alcott, Lane had a sarcastic streak, but like him, he was tyrannical, self-righteous, and monomaniacal. His hobby was thinking up new things to forgo, having already dispensed with sex, affection, and any remotely appetizing edible. From their first meeting in the front room of the Dove Cote, surrounded with trunks and boxes containing James Greaves's library, which Bronson had commandeered from Alcott House, Lane recognized an enemy in Abba. Her fierce mother lion devotion to her cubs betrayed all the deficiencies of mere human love and inhibited the growth of a detached, exalted, and improving sentiment such as the moral regeneration of society demanded. Lane discovered another enemy in Louisa, who was unreceptive to this stern teacher. He gave the girls morning lessons and tried to subdue Louisa's opposition by cold reason, but she simply grew to detest him.

Henry Wright, a rather weaker specimen of reformer, took a look at the size of Alcott's cottage, and the diet of apples and unbolted flour he was expected to eat, and hastily decamped. Lane, writing to an English friend, scorned Wright's desertion: "Nothing but fruit, grain and water was hard for the inside; then regular hours and places, cleaning up scraps, etc. was desperate hard for the outside."

The point of all this, Alcott explained over and over, was that "the evils of life are not so much social or political, as personal; and a personal reform only can eradicate them." If one gave up every individual inclination, one's reward was perfection. Alcott warned against coffee, tea, cocoa, milk, butter, pork, beef, mutton, warm water for baths, heavy clothes, lamps lit by animal oil, hiring workers, working for hire, religion, ownership, the enslavement of cattle, involvement in politics, and having children, writing: "Being in preference to doing, is the great aim, and this comes to us rather by a resigned willingness than a wilful activity, which is, indeed, a check to all divine growth. Outward abstinence is a sign of inward fullness; and the only source of true progress is inward."

Abba took this all rather badly. She found the coarse-bread-and-apple diet inadequate. Her teeth hurt and the apples were sour. She had never liked cooking much anyway, and cooking apples and bread for two Lanes and six Alcotts made it impossible for her to "consume that which cost me so much misery to prepare." After five months' freedom she found she was "almost suffocated in this atmosphere of restriction and form." She was easily grieved and touchy. The men excluded her from all decision-making and forced her to abide by a strict schedule, causing her to write: "I hope the experiment will not bereave me of my mind — The enduring powers of the body have been well tried. The mind yields, falters, and fails. This is more discouraging to me than all else. It unfits me for the society of my friends, my husband, and my children."

She added: "They all seem most stupidly obtuse on the cause of this occasional prostration of my judgment and faculties. I hope the solution of the problem will not be revealed to them too late for my recovery or their atonement of this invasion of my rights as a woman and a mother. Give me one day of practical philosophy. It is worth a century of speculation and discussion."

Bronson's homecoming had been considerably less edifying than Abba had desired. According to his biographer Odell Shepard, one of the many things that Bronson had renounced was sex. Abba, whom William Garrison described as a "practical Grahamite," was familiar with Dr. Sylvester Graham's suggestion that husbands and wives limit their sexual indulgences to once a month. Graham, a friend of Bronson's who had lectured at the Temple School, observed that American men were suffering from nerve deficiency, weakened brains, skin and lung ailments, and general debility. The source of this syndrome, Graham contended, was the loss of semen, an ounce of which was thought to be equivalent to forty ounces of blood. Alcott, influenced by Greaves's teachings on celibacy, suddenly found even monthly sex incompatible with the clean life. It is hard to imagine that, after many difficult pregnancies, Abba objected to Bronson's decision on the grounds of a lost pleasure. But she knew she was losing one of the only exclusive intimacies she shared with her husband. In the match with Lane to see whether Bronson was going to keep one foot in this world or plant both in the other, Abba lost the first fall.

Louisa became very upset and sullen in the month after her father's return. For her tenth birthday Bronson wrote her a note, explaining that he'd looked for a picture but hadn't found anything. Instead he offered her an exhortation to learn goodness from her father: "I would have you feel my presence and be the happier, and better than I am here. I want, most of all things, to be a kindly influence on you, helping you to guide and govern your heart . . . I live, my dear daughter, to be good and do good to all, and especially to you and your mother and sister[s]. Will you not let me do you all the good that I would? And do you not know that I can do you little or none, unless you are disposed to let me . . . " If she wouldn't, she would continue to be defined by "anger, discontent, impatience, evil appetites, greedy wants, complainings, ill-speakings, vileness, heedlessness, rude behaviour." Bronson's narcisism and arrogance aided him in selecting the approach least likely to win his daughter's confidence and affection. Louisa could only resent her father's thoughtless curtailment of her freedom and his systematic disregard for her wishes. She even lost Mr. Thoreau to her father.

Henry often visited the cottage to discourse with Lane and Bronson. One night as they began talking Emerson was amused to hear Louisa run to her mother, calling with alarm, "Mamma, they have begun again." Lane and Thoreau developed a cool respect for each other, although Lane excoriated Henry for coming near to sensualism in his love of nature, calling it the most "subtle and dangerous of sins; a refined idolatry, much more to be dreaded than gross wickedness, because the gross sinner would be alarmed by the depth of his degradation, and come up from it in terror, but the unhappy idolaters of nature were deceived by the refined quality of their sin, and would be the last to enter the kingdom." Henry suggested that since neither Lane nor Bronson knew the first thing about nature, they had nothing valuable to say on the subject. On the contrary, argued Bronson, it was precisely their abundance of spiritual love that happily prevented them, unlike Henry, from worshiping mere material nature.

These conversations, Louisa perceived, were not for women. If Lydian "Queenie" Emerson or Abba sat in, they were silent. If Mary Moody Emerson was there, she would silence a female with her withering regard and once remarked, "Be still. I want to hear the men talk." The women conspired to look respectful and alert while sharing their experiences of incomprehension, inferiority, and condescension. Increasingly, men appeared to Louisa self-absorbed, preoccupied in matters both unintelligible and impractical, unsympathetic, and cold. She was happier when they were not there.

If she could have understood and permitted herself the expression of malice, Louy, as the family knew her, would have agreed with Ellery Channing, who wrote that "me . . . does all thought ejected from the Alcottian syringe drive into dejection. Such work for nothing . . . alas for the unleavened wit!" But she couldn't allow out her real feelings for Bronson and had to endure as a silent spectator at her parents' scrimmage.

Abba was trying very hard to go along with Bronson, knowing that she had the power to provoke a truly major crisis. She could move out with the children and furniture and thus scotch all plans for a new Eden. Instead she worked for concessions, and got nuts added to the house diet. In December, she recorded her efforts to "live more internally" and less for her family. She took a trip to Boston with young William Lane and Louisa "to try the influence of a short absence from home." The visit and a loving note from Bronson made her momentarily more tranquil and resigned. On her return she felt "an unusual quietude — less tenacious of my rights, or opinions — I do believe that the miracle is about being wrought — to be truly quickened into spiritual life, one must die a carnal death."

In January 1843, Abba established a household post office for resolving daily grievances. Letters were distributed and read after dinner. Lane and Abba availed themselves of this contrivance to attempt to settle their respective hashes. Lane urged Abba to express her *"feelings* and *views* upon the whole subject of our future movements . . . " He assured her that her opinion was valuable and that her "excellencies" had not been "overlooked . . . Without your concurrence freely and kindly given, our work will hobble and halt."

Lane's gesture soothed Abba's indignation at the newly established dictatorship in the cottage. To Bronson it was "puerile and false sympathy," but to Abba it was "what I much need . . . It may betray weakness — well! I am weak — and I do not find that he is 'wise is *always* strong.' — I am but human and with many infirmities about me."

Lane was developing some sympathy with Abba. The extent of Bronson's indebtedness dismayed Lane, and he confessed that had he "been aware of the real state of things here, the probability is that I should not have come, yet no one has deceived me . . . " Lane was immediately drawn into financing the Alcott debt. Sam May was fed up. He pointed out that everyone had to work, why shouldn't Bronson. As Sam told Abba, "His unwillingness to be employed in the normal way — produces great doubt in the minds of his friends as to the righteousness of his life — because he partakes in the wages of others occupied in this same way — ." Lane found himself paying off $300 worth of Alcott's debts, and Sam signed a note for the other half.

Finally Abba agreed to try a communal experiment, and Lane and Sam May arranged to buy a disorganized, wooden farmhouse and one hundred acres in Harvard, Massachusetts, about fifteen miles from Concord. The house was settled halfway up a steep hill, facing across a gentle valley toward Mount Wachusett. Three spacious downstairs rooms formed an L; upstairs, the space was broken down into a disordered warren of sleeping quarters under the low eaves. The floors were joined by steep, narrow, pine staircases. In the winter, shallow fireplaces downstairs offered a little warmth, but the house was drafty and the wide plank floors grew very cold. "Fruitlands" was strictly an honorific, since there were no orchards, but there were wild wooded acres up behind and sloping down below the house.

On a rainy June 1, 1843, the "consociate family" slowly traveled the fifteen miles to their new home. They had packed a wooden wagon high with all their possessions. Bronson, despite his opposition to the enslavement of beasts, drove a small horse. With him sat William Lane, in his Dutch boy haircut, and Abba, jiggling along with the baby in her lap. Louy and Elizabeth played in the furniture behind, while Anna trudged on doggedly beside Charles Lane through the muddy, rutted road, sloppy from spring rain.

They were greeted by the bearded Joseph Palmer, a cantankerous eccentric with a pronounced New England drawl who was both a practical farmer and a well-intentioned man. He lived nearby and took a charitable interest in the vagaries of the visionaries, lending a hand or a cow when discussion failed.

Palmer pursued his principles single-mindedly, and although he was ridiculed and persecuted for wearing a full beard, he refused to shave. He was called the "Old Jew Palmer," since only Jews wore beards. Four men tried to shave him, but he resisted and spent the year 1830 in jail. He could have been released by paying a $10 fine, but he refused. Finally the town, realizing that his was an expensive martyrdom, had to let him go. Palmer refused to walk out and forced his captors to carry him out in a chair. He once spent a whole day shoveling snow off the Fruitlands path, which crossed a neighbor's land. Palmer was convinced he had the right of way. His neighbor, equally convinced, shoveled the snow back onto Palmer's path. The two continued it a for a full day until, exhausted and furious, they begged Emerson to arbitrate.

At the family's first meal of apples and cold water, they were joined by Samuel Larned and Abraham Everett, new volunteers. Larned, a twenty-year-old merchant's son, had worked in a counting house and was, wrote Lane, "what the world calls genteel." He was especially interested in dietary reform, and had himself existed for one year on crackers and for another on apples. The bill of fare at Fruitlands had seduced him away from the sensual extravagances of Brook Farm, where they allowed dairy products.

Everett was a taciturn man in his early forties who had many manual skills and no verbal ones. He had had, wrote Lane, "rather deep experience"; his family had incarcerated him in an insane asylum. Everett was the only man who helped Abba with the household chores.

Samuel Bower, a bearded Englishman, arrived suddenly with Abram Wood, whose particular reform consisted in calling himself Wood Abram. Bower wished the community to adopt nudity. His plan was discouraged, although he did make unclad forays into the woods at night. Bronson and Lane designed a brown linen costume, a tunic over a full pair of pants topped with a round, wide-brimmed hat. The use of cotton would have encouraged slavery, and the use of silk would have exploited worms.

The men spaded up turf for an herb and vegetable garden; they found the work so exhausting that they agreed to exploit Palmer's animals, just a little, to plant their crops. Palmer's team turned out to be a cow and an ox, but they got the job done. The family planted barley, rye, and wheat, all mixed together in consociate confusion. The farmers began their labors on a breakfast of porridge, unleavened bread, and water, had bread, vegetables, and water at noon, and ended the day with a big bowl of water, bread, and fruit.

In early July, twenty-three-year-old Isaac Hecker, another refugee from the worldliness of Brook Farm, arrived. Hecker, who later became a Catholic and founded the Paulist Fathers, was a member of a prosperous New York family of bakers and millers, his attachment to whom, Lane felt, would hinder his inner growth.

Within a week Hecker found that the place wasn't for him. He thought both Lane and Alcott superior in self-denial, but "they are too near me; they do not awaken in me that sense of their high superiority which would keep me here to be bettered, to be elevated."

Alcott wanted to know Hecker's opinion of Fruitlands and its inmates, and Hecker gave it to him. Of Alcott, he objected to "his want of frankness; 2nd, his disposition to separateness rather than win co-operation with the aims of his own mind; 3rd, his family who prevent his immediate plans of reformation; 4th, the fact that his place has very little fruit on it, when it was and is the desire that fruit should be the principal part of their diet; 5th, my fear that they have too decided a tendency toward literature and writing for the prosperity and success of their enterprise."

Hecker's accusation about the family's preference for literature over agronomy hit home. Lane and Alcott were preparing a work called "Days and Works at Fruitlands" and "The Consociate Family Life," as well as writing copious letters and journal entries.

Alcott, however, wouldn't hear Hecker's criticism and judged that he had, as he said to Lane, "flunked out." Lane disagreed and said that Hecker was right; "he wanted more than we had to give him." Lane felt that Alcott's cold, despotic behavior and his inflexible standards were likely to ruin the experiment. He wrote to a friend, saying, "Mr. Alcott makes such high requirements of all persons that few are likely to stay, even his own family, unless he can become more tolerant of defect . . . He does not wish to keep a hospital, nor even a school, but to be surrounded by Masters . . ."

Hecker never got over his dislike of Alcott, later writing that he was a man with an insinuating manner, but "of no great intellectual gifts or acquirements . . . I don't believe he ever prayed. Whom could he pray to? Was not Bronson Alcott the greatest of all?"

Consociate conversation took place with the regularity of meals, offering about the same amount of nutrition and variety. Hecker recorded one on the highest aim: "Mr. Alcott said it was Integrity; I Harmonic Being; Lane, Progressive being; Larned, Annihilation of the self; Bower, Repulsion of evil within us. Then there was a confession of the obstacles which prevented us from attaining the highest aim. Mine was doubt whether the light is light; not want of will to follow, or light to see." Often the little girls joined in when the conversation turned to self-criticism. Louisa wished to be rid of her impatience. Lane would ask the girls questions like "What is man?" Louisa put in her journal the suggested answers: "A human being; an animal with a mind; a creature; a body; a soul and a mind. After a long talk we went to bed very tired." Bronson would want to know what God's noblest work was. Anna answered easily "men," but Louisa said "babies" because they were never wicked and men often were; "we had a long talk, and I felt better after it, and *cleared up.*"

The little girls got up at five and helped their mother with the cooking and washing, but Abba was simply undone by the amount of work she found herself responsible for. Even Lane could see the problem and wrote to Henry Thoreau, who had gone to Staten Island to tutor Emerson's brother's children, asking him to send any likely woman to Fruitlands. "We may, perhaps be rather particular about the quality," he remarked.

Abba was turning into an embittered feminist. "A woman," she wrote in her journal, "may perform the most disinterested duties — she may die 'daily' in the cause of truth and righteousness. She lives neglected, dies forgotten. But a man who never performed in his whole life one self-denying act, but who has accidental gifts of genius, is celebrated by his contemporaries, while his name and works live on from age to age. He is crowned with laurel, while scarce a stone may tell where she lies . . ."

Abba reflected angrily on the necessities that mothered the emotional and philosophical differences between men and women: "There is certainly more true humility in woman, more substantial greatness in woman, more essential goodness, than in man. Woman's love is enduring, changeless. Man is fitful in his attachments. His love is convenient, not of necessity. Woman is happy in her plain lawn. Man is better content in the royal purple."

In August, stout Miss Page from Providence appeared. She was not a general favorite, but Abba found her "an amiable woman whose kind word and gentle caretaking deed is very grateful to me." Miss Page helped out with the household chores and gave the children music lessons. Louisa loathed her because she was "fussy." But Abba and Miss Page forged a kitchen alliance, and

Abba listened approvingly when Miss Page said that "a woman may live a whole life of sacrifice, and at her death meekly says, 'I die a woman.' A man passes a few years in experiments in self-denial and simple life, and he says, 'Behold a God.' "

Late in the summer Lane and Alcott, dressed in their Fruitlands finery, took a trip to New York City. There they described their venture to many friends including Lydia Maria Child. She asked them why they were in New York. Bronson replied, "I don't know. It seems a miracle that we are here." In great amusement, she wrote to a friend that "Lane divided man into three states, the disconscious, the conscious and the unconscious. The disconscious was the state of swine, the conscious a baptism by water, the unconscious a baptism by fire . . . They talked about mind and body, but as far as I could understand they seemed to think the body was a sham."

Bronson and Lane were on this disarrayed pilgrimage when the big barley harvest came due. Abba and the children, under threatening storm clouds, gathered in what they could in great sheets. The harvest wasn't as big as the hopes for it, since animal fertilizer was considered "disgusting in the extreme" and was not used.

Nearby was a Shaker community whose celibacy and neat, good order lured Bronson and Lane more than once. Alcott came back and lectured the family on the purity of Shaker ways, making a drawing of a Shaker cross on which, Abba recorded, "the lusts of the flesh are to be sacrificed" in order to produce the "utter subjection of the body to the soul." Abba visited the community, but, in light of the recent barley event, was less impressed with the tranquillity and sterility of the arrangements than she was plagued with questions about who did the work: "I saw but little of their domestic or internal arrangements — there is servitude somewhere I have no doubt — There is a fat sleek comfortable look about the men and among the women there is a stiff awkward reserve that belongs to neither sublime resignation or divine hope — wherever I turn I see the yoke on woman in some form or other — On some it sits easy, for they are beasts of burden. On others, pride hushes them to silence; no complaint is made, for they scorn pity or sympathy. On some it galls and chafes; they feel assured by every instinct of their nature that they were destined for a higher nobler calling than to 'drag life's lengthening chain along.' "

In some ways, life was better for Louisa at Fruitlands than in the close, humid atmosphere of the Hosmer cottage. Although she had two stern fathers, they were too preoccupied to watch her persistently. She could slip away for a run in the fields, pretend she was a horse or a bird, tease William, pick berries, sing, play with her doll, or race up the hill behind the house and hide out behind a thicket. She and Anna played games of make-believe, inventing characters, improvising wings for fairies and crowns for princesses. In the evenings she read Dickens or *The Vicar of Wakefield* or memorized poetry. At night she could see the moon from her bed, and if it stormed, the sound of rain falling on the roof close above her head made her feel cozy.

But she still had to contend with what Bronson called her demonic nature. Using her parents' vocabulary and perceptions, she expressed her dilemma in a poem:

> A little kingdom I possess,
> Where thoughts and feelings dwell,
> And very hard I find the task
> Of governing it well;
> For passion tempts and troubles me,
> A wayward will misleads,
> And selfishness its shadow casts
> On all my words and deeds.
>
> How can I learn to rule myself,
> To be the child I should,
> Honest and brave, nor ever tire
> Of trying to be good?
> How can I keep a sunny soul
> To shine along life's way?
> How can I tune my little heart
> To sweetly sing all day?

Louisa watched Anna, who at thirteen was considered a "heroine" by Lane. Anna walked with the men to Concord, where they all visited Emerson, and walked the fifteen miles back in five hours and "accomplished somewhat towards the liberation of animals," enthused Lane. It baffled Louisa. She grew angry with her sister, and wrote her mother little notes, saying, "O she is very very cross I cannot love her it seems as though she did everything to trouble me but I will try to love her better." She would avoid her sister "for fear she should speak unkindly and get me angry."

Louisa's journal is a record of her struggle with herself: "I felt sad because I have been cross to-day, and did not mind Mother. I cried, and then I felt better." Another evening after she had been cross and cried in bed she made "good resolution, and felt better in my heart. If only I *kept* all I make, I should be the best girl in the world. But I don't, and so am very bad."

Abba encouraged her small warrior in her internal battles. After Louy and Bronson had had a cross interchange Abba wrote: "My Louy, I was grieved at your selfish behavior this morning, but also greatly pleased to find you bore so meekly Father's reproof for it. That is the way, dear; if you find you are wrong, take the discipline sweetly, and do so no more. It is not to be expected that children should always do right; but oh, how lovely to see a child penitent and patient when the passion is over.

"I thought a little prayer as I looked at you, and said in my heart, 'Dear God, sustain my child in this moment of trial, that no hasty word, no cruel look, no angry action may add to her fault.' And you were helped. I know that you will have a happy day after the storm and the gentle shower; keep quiet, read, walk, but do not talk much till all is peace again."

Abba often wrote warm notes to her little girl, encouraging her to be more patient and loving. She would leave them on Louy's pillow so she'd find them at bedtime. Louisa responded with touching little presents — flowers, a bookmark, or an answering note. The bond between them was never stronger. Louy was despondent in the fall, when she thought Abba was going to Boston for a visit, because "no one will be as good to me as mother."

Parker Pillsbury, the abolitionist, came by and the consociate family talked about slavery. Bronson and Lane went to New Hampshire to preach. But increasingly, as September gave way to October, people stopped coming, and family members started leaving. Hecker was gone, Wood Abram/Abram Wood was gone. Bower was unhappy, thinking Alcott arbitrary and tyrannical. Lane tried to persuade him that he "must not complain nor walk off, but cheerfully amend whatever is amiss." Bower, however, went to stay with Joseph Palmer, whose standards of behavior were less demanding. Miss Page was sent packing, according to Louisa, for the sin of eating a fish tail at a neighbor's house.

On October 8, Abba's birthday, Louisa woke up thinking that she must be very good and wishing she "was rich, I was good, and we were all a happy family this day." Louisa helped out with the ironing and spent most of the day and evening husking corn in the barn. The family made an exception and allowed oil lamps to get the job done. In honor of the occasion, Louisa made up a verse about sunset:

> Softly doth the sun descend
> To his couch behind the hill,
> Then, oh then, I love to sit
> On mossy banks beside the rill.

In what was to become a characteristic remark about most of her writing, Louy said, "Anna thought it was very fine; but I didn't like it very well."

Louy could see that, however hard she wished, they were not all a happy family. Lane felt that Bronson must make a choice between the consociate family and the Alcott family. He was, wrote Lane, "rather wayward and notional than wicked and acquisitive, and more born down by this wife and family" than desirous of reneging on the vows he and Lane had shared. "Poor fellow between his cherished idiosyncrasies and his secular or social difficulties, his high moral principles have a sad time of it." As to Abba, she had "no spontaneous inclination towards a larger family than her own natural one, of spiritual ties she knows nothing, though to keep all together she does and would go through a good deal of exterior and interior toil."

On November 2, Bronson and Lane had a discussion, and Louisa wrote that "father asked us if *we* saw any reason for us to separate. Mother wanted to, she is so tired. I like it, but not the school part or Mr. L."

Abba and Lane had taken clear positions and Bronson had only to choose. His appeal to the children, while consistent with his transcendentalism, was very upsetting to the girls. Abba wrote to Sam that "come what may I shall try to see that the peace of these dear children be no more disturbed by discussion and doubts." But everything was deranged. Abba in disgust and bitterness boycotted the dinner table. Anna pleaded with her to come back. "I enjoy my meals much better when you are at the table," she wrote.

As the weather grew colder, chills and sickness plagued the

Fruitlanders, who had little insulation, physical or emotional. Louisa got sick with a cough and a headache. William suffered with a low-grade fever and debility so great that he could barely sit up. Lane wrote that he had to "nurse him while plagued with hands so chapped and sore that I was little more capable than the patient."

Sam May had finally had enough and refused to pay the note he had signed for Bronson's debt. Finally Abba delivered her ultimatum. She was going to move with the girls to a house provided by friends. She would take all the furniture. Lane understood that he and Alcott "could not remain together without her. To be 'that devil come from Old England to separate husband and wife,' I will not be, though it might gratify New England to be able to say it."

Once the decision was made, everyone but Lane cheered slightly. Louisa celebrated her eleventh birthday by playing in the snow before school and confessing to her father that her temper was her worst fault. Abba gave her a new journal and a note saying: "Your handwriting improves very fast. Take pains and do not be in a hurry. I like to have you make observations about our conversations and your own thoughts. It helps you to express them and to understand your own little self. Remember, dear girl, that a diary should be an epitome of your life. May it be a record of pure thought and good actions, then you will indeed be the precious child of your loving mother."

Emerson, who had visited in July, had been prophetic when he wrote: "The fault of Alcott's community is that it has only room for one . . . Alcott and Lane are always feeling of their shoulders to find if their wings are sprouting . . . They look well in July. We will see them in December. I know they are better for themselves than as partners . . . Their saying that things are clear, and they are sane, does not make them so."

December found the consociate family needing to find a home for itself, since the winter was going to be unendurable at Fruitlands. Bronson hadn't given up the ideals of Fruitlands, just the cold reality. He and Lane discussed the possibility of moving the venture, lock, stock, and apple, to Brook Farm in West Roxbury, but they were both repelled by the fleshpots and dairy delights there. Lane couldn't contain his disgust to find them "playing away their youth and daytime in a miserably joyous, frivolous manner."

In search of an alternative, Bronson visited Emerson, who was amused by the grandeur of his manner in spite of the fact that he "had been uniformly rejected by every class to whom he had addressed himself." Alcott was casting about for new roads to perfection. Not for the first time, he talked about abandoning the institution of marriage in favor of free love. Waldo replied, "as usual, that, I thought no man could be trusted with it; the formation of new alliances is so delicious to the imagination, that St. Paul and St. John would be riotous; and that we cannot spare the coarsest muniment of virtue." Bronson was deterred from meddling with marriage by the awesome wrath he knew he would touch off.

The dissolution of Fruitlands provoked a profound crisis for the Alcott marriage. Bronson wanted the freedom to experiment communally, spiritually, and physically. He discussed with his family the possibility of breaking up on many occasions. Louisa listened to him with the utmost alarm. After one session she wrote: "Anna and I cried in bed, and I prayed to God to keep us all together." Bronson's threat to abandon his family scared and scarred the little girl, further undermining her trust in men.

Frightened as she was by the possibility of a catastrophe greater than punishment, Louisa suddenly became very docile. When she went to see the neighbor Lovejoy's baby boy she tried not to wish she had a brother, "for Mother often says, if we are not contented with what we have got it will be taken away from us." She did her lessons with a good will and played cards without teasing Anna, "and when I went to bed I felt happy for I had been obedient and kind to Father and mother and gentle to my sisters . . ."

Bronson was rushing around, soliciting opinions, talking to friends, acting more and more distracted and "nervous and excitable." He went to Boston for Christmas, unable to stay still, and Abba and the girls celebrated by themselves. Abba tried to cheer up the apprehensive girls by letting them stay up late on Christmas Eve. On Christmas Day Louy got a stocking with some candy and a pointed jingle from her mother:

> Christmas is here
> Louisa my dear
> Then happy we'll be
> Gladsome and free

> God with you abide
> With love for your guide
> In time you'll go right
> With heart and with might.

On the night of Christmas, Joseph Palmer and his son and the Lovejoys came to sing carols. It wasn't much of a Christmas, but Louisa was too frightened to complain. Instead, she copied into her journal the hymns from *The Pilgrim's Progress* that she and her sisters had been singing. Bronson had been reading the book aloud to them just before he went to Boston. It was the foundation of his faith, and he tried to see that it became a familiar friend to his family.

The pilgrim offered Bronson an apt and flattering parallel with which to justify himself to his family. Christian alone sees the true path, and disregarding all danger, he follows the treacherous trail to righteousness, overcoming despair and temptation along the way. Not understanding his pure purpose, people mock him at every step, but he perseveres. Finally, after he has arrived, he manages to persuade his reluctant wife to follow with their children. They eventually meet him there, but he is the pioneer pilgrim and is greater than they for his righteous reconnaissance mission. To Abba, the analogy was clear if not always convincing.

To Louisa the message was, the harder the climb, the more glorious the view at the top. All privation and unhappiness had meaning. There was no gratuitous suffering, and if she was miserable it was because she hadn't learned to extract holy contentment from pain. The equation of misery with ultimate goodness tortured Louisa throughout her life, and she tried to bleed every travail for some of the peace and contentment that her father seemed to feel.

When Bronson returned from Boston he fell into an angry depression. He refused to eat and Abba was worried for his recovery. The failure of Fruitlands overwhelmed him. He had to give up his dream of a paradise on earth and return from his euphoric state to the realities of poverty and human needs. He blamed his family for inhibiting his ascension and took it out on them by making himself dangerously ill. He would do nothing for himself. Abba forced him off his vegetable regime, made him drink spearmint tea,

eat blackberries, and take shower baths twice a day. She wrote to
Sam that her ministrations had "restored him, but not made quite
whole this dying man." His mind was rushing along, hopping
dementedly from thought to thought, but his demeanor was
gloomy and "sepulchral." Abba suggested they take a "little quiet
journey in a chaise" without the children, but Bronson said no. Not
above a little vengeful melodrama, he added that he wanted to rest
for the present and that when he did journey "it will be a long one
— and *alone.*"

Bronson's withdrawal left Abba completely in charge. Bronson
was relieved to give up any effort to steer the family, and from then
on Abba made most decisions. She arranged with Edmund Hosmer to rent, for 50 cents a week, three rooms in one of his houses
in Still River. On January 16, 1844, the Alcotts moved, Abba noting with uncharacteristic understatement that "the arrangements
never suited me . . ."

"Beard" (as Abba called him) Palmer stayed to look after the
house. Eventually he turned it into a shelter for the needy, a variety
of Victorian crash pad. Charles Lane and his son had left two days
before to stay with the Shakers.

Bronson recovered enough strength to visit Emerson, to
whom he poured out his bitterness, loneliness, disappointment,
and suicidal thoughts. "The world was not, on trial," recorded
Emerson, "a possible element for him to live in . . . He had entertained the thought of leaving it, and going where freedom
and an element could be found." Emerson was very sorry to
see his friend distraught, but found him at the same time "very
tedious, and prosing and egotistical and narrow." He could see
the grandeur in Alcott's attempt, and the majesty of his vision,
but he could also see his inflexibility and the hauteur with
which he approached humanity: "I feel his statement to be partial and to have fatal omissions, but I think I shall never attempt to set him right any more. It is not for me to answer
him: though I feel the limitations and exaggeration of his picture, and the wearisome personalities." Alcott told his friend
about the poetry he had been composing during the winter. "I
fear there is nothing for me in it," wrote Emerson. "His overpowering personality destroys all poetic faculty." Such was
Emerson's habitual remoteness and Alcott's self-absorption that

during the next forty years of their friendship Bronson never noticed Waldo's disengagement. Emerson mused over Alcott's alienating character: "It is strange that he has not got the confidence of one woman. He would be greater if he were good humored. . . ."

10

Hillside

THE FRUITLANDS CRISIS PERMANENTLY altered the Alcott family structure. Bronson relinquished what little economic control he had exerted and retired deeper into his cave of grievances, protecting himself with a fence of rigid principles. He refused to earn a wage and refused further to own property or deal with those who did. He hoarded the wrongs done him and spent much time blaming the world for wasting his talents.

Abba stood by her husband in principle and in fact, but found it very taxing. She loathed poverty and its humiliations. Dunning her friends and family regularly, reminding them that she and her girls were close to starvation, made her ashamed and angry. Along with the donations, she inevitably had to submit to lectures about prudence and providence, which were more properly addressed to Bronson. Abba, who couldn't move him to help out, found the righteous advice of friends a grueling experience. Naturally nervous and touchy, she grew disproportionately suspicious and easily offended. She took out on Concord the resentment she couldn't show her husband. Her plight led her to ambivalent reflections on the female sex. When she heard that Louisa Bond, the orphan her parents had brought up with her, had just had a child, she wrote: "How thoughtlessly this domestic martyrdom is enacted in married life! What a volume might be written on the heroines of private life — There is a courage of endurance, as high as that of action — There are martyrs who wear no crowns and for whom no faggots burn . . ." Having children had been a great trial to Abba, and her girls were aware of this.

Abba alternated between seeing women crucified on the crosses of motherhood and self-sacrifice and seeing them as deficient in God's eyes. She told her husband that she thought there was "some mistake when she was created — it was an afterthought indeed." Woman, she went on, was constructed at Adam's suggestion for his companionship. She was the last animal designed. All the others were "pronounced *good* — but no such benediction was pronounced on her — but a tacit curse — and she has ever been an illogical indefinable medley of good and evil, angel and devil in consequence — I think God a little ashamed of this piece of his handywork — and therefore takes little account of us — We owe man a grudge for deriving us, and then caring so little for providing for us."

In the five years following the Fruitlands experience, while Louisa was going into and through her adolescence, her mother was in a nearly constant depression. She thought herself worthless except as a badly equipped provider for her girls. She was exacting, unhappy, overworked, and unrecompensed. No one would have willingly emulated her example of womanliness. Wherever Louisa looked, her mother's lot appeared unendurable. Abba was unappreciated, exhausted, embittered, and sorrowful. Her father seemed to make no effort to help. Louisa had nowhere to turn for advice or guidance except into the grief-stricken, complaining embrace of her fatigued mother. Here she found warmth, but also the unhappy prospect of dissatisfaction so deep that nothing could fix it.

Louisa's sexual awakening went unnoticed. As far as Abba was concerned, puberty made girls available to the hazards of childbearing, and was no great cause for hope or rejoicing. Her sexuality remained a mystery to Louisa, and Abba omitted all mention of it. Abba had strong sexual fears that got expressed in her frightened and overly stern attitude toward the frivolity of society and its ill effects on the innocence of women. She communicated her attitudes early by strict bans on any physical contact between her girls and the neighborhood boys. Later, as the girls grew, Abba's fears of men grew more pointed and articulate. Whatever Abba's sexual experience with Bronson had been, it did not make her sanguine about the existence of sexual feelings in men and their consequences for women.

Louisa channeled her nascent sexual energy into long runs through the hills, poetry, incessant fantasy, and reading. These activities characterized what she later referred to as her "romantic period." She felt shaken by great desires, inarticulate longings for love and unity to replace the disordered and shattered emotions that besieged her. She retreated farther into her imagination, attaching her yearnings sometimes to Henry Thoreau and sometimes to Waldo Emerson.

Louisa saw clearly the price of her mother's dependence, and it became her intention never to ask for anything in her life. She would never allow herself to need anything from anyone else since the chances of getting it were so slim and the costs prohibitive.

She dreamed of a gigantic love that would release her from her chaotic internal life and make her whole and contented in the worship of another. She understood from her mother that her salvation lay in subjection to a man. Abba believed that the best of her was realized through Bronson, the part of her that exercised the most self-discipline and goodness. Louisa learned from her mother that she needed to attach herself to a man who was better than she, and her problems would dissolve in the enormity and morality of the love she would feel. This powerful closeness, which Louisa identified as one she had shared from time to time with her mother, came to be her definition of love and the focus of her adolescent aspirations.

* * *

Louisa and Anna went to Miss Maria Chase's school in Still River, where they made friends with the Gardner and Haskell children. Often the girls didn't have enough to eat, and their friends shared their lunches with them. The town fathers complained about the Pythagorean diet and its effects on the Alcott children, and Abba wished "to see my husband a little more interested in this matter of support . . . Mr. Alcott is right in not working for hire, if thereby he violates his conscience — But working for Bread does not necessarily imply unworthy gains."

In April the family moved to "Brick Ends," a wooden house with brick walls at either end. For $25 a year they had five rooms, a kitchen, and three quarters of an acre for a garden. Here the girls entertained their friends, performed plays, and held hoop-rolling contests. Louisa dominated the children, dressing up as an Indian, declaiming poetry, and producing theatricals. In the Brick Ends woodshed Louisa was married to Walter Gardner. She wore an apron for a veil and slapped her spouse shortly after the ceremony, discovering that their temperaments did not match.

Alcott had not relinquished his hope of living communally, and throughout the winter and spring he and Abba made trips to communities at Hopedale, Oneida, and Northampton, looking for kindred idealists. They found nothing, but Abba turned up one day with a fourteen-year-old boy named Llewellyn Willis, who had hurt his hand on the door of the stagecoach they were sharing. She had comforted him, and within a week he had abandoned his boarding house in Still River and come to live at Brick Ends. He was motherless, with a father in debtor's prison, and he attached himself gratefully to the Alcotts, listening to Abba's woes, competing with Louisa, and being paired off with Anna.

In the summer, Bronson packed up and left with Anna to look west for "a new home established on truer and more elevated relations." Abba was despairing, suffering "soul sickness . . . I scarcely know where to begin to bring about a more joyous condition and yet it is wrong to indulge whilst my children are in no wise participators of my anxiety neither can they alleviate my suffering by their sympathy."

Louisa shared her mother's mood and wrote a poem about her separation from Anna:

> Sister, dear, when you are lonely,
> Longing for your distant home,
> And the images of loved ones
> Warmly to your heart shall come,
> Then, mid tender thoughts and fancies,
> Let one fond voice say to thee,
> "Ever when your heart is heavy,
> Anna, dear, then think of me."

The verses reflect the enervating influence of the genteel, sentimental ballad, Victorian America's most popular musical form, whose practitioners included Stephen Foster. The emotions were canned and the conventions insufferably trite. Nevertheless, for an eleven-year-old, the work demonstrates an excellent imitative ear and a facility for manipulating words. The poem doesn't reveal any original sentiment, but the leitmotif of Louisa's childhood was that her original sentiments violated popular and family assumptions, so they had to be squeezed into the clichés of someone else.

Alcott took Anna to Syracuse, where they visited Sam May, who recently had moved there. They stopped off to see Junius Alcox in Oriskany Falls and came home through Albany, where Bronson lost all of his papers, including everything that related to Fruitlands. He concluded "that the communities are not yet ready for us as now arranged or we are not adapted to them as now constituted — We must then take up the 'family' cross and work on isolated and poor a little while longer."

Failing to form a new transcendental family, the Alcotts decided to move back to Concord, where at least they would have transcendental neighbors. Abba tried to borrow money from Sam to buy a house, but he advised her to rent, and produced as much gratuitous advice as financial aid. Abba complained that although "they *aid,* they *censure* — and tho' they give cheerfully of their abundance, yet they feel that we should earn something ourselves — that dependence should not be the rule, but the exception of our condition."

On November 14, 1844, the family took a large, swaying coach from Still River to Littleton. Louisa sat on top of the flat roof, looking down at the enormous wooden wheels, feeling the shocks of the rutted road through the layers of suspended steerhide that acted as springs. There were square coach lamps on either side of the driver's platform and four strong horses to pull the accommodation along at about ten miles an hour, while the driver occasionally checked his "time-watch" to see how he was doing on this section of his run.

At Littleton they connected with the Fitchburg Railroad, which took them at about twenty miles an hour to Concord. The railroads were brand-new, resembling on the inside the conveyance they had just left. There were stiff narrow benches facing one another in the cars, which looked like coaches on platforms. At either end of the cars small stoves overheated the ends of the vehicle and left the center icy cold. The roof was usually a canvas platform and there was no ventilation. Tallow candles provided a flickering light and the passengers emerged covered with dust, cramped, and cold.

The family stayed with the Edmund Hosmers while they

searched for a home. They had three "good-sized . . . and neat" rooms, but felt very cramped in the noisy, lively Hosmer house. After a week, Abba was already at odds with her friends: "The family we are now associated with present a sad illustration of self indulgence and paternal rights! Oh no maternal wrongs!!"

In the winter Abba's father's estate was settled, freeing up $1000 for the purchase of a house. Emerson added $500, and with that Abba bought "Hillside," Horatio Cogswell's farm on the Lexington Road near Emerson's. Bronson would take no part in the transaction, being "dissatisfied with the whole property arrangement," Abba explained. He would, he announced, establish a working arrangement with the earth that he intended to use on sufferance, but not own.

Cogswell had been a pig driver who yarded his swine in front of the creaky, clapboard farm house. On one side was a spacious open porch, in the middle a semicircular room curving out, and upstairs a high, cupolalike dome. There were ramshackle outbuildings that Bronson reconstructed and attached to the basic structure. The house, which contained four large, low-ceilinged rooms supported by thick, unfinished beams, sat at the edge of the road on thirty wooded acres. Across the road, a grassy field slipped down to a brook. Bronson later planted the slope with willows to screen the family bathing spot.

On April 1, 1845, the Alcotts packed up again and moved to Hillside. Louisa and her sisters took the large upstairs room. Abba hoped the move would bring her peace and rectify "a constant almost invariable disappointment in my arrangements for life." In her own house she hoped she could lead "a quiet busy life to secure peace to my family and just relations to the world — Every day of my life convinces me more and more of the perversion — distortion of human nature. Life is a medly of care, hope, hate dissatisfaction — dissipation — trial and appeal — It will be no slight task to ravel out threads of these which have become woven into my own net of life — if I cannot do this I will destroy the whole fabrick and begin again on a different scheme."

Concord had firmly rejected her husband. "Even the little primary school was denied me," he wrote. "O God! How long wilt thou not permit me to be useful to my fellowmen? Suffer me to use my gifts for my neighbors children, if not for themselves, and thus bless the coming, if not the present generation. How long, O Lord! how long wilt thou try me, by this exclusion from the active duties of Church and State, and more than these, from the discharge of my duties to my neighbors, and my neighbors children?" Since Bronson refused any kind of occupation by teaching, and Concord refused him its schools, he resigned himself to gardening, work on the house, and his journals, in which he enlarged on his disappointments.

Abba and her husband still wished to expand their family, and Abba wrote to Junius, asking him to come back to Concord and move in with them. Abba explained that they didn't want to live selfishly but "to embrace many little charities for the good and the needy." In line with this plan, Llewellyn Willis came to spend the summer. And Sophia Foord, a teacher and amateur naturalist from Milton with whom Bronson hoped to open a school, moved in.

Louisa liked Miss Foord, a large, dark, pudgy woman in her mid-forties. Miss Foord took the Alcott and Emerson and Channing girls on outings around Concord. Once they made a trip to Flint's Pond in Lincoln. Louisa described the trek to a friend, telling her about wading across the mile-long pond, where they went "splashing along making the fishes run like mad before our big claws, when we got to the other side we had a funny time getting on our shoes and unmentionables, and we came bubbling home all wet and muddy; but we were happy enough, for we came through the woods bawling and singing like crazy folks." Louisa responded well to Sophia's energy and warmth, and she admired her dedication to high principle.

Sophia Foord nurtured a completely unreturned passion for Thoreau, so the atmosphere thickened when Henry came to visit the Alcotts. She later confessed to a friend that she thought "Thoreau's soul was twin to hers and that in 'the other World' her spirit and his would be united." Henry brutally rebuffed any ideas she might have cherished about their uniting in this world. He wrote to his friend Emerson that Sophia had bombarded him with letters: "She really did wish to — I hesitate to write — marry me. That is the way they spell it. Of course I did not write a deliberate answer. How could I deliberate upon it? I sent back as distinct a no as I have learned to pronounce after considerable practice, and I trust that this no has succeeded. Indeed I wished that it might burst, like a hollow shot, after it had struck and buried itself and made itself felt there. There was no other way. I really had anticipated no such foe as this in my career." Louisa watched Henry's usually gruff and brusque manner grow positively rude in Miss Foord's presence.

These developments interested Louisa, but she did not want more company. The last straw arrived in the form of Charles Lane. Louisa noted that "more people" were coming: "I wish we could be together and no one else. I don't see who is to clothe and feed us all, when we are so poor now." Louisa got little enough attention when the family was only six. She spent hours weeding with her father in his garden, finding this unspeaking sharing a peaceful kind of companionship. But more people turned her father to discussion and ideas while her mother's workload increased.

Abba worried for her antisocial girl and thought her excitable and anxious. She wrote her a fifteenth-birthday note on November 29, 1847, saying: "Light up your soul then to meet the highest, for that alone can satisfy your great yearning nature — your temperament is a peculiar one, and there are few or none who can intelligently help you."

With Lane's arrival, Bronson shook off some of his gloom and stopped telling Abba about how the world scoffed him and wanted to crucify him. He began to see Emerson more often and even arranged a May Day celebration, complete with a hayride and a maypole. He also devised a new routine and posted instructions for deportment: "Vigilance, Punctuality, Perseverance, Prompt, Cheerful, Unquestioning Obedience: Government of Temper, Hands and Tongue; Gentle manners, motions and words; Work, studies and play distinct; No interchange of labors." Everyone was to be up at five, eat breakfast at six, take lessons with Miss Foord until eight, when there was a break. At nine there were lessons with Mr. Lane until ten-thirty, when there was a half-hour recreation. At eleven Bronson gave lessons for an hour. After lunch there was a rest period till two, when they sewed, conversed, or read till four, when they had two hours for play and errands. Supper was at six, after which the girls could have conversations and play music till bedtime at eight-thirty.

Lane's presence made Louisa constantly upset: "I am so cross I wish I had never been born." One day she called Anna mean. Bronson told her to look the word up in the dictionary. She found that it meant "base" or "contemptible." She noted in her journal: "I was so ashamed of myself to have called my dear sister that, I cried over my bad tongue and temper."

Lane and Bronson catechized Louisa about her faults. Which ones did she wish to get rid of, asked her father? "Idleness, Impatience, selfishness, Wilfulness, independence, activity, vanity, pride and love of cats," she answered doggedly. What virtues did she need? "Patience, obedience, industry, love, generosity, respect, silence, perseverance, self-denial."

Lane would initiate Socratic quizzes:

> How can you get what you need?
> By trying.
> How do you try?
> By resolution and perseverance.
> How gain love?
> By gentleness.
> What is gentleness?
> Kindness, patience, and care for other people's feelings.
> Who has it?
> Father and Anna.
> Who means to have it?
> Louisa if she can.

Louisa watched Bronson give Anna a portfolio for her papers on her fourteenth birthday. He asked her to accept the present "as a neat disposition for her papers. Her father gladly encourages every indication of a love of habit or order and neatness, and would avail himself of all occasions to inspire and cherish these graces of womanhood." Louisa could see little Elizabeth reading aloud to her five-year-old sister, asking her father the meanings of words. He would help her draw pictures, and on her birthday Bronson gave her shoes and a note that read: "Your dear little head is so full of loving and quiet stillness, that I will not disturb its calm thoughtfulness by any words of graver wisdom: And so let me furnish your feet with a neat covering, in which your footsteps may be as light as your gentle heart, and swift as your obedience."

The girls showed their father their journals, which, Bronson observed, "they wrote very faithfully. Louisa was unfaithful and took her dinner alone." After a particularly grueling set-to, Bronson wrote: "Two devils, as yet, I am not quite divine enough to vanquish — the mother fiend and her daughter."

Lane tried more Plato:

> What are the most valuable kinds of self-denial?
> Appetite, temper.
> How is self-denial of temper known?
> If I can control my temper, I am respectful, gentle, and
>   everyone sees it.
> What is the result of this self-denial?
> Everyone loves me and I am happy.
> Why use self-denial?
> For the good of others.
> How shall we learn this self-denial?
> By resolving, and then trying *hard*.
> What do you mean to do?
> To resolve and try.

Abba would look into Louisa's diary and write notes. She was, she wrote, "hoping to see some record of more happy days. 'Hope and keep busy,' dear daughter, and in all perplexity or trouble come freely to your Mother." Louisa vowed to work for her mother, to be happy for her because she was "the best woman in the world." Louy wrote her mother plaintive notes about her efforts to be more contented. She wanted above all a room to herself to hide her unmanageable spirit, a place to defend herself against the swarming critics who plagued her: "I have been thinking about my little room, which I suppose I never shall have. I should want to be there about all the time, and I should go there and sing and think.

> But I'll be contented
> With what I have got,
> Of folly repented
> Then sweet is my lot."

Abba replied by telling Louy to rely on God and to remember that "Mother never forgets you, and your refuge is her arms." She asked her daughter to be patient and to be assured that "the little room you long for will come, if it is necessary to your peace and well-being. Till then try to be happy with the good things you have. They are many, — more perhaps than we deserve, after our frequent complaints and discontents." Abba encouraged Louy to write more poetry. "It is a safety valve to her smothered sorrow which might otherwise consume her young and tender heart," she wrote to Sam.

Toward the end of the summer, when the garden was yielding ripe melons, corn, beans, carrots, turnips, squash, and beets, Alcott was called to Spindle Hill to look after Junius, who had had a nervous breakdown. Alcott had hoped his brother and his family would join the Alcotts at Hillside and had been adding rooms onto the house for that purpose. Instead, the family was dwindling. Miss Foord announced her intention to go. Abba took it as proof that she had failed the test of community life again, but she was, all in all, relieved to be "thrown once more on my own efforts to do and be to my daughters what I believe I am capable of being." Miss Foord criticized Abba for taking on too many other responsibilities, which interfered with her family duties. She thought Abba "desultory" and the girls "indolent," "faulty specimens of parental impotence." But, Abba reflected, "a woman who has never known the maternal relation can know but little of the resources of a mother's love to bring about most important and desirable results . . ." Miss Foord had attacked Abba at her most vulnerable. She could fail at consociate living and loyalties. But her identity rested on being an indisputably fine mother. Miss Foord's critique prompted her to assure Louisa that "I am a busy woman, but never can forget the calls of my children."

That fall, after Lane and Miss Foord departed, Louisa and Anna began going to the local Concord school, where they were taught by John Hosmer, recently returned from Brook Farm. Bronson continued to teach the younger girls at home, while Louisa enjoyed her new freedom. He noticed that her mood had improved and that she was writing poetry often, as if to keep up with her emotional and physical growth.

In March 1846, thirteen-year-old Louisa got her own room. "It does me good to be alone," she wrote, "and Mother has made it very pretty and neat for me." Abba had filled the closet with sweet-smelling dried herbs. The room had a door that opened onto the garden and Louisa's desk and sewing basket sat under a window. She was very happy, the more so because the room was placed so that she could "run off to the woods when I like."

That summer the family made an expedition out to Walden to spend the day with Henry Thoreau, who had been there since the previous July. Although Thoreau came into town every day to visit his mother, Louisa rarely saw him. Alcott took long walks with his friend by the pond, where Henry read him sections from *A Week on the Concord and Merrimac Rivers.* Alcott identified with the young man, whom he considered to be the only one beside himself who "advocates the doctrine of resolute independency and an individual imperial self-rule — a surrender to the dictates of a religious conscience and a civil economy . . ." Thoreau liked Alcott, although he thought him rather silly. He admired his "hospitable intellect" which embraced "children, beggars, insane, and scholars . . ."

Her father's respect for Thoreau made him a uniquely romantic figure to the thirteen-year-old Louisa. That summer on the pond she listened to him talk about his friends the Indians and play his flute. He would test out lovely epigrams about the bluebird carrying the sky on his back, and the scarlet tanager flying through the green foliage as if to ignite the leaves. This was the man of whom she later wrote: "Broad-shouldered, strong-limbed, and bronzed by wind and weather. A massive head, covered with rings of ruddy brown hair, gray eyes, that seemed to pierce through all disguises, an eminent nose, and a beard . . . Power, intellect, and courage were stamped on face and figure, making him the manliest man . . ."

In the fall of 1846, Louisa fell into her adolescence with an unexpected jolt. Her mother could only stand by and watch, offering her for her fourteenth birthday a pen for poetry when the passion took her:

> Oh, may this pen your muse inspire,
> When wrapt in pure poetic fire,
> To write some sweet, some thrilling verse;
> A song of love or sorrow's lay.
> Or Duty's clear but tedious way
> In brighter hope rehearse.
> Oh! Let your strain be soft and high
> Of crosses here, of crowns beyond the sky:
> Truth guide your pen, inspire your theme,
> And from each note, joy's music stream.

Puberty aggravated Louisa's unsettled disposition. Displays of sexuality upset her deeply. There was a family prohibition on kissing, and when a boy tried to break the rule with Anna, Louisa came a little unstrung, called him "Mr. Smack," and couldn't stop carrying on about the incident. Louisa's new, unusual energy, her oppositional streak, her spontaneity and aggression, all convinced her that she was part boy. She later wrote to a childhood friend: "There was always something very brave and beautiful to me on the sight of a boy when he first 'wakes up' and seeing the worth of life takes it up with a stout heart and resolves to carry it nobly to the end through all . . . seeing defeats. I was born with a boy's spirit under my 'bib and tucker!' " Her confusion about her sexuality was exacerbated by the absence of any approval for her active spirit. Her father and sisters all seemed to have their passions under control, and her mother did daily battle with hers. Louisa's was an isolated struggle, and the only terms in which she could understand herself were that she was a freak, a girl-boy.

Sexuality — indeed, most physical expression—went unexpressed in the Alcott family. Bronson withdrew from contact with his girls, particularly from Louisa, whom he thought violent and too demonstrative. So Louisa came to feel an exaggerated awareness and fear of her physical expressiveness. If she were a boy, and her sexual and physical expressions were boyish, they were acceptable.

"I have made a plan for my life," she wrote after she had moved into her own room, "as I am in my teens, and no more a child. I am old for my age, and don't care much for girls' things. People think I'm wild and queer; but Mother understands and helps me. I have not told anyone about my plan; but I am going to be good. I've made many resolutions, and written sad notes, and cried over my sins, but it doesn't seem to do any good! Now I'm going to *work really,* for I feel a true desire to improve, and be a help and comfort, not a care, to my dear mother." What she meant by "good" was more "feminine," passive, yielding, and gentle. She meant turning her aggressive and sexual energy inward and becoming like Anna or Elizabeth. Instead of taking a run through the velvety grass by Walden Pond, she would sew for her mother and speak sweetly to her father.

One day at Emerson's she happened to read one of her parents' favorites, a translation from the German of Bettina von Arnim's *Goethe's Correspondence with a Child.* It purported to be a collection of letters exchanged by Goethe and a passionate fifteen-year-old girl. Bettina pours out her love and spiritual longings to her "Master." He receives her homage and white-hot idolatry with reserve and eventually turns away from her. Abba was struck by Goethe's coldness, and she generalized that men take and women give; men think, argue, and forsake, while women love instinctively and eternally.

Louisa was less taken by Goethe's distance, which seemed completely natural to her, than by Bettina's intensity and passion. She seemed to show Louisa that there was an outlet for her bottled-up excitement. Bettina did unthinkable things easily. She visited Goethe unexpectedly one night, and when she saw him, she stretched out her hand and fainted. He embraced her, "caught me quickly to his heart." She asked to stay on his sofa. "Then I flew to his neck, — he drew me on his knee, and locked me to his heart. Still, quite still it was, — everything vanished." Bettina was always rushing to him, kissing his hands, putting her head on his lap, and he would reward her with a "My child, my dear, good girl! Sweetheart!" Sometimes she would reproach him with coldness; other times she would convert her young, hungry sexuality into romantic transcendental imagery: "Ye steep mountains, ye bare rocks, ye bold, vengeance-glowing marksmen, ye desolated valleys and smoking dwellings, step modestly into the background and leave me to the absolute joy of touching the electric chain, which conducts the sparks from him to me; and countless times do I receive it, shock after shock — this spark of delight." The imagery was dangerous, but the ages of the correspondents and Goethe's marriage and aloofness gave Bettina the license she needed to display her passion with impunity. She fooled men into believing her sexless. Emerson wrote to Margaret Fuller: "What life more pure and poetic amid prose and derision of our time. So pure a love of nature I have never found in prose and verse." Bronson thought all young women should read Bettina, "that they may see how one of their sex has trusted the instincts of her nature, and what noble results have ensued." Bettina could do her sexual acrobatics because there was a net of sexless assumptions between her and the ground.

For Louisa the book sanctioned her fantasies. She wrote to forty-three-year-old Emerson letters derived from Bettina's. She found irresistible scenes like Goethe's coming to Bettina's at midnight, wrapped up in his cloak. Bettina lay silently on her sofa, and at first he didn't see her: "I uttered a low cry of amazement at my own bliss, and then — he had found me."

Louisa never delivered her letters, but she thought about the tall, thin essayist who shut his eyes when he laughed, whose serious, quiet manner lent itself to romantic fantasy. Emerson treated Louisa with grave politeness. He believed that women were better than men, and virgins better than other women. He scorned the Fourierist idea that women had a sexual component: "In their head it is the universal rutting season. Anybody who had lived with women will know how false and prurient this is . . . how chaste is their organization, and how lawful a class of people women are."

Bettina's book offered Louisa an expression of a tempting kind of heterosexual love, violently passionate but pure. Its intensity was heightened by the repression integral to it. Emerson, who in trying to justify his withdrawn manner told Lydian that a "photometer cannot be a stove," had the coldness and distance requisite to the equation, necessary to ward off Louisa's hot pursuit. If she couldn't trust herself to be female, hence asexual, still she could rely on him to fend her off. So she sat in a cherry tree at night and thought romantic thoughts, and dropped off anonymous bunches of wildflowers at Emerson's doorstep.

Louisa retreated before the tenacity of her own feelings. Her mother wrote to Sam that "nothing can exceed the strength of her attachments — particularly for her Mother — ." Louisa avoided people, fearing her overpowering feelings of attraction and repulsion. Her emotions and sexuality frightened her, so she spent her time reading in her room. "She will never endure anything like publicity," Abba went on. "She must have retirement agreeable occupation and protective provident care."

Louisa's ambivalence about attention made her mother treat her like an invalid, too sensitive to bear normal life. At the same time, she dreamed constantly of fame. She vowed that she would do something "by and by. Don't care what — teach, sew, act, write, anything to help the family; and I'll be rich and famous and happy before I die, see if I won't."

If she was rich and famous, then perhaps she wouldn't always feel in the wrong, desiring to hide her feelings and conflicts. Her mother didn't make womanhood look very enticing, but perhaps worldly success would help. Abba felt that God had withheld his blessing from women, delivering instead "a tacit curse — and she has ever been an illogical indefinable medley of good and evil, angel and devil in consequence — I think God is a little ashamed of this piece of his handywork — and therefore takes little account of us — We owe *one* man a grudge for deriving us and then caring so little for providing for us."

The continual Alcott chaos did nothing to clarify Louisa's ideas about being a woman. Her father had given up family leadership to Abba. He did occasional odd jobs for Emerson. With Thoreau, he looked after the grounds when Waldo went to Europe in 1847. He worked on a rococo summer house for his friend, a curiously pleasing structure that invited warpage and mosquitoes. Its curving lines contrasted with the brick and clapboard Concord geometry, and local people called it a "shanty," a "whirligig," "strangest thing I ever saw." Louisa observed that Alcott was, as Thoreau wrote to Emerson, "nowhere, doing nothing."

The girl could sense the tension between Waldo and her father. She had listened to enough of her mother's lectures on dependence, "that worst affliction of all conditions," which "mars friendship — chills love — destroys confidence" to be ashamed at the ease with which Bronson accepted his friend's handouts. Nor could she miss Emerson's antagonism toward Bronson, who "takes up this grating tone of authority and accusation" against people who worked for a living. "His unpopularity is not at all wonderful," Emerson noted in his journal after considering Bronson's continuing refusal to work and his insistence that he deserved to be supported by the community at large.

But angry as Louisa got at Bronson, she couldn't deny that he did good. He opened his house to a fugitive slave in February of 1847. John was thirty years old, only seven weeks from captivity. His stay, wrote Alcott, "has given image and a name to the dire entity of slavery. And was an impressive lesson to my children, bringing before them the wrongs of the Black man, and his tale of woes." With the help of Concord's underground railroad conductors, John reached Canada.

Louisa's response to the contradictory information she got was to withdraw into her room, where she indulged in her fantasies and read her favorite books. In this, too, she felt male, not female. Men withdrew — her father into his journals, Emerson into his metaphysics, and Thoreau into his beans and muskrats. Louisa could sense that men had an advantage in their ability to abstract and intellectualize, but the women who did it, Margaret Fuller and Elizabeth Peabody, were not household favorites, and were not considered feminine.

Louisa found the question of sexuality confusing and unfair. She heard the complaints that women took everything too personally. Emerson said, "Women. How difficult to deal with them. You must interfere continually to steer their talk or they will be sure, if they meet a button or a thimble, to run against it and forget all in the too powerful associations of the Worktable and the pantry. Can't keep it impersonal." Abba agreed with him, and blamed faulty education for leaving women without intellectual balance. She thought women didn't see "clearly, hear distinctly . . . Thus when they desire anything they are not quite sure of the distance or colour . . . girls are taught to seem, to appear — not to be and *do* . . ." But Louisa could do very little without running counter to her father's definition of what was womanly behavior.

At the end of 1846 Abba reviewed family expenses and found that they had earned and received as gifts $478 and that they owed $254: "My friends are wearied with my applications for help — and it does not seem to occur to them that each putting a fraction at interest for me, would relieve all this distressing embarrassment and give us a comfort which we deserve at their hands."

She was constantly on the alert for a way to make money. She took in a deranged adolescent, Eliza Stearns, whose family paid her $16 a month. And although the girl was a "great hindrance," they managed for one month to live on that income. Abba felt her children were old enough to contribute to the family support. She considered sending Louisa to learn how to paint bronze. Someone had offered her free lessons and Abba thought she could "furnish articles for the fancy stores — in her own room . . ." Anna could read German, and if Elizabeth could teach piano, Abba envisioned opening a small school where the Alcott women could teach their various skills.

Alcott advised Abba to relax and let the Lord provide jobs for the girls. Abba, seeing how casually he had provided so far, was not sanguine, but cousin Elizabeth Wells suddenly invited Anna to come to her house in Walpole, New Hampshire, as a governess, and Bronson's faith was vindicated. Bronson had abdicated from any plan-making. Abba wrote to Sam that she wasn't sure she would be a successful captain, "but at least I think I shall keep better soundings — and ascertain oftener and more correctly whether I am fairly in deep waters or shallows — We have nearly wrecked twice — ." Bronson advocated that the family do a Thoreau on Walden Pond, but "will yield to any plan of mine — he is helpless here as things now are — we must either abandon the place or remodel our plan — ." Bronson wanted to go to Alcott House in England, but Emerson, irritated, refused to support the trip when his family was in such straits.

In May 1848, Abba packed up little Abby and demented Eliza Stearns and made the long trip to Waterford, Maine, where she had accepted the matronship of a water therapy spa. She sent Abby home almost immediately, feeling the secular atmosphere was bad for her. Then she worried because the little girl adjusted so poorly to her absence. Abby wrote to her mother that she was "so disappointed when Father told me there was no letter for me that I cried outright. I could not help it. I felt jealous. The girls all had letters, but there was no letter for me . . . I wish you would come home . . . I wish I had stayed with you. Father asked if I worried you, and that made me cry, it seemed unkind . . . I shall not send the least bit of love till you write me."

Abba had high hopes for the Maine venture. As she wrote to a friend, she hoped to "facilitate . . . the emancipation of my children from this dependence on friends, and charities — I am not afraid of labour, but I sicken and perish under reproach." She observed Eliza Stearns's progress with water therapy. The girl had been, in Abba's words, "stupid" before arriving at the spa, and the treatments, dormitory life, and excitement were bringing her to a pitch of active confusion. Abba thought it might be the crisis before her recovery, but it proved to be merely a stirring up of the poor girl's addled wits, bringing her no closer to comprehension. Abba realized the damage occurring to her charge, and by the third week in July she had returned home with the girl. Abba collapsed from her overexertion of the previous nine weeks. She wrote to her cousin Samuel Sewall that her "labours were incessant and both satisfaction, and compensation too small, to make it worth my while to leave family and domestic comfort for either."

As the summer wore on, the Alcotts spent their time discussing where to go. Bronson recorded that Abba was "almost frantic" at the idea of spending the winter in Concord. She considered the town her own personal purgatory and hated the location of her poverty and humiliation. Bronson liked Concord, for he could always find company for talk. He considered staying there while Abba moved with the girls to Boston. Her friends were urging her to return to the city, where she could find work and live closer to her network of relatives and supporters. She was eager to leave. In the summer the family had almost enough to eat from Bronson's vegetable garden, but with winter coming there would be no income and no more credit. Abba prevailed. The family rented out Hillside and took rooms in the South End.

During this move, Louisa had gone to visit friends in Hopedale, Massachusetts. On her sixteenth birthday, the tall, shy, dark-eyed, dark-haired girl received a letter from her father announcing that the family had settled on Dedham Street in Boston and that he was holding a conversation in his rooms on West Street above Elizabeth Peabody's bookstore. He sent her a circular of his conversation, adding: "If you were here, the spectacle, if nothing more, might please your own curious eyes once in a week. Anna means to find some corner, and become invisible to overhear the talk, and laugh at our wise nonsense. I wish we may all be as diffident and unpretending as this sister of yours, and so escape the terrors of meeting."

II

Midcentury

LOUISA DID NOT WISH TO MOVE TO BOSTON, but there was no alternative. Abba had to be near her patrons. So the girl had to give up her walks and runs and her favorite retreat, an old cartwheel partially buried in tall grass where she went to write, do homework, and think. She had to leave the beautiful Concord woods for dark, cramped city rooms. In Boston, she would have no chance encounters with Thoreau and no Emerson close by to admire. Louisa's greatest sacrifice was her solitude, essential to her rich interior life. For her most pleasurable moments had always been acts of her imagination, by which she obliterated her impoverished surroundings and painful feelings. Deprived of easy access to nature, Louisa had to work much harder to will away her environment and unhappiness.

She later remembered her first experience of Boston: "I was left to keep house, feeling like a caged seagull as I washed dishes and cooked in the basement kitchen, where my prospect was limited to a procession of muddy boots.

"Good drill but very hard; and my only consolation was the evening reunion when all met with such varied reports of the day's adventures, we could not fail to find both amusement and instruction.

"Father brought news from the upper world, and the wise, good people who adorned it; mother, usually much dilapidated because she *would* give away her clothes, with sad tales of suffering and sin from the darker side of life . . .

"Then we youngsters adjourned to the kitchen for our fun,

which usually consisted of writing, dressing, and acting a series of remarkable plays . . . But we were now beginning to play our parts on a real stage, and to know something of the pathetic side of life, with its hard facts, irksome duties, many temptations, and the daily sacrifice of self. Fortunately, we had the truest tenderest of guides and guards, and so learned the sweet uses of adversity, the value of honest work, the beautiful law of compensation which gives more than it takes, and the real significance of life."

The sweetness of adversity was not Louisa's main preoccupation when she first arrived in Boston. She found her mother and sisters, that winter, in dingy rooms on Dedham Street in the new South End. The city had changed dramatically in the ten years since the Alcotts had lived there. The 1850 census counted 131,881 residents, with an Irish population of 35,000 that grew to 50,000 by 1855. To cope with this expansion, Boston was filling in its tidal marshes. Part of this growth occurred in the section that is now Roxbury. There, during the Revolution a tidal wall had been constructed around the South Cove, and in 1847 the southern part of the city, called the Neck, was filled in. In the 1840s it looked as if this flat, grassy section with the large, bow-windowed, mansard-roofed houses going up was to be the new locus of fashionable Boston. People built homes of brick and brownstone with high stoops, planted gardens, and hemmed them in with iron fences. The land was plentiful and cheap for the moment. Peter Parker, a rich merchant, began erecting in 1848 a dazzling, French-designed brick mansion on Washington Street, perpendicular to Dedham Street. The enormous house was surrounded by a high brick wall and sported Boston's first porte-cochère. The rooms Abba had found, rather less imposing, were in a modest house a block from the Old Colony Railroad, which had connected Boston and Plymouth since 1845.

From Dedham Street, for six cents Louisa could take a horse-drawn omnibus to West Street, where Bronson had rented rooms right next to Elizabeth Peabody's bookshop at Number 12. West Street, formerly a cowpath, led to the Common from the south. At Miss Peabody's store, Bronson could meet friends and sit and read the transcendental periodicals that he couldn't afford to buy. He had a good view of the Common and could see the October 25, 1848, "Water Celebration," commemorating Boston's piping water from Lake Cochituate in Natick into the city's water system. A long procession marched across the Common to a platform suspended over the Frog Pond. Mayor Josiah Quincy, Jr., balanced above the horned-pouts and shiners, presided over the ceremonies, which included conscripted schoolchildren singing James Russell Lowell's ode, written for the occasion, and the release of an 80-foot column of water, shooting out of the Frog Pond, direct from Natick, Massachusetts.

Louisa found that the "bustle and dirt and change" of Boston "send all lovely images and restful feelings away. Among my hills and woods I had fine free times alone, and though my thoughts were silly, I daresay, they helped to keep me happy and good. I see now what Nature did for me, and my 'romantic tastes,' as people call that love of solitude and out-of-door life, taught me much." But Louisa had to shelve her long reveries by the Concord River. At Dedham Street she had no room of her own and no privacy. The family gathered in the kitchen for lack of a parlor. Louisa mourned for the mental elbow room of Concord.

But she devised a new way to remove herself from the oppressive South End realities. She organized her sisters into a production company to perform the tragedies she wrote and directed. Anna built the sets and props and Lizzie sewed costumes. Louisa's dramas included "Norna; or, the Witches' Curse," "The Captive of Castille, or the Moorish Maiden's Vow," "The Greek Slave," "Bianca," and "The Unloved Wife, or Woman's Faith." The plays usually feature a strong, tender heroine afflicted by some vile scoundrel, either her father, lover, or husband, who is determined to ruin her. The women undergo giant injustices at the hands of men, but love on. The heroines say things like, "Dost thou not know the more a woman's heart is crushed and wounded the more tenderly it clings where first it loved; and though deserted, ay, though hated, I had rather be the slighted wife of him . . ." In short, the playwright's inspiration came from her own tragical sense of being unloved.

Louisa played the male roles, with lots of mustache-twirling and stomping of boots, to Anna's breathless leading ladies. Louisa wrote about women's heartbreak, but she dissociated herself from it at the performance, lining herself up on the side of the strong, who are not victims of their hearts.

The family stage was a tremendous relief for Louisa. It provided a pause in her everyday pain, anger, anguish, dreariness, and hopelessness. Just being Louisa, she found intolerable. Her problems obsessed her except when she could ride her imagination roughshod over them. In performing she found a replacement for the solitude of Concord as well as a method of putting her fantasy life to use. She received attention and admiration in exchange for transforming reality. The success of these dramas began to shape Louisa's personal style. She became more dramatic in her daily life, speaking in mannered and humorous asides. Stagy locutions offered her a hide-out. She could express herself, but in disguise she took fewer risks than if she were unreserved and natural.

Short of entertaining, Louisa had trouble disposing of herself. She was a somber, sober young girl who maintained an impenetrable silence in the presence of strangers. A young man who met her for the first time in Boston recalled that she had a melancholy expression, an earnest manner, and no interest whatsoever in conversation. She couldn't manage neutral chat for casual acquaintances. She could articulate her deepest philosophical beliefs and describe the emotions she was feeling, but she experienced little in the unmined middle ground of life. The requisite peace of mind for absorbing objective information eluded her.

At his West Street rooms, Bronson held a series of conversations for young women on various aspects of man, "Monadic, Embryonic, Natural, Demonic, Human, Intellectual and Divine." On March 20, 1849, a group of men gathered at his rooms to discuss forming a club. Alcott's voice, according to Emerson, faltered and he became overwrought with gratitude as they discussed making him permanent secretary and paying the rent for his rooms. The thirty founders of the Town and Country Club included the main man Emerson, William Lloyd Garrison, the poet James Russell Lowell, Jones Very, Samuel Gridley Howe, James Freeman Clarke, the Reverend Theodore Parker, and later an editor of the *Atlantic Monthly*, Thomas Wentworth Higginson. Higginson recalled that Alcott wanted to call the club Olympian, or the Pan Club. Lowell suggested, when the issue of women members was raised, the Patty-Pan Club. Emerson emphatically decided that question by drawing a line through the names of the females suggested.

Bronson and Abba were informally separated, she trying to support herself and the girls, he attempting to shift for himself. On Christmas 1848, Abba took some pride in the fact that neither she nor the girls were freezing or starving. She had come to the city, assured by her cousin Hannah Robie that she could earn $25 a month by distributing charity to the poor. Miss Robie had organized a group of philanthropic women willing to fund Abba to this amount. Abba collected bundles of clothing and food and handed them out at the relief room she hired on Washington Street. She badgered rich people into contributing to aid the poor. From her parents she had inherited a zeal for personal philanthropy at whatever cost to her own children: "I cannot always stop to count consequences when starvation and destitution is at my door wailing its want — and pleading its necessities — I must stop the wail with a slice of my loaf." Three evenings a week she, Anna, and Louisa taught a group of black adults reading and writing. Abba was discovering Boston's racism, which kept black people almost invisible. She was appalled that there were no adequate schools for "our coloured brethren."

Abba was not so charitably inclined to the numerous Irish, whose Catholicism and drinking repelled her. She considered them deceitful, slothful pagans and reviled "Victoria and Albert, laughing behind their crown while they contribute five-hundred pounds to the Emigration Society who ticket the halt, maimed and blind to send them to America."

After one month Abba read a long, perfervid account of her activities to her employers at Bronson's rooms. Her tone of righteous indignation and exhortation must have come as an unpleasant surprise to the good ladies, who fancied they were doing Abba a favor. With aggressive precision she listed the forty-nine persons she had visited, the twenty-two from whom she had solicited aid, the nine who refused her, the $143 she had received, and the $53 she had disbursed; "I have also distributed four Bibles and twenty tracts, with such readings as people do appreciate." Like her father, she was not satisfied with the dole. She wished to eradicate the cause of poverty, not just minister to its symptoms. She told her circle that the poor must be lovingly understood and warmed by a desire to help themselves, not merely fed and clothed. "Believe me," she concluded, with feeling born of personal experience, "it is more frequent that despair paralyzes the heart than that hunger starves the body."

Abba's work fed her voracious appetite for being good. Her house became a shelter for wandering indigents. One day she found an eleven-year-old girl at Bronson's rooms whose father had "no moral sense or sentiment." Abba took her home for a few days finding, when she got home, another destitute child waiting for her. She was particularly anxious to save young girls "from the sharks and lust that wait." She grew gloomy over the crowds of young women who wandered about aimlessly with no thought except for finding a husband. She lectured every girl she could on her duty to learn a trade. Unprotected adolescent girls weighed on her mind. She worried for their chastity, and wished to keep them from the temptations of the flesh. Without firm guidance like hers, she believed, they would fall into sin through their own weakness and the wickedness of men. She could hardly have worried more about her own girls, and she used every young woman as the source of a lecture on the evils of lasciviousness. Abba transmitted her sexual fears effectively to her daughters, and inexperienced Louisa came to believe in the essential baseness of men.

Seventeen-year-old Louisa had grown to her full five feet six. She wore her beautiful, thick chestnut hair in a snood or piled on top of her head. She looked out with sadness and suspicion from large, dark, deep-set eyes. She had a strong, handsome face and a healthy complexion and would have been the prettiest of her sisters had she been less severe- and angry-looking. Tall for the era, with a full figure and broad shoulders, she was restless and taut with the contradictory demands of puberty and confinement.

Abba's work took up her attention, and Louisa was lonely and hungry for affection. She spent most of her time with Anna, and when Anna was busy, Louisa read Dickens or the Swedish mistress of the soap opera, Fredrika Bremer.

The family split and regrouped several times during the spring of 1849. Louisa and little Abby spent several weeks out of Boston with the Sewall cousins while Abba and Bronson took rooms on Temple Place, the twelve-foot-wide passage near Bronson's old school. In May they all moved into the house of Colonel May's brother Samuel, a large home on Atkinson Street, in the older part of the city near West Street and the Common. The house, a gracious, comfortable establishment, was set in among elegant seventeenth- and eighteenth-century homes on quiet, wide streets overhung with trees. There the family waited through the epidemic of Asiatic cholera, which took more than a thousand lives that summer.

Abby, at nine, was a blonde, blue-eyed child, full of life and determination. Unlike the other girls, she asked for and frequently got her way. Louisa found her something of a trial. The contrast between their experience was extreme, and Louisa resented Abby's demands. It wasn't the facts so much as Abby's assumption that she had some importance and that her desires were worth articulating. To Louisa, who had never felt this assurance, it was galling to see her baby sister asserting her will and succeeding.

Bronson took the girls on walks through the Common morning and evening throughout the summer. On the last Wednesday in May, they witnessed the arrival of the black voters who lived on the north side of Beacon Hill, coming to participate in the General Election. In early June the all-white Artillery Election took place and was celebrated by a promenade concert and children's dance. Throughout the summer there were band concerts, which were occasionally disrupted by boys shooting off firecrackers. A corner of the park was devoted to smokers, who were not allowed elsewhere on the Common. Occasionally Louisa would find herself near a rough rock on the northeast side of the park where children made wishes. From there she could watch the lovers circling Frog Pond and the children throwing balls and flying owl-shaped kites.

That summer, in Sam's spacious house, Louisa started a family paper called "The Olive Leaf," to which she contributed poems, stories, and articles. Her father's behavior distracted her somewhat. He ate so little during July and August that he began hallucinating, and once he saw the universe as a long spinal cord. Abba became sufficiently alarmed to pack him off to Concord, where he spent several weeks recuperating. He had long walks and talks with Thoreau and Emerson and reflected on how fortunate he was that Abba could provide for him so well, "and rendered me not wholly dependent on others for a subsistence which I have no means of earning." He was clearly getting better when, at Emerson's one night, when Waldo was carving roast beef and discoursing on the horrors of cannibalism, Bronson replied, "But Mr. Emerson, if we are to eat meat, why not eat the best?"

In the fall the family moved back to the South End to rooms on Groton Street, which extended south to the South Boston Bridge.

Built in 1805, the 1500-foot wooden bridge joined the South End with Dorchester Neck (now Dorchester). The bridge, a favorite promenade for lovers, became known as the Bridge of Sighs. It afforded a comprehensive view of downtown Boston across the water, and provided discretion-conscious lovers with some seclusion. Groton Street, several blocks north and east of Dedham Street, was near the train yards and next to noisy, trafficky Dover Street. After Sam's fine house, Louisa was dismayed with these dreary new surroundings.

Louisa assisted Anna in teaching a few children on Canton Street, a block away from their Dedham Street home. Often, in the morning, Bronson would stop in to look over the girls' work. Louisa disliked teaching and dreamed of running away, but forced herself to keep at it. After school Anna needed her to clear up and get ready for the next day, so she had no free time and no peace. "I think a little solitude every day is good for me," she wrote wistfully. "In the quiet I can see my faults, and try to mend them: but deary me, I don't get on at all."

Even her journal wasn't a private experience; even it was critically appraised. Bronson remarked that Anna's concerned others and Louisa's was about herself. Louisa thought she kept a selfish diary, in part because she didn't *talk* about herself. Instead, she was always thinking about the "wilful, moody girl I try to manage, and in my journal I write of her to see how she gets on. Anna is so good she need not take care of herself, and can enjoy other people. If I look in my glass, I try to keep down my vanity about my long hair, my well-shaped head, and my good nose. In the street I try not to covet fine things. My quick tongue is always getting me into trouble, and my moodiness makes it hard to be cheerful when I think how poor we are, how much worry it is to live, and how many things I long to do I never can." Vanity was big game in the Alcott family, and Louisa was forbidden to enjoy her somber, almost Mediterranean beauty. Instead, she forced herself to contemplate the virtues of the bovine Anna.

Abba's absorption in her charities left Louisa without any resources. Her mother's involvement and encouragement were vital to Louisa's attempts at self-improvement. Abba had made her participation a condition for Louisa's equanimity, and without her there was anxiety and depression for the girl. Louisa felt blamed for worrying about herself at all, and doubly blamed for wanting to share her worries with her mother, who had so many of her own. At seventeen, her impoverished life looked so gloomy that she wished it were ended: "So every day is a battle, and I'm so tired. I don't want to live; only it's cowardly to die till you have done something."

Abba was very good at her job. She was a capable organizer, kept clear, meticulous records, and effectively shamed acquaintances into becoming generous donors. She loved the responsibility, and took great satisfaction in stepping out of the family closet into a position of public self-sacrifice: "My efforts hitherto have been acceptable — and successful to both rich and poor . . . the work of dispensing charity is one of the most arduous and least understood of any philanthropy." Despite the job's satisfactions, she felt exploited by her low salary and disappointed with her employers for not doing more to wipe out the causes of poverty. She lectured them regularly, shaking a self-righteous forefinger at their inactivity.

Abba accused the board of interest in "sympathizing in the details of wretchedness and want" but overlooking the *"causes* of so much poverty and crime . . . And for myself I feel that I have much to do to prevent myself from yielding to a false sympathy with the symptoms, rather than making a stringent effort to overcome the necessity for so much begging and Almsgiving." With every blanket, loaf of bread, and rent payment, Abba supplied a lecture on Malthusian principles of overpopulation and the importance of temperance and self-reform. The spectacle of the almslady coming with stern advice on self-improvement alarmed the poor, although they had to put up with it. It enraged the kind-hearted philanthropists, who thought Abba unkind to individual paupers.

Abba complained of fatigue and "cost to mind, body and estate." Her supporters began to drop away. Abba railed but was proud of her position: "I stand alone, my heart unbiassed, and my mind my *own.*" She told her subscribers that she wished to be elected "Prima Donna of a watercure, to which, ladies, in your summer rustication, I invite you most cordially. You shall each and all be welcome to a plunge, spray, and shower, and a rub with a crash mitten, the best of all remedies for warm talks and cool friendships." Sarcasm didn't prevent her losing her job in April 1850.

Abba had made the same emotional journey as her father, from an intense interest in relieving immediate suffering to disgust with the individual profligacy and weakness that, both agreed, resulted in want. Out of this disgust grew the urge to change people, to renovate their habits and improve their goals. Colonel May had treated all his petitioners (and children) this way, and his daughter continued the tradition.

In March, Abba complained of the onset of a periodic depression, brought about, she thought, by overwork and "no rest . . . have been called upon for any office to sick, dying, or dead . . ." In a letter to Sam, she told him of her weakened, rattled condition and begged him for more help. She acknowledged how much he had already done, "but do you realize how important to *me*, to my four daughters, is the counsel and encouragement of our friend, a right understanding of my husband — a just appreciation of his excellencies not a tacit cold disclaimer of his virtues — because they are not producible of *bread and cloth.*"

She told Sam that he ought to have sought out Bronson if only to find out how to explain to the world what Abba was at a loss to explain — Bronson's inactivity. She wanted to figure out how they could live together — "we have tried separation — death is more tolerable . . . Is there not superfluous means somewhere that can keep us where we belong . . . must we be driven to denounce society for its selfishness — and individuals for their forgetfulness . . . I make this appeal to you, my brother: *Think* for us — be to us an earthly Providence — your better wisdom of what, where, how to *do* — We ask no man what or *how* we should *be.*" In closing this excited petition, Abba asked for all Bronson's and her letters: "He is collecting his autobiography which some day may be a gem in literature . . ."

The family scattered among cousins while they decided what to do. In the evenings they would gather at Samuel Sewall's large house on Chestnut Street to discuss arrangements. Bronson didn't mind being considered a useless prophet, but he noted that "to the thinker's family . . . it is no small matter . . . for the wrongs *it* suffers, there is nor can be, no recompense." He was clear, however, that there was nothing for it: "I am an unsaleable commodity . . . an unprofitable servant, as are all thinkers and idealists, to merchantmen and citizens of the senses."

Alcott noted in his journal that the poet James Russell Lowell "begged" him to write his autobiography. Bronson intended to do so "to clear my existence of the charge of unproductiveness which might be quite honestly preferred against it by those who are not in my secret — ." So Bronson arranged his papers in his room at the Sewalls'. He never completed the autobiography, but his preparations were extended and voluminous.

Among those not in on Bronson's secret was Sam May, who wrote to Abba that he really failed to understand why Bronson couldn't find any way to help his family. As for himself, Sam generously promised to continue whatever aid he could manage.

Abba's Uncle Samuel May gave them his big Atkinson Street house for another summer. The Alcotts moved to Mr. May's house with alacrity, for the Sewalls, to whom Abba referred ominously as "some persons," seemed to her to "take pleasure in asking me painful and inquisitorial questions . . ." Louisa looked forward to enjoying the large house, and hoped that by the end of the summer she would have something to show for herself: "Seventeen years have I lived, and yet so little do I know, and so much remains to be done before I begin to be what I desire, — a truly good and useful woman."

The summer began inauspiciously when the family all came down with smallpox, infected by one of Abba's charity cases. The girls had light attacks, but Abba and Bronson were very sick. On June 7, Bronson described the pox "crimsoning and knitting over the face, with tapestries." Ten days later he was better and complaining that he didn't look well with a beard and mustache.

Abba had hardly recovered before her friends started telling her that Bronson's idleness was disgraceful and that he must be a heartless man to let her support the family. She reported these remarks to Alcott, and he replied that he "must stand, for the time, as a thriftless, if not heartless and incapable fellow."

The oldest girls, however, went to work. Anna left home for Lenox, Massachusetts, where she was to assist the Tappan family, who had a new child. When Anna had fully recovered from the pox at the end of June, she left on the stage for western Massachusetts.

Louisa was doggedly running a little school in the South End, on Suffolk Street. Bronson would drop in and read sections from *The Pilgrim's Progress*. Louisa took some pride in the achievements of her pupils, but she didn't enjoy the hot, dusty commute or the labor. She read in her spare moments.

That summer James T. Fields, a round, bearded, jocular book-seller, in partnership with William D. Ticknor, published Haw-thorne's *Scarlet Letter*. Fields had visited the Hawthornes in Salem, where they had gone after leaving Concord. Fields found the completed manuscript in a bureau drawer and cozened the coy author into letting him publish the novel. It was an immediate success, and Louisa and her mother discussed the complexities of Pearl's character and what Abba called "the shammery of what is so falsely called religion and the beauty, power and sublimity of contrition, love and truth." Unlike her mother, who preferred Fredrika Bremer's tales of domestic morality, Louisa responded to the quality in *The Scarlet Letter* that she called "lurid." Over the years this word came to define for her everything in fiction and life that seemed spontaneous, lively, and hence evil and forbidden. Hawthorne wrote about the commission of sin and its attendant guilt with an almost sensual pleasure. His fascination with amoral energy under the coating of morality appealed to Louisa. She enjoyed the freedom and rebelliousness of dealing with evil before it had been judged and processed into the moral compensation mechanism. She was temperamentally suited to understand the chaos of an active emotional life. Her own deep and contradictory feelings resonated with Hawthorne's tortured characters. She was compelled to organize her confusion of emotions under her fa-ther's rules, but she could never pretend she didn't have them. She was to write many of what she called "lurid" stories, dealing with powerful feelings and the expression of evil. But she always wrote them under a pseudonym. For Louisa Alcott, issues of behavior had to be black and white, a demand that forced the writer to remain forever in her adolescence.

Louisa guiltily curtailed her pleasure in reading Hawthorne's lurid work and resolved to read fewer novels. She listed her favor-ite books. They were eminently transcendentally acceptable: Car-lyle, Goethe, Plutarch, Milton, Schiller, Madame de Staël, Bettina von Arnim, Harriet Beecher Stowe, and Emerson's poems.

When she was teaching or reading, Louisa worried about Anna and her mother. Anna's letters to Louisa confessed how feeble, miserable, and homesick she was. She missed Lizzie, her "con-science, always true and just and good." She begged her sister not to let her mother know of her distress. Louisa bore the burden. She daydreamed of buying a little home for Anna, her mother, and herself. She brooded in her journal about her mother's hard life since her marriage, and she tried to cheer her up. Occasionally Abba would write a note in Louisa's diary, as she had done at Fruitlands, and it gave Louisa encouragement.

Anna's misery was casting a pall over the Tappan nursery, and she and Mrs. Tappan agreed, after some unpleasantness, that Anna should go home. Anna felt grievously unappreciated by her employers and left her wages in the nursery. Mrs. Tappan was insulted and wrote to Abba, forwarding the wages. "I am sorry," Mrs. Tappan concluded, "if I said anything which led Anna to leave the money. I was troubled by her being here — her unhappiness was a weight upon my thoughts and spirits from the first hour she came — indeed it affected everyone in the house." The Alcotts received Anna as a heroine and a martyr. Bronson wrote that she had "accounted herself nobly to conscience and the facts, and all the wiser and more admirable for this enterprise . . ." The Alcott girls were unfitted for existence anywhere but home. From years of poverty, pride, and Abba's denunciations of society, their skins were so thin, and their sensitivity to criticism so high, that they never felt anything but pain from their employers. They looked for and found unfairness, selfishness, and abuse.

In late July, the news of Margaret Fuller's death shocked the Alcott family. Margaret had gone to Europe in 1848, finding New York and Horace Greeley's *Tribune* too limiting for her expansive romanticism. The Risorgimento drew her to Italy and Mazzini became her close friend. There she took a lover — and, she claimed, a husband — in Count Ossoli, whose manners were indisputably excellent, although there was some controversy over his intelligence. Hawthorne, who never met Ossoli, maliciously circulated stories that he was little better than a moron, but Hawthorne's sexual antagonism for Margaret was pathological, and it suited his problem to see Margaret throwing intellect to the winds and lusting after some inarticulate halfwit. In any case Margaret, forty years old, sailed home with Ossoli and their infant son. She was gravely apprehensive about the journey, uncertain of her welcome in this country, and unsure of her future. When the *Elizabeth* went aground off Fire Island, she said, "I see nothing but death before me, I shall never reach the shore." She made no effort to save herself and went down with her son in her arms. Emerson dispatched Thoreau immediately to salvage whatever he could find, but there was no trace of the book on which she had been working.

Abba wrote to a friend, marveling that Margaret's talent and genius had not "unsexed" her. She disagreed with James Russell Lowell, agreeing with Emerson that Margaret had a big and generous heart: "Sometimes . . . men are apt to think there must be a diminution of affection as there is a preponderance of intellect. What folly! is not God love and who so wise?" Abba thought perhaps it had been just as well for Margaret to end her life so artistically. Otherwise, she thought, "care and sorrow might have invaded her domestic relations: cold criticism or neglect might have blighted her literary aspirations — and what more melancholy than the victim of outraged genius or neglected worth."

Bronson and Margaret had sniffed around at each other with as much suspicion as affection, for Margaret was too serious and exacting in her own right for Bronson's comfort, but he had honest admiration for her and mourned her death: "She has been more to many women, and to many men, I may add, than any woman else, of these last years, nor is there any to fill and make good her place."

Margaret's feminism, best expressed in her life and in *Woman in the Nineteenth Century,* was essentially a plea for women to develop all aspects of themselves, not just the domestic. "Woman, self-centered," she had written, "would never be absorbed by any relation; it would only be an experience to her as to a man. It is a vulgar error that love, *a* love, to Woman is her whole existence; she also is born for truth and Love in their universal energy." That was one of the themes of Louisa's life and fiction. Years later, the heroine of *Rose in Bloom* tells her male cousins that women have "minds and souls as well as hearts; ambition and talents, as well as beauty and accomplishments; and we want to live and learn as well as love and be loved. I'm sick of being told that is all a woman is fit for! I won't have anything to do with love till I prove that I am something beside a housekeeper and babytender!"

In the fall, the Alcotts sadly relinquished Uncle Sam's comfortable house, taking rooms a block away on High Street, a wide thoroughfare two blocks from the wharves. High Street sloped up to Fort Hill, which still had remnants of Revolutionary fortifications. At the top of the hill, brick townhouses encircled a park. What had once been an expensive residential area was turning into a slum for Irish immigrants. Owners were subdividing and subletting their houses, turning them into overcrowded tenements. Josiah Quincy, Boston's mayor and Harvard's president, had once grown honeysuckle and damask roses by his spacious home on High Street. But as the warehouses went up and business from the wharves increased, he and his wealthy neighbors moved to quieter parts of Boston. Over two streets, India Wharf extended almost 1500 feet into the harbor, rising on great pilings out of water deep enough for the most heavily laden ships. At right angles to the wharf, along Broad Street, stood the classical five-story granite warehouses, behind which against the sky appeared delicate fences of masts and rigging. Down on the piers vendors sold oysters, to be eaten with vinegar and pepper and plates of hard biscuits.

From there Louisa walked or took the horsecar with straw on the floor to Suffolk Street to teach. Anna commuted a little farther south to Jamaica Plain, where she looked after the children of ex-Brook Farmer George Minot. Abba set up an intelligence office, a matching employment service for working women and women who needed domestic help. As Louisa put it, they were "poor as rats and apparently quite forgotten by everyone but the Lord."

An elderly lawyer named James Richardson applied to Abba for a companion to his sister and aged father. Instead of giving him one of her "Californians, Germans, Irish or coloured girls," Abba suggested the job to the doleful Louisa. She agreed to try it, although, as Abba wrote to Sam, "every sentiment of her being revolts at it — and I am not sure how long she will remain." Seven weeks, it turned out, until she could no longer bear labor she considered degrading. She found herself expected to shovel snow, black boots, and, worst of all, listen to the poetry of her employer. She left Dedham, Massachusetts, and headed home with her salary. When she discovered that they had sent her off with only four dollars she was enraged, and, in the tradition of Anna, she sent it back. The family applauded her decision. Emerson noted his approval of her homing instincts. And Abba was proud that "Louisa scarce acknowledges the office of mistress . . . she is too free to recognize service — and I am glad the connexion was so loosely sustained, so soon dissolved — I believe there are some natures too noble to curb — too lofty to bend — of such is my Lu."

Louisa later wrote the story "How I Went out to Service," in which she implied that Richardson's poetry was a sexual preliminary. She made much of her mistreatment, and there is no reason to doubt that her employers were callous and demanding. Whether Richardson actually hoped to threaten Louisa's virtue, or whether Louisa was suffering from an overdose of her mother's hysterical sexual fears, is impossible to determine. It is clear, however, that Louisa was profoundly aware of and troubled by her sexuality. Thanks to Bronson and Abba, she felt unsafe in the presence of men.

* * *

Some of the difficulties Louisa was undergoing in becoming a woman were suddenly topics of general concern to the reform community. Since the Seneca Falls convention in 1848, there had been agitation for a more widely based meeting to discuss women's issues. At the close of the Anti-Slavery Convention in Boston in 1850, interested members stayed on to discuss a national women's convention. Quaker abolitionist Lucy Stone, wealthy Paulina Wright Davis of Rhode Island, Boston's Dr. Harriet Hunt, who had been practicing since 1835, and several abolitionists circulated a petition calling for a meeting. Bronson signed it, along with Theodore Parker, Wendell Phillips, William Lloyd Garrison, and Rev. Sam May. The first National Women's Rights Convention was held at Brinley Hall, Worcester, Massachusetts, on October 23, 1850, and was called to order by Sarah H. Earle, the wife of a newspaper editor. The speakers included Lucretia Mott, Garrison, Lucy Stone, the Reverend Antoinette Brown, and Frederick Douglass. Conventions were called annually through 1857, and the complaint was raised that nothing happened but talk. Critics missed the point that women talking in public about their oppression constituted in itself a social revolution.

Bronson attended the 1853 convention and wrote that the women had imitated men at their worst, and poorly at that. They had naïvely mistaken parliamentary procedure as a superior method to the "potent persuasions of the parlor, the conversation, prevailing manners . . . the suggestions of literature, religion and of pure art. Not that a woman shall not use any armor, but use it in a superior and womanly way. The Convention if she will, the ballot, the pulpit, the professorship: all these are hers if she will grace them well or show man how to become them better." Bronson's feminism derived directly from his transcendentalism. He offered women the opportunity to become sublime, but denied them the chance to be human. It is not fair to accuse Bronson of standard sexual bias, however. He wanted his women to be ladies, but he wanted his men to be ladies, too. He only kept company with Waldo, he said, because the "best of Emerson's intellect comes out of its feminine traits, and were he not as stimulating to me as a woman, and as racy, I should not care to see and know him intimately nor often."

Unlike Waldo, who viewed the admission of women to the Town and Country Club as "quite fatal," Bronson wanted female members. Some women were his best audience. He grew exceptionally gluey and, to rephrase Thoreau on the prose of Ellery Channing, sublimo-playful in describing the ladies: "Woman is an allegory; a myth sleeping in a myth; a sheathed goddess and a blazonry; a Sphinx's riddle, devouring and devoured; an ambush and retirement, a nimbleness, a curiosity, a veil behind a veil, and a peeping forth from behind veils; a crypt of coyness, a goal of surprises, and an ambuscade."

This combined reticence and nonsense betrays Bronson's desire to keep women out of focus. He idealized the qualities of ambiguity, artfulness, discretion, deference, shyness, and religiosity. These were distinctly not Louisa's traits. She tried to understand and adapt to her father's fuzzy adulatory feminisim. His sympathy sanctioned her interest in women's rights, but her failure to be his kind of woman left her politically inactive.

Bronson sensibly judged that, whatever a woman could do better than a man, she would, and that there was no lasting danger of "confusing sexes or spheres . . . Absurdities are short-lived . . ." He referred to the bloomer, of anonymous invention. The garment was promoted by Amelia Bloomer, editor of the *Lily,* a journal subheaded "Devoted to the Interests of Women," one of a number of feminist papers that appeared in the 1850s. The bloomer consisted of a knee-length tunic that was loosely belted over a pair of full harem pants and gathered at the ankle. Elizabeth Cady Stanton and Susan B. Anthony gave the outfit a valiant try

and found it a physical comfort but a psychological agony. Harass-
ment was incessant, and Mrs. Stanton wrote to Susan Anthony that
she thought it wise to give up the experiment to preserve their own
strength for greater battles.

The costume was designed to relieve women of the weight of up
to thirty-nine pounds of horsehair, crinolines, wire, and whalebone
under which the well-dressed were expected to stagger. The
Crinoline Period officially opened in 1852, and skirts grew to include twenty-five yards of fabric and carried as many as fifteen
flounces. Steel hoops supported the bulk of crinolines, quilted
petticoats, and woolen underskirts. Lacing was tight and getting
tighter to display nonexistent waists under skinny bodices and
fetching berthas.

Louisa was taught to disdain fashion, but her attitude was colored by the regrets of poverty as she daily passed shops displaying
cauls for the hair of gold thread with beads, folding fans of gauze
or painted silk inlaid with mother of pearl, painted ostrich feathers,
velvet bands for neck and cuffs, silver bouquet holders for the
evening, and lace and kid gloves in soft pastels. She told herself
that only shallow, silly women coveted these ornaments, but often
that was chilly satisfaction.

Louisa was bringing home a little money from looking after a
child on Beacon Street. She contributed her whole salary to the
family needs. Anna set aside her money from the Minot children
for eleven-year-old Abby's schooling. Lizzie, who was too shy to go
to school even if there had been money enough, stayed home to
look after the house. Louisa called her "our angel in a cellar
kitchen." Abba kept up her employment service and invited Llewellyn Willis to board with them while he prepared for Harvard
Divinity School. In the spring of 1851, Uncle Sam organized a tiny
Alcott Fund to ease matters.

Bronson laughingly considered putting down his pen "and philosophy" to emulate Abba's good works. He joked that he would
take "the office below stairs, to furnish gentlemen with grooms,
coachmen, and general domestic male help." Instead, he remained
engrossed in what Ellery Channing of the wicked tongue referred
to as his *"Encyclopédie de Moi-même en cent volumes."* Bronson's journal for 1851 ran to 1338 pages, and he was perfectly accurate when
he wrote: "This diary is taking the best out of me." Occasionally

he railed at Boston, where he had done "some of my best things" and still couldn't find a reward. But he was grateful that he didn't mind poverty and even came to enjoy the position of dignity he occupied as a debtor. He found he rather liked meeting his creditor "with a civil *'nothing'* for his honest demand" and was pleased that he had yet "to receive the first incivility from that class, to whose better knowledge of business I owe more than is put into the bill. A civil dun is one of the finest pieces of courtesy I know of."

In September 1851, *Peterson's Magazine* obliged Louisa by publishing her first poem, "Sunlight," under the name Flora Fairfield. *Peterson's* had been issued in 1842 to compete with the vapid fiction, genteel engravings, and colored fashion plates of Louis A. Godey's *Lady's Book*. The monthly sold for two dollars, a dollar less than *Godey's,* and rapidly became the nation's most popular women's magazine, specializing in tales of virtue, beauty hints, and an occasional thrilling, real-life episode of rescue or daring.

Louisa was delighted with her beginning, and it encouraged her to indulge in hours of speculation on a life of fame. She was more eager to go on the stage than become a writer. The rewards seemed more immediate. Anna shared her ambition. "We could both have plenty of money perhaps," reasoned Louisa, "and it is a very gay life. Mother says we are too young, and must wait."

While she waited, she found herself heated by the enthusiasm of the abolitionists. With them she found a cause in which to unstop her anxiously contained passions into waves of righteous rage, despair, and hope. Daniel Webster had outraged his antislavery constituents by collaborating in the Compromise of 1850. The most heinous provision in the compromise concerned the new tight federal control on the return of slaves. The bill also left open to slavery the territories gained from the Mexican War while admitting California as a free state. Its passage was greeted by official Boston with relief and a one-hundred-gun salute, but the Fugitive Slave Law helped to hasten the Civil War. Apolitical Emerson, with creaky but sincere emphasis, announced: "This filthy enactment was made in the 19th century, by people who could read and write. I will not obey it, by God." The philosopher, by nature an aristocrat, had been wrenched out of his instinctive admiration for Webster's elegance, prose, and breeding. Emerson astonished himself with his vehemence, saying that "the word *liberty* in the mouth of

Mr. Webster sounds like the word *love* in the mouth of a courtezan."

On the fifteenth of February, 1851, a black man named Frederick Jenkins, called Shadrach, who was working as a Boston waiter, was seized under the new bill by slavecatchers. The lawyer and writer Richard Henry Dana, Jr., tried to use legal means to get Shadrach free, but before reaching the courthouse to file his plea he heard a shout go up from the crowd and "down the steps came two huge Negroes bearing the prisoner between them with his clothes half torn off, and so stupefied by the sudden rescue and the violence of his dragging off that he sat almost dumb, and I thought had fainted . . ." Shadrach got to Cambridge that day, and Concord the next, where he was sent on to Canada by the village blacksmith, an engineer on the Underground Railroad. Next came Henry Williams, Shadrach's friend, who had escaped from Virginia. He found his way to Henry Thoreau, who sent him "into the cars for Canada." The Underground Railroad had grown so efficient in response to the challenge of the Fugitive Slave Act that it boasted a two-day trip from slavery to Canada.

But the Boston Vigilance Committee, established to protect blacks from being returned to the South, failed with a runaway named Simms. After the escaped slave was arrested, Louisa went to a meeting where she heard Wendell Phillips. He had taken Garrison's place as Boston's leading abolitionist, since Garrison's pacifism prevented him from endorsing any rescue or defensive violence. "People were much excited," Louisa reported, "and cheered 'Shadrach and liberty,' groaned for 'Webster and slavery,' and made a great noise. I felt ready to do anything, — fight or work, hoot or cry, — and laid plans to free Simms." But despite the plans and Dana's defense, the man went back into slavery.

Throughout 1852, Louisa looked after some children on Beacon Street from ten till two. The family remained at 50 High Street, where Lizzie ran the kitchen and Abba her bureau. "Father idle," commented Louisa, adding with acerbity, "Ab doing nothing but grow."

In the summer, Bronson took a trip to his birthplace at Spindle Hill, Connecticut, where he gave conversations. Abba wrote to him of her weariness and doubts concerning her ability to continue "the active partner of an establishment."

To make matters easier, the Hawthornes decided to buy Hillside in Concord, giving Abba enough cash to rent 20 Pinckney Street, on Beacon Hill. She wrote to her brother that they finally had what they had wanted since they had moved to Boston, "a *respectable* position. Nobody can work in this City without a *position,* a comfortable house in a good neighborhood."

The Mount Vernon Proprietors had laid out Beacon Hill just before the turn of the century as a group of scattered, costly, free-standing town houses and mansions decorating the hill above the Charles River. By midcentury, fewer gardens and more red brick houses climbed the slope to the State House. The Alcott's house stood on the corner of gracious Louisburg Square, halfway up the hill, where four-story brick townhouses enclosed a tiny park.

Here Anna and Louisa opened their own school. Abba took in boarders and Bronson received acolytes. Franklin B. Sanborn, a twenty-three-year-old Harvard student, often came with friends and listened to Alcott or played whist with the girls. A mild, thin, tall young man, he was something of a sycophant and became Alcott's biographer and the unofficial historian of Concord's literati. Sanborn, who was secretly engaged to a dying girl, was struck on meeting Louisa by her "earnest face, large dark eyes, and expression of profound interest in other things than those which usually occupy the thoughts of young ladies." Sanborn had probably never met a handsome, intelligent, vital young woman who had been trying to help support her family since her fifteenth year. Louisa had little in common with girls her age. Her eccentric upbringing had given her a serious, worried demeanor, and none of the irresponsible, gay traces of childhood showed on her adolescent face. The dark-haired girl had no social graces: she talked little and abruptly to strangers and stared at the floor. Her expansive, lively, humorous side emerged only with the love and encouragement of her mother and sisters.

Occasionally on Sunday mornings Louisa would walk across the Common to the brand-new Music Hall on Winter Street, near the former Temple School, and listen to the sermons of the Reverend Theodore Parker. A compact little man in spectacles with a rapid-fire delivery and a preference for big words, he was an acquaintance of her father's, a dedicated reformer, and an abolitionist who preached an unorthodox, practical Christianity. At forty-two, Parker was at his rhetorical height. He was both a rational and an emotional man in command of a lively imagery and a dramatic voice. His disregard of fatigue prompted a friend to compare trying to take care of his health to trying to put "a young steam engine to bed, cover it up and give it a physic." Parker rated his health A if he could write his sermon Monday morning, A/2 for Monday evening, and so on through F/2 for Saturday night and o if not at all.

Like many other reformers, Parker enjoyed considering himself the most unpopular man in America. When people suggested that he run for Congress, he suggested that "no town in Massachusetts would give me any post above that of *Hog-Reeve*, and I don't feel competent for that office — a man in spectacles would not run well after swine."

Most of all, Parker liked women, especially attractive ones: "Is it their affection or their beauty of mind that attracts me to them? I love to look at a handsome woman. I love the subtlety of woman's mind. I like not this dazzling subtlety in men." Like most transcendentalists, he thought men were smarter but women better, and that woman's function was "to correct man's taste, mend his morals, excite his affection, inspire his religious faculties."

Parker and his simple, adoring wife, Lydia, opened their home to friends on Sunday evenings. Alcott came sometimes, although Parker privately found him "unbearable," and Bronson closed up when Parker taxed him with sharp, factual jabs. Louisa, however, worshiped the courageous organizer of Boston's Vigilance Committee. Twenty years later she used him as a model for the saintly Reverend Mr. Power in her novel *Work*. In December, Parker's sermon on the dignity of working women gave the desponding Louisa a lift. In her diary she noted that between teaching and sewing she had earned $105 in 1852.

In January, Abba greeted the new year by coming down with the mumps. "The girls enjoy it very much," she wrote to Sam, "when mother has to keep still — it's beautiful to have the fat old lady keep quiet." Anna and Louisa held classes for a dozen students in the second-floor parlor on Pinckney Street.

On May 26, Louisa left to stay with May cousins in Leicester, Massachusetts. As a "second girl" she earned two dollars a week doing wash; she remained there until October. Anna had gone to her Walpole cousins and Abba to Syracuse, to relax with Sam and his family. Bronson stayed in Boston, where Elizabeth kept house. He spent a rainy Sunday with Emerson discussing a trip west to give conversations. Emerson offered to give him travel expenses, so Bronson asked Abba for her advice, and whether "we shall try to find some decent outfit of clothes" so that he could set off in September.

Abba returned from Syracuse, rested and hopeful about Bronson's speaking junket. Louisa came home from Leicester with $34, and Anna returned from Walpole, horrified at the meagerness of her Boston life after the comforts of Walpole, where her cousins had a large warm house and pretty clothes. Abba wrote to Sam that Elizabeth and Louisa were of "rather higher metal and their mother is true steel . . . but Anna suffers when there is no order — gentleness and genteel surroundings — her big eyes see the battered furniture — the odd chairs — Mother's 'unkempt' head at the breakfast table — I often threaten to banish her from the premises until 'Our Ship' arrives." Instead she sent Anna up to Syracuse, where the girl tried to teach her cousins, study German, and not be homesick. Louisa took on ten pupils in Boston and her mother invited boarders again. Unfortunately, one of them fell in love with Elizabeth, and Abba sent him away. On the whole, Abba's boarders were not worth the money they paid, and by Christmastime they had all left.

Louisa had dramatized her experiences as a servant in Dedham and took her story to James T. Fields at his offices above the Old Corner Bookstore on School Street, around the corner from the Music Hall. Fields worked on the floor above the store where long counters piled with books ran from front to back, lit by gas lamps bracketed along the walls. Next door was Mrs. Abner's Coffee House, where Fields took authors and friends for hot buns and mugs of coffee. His office was behind a green curtain and his window looked across School Street to the spire of the Old South Church. The thirty-five-year-old Fields, a full-lipped man with a high forehead who wore heavy tweeds, was determined to turn the bookstore into a renowned, literary publishing house. He had begun with Thomas De Quincey's *Confessions of an English Opium Eater* and had followed that success with *The Scarlet Letter*. Eventually, his extraordinary stable included Emerson, Thoreau, Longfellow, and Horace Mann. He was personally kind to Louisa, and made jokes and spoke affectionately of her father, trying to put the tense and intense young woman at her ease. But he didn't envision her among the luminaries he was bent on collecting. He advised her to stick to her teaching, that she had no talent for writing.

Fields's rejection stunned Louisa. She wasn't happy, rich, beautiful, or beloved, but at least, she had reasoned, she could write herself into money and fame and happiness. To have Fields summarily dismiss not only her story, but also her ambition, left her breathless with despair.

But Louisa recovered quickly in the load of family responsibilities she undertook. She rallied out of what she called her "slough of despond." Her mother sensed her daughter's growing strength and, little by little, began to lean on her. She wrote to Bronson that Louy was "stronger and braver" than Anna and Elizabeth, who were not "so firm in health and there is a more dependent feeling on their parents." Abba needed a self-reliant Louy, for she more and more resented being "a mere tool by which other people can live." She was angry about "the oppressive circumstances of my muddled life" and felt like an "intelligent fragment of a body whose other members are harnessed, and move only by the spur of necessity."

Bronson arrived home in February of 1854 after his conversation circuit had taken him to Rochester, Cincinnati, Buffalo, Cleveland, and Syracuse. In November he had sent home a draft for $150, suggesting that perhaps Abba pay the dentist for his teeth with his first talking earnings. In December he sent $25 in cash and sewing notions for Abba, Louisa, and Lizzie, with a gold cross for Abby. He wrote that he would come home with enough money, added to the $1000 that Emerson had promised, to pay all their debts.

Louisa's account of this homecoming offers a clear view of her perspective on "the pathetic family," as she had begun calling them: "Father came home. Paid his way, but no more. A dramatic scene when he arrived in the night. We were waked by hearing the bell. Mother flew down crying 'My husband!' We rushed after, and five white figures embraced the half-frozen wanderer who came in hungry, tired, cold and disappointed, but smiling bravely and serene as ever. We fed and warmed and brooded over him, longing to ask if he had made any money; but no one did till little May said, after he had told all the pleasant things, 'Well, did people pay you?' Then, with a queer look, he opened his pocket-book and showed one dollar, saying with a smile that made our eyes fill, 'Only that! My overcoat was stolen, and I had to buy a shawl. Many promises were not kept, and traveling is costly; but I have opened the way, and another year I shall do better.'

"I shall never forget how beautifully Mother answered him, though the dear, hopeful soul had built much on his success; but with a beaming face she kissed him, saying, 'I call that doing *very well*. Since you are safely home, dear we don't ask anything more.'

"Anna and I choked down our tears, and took a lesson in real love which we never forgot, nor the look the tired man and the tender woman gave one another. It was half tragic and comic, for Father was very dirty and sleepy, and Mother in a big nightcap and funny old jacket."

Louisa adopted toward her parents a tone of sentimental pity that gave everything a heartbreak flavor, but that didn't necessarily correspond to reality. She chose to see them as baffled children, buffeted mercilessly by arbitrary winds. This is the tone familiar to readers of *Little Women*, and it derives from Louisa's need to find a sentimental, loving vocabulary for articulating the family events. Rage, anger, and disappointment were not allowed, so she had to reduce everyone, and especially her father, to the stature of a large, bumbling, adorable baby. By making him like an infant, as Abba did, Louisa justified his outrageous irresponsibility.

Louisa practiced this tone in family letters. In a more sober, self-conscious voice, she began setting down in poetry and prose the fairy stories she had told Ellen Emerson in Concord. She worked on these through the spring and summer of 1854 while all around Boston bonfires of abolitionist sentiment were flaring up.

The aftershocks of the Fugitive Slave Law were turning out to be of greater intensity than the original tremor. Samuel J. May had written a tract, *The Fugitive Slave Law and Its Victims*, castigating Daniel Webster and relating deeply moving case histories of hundreds of people returned to slavery. In 1854 the Kansas-Nebraska Act dangerously heightened the tensions by opening to slavery lands north of the old Missouri Compromise line. Free-soilers and abolitionists took up arms against those who would own slaves, and the nation watched violence grow in Bleeding Kansas. In Boston's abolitionist circles stories circulated, like the one about Margaret Garner, a black woman who killed her little girl rather than let her be returned to servitude. People talked of fiery Theodore Parker performing the marriage of William and Ellen Craft on "Nigger Hill" behind the State House. Slavecatchers were after Craft, and Parker, finding in Craft's home a sword and a Bible, put the Bible in the groom's right hand and told him to use it. He put the sword in Craft's left and told him to protect his wife's liberty and life with it if necessary.

On the twenty-fourth of May, 1854, Anthony Burns, a runaway from Virginia, was arrested in Boston for allegedly robbing a jewelry store. Six men carried him bodily to the courthouse, where Richard Henry Dana, Jr., found him "cowed and dispirited." Burns was an intelligent, literate, courageous man, branded on his cheek, with the self-possession to overlook the bone sticking through his hand, newly broken by his captors.

That night Alcott went to Worcester to inform Thomas Wentworth Higginson, commander of Boston's Vigilance Committee, of Burns's arrest. Higginson came to Boston immediately, and on May 26 there was an effort to free Burns. The leaders of the assault broke through the door of the jail, but the marshal's posse forced them back and took up a position at the foot of the steps. The crowd regrouped in the shelter of a nearby stairway. In the following pause, Bronson Alcott walked up the deserted, brightly lit jail stairs and turned to the crowd, asking, "Why are we not within?" He was told, somewhat irritably, that there was no support for the attack. Alcott continued his climb, carrying his cane and his serenity. At the top, quite alone, he heard a pistol shot from inside the prison. Unhurt, unhurried, and unaided, he came back down with all the majesty with which he had ascended. As Higginson said, "Under the circumstances, neither Plato nor Pythagoras would have behaved more coolly; and all minor criticisms on our minor sage appear a little trivial when one thinks of him as he appeared that night."

Burns went to trial with a bodyguard of 125 men selected, Samuel May reported, "from the vilest sinks of scoundrelism, corruption and crime in the city," men "with every form of loathsome impurity and hardened villainy stamped upon their faces." Cocounsels for the defense, Richard Henry Dana, Jr., and Charles

McEllis, tried to prove that Burns had been in Boston a month before his alleged escape. The prosecution, which was in constant communication by telegraph with President Franklin Pierce, executor of the Fugitive Slave Law, won its case. Burns's owner refused a $1200 offer for his former slave. Louisa saw the man marched through black-crepe-draped streets between rows of troops especially gathered in Boston to ensure his return. Bronson said nothing but grace for twenty-four hours after Burns's ship left for Virginia.

In June, Anna and Louisa closed their school, and on June 15, Anna left to spend the summer in Syracuse. Louisa followed in August. Bronson spent the latter part of September with friends in Plymouth, Massachusetts, meeting Henry Thoreau, who was passing through. In October, Abba sent him $1.12 for the train and 37 1/2 cents for a hack to cart him and his voluminous journals from the station to 20 Pinckney Street.

Louisa came home in early October and Anna followed later, staying on despite homesickness to earn more money. Louisa set to work in the third-floor room, writing. She finished "The Rival Prima Donnas," which was published on November 11, 1854, under the name of Flora Fairfield in the *Saturday Evening Gazette.* The *Gazette* advertised itself in 1857 as "the best theatrical journal in the country" and was a miscellany, issued Saturday afternoons, that included articles on the theater, book reviews, humor, and stories. It existed from 1814 till 1864 and attracted a somewhat raffish readership. Its editor, Mr. Clapp, paid Louisa $10 for her first story, which she called "rubbish" and would later have called "lurid." It featured two women performers pitted against each other professionally and personally. The dénouement involves considerable carnage and awful retribution.

Shortly afterward Louisa went legitimate with the first volume to which she put her name. *Flower Fables,* the fairy stories she had written at sixteen for Ellen Emerson, were published on December 19, 1854, by George Briggs, who brought out an edition of 1600. The volume opens with a quotation from Emerson's *Woodnotes* and is dedicated to Ellen. The stories and poems are moral fables, all rather windy and obvious but emotionally revealing. Violet, a fairy in the opening story, goes on a mission to try to love the Frost King into letting flowers live during the winter. The Frost King's heart "is hard as his own icy land; no love can melt, no kindness bring it back to sunlight and to joy." Violet, however, through patient suffering, turning many cheeks, and persistent warmth, eventually thaws out the chilly ruler. His cold servants beg him to "grant the little Fairy's prayer; and let her go back to her own dear home. She has taught us that love is mightier than Fear."

The message of subsequent tales is not to covet external beauty, but to work quietly at beautifying one's soul. A mother rose tells her bud:

> Why shouldst thou seek for beauty not thine?
> The Father hath made thee what thou now art;
> And what he most loveth is a sweet, pure heart.
> Then why dost thou take with such discontent
> The loving gift which he to thee hath sent?

Several tales teach that cruelty and selfishness must be atoned for and that reformation brings content and peace. Anger and discontent must be overcome through diligent self-reform. Gentleness and good deeds bring their own rewards.

The final tale concerns an angry, selfish little girl who is given a fair flower to help her be good. She abuses the gift, and the fairy queen sends her a dream showing her how her nasty words and unkind thoughts look as "dark unlovely forms." As Bronson would have said, the words and thoughts were "imaged forth." "Some of the shapes had scowling faces and bright, fiery eyes; these were the spirits of Anger." There were others of pride and selfishness, all growing until they had "a strange power over her . . . rising slowly round her Annie saw a high, dark wall, that seemed to shut out everything she loved . . . Higher and higher rose the wall, slowly the flowers near her died, lingeringly the sunlight faded; but at last both were gone, and left her all alone behind the gloomy wall. Then the spirits gathered round her, whispering strange things in her ear, bidding her obey, for by her own will she had yielded up her heart to be their home, and she was now their slave."

Louisa spelled out her nightmare, the enemies she battled, her fears of being isolated behind a wall of sins of her own making, and the terrifying nature of some of her impulses, which she had to shut away. In each fable the sinner repents and gains great love, and often a coveted journey home. She is received with great joy and warmth. The self-abasement produces a resolution and peace. Hard, patient, uncomplaining work always wins love, even from the Frost King. Each tale is a pathetically simple fulfillment of a wistful desire for love. This love always depends on goodness or repentence, charity, selflessness, and a lack of vanity. The tales are inept, with no well-developed drama or incident, but each one provides moral satisfaction. The relentlessly pointed endings were part of Louisa's practice drill to learn admission to her father's ideally just world.

Anna came home from Syracuse in the winter of 1854–1855 to help Louisa with her school. Abba insisted that she come, anxious that Louy the author have help with the work she found so repugnant. Louisa had inscribed her fables to Abba as a tiny promise of things to come, and Abba wanted to give her daughter the occasion to realize her promise. So Louisa had more time in the garret, writing for the *Gazette* at five dollars a story. She often went to the theater with young Hamilton Willis, her cousin. Hamilton was the son of Abba's sister Elizabeth, who had died in 1822, and her husband, Benjamin Willis.

Louisa's enthusiasm for the theater induced her to dramatize *The Rival Prima Donnas* and quickly write *Nat Bachelor's Pleasure Trip,* a farce. With another cousin, Dr. Charles Windship of Roxbury, the only child of Abba's dead sister Catherine, Louisa discussed the chances of getting her plays produced. It was hardly unthinkable. American theater was young and open. Standards were low and actors and playwrights paid practically nothing. Often plays were written in a few days, as Louisa's were, barely rehearsed, and performed only a few times. Boston had five theaters and had to scramble to fill them, offering Shakespeare one night and a juggling act the next.

Louisa and her cousins often went to the Boston Theater on Federal Street. Its manager, Thomas Barry, booked clergymen, ballet dancers, minstrel shows, orators, and athletes. Louisa could see uplifting melodrama, like William Henry Smith's *Drunkard,* with its famous delerium tremens scene. This was one of a number of dramatized moral works, like Mrs. Stowe's *Uncle Tom's Cabin,* which made the theater a legitimate experience for a young Victorian woman.

In 1854 Louisa followed Barry's Boston Theatre Company to its new location on Washington Street, where an immense chandelier with thousands of cut-glass prisms hung in its lobby. Over the proscenium was a unique German paneled clock. Louisa spent as much time as she could absorbing the theater's atmosphere and dreaming of fame.

Louisa couldn't wait for Barry to make her rich, however. The family money had, once again, run out. Emerson had established an Alcott Fund and enlisted contributors like Longfellow, Lowell, and Frothingham, but there wasn't enough to pay the rent at Pinckney Street. They discussed moving to Wolcott to live with Bronson's mother, an idea that Uncle Sam favored. Once again, Bronson desired to sail for England, but Louisa was opposed to such an extravagance. At the suggestion of Hamilton Willis's sister, Elizabeth Wells, the family decided to move to Walpole, New Hampshire, where Anna had summered years before.

12

Beth

On July 10, 1855, the Alcotts took the Fitchburg and Cheshire train, traveling the last part of the journey by stage to Walpole. This New Hampshire town of about 1500 was located on the Connecticut River, just across from Vermont and about twenty-five miles north of the Massachusetts border. The countryside is mountainous, green, and tree-covered, with fertile soil and fresh, sweet air. Black bears and rattlesnakes still occupied nearby Kilburn Mountain. Moose, red deer, and gray wolves ran through the forests of beech trees, white birches, and white pines. Two miles north, a mineral spring had attracted developers the year before, and the town anticipated a prosperous resort-future. The bulky coach left the family in front of a two-story tavern on Washington Square, the center of Walpole. Around the square stood two village stores, one for Whig and one for Democratic discussion, Slade's meat market, the post office, and a barber shop, where you could also get candy, nuts, root beer, and harnesses.

The Alcotts moved to a cottage near a ravine not far from the large, square Wells house, where Anna had taught in a downstairs room. Bronson began laying out an elaborate garden. Local people took their flowers and vegetables seriously, and Alcott observed many neat gardens, with paths marked out with trees and boxes of petunias, phlox, verbena, and sweet William. Orchards grew peaches, plums, apples, Bartlett and sickle pears, several varieties of grapes, and cherries. Bronson set in beans, peas, asparagus, squashes, beets, potatoes, sage, cucumbers, and corn. He erected a trellis and coaxed up tomatoes. Abba and her daughters scrubbed the house. They found whale oil too expensive and inefficient and so dipped their own candles, lowering cotton wicks into a kettle of hot sheep tallow and hanging up the finished candles to dry.

The family visited often with Eliza Wells, a sweet-natured woman married to an intelligent but discontented man whose business failures had left him a ragged temper. Eliza's father, Benjamin Willis, had suggested in 1845 that the family move to Walpole. The town story was that, when Willis arrived, he bought a pipe (sixty to a hundred gallons) of Dutch gin from the tavernkeeper, drank his way through the purchase, and, when he was done, packed his belongings and left. It was, in any case, no secret that Willis was partial to his toddy and that he often became talkative and sometimes angry of an evening. Willis's father, a cantankerous man in his eighties, also lived with the Wellses, along with the four Wells children. The townsfolk were fond of Eliza and thought she had all the female virtues except beauty. They pitied her life with three such unpleasant men.

Anna quickly picked up with her earlier acquaintances, and she and Louisa founded Walpole's first Amateur Dramatic Company. They performed *Box a Cox, Rough Diamond,* and Sheridan's *Rivals.* Anna loved the stage, and only her slightly impaired hearing prevented her from pursuing a professional career. Louisa began work on *The Christmas Elves,* which Abby illustrated.

Walpole was not entirely cordial to Bronson and took disapproving note of the excellent-quality, unlined, cream-laid, high-finish legal cap on which he copied his journals. They found it inexplicable that Willis cut up and gave winter firewood to Alcott, who then gave it to his poor neighbor Owen Burns and went back to Wells for spare sticks.

Anna left in October for Syracuse, where she had been offered a job in Dr. Wilbur's Idiot Asylum. Bronson cautioned her to avoid: "1. Late hours, 2. Close rooms, 3. Superfine bread, 4. People too many, 5. Suffering from diffidence, 6. Spending too little for self, 7. Routine; and to take: 1. Early bed, 2. Daily walks, 3. Brown bread, 4. Bath often, 5. Pure amusements, 6. Good readings, 7. Heed conscience."

In November, Louisa packed herself up and left for Boston with $20 from her *Saturday Evening Gazette* stories, her manuscripts, and a trunk of hand-sewn clothes. She stayed in Boston with her "Auntie" Louisa Bond, a middle-aged woman whom Abba's parents had raised. Louisa had been cramped and frustrated in Walpole. Her older sister was off earning money and she felt the anxious urge to produce. She also desired to be free from the family confines. Boston offered both work and entertainments. Louisa wished to be out from under the family blanket and listen to herself and her own moods at her leisure.

Ironically, Louisa was uneasy with freedom and vacillated throughout her life between independence in Boston and Alcott home life. With her independence she earned money, which increased her family's dependence on her. She transformed her freedom into indentured service, but still she had the experience of emotional time and territory to herself with no accountability for her moods. The absence of restriction and familial reference points made her at once giddily excited and apprehensive. After a while, usually two to four months, the anxiety would bleed into the area occupied by excitement and she would find herself needing to go home.

Just after her arrival in Boston, Louisa wrote to her father to commemorate their birthdays, his fifty-sixth and her twenty-third. It was a long, wry letter in which Louisa, with some sadness, sketched the differences between them: "I know *you* were a serene and placid baby when you began your wise meditations in the quiet little Spindle Hill farm house . . . and nothing but the lines on his face where the troubles have been and four tall women at his side, show that years and trials have changed the wise little child into a wise old man. Surely dear father some good angel or elf dropped a talisman in your cradle that gave you power to walk through life in quiet sunshine while others groped in the dark. I wish you could teach its magic . . .

"*I* was a cross crying brown baby, hawking at the disagreeable old world where on a dismal November day I found myself . . ." Louisa continued, describing her difficult childhood and her unwilling ascent into adolescence, concluding that "the topsey turvey girl shot up into a topsey-turvey woman who now twenty three years after sits big brown and brave, crying, not because she has come into the world, but because she must go out of it before she has done half she wants to, and because it is such hard work to keep sunshiny and cheerful when life looks gloomy and full of troubles, but as the brown baby fought through its small trials, so the brown woman will fight through her big ones and come out I hope queen of herself though not of the world."

The significance of "brown" in Louisa's letter came from Bronson's deranged and harmful theory of complexions that blond, blue-eyed people, like himself, were godlike, whereas dark-haired, dark-eyed people, like his wife and Louisa, were, as Emerson paraphrased him, "a reminder of brutish nature." It was a theory that rightly appalled many of his friends. How seriously Louisa took this bizarre racism it's impossible to say, but she didn't reject popular phrenology, and there is no reason to assume that she was immune from some pernicious fallout from this doctrine.

She went on to say that her life was quiet and busy, although hard and full of unsatisfied longings. She was sewing shirts for the Reverend Ezra Gannet, the inheritor of Dr. Channing's sublimity at the Federal Street Church. She was working on her stories and going to the theater with Hamilton Willis. She had seen Edwin Forrest's *Macbeth* and found American's best-known actor lacking subtlety. The short, stocky actor's style was high-volume histrionic and his range went from gasping and panting to snorting and gurgling. She preferred Edwin Booth's more controlled technique and his slender, poetic charm, but even he, she found, didn't make Shakespeare the glistening experience of her imagination. She had given up the idea of trying a career on the stage, deciding the physical and moral costs were too high, and "shall try to be contented with the small part already given me . . .Can you not write to me and send some of your quiet in a letter?" she asked her father wistfully.

Louisa spent her Sunday evenings at Lydia and Theodore Parker's, where she met gray-eyed, little Frederic Hedge, the German scholar and minister who had memorized Virgil at seven and was the only American to have read Kant in the original. "A face like a rock, a voice like a howitzer," said Thomas Carlyle affectionately.

She also met Charles Sumner, Parker's phlegmatic friend and soon to be Massachusetts's abolitionist senator, whom he lectured shamelessly. Parker said he expected "heroism of the most heroic kind" from Sumner and made every effort to keep him honest.

Sumner told Parker that he was in morals, not politics, and Parker never let him forget it.

Parker had pulled out all his semantic stops and described slavery as "the most hideous snake which Southern regions breed, with fifteen unequal feet . . ." which "wormed . . . along its track, leaving the stain of its breath in the people's face . . ." Parker's sinewy abolitionism had made him many an articulate enemy. "Hell never vomited forth a more blasphemous monster than Theodore Parker," remarked one minister. Another prayed with his congregation that "God will put a hook in this man's jaws, so that he may not be able to speak." And a third told Parker that "your clerical robes are too transparent to conceal the viperous serpents that nestle in your bosom and twine around your heart."

Louisa was impressed by Parker's vehemence and by his conviction that there must be a slave rebellion. "It must be tried many times before it succeeds, *as at last it must,*" he announced. She was overpowered, awestruck, by the little coughing man in glasses. His foes wished to crucify him, and still he took the time to come over and talk to her of a Sunday, to wish her well and ask about the family. Like all men she admired, she could barely talk to him from constraint and shyness, but she sincerely reverenced the passionate evangelist.

At Parker's, Louisa met his good friends, the handsome Samuel Gridley Howe and his wife, Julia Ward Howe. Julia was interested in the emancipation of women as well as abolition. Louisa's feminism, though never so codified as Mrs. Howe's, eventually came to resemble the older woman's doctrine that women should be allowed to study only after completing their domestic duties. If they had three hours a day they should pursue "art, literature and philosophy, not as they are studied professionally, but in the degree involved in general culture." If they had only one hour they should read philosophy or learn languages. And if they found themselves with only fifteen minutes, they were to "read the Bible with the best commentaries, and daily a verse or two of the best poetry." No intellectual interest should interfere with "the household gifts and graces. A house is a kingdom in little, and its queen, if she is faithful, gentle, and wise, is a sovereign indeed."

To Anna in Syracuse Louisa wrote long letters, explaining her earnings and expenditures and announcing by their tone her gradual assumption of extraordinary responsibility for the family. She had bought a shawl for her mother and a red bonnet ribbon for Abby. She had shifted to her youngest sister her desires for herself: "She is so graceful and pretty and loves beauty so much, it is hard for her to be poor and wear other people's ugly things. You and I have learned not to mind *much;* but when I think of her I long to dash out and buy the finest that the limited sum of ten dollars can procure." She took her cousin Lizzie Wells's discarded ribbons and decorated her own old straw bonnet for Abby. She planned to buy a new dress for Beth, Bronson's name for Lizzie, who was wearing all her and Anna's hand-me-downs. For her father she was sending more paper so he could "keep on with the beloved diaries though the heavens fall."

Boston was full of money and fine clothes, and Louisa had the passionate style consciousness of the deprived. She wore her hair fashionably, with a center part and protrusions over each ear, the bulk gathered in a chignon in back. She later displayed her love of clothes in her novels in meticulous, lingering wardrobe descriptions. With Abby's curiosity and desires as a rationale, she noted the heavy amber, crystal, and Venetian glass jewelery, the heavy bracelets, the long earrings and bandeaux for the hair. She watched women wearing brilliant daytime colors touched with lace, bodices covered with paisley cashmere shawls, hats decorated with ribbons of velvet and taffeta. She saw black kid boots buttoned with pearls, with scarlet French heels. At the theater women wore silk and shot silk and, after 1855, jet trimming. Winter furs came in mink, ermine, seal, beaver, and astrakhan. Slightly shorter skirts meant more detailed hose — a lace inset for evenings, horizontal stripes for daytime. Shirtwaists and blouses could be shimmeringly fastened with steel or silver buttons set with colored stones. Louisa learned these tantalizing lessons and, knowing that even if she could afford such luxuries she couldn't have them, wrote about them and tried to buy them for her vain alter ego, Abby.

Louisa advised Anna to look after herself, to spend a little on her own wardrobe, "for it makes me mad to know that my good little lass is going around in shabby things, and being looked down upon by people who are not worthy to touch her patched shoes or the hem of her ragged old gowns." The tone is peremptory and loving-admonitory. It resonated with the change that was coming over

Louisa as, more and more, she took charge of family affairs. She had cast her sisters and parents into stiff "Pathetic Family" caricatures, and she herself assumed the part of strong provider who could never relax or rely on anyone else.

In April 1856, Bronson came to Boston and found Louisa cheerful, hoping to see her play produced and waiting for Anna to come from Syracuse. Together they left for Walpole for the *"leisure and rest,"* which their father wrote them, "you cannot get away from home."

The mountain-cool spring and a tired, anxious mother welcomed them. Walpole was a great bog from melting and rains. The roads had no drainage and the town's main square was a treacherous, rutted mire. At home there was spring cleaning. The family made soap out of an ecumenical collection of bones, grease, fragments of suet, and damp wood ashes, boiled in lye. The pungent smell lingered for days while the viscous substance stood in an open barrel.

The dramatic society reconvened, including summer people like Howard Ticknor, the son of James T. Fields's partner, and local regulars. That summer the players had the use of an attic of an inn on Washington Square.

At home, Lizzie was the ailing centerpiece. In late May she contracted scarlet fever from a neighbor whom Abba had been nursing. Bronson and Abba watched her "night and day," painfully worried. On the first of June she was, according to her father, "alarmingly ill." Abba thought she had suffered some "collapse of the brain — at times she seems immovable — almost senseless." Gradually she began to convalesce, but seemed to have lost what little animal vitality she possessed.

Lizzie, so quiet and shadowy, dropped into confused absentia. She wanted nothing, wouldn't go out. She had always been a noncombatant in a warlike family. Temperamentally she was more like Anna than her other sisters, but unlike Anna, was always overlooked. A frightened, passive spirit, Elizabeth found invalidism and began to fail.

Anna, meanwhile, was miserable at being away from Syracuse, which had she grown to love. She wrote her Syracuse friends long, unhappy letters, asking for news and re-creating "the jolly talks over the fire at night, the stormy days when we used to talk pictures

LOUISA MAY ALCOTT
Concord Free Public Library

BOSTON, 1841, FROM DORCHESTER

I. N. Phelps Stokes Collection, Prints Division
The New York Public Library, Astor, Lenox and Tilden Foundations

THE WATER CELEBRATION ON BOSTON COMMON, 1848

I. N. Phelps Stokes Collection, Prints Division
The New York Public Library, Astor, Lenox and Tilden Foundations

AMOS BRONSON ALCOTT
Concord Free Public Library

LOUISA MAY ALCOTT
Concord Free Public Library

THE YOUNG THEODORE PARKER
The Boston Athenaeum

HENRY DAVID THOREAU, 1856
Concord Free Public Library

RALPH WALDO EMERSON
Concord Free Public Library

EMERSON'S HOUSE,
CONCORD, MASSACHUSETTS
Concord Free Public Library

CENTER OF CONCORD, MASSACHUSETTS, ABOUT 1865
Concord Free Public Library

ORCHARD HOUSE, CONCORD
Concord Free Public Library

BRONSON ALCOTT'S SKETCH OF HILLSIDE, 1845

Concord Free Public Library

ABIGAIL MAY ALCOTT

Concord Free Public Library

AMOS BRONSON ALCOTT

Concord Free Public Library

JOHN BROWN

The Boston Athenaeum

NATHANIEL HAWTHORNE, 1841,
OIL BY CHARLES OSGOOD

*Courtesy of the Essex Institute,
Salem, Massachusetts*

THOMAS CARLYLE

By permission of the Houghton Library,
Harvard University

SOPHIA PEABODY HAWTHORNE

The Boston Athenaeum

HENRY JAMES, SR.
The Boston Athenaeum

MARGARET FULLER
The Boston Athenaeum

JONES VERY

The Boston Athenaeum

COLONEL JOSEPH MAY

The Boston Athenaeum

WILLIAM LLOYD GARRISON

The Boston Athenaeum

and plays all day long, feasting on roast potatoes and unnameable puddings, the nice walks, and best of all the beloved theatrics with the fussing and scolding and drilling and rehearsing, all so dear and delightful and it seems as if I *must* go back."

In mid-September 1856, Bronson left on an extended trip to visit his mother in Connecticut and to go on to New York City, where he planned to give conversations and try to make a new arrangement for the family. After more than a year, the Willis-Wells charity was drying up. Benjamin Willis had stopped speaking to Abba and the rest treated her with careful manners. "I am not a worm," Abba wrote to her husband, "therefore shall not turn when trodden on, but my head erect with eye fixed on the future for relief and release." It was the most selfish community she had ever lived in, she wrote to her brother, and she prayed not to give in to her hunger for "revenge and retaliation." The Wellses and Willises had grown tired of their wards and their economy had become *"penuriousness."* Abba had fallen into her it's-all-over-but-my-funeral tone and told Sam that the "remnant of my days which are obviously numbered — will be soothed and comforted by my beloved girls and most exemplary husband — I shall leave Walpole just as soon as I can see a safe harbour for my poor frail bark to moor a little longer." Her cousin Samuel Sewall told her that she could only count on about $200 annually from friends. "Thus I am thrown back on all the vicissitudes and uncertainty that must arise from self-support — and all the embarrassment attendant on my own efforts — ."

In October, Louisa set out again for Boston, leaving behind faces on which she saw "love and hope and faith." They were all depending on her, she thought, to make it better. "I *can't wait* when I *can work,*" she wrote, "so I took my little talent in my hand and forced the world again, braver than before and wiser for my failures."

She moved into a boarding house on Chauncy Place, southeast of the Common, though not as far south as their old Dedham Street house. Her top-floor room looked out on the steeple of the First Church. She was centrally located, so that to get to Parker's and most friends she didn't need to take the new horse-drawn cars that clopped along the dirt streets. She paid the three dollars' rent out of her writing and sewing and saved enough to send her mother a basket of treats, a blanket shawl, and gloves and pretty trimmings for Anna and Beth. She often spent evenings with her sister Abby, who had come to Boston to stay with Auntie Bond and study drawing with Mrs. Richard Hildreth, the wife of the historian.

In October, while in New York, Bronson learned that Harper's would not publish Louisa's *Christmas Elves*. She swallowed this great disappointment as well as her mother's stream of advice, names of papers to write for, and warnings to be "careful about capital letters and punctuation in any manuscripts you send to be printed." Abba offered critical evaluations and suggested improvements: "I think one more incident would have improved it — such as the death of the old man and the filial devotion of the restored daughter — the contrition of the old man and the bequest of all his property to Mother and Child leaving the inference '*this is the holy family at* Christmas' — something of that kind." Louisa's writing had always been a family affair. Something of their excessive involvement and the burden that carried comes across in Abba's remarks on the chance of Louisa's play being produced: "The thought of that performance on the Boston stage is too much for maternal pride to stagger under, — and your sisters are ecstatic with delight — I believe Lizzy lives so much in the success of her sisters that any defeat would most kill her."

The performance of Louisa's *Rival Prima Donnas* remained in arbitration for another season, but deaths of actors postponed things. Hamilton Willis and Louisa's cousin Windship were active diplomats in the negotiations, and Louisa got a free pass to the Boston Theater for her troubles. She wrote: "This was such richness I didn't care if the play was burnt on the spot, and went home full of joy." She noted cynically that her pass made previously distant gentlemen eager for her company. She was managing, she wrote to her father, and proving that "though an *Alcott* I *can* support myself. I like the independent feeling; and though not an easy life, it is a free one, and I enjoy it. I can't do much with my hands; so I will make a battering-ram of my head and make a way through this rough-and-tumble world." The violence of her intent, and the hardly concealed anger linked with her father's name, reflect her worry for the Walpole dependents.

Bronson was worried, too, but his adventures absorbed and

gratified him. In New York he met and enjoyed Walt Whitman, whose *Leaves of Grass* had scandalized Abba and the rest of the country in 1855. Bronson saw him several times, called him "the Satyr, the Bacchus, the very God Pan." He was fascinated by Whitman's disregard for convention and his romantic expressiveness. Bronson detailed his red flannel undershirt, his "man Bloomer in defiance of everybody," his beard, open collar, brawny neck, "striped calico jacket . . . the collar Byronical, with coarse cloth overalls buttoned to it: cowhide boots; a heavy roundabout . . . and a slouched hat for house and street alike." Whitman's gray eyes and deep voice, "tender sometimes, and almost melting," intrigued Bronson, who was pleased to find a good listener: "inquisitive very, overcurious even, inviting criticism on himself, on his poems, pronouncing it *pomes:* in fine an egotist incapable of omitting, or suffering anyone long to omit noting Walt Whitman, in discourse."

He introduced him to Thoreau during his New York visit. Thoreau thought Whitman a "great fellow," and the two men formed a distant, rather romantic attachment. Thoreau discussed him at length with Alcott and wrote to his Vermont friend Harrison Blake that Whitman was a "remarkably strong though coarse nature, of a sweet disposition . . . Though peculiar and rough in his exterior, his skin . . . red, he is essentially a gentleman. I am still somewhat in a quandary about him, — feel that he is essentially strange to me, at any rate . . . He is very broad, but, as I have said, not fine. He said that I misapprehended him . . . He told us that he loved to ride up and down Broadway all day on an omnibus, sitting beside the driver, listening to the roar of the carts, and sometimes gesticulating and declaiming Homer at the top of his voice."

Bronson tried to help out at home. He sent $50, wishing it were more, "twice fifty, three times, four . . ." He discussed the possibility of the family moving to Eagleswood, an experimental community in New Jersey. He buttonholed philanthropists, trying to find a suitable situation. Meanwhile he sent home reports of his meetings with Lucy Stone, Lucretia Mott, and Susan B. Anthony. He sent along a circular from the Blackwells about their hospital for women and children. He mentioned meeting Stephen Pearl Andrews, later notorious for his column on free love in *Woodhull and Claflin's Weekly.* The paper advocated a woman's right to take a new lover every day if she wished, scorning the monotony of monogamy. Andrews insisted on selective breeding, wishing only the best men to impregnate women, thus producing the finest children.

Louisa made a quick visit home to what her mother called the "drowsy Depot" in mid-February and found Lizzie very unwell. Anna was miserable, too, "not quite sure for what she was created, and by no means sure that she ought even to have been born," Abba wrote to her husband. Anna had turned twenty-six on March 16, 1857, and wrote to her father that she was cross and unhappy and discouraged, but that she tried to keep cheerful by gossiping "about town . . . Lizzie is miserably and tho' better today is all out of sorts bodily and thin as a rail, but hoping much better from the warm days and sunshine of which we see very little just now."

Louisa returned to Boston and kept house for her Sewall cousins. Bronson found her there in April, and father and daughter set out househunting in Jamaica Plain, Roxbury, and Cambridgeport. Bronson wrote to his wife that the Sewalls thought "$200 or $250 will give us a comfortable house (including my garden of course) within walking distance of the city attractions." At the end of April, Abby returned to Walpole with letters from Bronson and some of her own work, which surprised the family by its skill.

The first week in May, Bronson and Louisa started for Walpole, stopping in Concord for a night. They spent Sunday evening with the Emersons. They missed Thoreau but saw Sanborn, and the men discussed plans for a philosophical college to be established in Concord.

When they arrived home, they found Elizabeth weighing little more than ninety pounds. She had been unwilling to eat anything substantial for weeks, and barely left her room. The village doctor, Kittredge, thought she would get well, but some of her scarlet fever symptoms were returning and, as Bronson said, the illness had made "very perceptible ravages upon her frame, and we cannot but fear sometimes it's wasting her away." Kittredge advised sea air, so, on August 4, 1857, Abba took Elizabeth to Lynn, Massachusetts, on the North Shore.

They took rooms in a boarding house. Abba encouraged Lizzie to take saltwater baths and took the frail girl out for a drive, but she was quickly exhausted and liked to lie on her bed and listen to Abba read to her. Abba's anxiety was very high, and her journal alternates with detailed accounts of Lizzie's progress, or rather the progress of Lizzie's degeneration, and imprecations against the medical profession. Medicine, she concluded, "is a prolonged guess." She got letters from the family discussing various plans for the fall, but she refrained from entering the fray. "Boston seems singularly absent in interest to me — I have cared to see but little of anybody — How soon the mind becomes intensified on the object of its affections if danger approaches — particularly in the shape of an insidious disease or somewhat dubious ill!" She wrote home that her daughter was comfortable, but "thinner than ever and looks the incarnation of frailty. Her smile is sweet but ghastly — and at times she is dreadfully distressed." Lizzie wrote to her sisters that she was sure they were glad not to have to run to the sound of her bell every five minutes or keep quiet all the time; "I know you miss your little skeleton very much don't you?" she asked pathetically.

Every four or five days Bronson wrote to Abba about theatrical and culinary triumphs, the family's morning walks, and the rich vegetable harvest. At the end of August, Bronson went to collect Abba and Lizzie, whom he found thinner but "for her, communicative." She had contracted a slight but troublesome cough that worried everyone. Despite the doctor's failure to find an organic cause for her sickness, the case was, Bronson saw clearly, *"a critical one."* In addition to her physical ailments, she was becoming emotionally unreachable.

Bronson took his wife and child to the Sewalls' in Boston, where he tried to determine the next step. The Sewalls offered them a plot in Malden to build on, and Bronson told the girls he would consider Boston and its suburbs, "nor do I omit Concord from the possible sites of our future home." It quickly emerged that he wanted very much to live in Concord. He also desired to "take the reins a little more firmly in hand," he wrote to Walpole, "and think you may rely on me for supports of labour and money in the years to come . . . I will press nothing, but only state frankly my views and preferences . . . I can do more for you, and for myself, from the Concord position . . . Let me be the central figure of the Group, and try our family fortunes so, for a little time." Lizzie wanted to go to Concord, and although no one else was very happy with the idea, Bronson prevailed. He pleaded that "if you will trust me for once a little," he could arrange things satisfactorily. "I cannot but think your mother's reluctances will be somewhat overcome and softened by time and the experiment, as well as yours."

Bronson selected a ramshackle farmhouse set about with elm and butternut trees. It came with ten acres, lumber for winter fires, and an orchard of forty apple trees that produced annually a twenty-barrel crop. Thoreau promised to survey the land on which it sat, next door to the Hawthornes' Wayside (originally the Alcotts' Hillside). The house, although old and in dire need of attention, had a sound cellar and a good well and cost only $950. Emerson put up $500 and Alcott had friends to supply the rest, "and so leave your mother's investments untouched."

Abba and Lizzie stayed with Nathaniel Peabody, Elizabeth's father, who was living with Elizabeth at Wayside while his daughter and son-in-law were in England. Bronson went to Walpole to help close up the house and wait for Sam May's check to pay off their debts. He and the three young women met Abba in Concord, where they rented half a house by the train station while they waited until spring for their own house to be habitable.

Abba had put Lizzie under the care of Dr. Christian Geist of Boston, who dosed her with medicines, including opium. The drug-induced rest seemed to do her good, and Bronson thought her improvement sufficient for him to leave. In mid-November he set off on another conversation tour.

Lizzie's illness dominated the household. She grew ethereal-looking. The doctor told Abba that her condition was due to a lack of proper care during her convalescence from scarlet fever. Abba was tortured with guilt for having infected her child in the first place and could barely deal with the additional accusation. She coped by pretending that Lizzie would get well, and she pleaded in her journals for justification. She had done the best she could. "I watched her with jealous care — And I think the cold, and perhaps want of more cheerful society — as well as absence of certain nutritive diet may have caused this sad wrench of her frame — but I hope soon to . . . have the return of cheerful quiet days . . . "

In December, Lizzie, sensing that she was dying and hideously tired of pain, grew angry, fretful, and upset. She refused to let Abba near her, thought Anna "horrid," and asked to be allowed to sew in peace. Louisa would carry her downstairs, but Lizzie grew too restive and anxious for anything but her room. Mr. Emerson and the Alcott's landlord both left their carriages at Abba's disposal, but Elizabeth's withdrawal increased. Abba tried no longer to restore her, just to tempt her: "Nothing now but comforts — bed, armchair, couch, raw beef, milk toast, cocoa, a wood fire day and night." Opium kept her sedated.

Louisa watched her sister's decay with stark horror. Lizzie's long, punishing death was the focus of the house, and Louisa could draw no compensation from the agony of the emaciated, semicatatonic, half-deranged girl. Louisa barely recognized her sister in the skeleton with the hot, enormous eyes that looked vacant or suspicious. In one way Lizzie was more real to her, revealing for the first time in her life her resentments and desires. In life she had been passive, undemanding, and therefore, in family terms, blameless. In dying she was angry, frightened, and complaining. Suddenly Louisa had a different, if not clearer, view of her sister's life. She came to value Lizzie's pacific, almost invisible ways more than she had, and with this came hindsight guilt for not appreciating her more than she had, before it was too late. Louisa resented losing Anna and her mother to Lizzie's endless needs, and was horrified at herself for her own selfishness. She tried to sacrifice cheerfully for her sister, but the months were long and hard for Louy, unrelieved by diversions. "A hard thing to bear, but if she is only to suffer, I pray she may go soon," wrote Louisa.

Anna wrote to Bronson in January that he should come home soon: "It is evident to us that Lizzie is failing, and I fear she cannot remain with us very long. She is glad it is to be so as she is ready and willing to go any time, and I think she is." The doctor had called the case "hopeless," and Abba wrote that "now I feel that my darling will be in safer hands than her Mother's . . ."

Louisa tried to be brave for her sister's sake. She and Anna gave up their theatricals, and Anna took over the household chores so Louisa and Abba could be full-time nurses. Louisa could hardly endure seeing Lizzie try to get through the rest of her time without troubling anyone. She sat with her sister in her room during the day and kept the fire going at night.

When Bronson got home, he wanted to know if Lizzie had considered the thought that she might not get well.

"Yes, nor have I believed otherwise for a long while past. It will be something new in our family, and I can best be spared of the four," she replied.

"I shall see Dr. Geist, and hear what he says of your prospects, Elizabeth."

"Twill be as well one way as the other, with me as with the rest of you."

"Have you some notions of your state after the change?" asked her father, always curious about the hereafter.

"Not so clear as I could wish, but you will have me none the less, and I prefer going as soon as may be."

In the first week in March, Beth complained that her needle was too heavy and put it away. She gave away her possessions. Abba was not especially worried by this obvious decline, having seen her rally so often before. She asked Bronson to take her in his lap, asked the family to gather around, breathed deeply, and asked for the window to be opened. "All here," she said, and she kissed them all, saying, "Oh, heavenly air," before asking to be laid down. She seemed stronger but excited, and she asked for ether and morphine, although both had lost their effect. She drank a good deal of wine, which seemed to ease her. That night Abba gave her ether and she slept, waking up at eleven to ask who was on the couch. Abba told her it was Anna.

"Anna has never slept here before."

"No, dear," her mother said, "because she is deaf and I have been afraid she would not hear you if you spoke."

"Well now mother, I go, I go. How beautiful everything is tonight."

"Yes, because you are free from suffering."

For two hours she held a barely audible monologue with herself until at one o'clock Abba waked Anna, seeing that a change was occurring. Abba gave Beth water and she smiled. At two Abby and Louisa came in. Her mother wrote: "She seemed to sleep — her breathing became intermittent — and at 3 o'clock ceased altogether — her eyes opened spasmodically and all was over."

Louisa recorded a phenomenon that she and her mother witnessed: "A few minutes after the last breath came, as Mother and I sat silently watching the shadow fall on the dear little face, I saw a light mist rise from the body, and float up and vanish in the air.

Mother's eyes followed mine, and when I said 'What did you see?' she described the same light mist." Both women concurred that it was Lizzie's life, her spirit making its exit.

That night the women dressed her in her gown and cap and laid her out. The twenty-three-year-old woman, hairless and shrunken, looked at least forty to them. She had chosen to be buried at Sleepy Hollow, a new cemetery in Concord, not far from the center of town. Mr. Emerson, Henry Thoreau, Franklin Sanborn, and Anna's friend John Pratt carried her to her grave. Louisa struggled to cram the horror inside a meaning: "So the first break comes, and I know what death means, — a liberator for her, a teacher for us." For Abba there was only intermittent release: "I dare not dwell on the fever which I carried to my home, which devoured the freshness of her life . . ."

After the exhaustion of nursing Beth for so long, Louisa sank into a depression. She mourned for her sister, but couldn't shake her feelings of guilt and incomprehension that the girl who had been so good, so much what a girl was supposed to be, had suffered lengthily and died. Louisa, who so dramatized her own sinfulness, could make no sense of her survival. She was quiet and despairing, abandoned by Beth and soon to be deserted for marriage by Anna. Her own treasonous sisters were betraying her and attacking her hard-won identity as the indispensable family prop.

13

"Love and Self-Love"

THE FAMILY TOOK OVER ORCHARD HOUSE in the spring of 1858. It was a two-story clapboard farmhouse with small windows, small rooms, and plank floors. Set back from the road, the house stretched laterally along a gentle hill. " 'Tis a pretty retreat," wrote Bronson, "and *ours;* a family mansion to take pride in, rescued as it is from deformity and disgrace by these touches of grace and plain-keeping which I have contrived to give it, against the journeyman's jibes and joiner's void of taste or carpenter's skill." Bronson's decorating notions, while disastrous for his prose, were just right for Orchard House. He made alcoves for busts from the Temple School, touched up the staircases, built bookshelves and a studio onto the back for Abby's painting. He constructed a curvacious fence, using, according to local kibbitzers, more nails than anyone normally used to build and roof a two-story house. But the fence, rounded and fantastical, was pleasing. Louisa, Abby, and Anna painted and papered. Abby drew brilliant birds and flowers on black panels, surprise moments of vivid color and drama in an otherwise pastel environment.

There is some confusion between the dates in Abba and Bronson's journals, but it seems that on April 7, 1858, three weeks after Lizzie's death, Anna went to her mother and asked her advice about marrying John Pratt, her twenty-four-year-old suitor. John was the son of Minot Pratt, a printer by trade, who had been one of the three directors of Brook Farm in 1844. After Brook Farm began its Fourierist experiments, Minot Pratt brought his family to Concord. Pratt was a quiet man who was interested in botany and transplanted many kinds of plants to Concord. He was a rose lover, and planted rose bushes hit-and-run fashion in odd parts of the township.

John, like his father, was a sweet, friendly, unambitious man. He worked for an insurance firm. John had acted in many theatricals with Anna, including *The Loan of a Lover,* in which he had played a Dutch peasant. Anna had come to corn-husking parties and had shared with him popcorn, brown bread, gingerbread, and pumpkin pie at the Pratt farm on Punkatasset Hill. She had sat with him under their elm, which Thoreau called "stupendous . . . like vast thunderbolts stereotyped upon the sky, heaven-defying, sending back dark, vegetable bolts, as if flowing back in the channel of the lightning."

Abba told her daughter that she was twenty-seven and must decide on her own. For her part, she considered John "a man of most unimpeachable character — Seldom seen a person with fewer faults or more decided principles of honor and goodness — I hope on knowing him more we shall love him still better."

Anna decided in favor of John. He came to speak with Bronson, who wrote: "I think well of him and doubt not of his power of being the good friend and companion of my good daughter. Still the thought is more than I am ready for at this moment." He couldn't let his first child go so soon after Beth's death and told Anna and John to wait a couple of years. Abba confessed in her journal that Anna had been theirs "so exclusively we have forgotten that she is her own for any destiny she pursues."

For Louisa, Anna's engagement was another death: "I moaned in private over my great loss, and said I'd never forgive J. for taking Anna from me; but I shall if he makes her happy, and turn to little May for comfort." This edited journal entry doesn't convey the violent anguish Anna's announcement gave Louy. The family was the only organization she understood and in which she felt secure. She had prepared for Beth's departure; but that Anna should *choose* to go toppled her tower of assumptions. She defined herself as a part of a unit that couldn't survive without her. John was a demonstration that she was replaceable. She had accurately assessed Anna's capacity for perpetual dependency, but hadn't anticipated the chance that her sister might lean on someone else.

Also, as long as the family remained intact, Louisa didn't have to confront her spinsterhood. Anna had represented confirmation that being single was an acceptable alternative. But Anna's decision to marry forced Louisa to acknowledge that she had no man, only daydreams.

For Louisa loving a man was to be rejected and melancholy, to try without success to please. Her experience with her father had taught her that men were inaccessible and impossible to influence. Consequently her attitude toward marriage was childishly oppositional, in direct proportion to her deep fear of men.

Without a husband, however, it was extremely difficult for Louisa to feel justified. Victorian single women had not so much a role as a caricature to play. And while the transcendentalists idealized women, it was their qualities in contrast and in relation to men that preoccupied them. They were not concerned with the woman by herself, as an assortment of human characteristics. She was defined in terms of her pliability, her maternal qualities, her ability to soothe, comfort, support, and respond to men. Her own desires, talents, and concerns were of no weight in measuring her social desirability.

As a woman, Louisa could take only minimal satisfaction from her work. She always underplayed its importance, concentrating on her failings as a female rather than on her achievements as a writer. As a woman first, she could only value herself for what she could give others. But even there, despite her sense of self-sacrifice, she met rejection. Anna relinquished her sister's support for that of a husband. Louisa, at an age when she should have been enlarging the circle of people she trusted, contracted it instead. Anna's betrayal left only Abba and Abby to depend on her, and hence give her the definition she had to have.

Anna had always intended to marry: "When I used to build castles in the air, a wedding scene always found a place among my pictures . . ." As she grew older the determination grew, at least in part in response to the continual and frightening strife at home: "In a household like my father's where poverty and trial and disappointment have been continually trying the tempers and hearts, *very quick tempers, very warm hearts,* there has necessarily been much disquiet, and *great clashing* of *wills,* and though we have always loved and dearly labored for each other, there has been a want of that harmony which is the great charm of family life." Working had always been a bitter and painful experience for Anna, who never found any that satisfied her. Marriage represented many attractions to a woman inclined to be dependent.

In John she found a diffident, mild man to whom she could devote herself and retire from the possibilities of conflict. He was a self-effacing soul who was quite dazzled by the Alcotts, particularly his prospective father-in-law. No Alcott ever mentioned John with more or less than a remark about his good character. He was quiet, undistinguished by any brilliance or originality, but reliable and faithful. The Alcotts quickly annexed him and his dependability, absorbing him into their complex feudal arrangements.

Abba watched her oldest daughter fall into the absorption of her new love. She had, her mother thought, "a large *love* nature and her affections are pure and free from selfishness — this is the key note to the conjugal relations — the conditions are all tolerable when love breathes through the details of life — it becomes to the household *bread for food, wine for weariness,* peace for troubles."

John shyly slipped into the family. He stayed with Abba and Anna when Bronson made a conversational tour in 1858–1859. Anna wrote to her father that she and Abba were loosening him up:"He is growing as chatty as any of us, and reads aloud, tells the news, and really talks without being asked . . . he makes good your place to us better than anyone else could, his gentle womanly ways are so like yours. Your mention of him in your letters gratifies him very much, and always makes him blush with pleasure, for Papa Alcott has always been a mystery to him and he isn't quite sure that he will be a welcome inmate to the old gentleman."

Louisa surrounded herself that summer and fall with boy students from Sanborn's school. She had little use for Sanborn himself, although her parents had encouraged a union between them. In December 1857, Sanborn had distinguished himself in Concord for the first, but not the last, time by making a strong abolitionist speech at the antislavery society meeting. Garrison attended and said, "Sanborn is very tall, but when he made that speech, he towered to the roof."

Sanborn came often to Orchard House; he read German with Anna and organized the Concord Dramatic Union. Anna, John Pratt, his sister Carrie, Louisa, Abby, George Bartlett, son of the town doctor, and some favored pupils from Sanborn's school all participated.

Louisa much preferred the company of young Alfred Whitman,

a somber schoolboy, to that of the officious, outgoing schoolmaster. Sanborn's optimism, his toadying to her father and Emerson, and his gossipy good nature disagreed with her, whereas she resonated sympathetically with Whitman's reserve and melancholy. For his part, Sanborn was put off by Louisa's jerky, no-nonsense manner. She always, he said, had "to contend against certain infirmities of temper, from which her father was free." So the young man and woman eyed each other with puzzlement and suspicion. Meanwhile, Louisa formed a safe and firm attachment to Alf Whitman, her "special boy," who was "proud and cold and shy to other people, sad and serious sometimes, when his good heart and tender conscience showed him his shortcomings, but so grateful for sympathy and a kind word . . ." Alf was living with the Pratt family and spent many evenings at the Alcotts'. He offered Louisa a special combination of ingredients packaged to appeal to her. She could establish a unique, maternal relation with him, duplicating the kind she shared with her mother. She was Alf's only confidante, the only one to bring him out. In his dependency she found satisfaction and security. This was the kind of emotional bond she understood and trusted.

On Monday evenings the Alcotts held open house. Abby, who had begun calling herself May to distinguish herself from her mother, would play their old and infirm piano while friends sang. Bronson enjoyed holding forth to Sanborn and whoever else would listen. He was known as "The Sage of Apple Slump," Louisa's rendition of Orchard House. An anonymous verse circulated about his feeding habits:

> Give him carrots, potatoes, squash turnips and peas,
> And a handful of crackers without any cheese,
> And a cup of cold water to wash down all these,
> And he'd prate of the spirit as long as you please . . .

Occasionally there was dancing, a polka, waltz, the lancers, or a schottische. Groups sat around the large parlor table playing long-whist, euchre, or old maid. Abba served her homemade root beer, gingerbread, and deep-dish pies. Louisa, if she was in sufficiently good spirits and if she was begged prettily enough, would tell chilling ghost stories performed with dramatic gimmicks, screams, dousing of lights, and eerie rappings. She also had a "Lecture of

Strong Minded Women," a parody of women's rights speakers, and a bogus philosopher's talk featuring a "Mr. Emerboy."

One of the family's favorite and most indulged pastimes was the discussion of personalities, or gossip, for which the town offered rich material. In 1858 Waldo's eighty-four-year-old Aunt Mary Moody Emerson arrived in Concord and often visited the Alcotts. She found Bronson's metaphysical peregrinations intriguing and he thought her "sprightly, entertaining, and a lady of much wit and genius." Emerson had more experience of her and consequently more wariness: "If Aunt Mary finds out anything is dear and sacred to you, she instantly flings broken crockery at that."

Mary held on to her grudges like capital investments. Once, after saluting a person who had, years before, offended her, she went to him and said, "I did not know who you were, or should never have bowed to you." Elizabeth Peabody displeased her sometime in the 1830s, and for the next three decades Mary referred to her disdainfully and in the lower case as "Miss pea."

One Concord woman, a friend of Emerson's, remarked to him that Mary "thinks much more of her bonnet and of other people's bonnets than they do." Indeed, bonnets tormented Mary's days as she endlessly shopped for the elusive nonconformist bonnet. In between shopping expeditions she offered critiques of vulgar conforming bonnets.

Mrs. Thoreau, Henry's mother, provoked a bonnet crisis one day when she called on Mary. The latter kept her eyes screwed shut for ten minutes, when she finally said, "Mrs. Thoreau you may have noticed that while we were speaking of your admirable son I kept my eyes shut."

Mrs. Thoreau acknowledged that she hadn't overlooked this circumstance.

"It was because I did not wish to look upon those ribbons of yours, so unsuitable at your time of life and to a person of your serious character."

In the fall of 1858, a veteran Bronson-baiter in the form of Henry James, Sr., came to Concord. James was elegant, urbane, and scholarly, and although his philosophy was not more systematic or comprehensible than Bronson's, still he adopted the appearance of precision and logic, and couldn't excuse in Alcott the vagaries and self-indulgent half-meanings he also committed.

They had faced off numerous times, when Alcott would say things like, "Life is the dispersion of the identities and the concentration of the diversities." James became furious when Bronson talked of his divine paternity. James said, "My dear sir, you have not found your *maternity* yet you are an egg half hatched, the shells are yet sticking about your head." Bronson gathered himself together and replied, "Mr. James you are *damaged goods* and will come up *damaged goods in eternity.*" James had little use for Concord's eccentrics; he considered Thoreau guilty of "mountainous inward self-esteem" and saw Hawthorne as having the look "of a rogue who suddenly finds himself in a company of detectives."

He attended one of Alcott's conversations at Emerson's with the cunning of a Jesuit at an encounter group, and proceeded to disrupt things. He upset Bronson by interrupting him with witticisms until Alcott fell into a petulant silence. Thoreau tried to head James off, but he continued talking paradoxes until he made Emerson furious by denouncing moral law. Emerson got inflamed and personally attacked James, at which point Mary drew herself up to her four feet three inches, placed herself directly in front of James, and said, "Let me confront the monster." She clasped her hands, raising them to her left temple, touched her black hairband, and proceeded to set James straight and rescue her glowering transcendentalists from their humiliating rout. Bronson reported that her "gifts of speech and mode of handling poor James, win the admiration of the party and the thanks of everyone present."

Mary preferred the company of men, and persisted in the convictions, which she had shared with Waldo twenty-five years before, that "sexual influence . . . has done the most injury to men and women since the allegory of Adam" and that "the waste of hours in female society" took from man his highest honors. She told Thoreau that "men are more likely to have opinions of their own" and that women were "frivolous almost without exception."

Unlike Mary, Bronson pitied Thoreau for being womanless, "aloof . . . alone without his Eve building from inside to animate and humanize the wilderness of his Paradise which without woman is solitary and desolate. — For Nature, unless wooed and won through the womanly love, is ever the fanged Dragon to snap up the mortal man or woman drawn toward her by the brute affections, these never solving life's riddles." Bronson sent this arch dirge to Abba as a comment on the loneliness of both Henry and Ellery Channing, whom he had met in New Bedford in 1857. Channing had left his wife and four children and was living, no one knew where, "saner and sounder than heretofore," Bronson thought, but sad and lonely.

When he lived in Concord, Channing and Thoreau had a close, if uneasy, friendship. Ellery is the poet mentioned in Walden, and he and Thoreau were inseparable for a time. The two took long walks, Thoreau making notes in his precise way. Ellery imitated the habit, but lacking a genuine desire to observe anything, he got fed up and threw away his notebook. He announced with peevish bravado, "I am universal; I have nothing to do with the particular and definite." Channing called his walks along the Concord river-banks "riparial excursions." Henry, all-too-easily influenced, got edgy with such terminology. He felt that Channing's reckless diction tempted him to "more harsh, extravagant and cynical expressions concerning mankind and individuals than I intended . . . I think it is because I have not his sympathy in my sober and constant view. He asks for a paradox, an eccentric statement; and too often I give it to him . . ."

Emerson had thought for a while that the extremely clever, witty poet might be a genius, a mistake he felt he had made about Thoreau already. Channing's verse, rife with classical allusions and self-consciousness, leaning for its effect on adverbs, left its originality covered by mannerisms. Thoreau, in a wicked revel, called the poems "sublimo-slipshod," and Edgar Allan Poe refused to call them "precisely English, nor will we insult a great nation by calling them Kickappo; perhaps they are Channingese."

Ellery was a confused, unhappy man who had wildly unstable feelings about everything, especially women. He thought Waldo's daughter Ellen a talented young woman, and yet told Sanborn that it was precisely her talent that was "so unattractive in a woman, that I often think it a bad possession for its owner. Unmarried women are so odious. . . ."

Unlike Henry, Ellery had tried to reconcile his ideal view of women with the reality of a wife. The marriage was painful and ended when Ellen Fuller Channing moved to Worcester with her four children to stay with her cousin Thomas Wentworth Higginson. Ellery dressed up in his party clothes and went to a tea, where he danced and escorted a woman home. Abba wrote to Bronson that he must be crazy "to conduct so — wanting peace himself, he forced his fierce dissatisfaction on his tender, weaker wife . . . He holds himself aloof in savage isolation . . . I pity pity him — capable of so much beauty — yet gravitating to so much that is low and ugly." After the breakup of his marriage, Ellery could share Thoreau's unrelenting misogyny with no distraction.

Louisa didn't trust or admire Channing, agreed with her father that he was a "mood once claiming to be a man," but was fascinated by his friendship with Henry Thoreau. She envied their tramps, canoe trips, and travels, their easy companionship and liberty.

Occasionally Thoreau came over for dinner and talk. Bronson had a very high opinion of him, and he recognized the same man Louisa idolized: "His senses seem double and give him access to secrets not read easily by other men, his observation is wonderful, his sagacity like the bee and beaver, the dog and the deer, the most gifted in this way of any man I have known . . . I am proud of him. I should say he inspires love, if indeed the sentiment he awakens did not seem to partake of something yet purer, if that were possible, and as yet nameless from its rarity and excellence. Certainly he is better poised and more nearly self-sufficient than other men."

This was the Thoreau of Louisa's heart, not the Henry who left Walden Pond every day to see his carping mother; not the frightened man whose mother, out of jealousy, banned Channing from her house; not the rude lump Emerson accused of stealing his thoughts. Louisa saw the magnificent idealist, whose silences she thought magical. Oliver Wendell Holmes might complain that Henry had bad manners, but to Louisa his disregard of conventions was an Indian love call.

Louisa understood and shared his antisocial demeanor. She felt a sturdy bond with Henry and he occupied the foremost spot in her fantasy life, as her fiction would show. His coldness excited her desire to please, and his bluntness she interpreted as honesty, not hostility or fear. His inability to approach made sense to her. She knew the pain of dependency and shared his horror of intimacy. She admired the uncompromising public Thoreau, the active engineer on the Underground Railroad. She listened with interest when he told her father about the visit of a Connecticut abolitionist named John Brown, who had lunched at his mother's boarding house in March 1857. Everything Henry said and did was important to her. She had a passion for the broad-shouldered man with the sad eyes.

Although Emerson later said that Thoreau hated Alcott, that reflected more of his own disillusionment with his friend than Henry's. On the contrary, Henry often supported Louisa's sweetest view of her father, thereby giving her further reason to worship Henry. He thought Bronson "the man of the most faith alive. His words and attitudes always suppose a better state of things than other men are acquainted with, and he will be the last man to be disappointed as the ages revolve." Henry's admiration for Alcott confirmed Louisa's belief that her negative feelings about Bronson reflected her own inadaquacy, not his.

Thirty-nine-year-old Henry had usurped Emerson's place in Louisa's fantasy life. She still revered the philosopher, but his relation to her father made her wince slightly: "Father had four talks at Emerson's; made thirty dollars; Emerson probably put in twenty . . . A true friend this tender, illustrious man." But also an almsgiver. Louisa could sense, if she did not know, that Emerson was tired of her father. "Could he formulate his dogma?" asked Emerson wearily. "A horse doctor could give a prescription to cure a horse's heel. Had he no recipe for a bad memory or a sick angel?" Just as his son was beginning to do his Latin without him, Emerson noted that he was "coming to do without Plato, or Goethe or Alcott."

In the fall of 1858, Bronson left for the West and Louisa went to Boston "on my usual hunt for employment, as I am not needed at home and seem to be the only breadwinner just now." She had a very hard time finding work; one thing fell through and then another, until it looked as if there were nothing. Louisa was stricken all at once with her helplessness and real isolation. Suddenly Beth's death seemed "beautiful; so I cannot fear it, but find it friendly and wonderful." She took a walk along the Mill Dam, which created the Back Bay, and considered leaping over it into the noisome water. The dam, built in 1821, was fifty feet wide and a mile and a half long, extending through water that has since been drained to form the Back Bay residential area. As Louisa walked southwest across the bay, the sluggish receiving basin was on her left and the Great Bay of the Charles River was on her right. The air was stagnant, and the sluices emptying water into the receiving basin kept it from drying up entirely and sending clouds of dust into Louisa's face. Somewhere the depressed woman found the strength not to kill herself, "for it seemed so cowardly to run away before the battle was over . . ." She went back to the Sewalls' house up on Beacon Hill, away from the tempting Back Bay.

The following Sunday she heard Theodore Parker's sermon, "Laborious Young Women." He preached: "Trust your fellow beings, and let them help you. Don't be too proud to ask, and accept the humblest work you can find." Louisa discussed her problems with Mrs. Parker, and within a few days she was offered the position she had originally applied for, governess to the invalid Alice Lovering. She was to receive $250 a year for light work and had a carriage available for Alice's outings. Her spirits lifted considerably, and when May arrived in Boston to study art, Louisa had a companion and an object for her persistent charities.

Louisa committed her self and wages to keeping Orchard House: "The old people need an abiding place. . . ." Staggering under these overwhelming responsibilities gave Louisa a renewed sense of self-justification, a reason to persist in her joyless life.

In her leisure hours Louisa wrote a story for the *Saturday Evening Gazette* and another called "Love and Self-Love," which she had her father take to the *Atlantic* offices. The story concerns Effie, a poor, friendless sixteen-year-old whose female protector dies, leaving her in the care of a stern, cold, older man. Basil Ventnor marries his young ward, but confesses that he should have "been a father to the child, watchful, wise and tender," but was "too young to feel a father's calm affection to know a father's patient care." Instead of giving the girl friendship and guidance, he was "a master, content to give little, while receiving all she could bestow." Ventnor admits to the girl his inability to love her properly. She tells him she will no longer trouble him for adult affection and involvement. She will try to be "your merry girl again," and begins to call him "father" to release him from any grown-up responsibility toward her.

But Effie cannot entirely suppress her womanly needs, and after trying unsuccessfully to live with Ventnor without wanting anything from him, she tries to kill herself. Basil suddenly awakens to

his own love for young Effie: "But through the darkness of my
anguish and remorse that newly kindled love burned like a blessed
fire, and while it tortured, purified. By instinct I saw the error of
my life: self love was written on the actions of the past, and I knew
that my punishment was very just."

Ventnor, awake to his narcissism, suddenly sends Effie away as
his first act of genuine, if misguided, love. She leaves, misunderstanding his reasons, and thinks he is rejecting her. In time, Effie
hears that he has lost his money. Meanwhile, she has come into her
grandfather's fortune, and she returns to her husband, armed with
dollars. Ventnor and Effie confess their mutual love and Effie
throws in her fortune. "Take it, Basil," she says, "and give me a
little love."

Louisa's dream, heavily influenced by Bettina von Arnim, almost
overwhelms the reader with its pathos. It is a more sophisticated
version of the theme of *Flower Fables,* in which a poor, lonesome
girl must thaw out a stern, cold man. The girl must overcome her
inherent, God-given worthlessness by gigantic sacrifice and labor.
She must offer everything and want nothing back. For her efforts
she will receive some affection and attention from her father-hus-
band.

In order to wrench Basil's attention away from himself, Effie
must try to commit suicide. A woman's weapons are negative ones,
passive acts of endurance or self-destruction. Effie forces Basil
Ventnor to face his selfishness by her superhuman generosity. In
Louisa's fiction the sacrifice pays off, whereas in real life *no* effort
of Louisa's ever dented her father's unshakable narcissism.
Louisa's acts of self-abnegation only sharpened her own resentments. Bronson accepted them casually as willing and understandable demonstrations of her helpfulness. Louisa was like an uncomprehending Calvinist trying to win her salvation by good works,
when only faith would do the trick. Bronson did not share Louisa's
interpretation of her life as a sacrifice; this left him insensitive to
his effect on her and left her doomed to persist in seeking an
impossible resolution from him.

Louisa went home at Christmastime to find her mother sick.
John and Anna formed a unit and she felt left out, although she
was, according to Anna, "the greatest blessing and comfort." Anna
wrote to her father that Louisa had taken John "to her heart most

cordially," but Louisa still felt buffeted by her moods and isolated in a new, adult way. She found in her work "salvation when disappointment or weariness burden and darken my soul . . .

"A great grief has taught me more than any minister, and when feeling most alone I find refuge in the Almighty Friend . . . After my fit of despair I seem to be braver and more cheerful, and grub away with a good heart. Hope it will last for I need all the courage and comfort I can get." In January, when Abba was better, Louisa left for Boston and dreamed of writing a great book, for which she began to feel ready.

On Louisa's return to Boston, Parker was no longer preaching. He felt sick on New Year's Day, but delivered his sermon. The following Sunday he sent his congregation a message saying that at 4:00 A.M. he had had "a slight attack of bleeding from the lungs or throat. I intended to preach on the religion of Jesus and Christianity of the Church, or the superiority of Good Will to Man over Theological Fancies. I hope you will not forget the contribution for the poor, whom we have with us always. I don't know when I shall again look upon your welcome faces, which have so often cheered my spirit when my flesh was weak." Parker never saw his parishioners again. He went to Cuba with Julia Ward and Samuel Gridley Howe. When the tropics failed him, he traveled on to Europe. In Rome, the following spring, he wrote to his friend Ripley, "O George it is idle to run from Death. I shrank down behind the sugar canes of Santa Cruz, Death was there too; then I sneaked into a Swiss Valley, there he was; and here he is at Rome. I shall come home and meet him on my own dunghill." He died on May 10 in Florence. Louisa attended a memorial service for him at the Music Hall "which was very beautiful, and proved how much he was beloved . . . I was very glad to have known so good a man, and been called 'friend' by him."

In the spring Louisa completed her term of service with the Loverings and returned to Concord in time to hear Sanborn's friend Captain John Brown speak on May 8, 1859, at Town Hall. He described the desperate, embattled conditions in Kansas and what he had been doing there. Emerson and Thoreau were in the audience and afterward Bronson stopped to talk to the gaunt abolitionist. With Sanborn's covert help, Brown managed to raise $2000 there and in Boston for what would be his astonishing venture at Harper's Ferry.

His stern being and the fervor of his belief roused Louisa's blood. In September she was excited when a number of Massachusetts regiments made camp near Concord and trained close to town: "Town full of soldiers with military fuss and feathers. I like a camp and long for a war, to see how it all seems. I can't fight but I can nurse."

Louisa's desire for war was instinctive as much as political. Her violent tensions and moods found no full release in self-expression, anger, physical activity, or sexuality. Only exhausting housework or nonstop weeks of writing could wear her out or calm her down. War seemed to offer a righteous release. She craved the simplicity of physical heroism, and often wrote about brave, cheerful war deaths. The risk of bodily danger had none of the terror for her that emotional hurt could bring. The punishingly unstable ride of her moods made her physically reckless in search of relief and oblivion. Bloodshed, violence, depletion, all seemed to promise the tranquility she rarely experienced.

The news of the Sunday, October 16, raid on Harper's Ferry made the month "memorable" for her: "Glad I have lived to see the Antislavery movement and this last heroic act in it. Wish I could do my part in it." She felt no doubts about the need for bloodshed. The futility of Brown's raid and the slaughter it entailed gave her no qualms. Her morality was without compromise or ambiguity, which afforded her all the strengths of the righteous and the limited vision that that implies.

Brown was tried and sentenced to hang on December 2, 1859. Sanborn, one of the original conspirators, suggested to Alcott that he go to the Virginia jail where Brown was imprisoned to see if he wanted a company to rescue him. Bronson didn't go, but hoped that Thomas Higginson would take troops to free the man. Meanwhile, Abba's childhood friend Lydia Maria Child had applied to Virginia's governor to visit Brown and treat his wounds. Elizabeth Peabody begged the governor in person, and in vain, to spare one of the raiders. Everyone the Alcotts knew rallied for the captives.

The rhetoric was rising to wartime levels. Abba, whose style tended to be millennial in the most peaceful times, grew quite biblical. Brown's raid, she wrote, had shaken the confederacy "to its foundation. The south have been made to believe that there are brave men in the North. The hour and the man both came at last to reveal to the South their sin and to the slaves their saviours.

He came to them with a sword but he has slain thousands by his word . . ."

After Brown's hanging, Concord held memorial services at Town Hall on Friday, December 2, 1859. The bells were not rung. There was music, a prayer, and hymns. Alcott and Emerson read aloud. Thoreau gave an oration that wandered a little into his private battlefields, but that stirred Louisa nevertheless. "So universal," Henry began, "and widely related in any transcendent moral greatness — so nearly identical with greatness everywhere and in every age, as a pyramid contracts the nearer you approach its apex — that when I now look over my commonplace book of poetry, I find that the best of it is oftenest applicable, in part or wholly, to the case of Captain Brown." Brown, he said, "did not go to the college called Harvard, good old Alma Mater as she is. He was not fed on pap that there is furnished. As he phrased it 'I know no more of grammar than one of your calves.' . . . he permitted no popularity; no man of loose morals was suffered to remain there, unless indeed, as a prisoner of war. 'I would rather,' said he, 'have the small-pox, yellow fever, and cholera, all together in my camp, than a man without principle . . .' "

Louisa joined Thoreau in funeral eloquence, contributing a poem that the *Liberator* published on January 20, 1860:

In the long silence of the night,
Nature's benignant power
Woke aspirations for the light
Within the folded flower . . .

Then blossomed forth a grander flower
In the wilderness of wrong,
Untouched by Slavery's bitter frost,
A soul devout and strong . . .

No monument of quarried stone,
No eloquence of speech,
Can grave the lessons on the land
His martyrdom will teach . . .

Thoreau held Louisa and the family spellbound with his story of X, one of Brown's raiders, who reached Henry the day after the services. He was deranged, talked unceasingly, thought Thoreau was Emerson — "But then Emerson wouldn't lie" — and discussed his lunacy. Francis Jackson Merriam made it to freedom in Canada with Henry's assistance.

In the fall of 1859 the *Atlantic Monthly* accepted Louisa's "Love and Self-Love." James Russell Lowell, then editor, thought Louisa's story so unusual and unlikely that he asked if it were a translation from the German. Lowell tried to be progressive in his thinking about women, and published a piece in favor of women's education by Thomas Higginson in 1859 ("Ought Women to Learn the Alphabet?"), but he was not sure how equal the sexes were, and wrote to Higginson that he wanted a "perhaps" "where you speak of the natural equality of the sexes . . . because I think it not yet demonstrated."

Louisa was grudgingly pleased with her achievement: "People seem to think it a great thing to get into the *Atlantic;* but I've not been pegging away all these years in vain, and may yet have books and publishers and a fortune of my own." The *Atlantic* was two years old, and "purely literary as it is, it has a subscription list, daily increasing, of 32,000," wrote the promoter and editor James T. Fields. "The *Atlantic Monthly* is a striking feature just now in American life," he continued with smug accuracy. The magazine represented much of the best New England writing, and Louisa was in excellent, if parochial company.

Louisa's parents celebrated her accomplishment. Bronson judged her stories "lively, wholesome, and American." Abba thought her "creative as well as her descriptive faculties are quite remarkable. She gives you the natural common traits without any of the vulgar shades which it is so difficult to avoid . . . Perhaps," added Abba, never wholly satisfied, "her shades are a little too dark, tragic, her light a beam too rosy." Louisa got her $50 and on her twenty-seventh birthday, November 29, 1859, she wrote: "Success has gone to my head and I wander a little." She was, for a change, "very happy."

The $50 didn't make the family rich. Caroline Dall, a Boston reformer, was looking for a matron for the Boston women's jail. Penal reform had been popular for three decades, and Abba felt strongly that "women need protection from the vulgar men often attached to these 'lock ups' . . ." Elizabeth Peabody wrote to Mrs. Dall, recommending her friend for the job:

"I believe that she is the woman to do the most difficult duties best. I never saw such humane sentiments united with so practicable a mind — and such singular extent of information in regard to the 'perishing classes.' " It seems a dubious position for which to recommend a sixty-year-old woman, but it stemmed from Miss Peabody's earnest admiration. Abba found herself too plagued by rheumatism to make the effort and wrote to Mrs. Dall that she had "no courage left to attempt anything away from my home—while any decent comfort can be maintained here."

Abba noted that she was slowing down slightly, but her troubles had lessened slightly, too: "The absence of money and the merchantable faculty of earning it, honestly seems to be the cause of most of our discomfort," she wrote, just as she might have written twenty-five years before.

Things were considerably better, however, and Louisa was selling stories to ensure Abba's comfort. On February 17, 1860, Bronson arrived from Boston with a copy of the March *Atlantic,* which contained "Love and Self-Love." She had completed another, called "A Modern Cinderella," a story of courtship based on Anna and John. And, after years of delay, Louisa's farce "Nat Bachelor's Pleasure Trip" was produced on May 4, 1860, at the Howard Atheneum. Louisa shared a box with Anna, and their cousin Dr. Windship sent the author flowers. The piece was performed only once, as a companion to a longer farce called "The Romance of a Poor Young Man." Louisa's name appeared on the playbill as "Adcott," which indicates the slightly watered satisfaction she got from the hastily thrown together production.

That was one of Louisa's last outings with her sister as a single woman. Anna had picked her parents' thirtieth wedding anniversary, May 23, 1860, for her marriage to John Pratt. The Emersons, Thoreau, Sanborn, and the families arrived a little before 11:00 A.M. on a brilliant, warm day. Anna had planned to wear white but decided on a silver-gray riding dress at the very last minute, "knowing myself to be neither young nor pretty." Louisa ornamented her sister's hair and dress with lilies of the valley. The couple spent a few moments together before the wedding, and John asked, "Annie, are you happy?" She was too happy to answer: "He told me how hopeful he felt, how tranquil and full of love, and we went down among our friends at peace with one another and all the world feeling that no ceremony would make us more married than we already were."

Louisa had made the house fragrant with flowers and wreaths. Uncle Sam May performed an unadorned service and Abba sobbed loudly. There was kissing and dancing under the elms on the front lawn, cake and wine and a large wedding dinner supplied by a neighbor. Finally a carriage arrived, and Anna and John left her red-eyed family and well-wishing friends: "Very quietly we came to our little married home, we two alone, and peacefully we sat through the summer evening with the moon looking down upon us, not more serene than were our hearts . . ."

Louisa's heart was not serene as she saw her sister off. She called her bridesmaid's dress sackcloth "and ashes of roses; for I mourn the loss of my Nan, and am not comforted . . . Mr. Emerson kissed her; and I thought that honor would make even matrimony endurable . . ."

The separation between Anna and the family was too painful to be completed. Anna's allegiances remained at home, as she said in her wedding note to her mother, assuring her "that I shall ever consider myself your Annie as long as I keep myself good enough to deserve the name of daughter to so excellent a mother . . ." Anna aptly described the family feeling as "anxious affection," and her father found himself so moved that for the first time in his journals he noted: "I cannot yet write about it."

Abba visited the couple in Chelsea, Massachusetts, the next week, establishing a persistent pattern. Bronson, on her return, was ready to ruminate on his favorite child: "I am sure she is one of the best women I have known, with all the wealth of heart her mother gave her: the simplicity and sincerity of a saint . . . I have not lived in vain, nor her mother to be thus blessed: without any defect of mine, she has every social excellence I may covet, and is a treasure for the heart."

Abba lived for Anna's letters, and her visits home focused the lives of both mother and daughter. "I think," wrote Anna, "the family will always be the same to me as it was when I worked for them as if they were the only thing in the world." She was ashamed of being comfortable when they were in want. She knew her duty was to her husband, but she felt wicked not going home and working.

Anna's journal is full of stories about leaving John with a somber face and rushing home, where she had a welcome "as only Alcotts know how to give, Mother seemed perfectly wild with joy and flew round . . . while Lu could hardly express her happiness and kept grabbing me to make sure I was there. Certainly there is nothing so nice as going home."

She was a very reclusive bride, and although she knew it troubled John, she wouldn't join in parties or social evenings. She found people uninteresting, and blamed them rather than examining her own retreat. She was at a loss without John or her family. If forced to attend a party, she would sit in a corner and watch, "though I find it hard to understand how people can enjoy anything so silly and noisy." One Sunday, when John wished to hear Wendell Phillips speak in Boston, Anna wouldn't consider going. John continually changed his mind about whether or not to go, balancing Anna's loneliness against her urging him to go. At last he left, and Anna wrote: "I felt lonely enough and would have given a good deal to have had him back again, but I knew it was best he should go . . ."

Anna's relation with John had to accommodate her position in the family. It was as family members that the women found their identities, and no external tie ever challenged that structure. For the most part, neither Anna nor Louisa attempted to include anyone in their lives. Once Anna had admitted John, she closed off others forever. Louisa only made tentative friendships and stored up fantasies.

The only suitors Louisa allowed to find her were utterly unacceptable. Her manner held no encouragement, and she was so convinced of the special mission allotted to the Alcotts that she couldn't countenance a man as ordinary, say, as John Pratt. When she did meet men, her father unthinkingly polished them off with a transcendental remark or two. One day in Concord Louisa admired the work of a young blond artist. They discussed drawing techniques, and he pleased her by admitting to painting by instinct. She introduced him to Bronson, who also painted without formal training. "Young man," said Bronson, observing his blond hair, "you are a child of light, a child of God." Oblivious to everyone's discomfort and incomprehension, Bronson pointed to some colorful flowers and proceeded, "These are God-like; they represent all that is good, but the night-shade, belladonna and others of like nature are of darkness, of evil."

In June, the return of the Hawthorne family to Concord made Louisa's social life gayer. Sixteen-year-old Julian Hawthorne liked both Alcott sisters and was young enough to be a perfect companion for Louy. She was twenty-eight when he first met her, and he saw a dark-haired, dark-eyed young woman, with red cheeks, a strong jaw, and hearty laughter. He found her a woman of good will, common sense, and a well-developed sense of humor.

Julian paired off romantically with May, just four years older than he. He took her to see the water lilies open at dawn. He organized coeducational swimming parties. All the women came enflanneled from head to foot. All but Louisa coiled their hair into caps. She went barefoot and let her long chestnut hair float free. She also managed to capsize a punt while climbing in and split her pantaloons from hip to knee. Easily scandalized Ellen Emerson took her to the changing tent and mended while Louisa laughed.

The Hawthornes added a square tower to their Wayside, and planted a path to facilitate traffic between their house and Orchard House next door. Julian came over and flirted with May, who squelched him by promising to marry the first man who would take her to Europe to study art.

One day Julian found May with a darkly mustached young man who had his arm about May's waist. May explained hastily that it was her cousin from England. The young man drawled offensively, "Well, well! So this is our young friend Julian; quite a well-grown boy. I was expecting something a little less mature. But I'm pleased to see you, my child, and when you've had an opportunity to change your attire, I shall be happy to improve our acquaintance." May, who could no longer carry on, rushed inside, leaving Julian to recognize Louisa behind the mustache.

The senior Hawthornes and Alcotts got on somewhat less well than their children. Abba rushed over to Wayside to sit with Nathaniel and Sophia while their daughter Una lay sick that June. Abba thought Sophia sweet, but cold and immobile: "Her heart early had a paralytic shock and with her classic head within and without she is one — ."

Nathaniel was elusive. He visited the Alcotts no more than twice and left quickly. Bronson would have liked a friendly neighbor and wrote wistfully: "Nobody gets a chance to speak with him unless by accident." Hawthorne spent most of his time in his new tower, writing and smoking his cigars. "Still he has a tender kindly side, and a voice that a woman might own, the hesitance is so taking, and the tones so remote from what you expected."

Channing and Thoreau once took Hawthorne to a densely grown and overhung pool. Channing recalled, "It was a choice walk to which Thoreau and I did not invite everybody." Hawthorne was silent for a moment, then looked around him and said, "Let us get out of this dreadful hole!"

Oliver Wendell Holmes tried to draw Hawthorne out, and invited him to his club. Hawthorne replied that he would like to but he couldn't drink. Holmes said it was no problem, neither could he. Hawthorne tried another tack, saying he couldn't eat. Holmes insisted that they would like to see him. "But I can't talk either," said Hawthorne desperately.

Herman Melville later explained that the morbidity in his friend "derives its force from its appeals to that Calvinistic sense of Innate Depravity and Original Sin, from whose visitations, in some shape or another, no deeply thinking mind is always and wholly free . . ." This set Hawthorne apart from his Concord neighbors, who, although they rather liked the man, had little use for his views. Emerson thought Hawthorne's reputation as a novelist "is a very pleasing fact, because his writing is not good for anything, and this is a tribute to the man." "Mere mush," he called Hawthorne's most recent novel, *The Marble Faun.*

Hawthorne's feelings about women were similar to Ellery Channing's and Thoreau's. Sophia was devoted to her husband and family and nothing else. She had terrible nerves and an expressionless demeanor. Channing, who thought her "one of the best of women," said that her struggle with illness had given her that unnatural self-restraint and accounted for her "mechanical" seeming manners. She spent her strength trying to control herself into a Victorian vision of female sanctity and quiescence. She agreed entirely with her husband, who wrote his publisher, James T. Fields, that *"all* women as authors are feeble and tiresome. I wish they were forbidden to write on pain of having their faces deeply scarified with an oyster shell."

The Hawthornes had other opinions equally unpopular in Concord. Nathaniel Hawthorne's closest friend for years was Franklin

Pierce, a President of whom all abolitionists disapproved. While the Hawthornes were in England, Elizabeth Peabody pelted her sister and brother-in-law with her abolitionist tracts. Hawthorne returned one tract that Elizabeth had written. Elizabeth doggedly sent it on again. Hawthorne wrote that he didn't think it "worthy of being sent three times across the ocean; not so good as I supposed you would always write on a subject in which your mind and heart were interested." Reluctantly, he passed the pamphlet on to Sophia. She wrote, aghast at the potential injury to Una: "And you would display before her great innocent eyes a naked slave girl on a block at auction (which I am sure is an exaggeration for I have read of those auctions often and even the worst facts are never so bad as absolute nudity) . . ." She found a naked body more horrifying than slavery and retreated behind her husband for protection from her sister. He wrote, advising Elizabeth to stop writing to Sophia: "I entirely differ from you in the idea that such correspondence is essential to her peace of mind; but not that she loves you deeply and sincerely . . . But it is a solemn truth, that I never in my life knew her to receive a letter from you without turning pale . . ."

Abba was too much like Elizabeth for Sophia to feel comfortable with her. But she liked Bronson, and their friendship survived his impractical delinquencies. One day Sophia and an Italian designer climbed her hill to plan a wooden shrine. Bronson, still triumphant from the summer house he had built for Emerson, came along to advise. He picked up a long board and set it on top of some loosely planted columns. He had shaken the columns into the attitude he desired when, as Sophia wrote, "the board obeyed at once the eternal laws, and came thundering down upon the head of . . . Sophia Hawthorne . . . I held my cranium together and descending the hill, hearing Mr. Alcott gently say, 'I fear you are very much hurt, Mrs. Hawthorne.' I thought I was. But as usual in great straits, I was very quiet and kept as far out of my body as possible, till I had plunged my broken crown into a basin of arnica and water."

* * *

The coming war was never far from Concord. Sanborn had been subpoenaed to testify in Washington about John Brown. He refused to go, and on the night of April 3, 1860, four slavecatchers tried to handcuff him and drag him off without a warrant. Sanborn, in his bare feet, yelled, "Murder," and fought the thugs, who were trying to force him into a carriage. Sanborn's sister flew out of the house and tried to startle the horses into flight. Sanborn braced himself against the vehicle with his feet and stubbornly held on while a crowd of thirty or forty gathered. Emerson accosted the chief assailant and demanded, "Who are you, Sir? By what right do you hold this man?" After much confusion, a hasty writ of habeus corpus freed Sanborn. Townsfolk chased the failed abductors away, and the Sanborns went back to bed after borrowing a gun. "Great ferment in town," commented Louisa. She was subsequently appointed to a vigilance committee to protect Sanborn. Later that spring she heard Harriet Tubman, the escaped slave called Moses, speak of her many trips south to rescue other slaves. Louisa was profoundly stirred by the woman's courage and patience. Unfortunately, her rendition of the woman in her late novel *Work* is dismayingly sentimental. Like many abolitionists, she never examined her own racism.

Early in the summer of 1860 John Brown's widow arrived in Concord, and the Alcotts held a reception for twenty, at which forty-two appeared. Louisa admired the pale, quiet Mrs. Brown from a distance. She was indignant with the gatecrashers and looked after her favorites, Mr. Emerson and Uncle Sam May. After loading them down with tea and food, "feeling that my mission was accomplished, I let the hungry *wait,* and the thirsty *moan* for tea, while I picked out and helped the regular Antislavery set . . . We got through it, but it was an awful hour; and Mother wandered in her mind, utterly lost in a grove of teapots . . ."

In August, Louisa sat down for four solid weeks of work on her adult novel *Moods,* a love story about Henry Thoreau. She had been thinking about the book for a long time and worked with uncommon speed, tearing through a first draft: "I was perfectly happy and seemed to have no wants. Finished the book, or a rough draft of it, and put it away to settle. Mr. Emerson offered to read it when Mother told him it was 'moods' and had one of his sayings for a motto." The book went through many transformations before anyone read it. Louisa's four-week "vortex" satisfied her for a time, and, having released a great deal of psychic and physical tension working day and night for a month, she could relax for a time.

In September, Dio Lewis, an instructor in gymnastics and hygiene, arrived in Concord. The short, stocky, yellow-haired man, with a thick blond beard and passionately erect posture, sent his card to everyone in town. He hired Town Hall for an evening and Sanborn introduced him and his wife, whom Lewis used as a punching bag to demonstrate his activities. Louisa and May took the course, and Louisa was proud that the "delicate vegetable productions" did so well while "the beef-eating young ladies faint away and become superfluous dumb-belles." Everyone in town had become a "perambulating windmill . . . and the most virulent cases present the phenomena of black eyes and excoriations of the knobby parts of the frame, to say nothing of sprains and breakage of vessels looming in the future . . ."

On Thursday, October 18, Louisa was in Boston on the Common for the visit of Lord Renfrew, Prince of Wales, the future King Edward VII of England. The prince, in a colonel's uniform, rode an impressive black horse the length of the Beacon Street mall. He was greeted by an artillery salute. Louisa found the boy prince engaging, and referred to him as frequently as possible as the Prince of Whales.

She went back to Concord to take care of the house while her mother visited Uncle Sam in Syracuse. She baked bread and produced satisfactory applesauce and cocoa, according to her father. Bronson wrote to Abba that both May and Louisa finally seemed to have learned housekeeping from experience, "if not born to the act." He was taking advantage of the fine Indian summer to set in strawberry plants, transplant some evergreen shrubs for the Hawthornes, look after Abba's rosebushes, and harvest the beets, turnips, and parsnips.

That fall Louisa heard Charles Sumner open Concord's lyceum, a self-supporting, voluntary society for public education. The lyceum, the century's most popular method of education, was also one of Concord's social centers. The town had a particularly stimulating roster of speakers, beginning, of course, with its most famous native lecturer, Emerson.

Abba returned to exchange places with May, who went to Syracuse to teach drawing and piano at the Idiot Asylum. Louisa told her mother about a new $50 from the *Atlantic,* which had accepted "A Modern Cinderella." Despite that cash, Christmas was bare and pinched. The family exchanged flowers and apples and discussed the violence in the Kansas-Nebraska territory. Emerson had said that he knew people who were cutting down on their personal expenses "to save and earn for the benefit of Kansas emigrants." The slavery and free-soil forces had been fighting long, bloody skirmishes since 1857. The settlers were so distracted by conflict and the Kansas weather so uncooperative that there was starvation everywhere. They had no celebration, and grieved for Anna, May, and Beth. "But we are used to hard times, and, as Mother says, 'while there is a famine in Kansas we mustn't ask for sugar plums!' " Louisa observed.

That December Henry Thoreau went out in a snowstorm to study the rings of a tree. He fell sick with the pulmonary complaints from which he had suffered twice in the early 1840s and once in 1855. After a slight recovery, he left on a convalescent trip to Chicago with seventeen-year-old Horace Mann, Jr., a student of Sanborn's and Hawthorne's nephew.

Louisa spent January looking after Abba, who was ill. She began work on an autobiographical novel called *Success,* which she dropped after a few weeks in favor of revising *Moods.* She worked steadily, stopping only to take a run through the woods in the late afternoon. Her mother had sewn her a hat of green silk with a red bow, which she wore with a faded green and red party cloak. Louisa was too excited to eat and barely noticed her mother's appearances with cups of tea and pieces of gingerbread. Bronson appeared from time to time with a cup of cider or a shiny red apple. Louisa commented: "All sorts of fun was going on; but I didn't care if the world returned to chaos if I and my inkstand only 'lit' in the same place."

After three brutal weeks Louisa had to stop to rest. She found her mind was still pelting on, but her body had protested. She had a dizzy, ringing head, wobbly legs, and insomnia. Nan came home and distracted Louisa, who treated herself with a regimen of cold baths and long wintry hikes.

She read the new version of her work aloud and basked in familiar praise. Abba told her it was wonderful, and the ever-loyal Anna "laughed and cried, as she always does, over my works, saying 'My dear, I'm proud of you.' " Her father thought her metaphysics divine and wanted to read it to Emerson. "She writes with unusual ease and in a style of idiomatic purity," he observed from

a long apprenticeship with letters and diaries. The book was especially attractive to him, he decided, because of the family history
she had interspersed in the love story and philosophy.

Anna and Louisa stayed on to see the March 18, 1861, festival
that Concord students had planned to honor Bronson. He had
served the last two years as a superintendent of schools, visiting
classrooms, observing teachers, making suggestions, talking with
pupils and parents, and writing voluminous, humane, and considered reports. Bronson had finally earned recognition for his teaching theories. Concord, long disposed to dismiss him, had found his
devotion to education both praiseworthy and instructive. The students added a surprise to the celebration, and when a committee
of schoolchildren presented Bronson with copies of George Herbert's poems and, of course, *The Pilgrim's Progress,* he blushed and
grew teary, hugging the books to his chest.

Louisa had written a song for the occasion, the second verse of
which contained a reference to John Brown. The town made an
effort to suppress that stanza, but Sanborn told the Alcotts to
remain firm and Emerson declared it would be sung, *"and not only
sung but read first and I will read it."* Emerson did precisely that, and
Abba found herself on the verge of tears with the grandeur of the
moment and the honor done her family. Anna said, *"Dear Lu. I do
so love to see her appreciated."*

Louisa was moved by the public gratitude expressed for her
father and found that she, too, had grown enough to see "much
of the beauty of my father's life." She was beginning to experience
some measure of peace within herself about her complex feelings
for the idealistic narcissist who was her father, and she had arrived
at a time when she could start to accept both her good and bad
feelings about him: "I believe that father is one of those for whom
the world is better though it knows little of them, for their power
is not so much in thought, word, or act, as in the silent influence
of character. An influence often unconsciously possessed and
used, receiving small returns and no applause for its reward yet
lasting gracious to the end and leaving life the richer for a presence
which unwittingly achieved a beautiful success.

"Even we his family often misjudge and reproach him, unjustly
perhaps, for he seems to live by a higher law than any we can see,
and if he had done nothing else he has kept his heart young, and

his soul serene through sixty years of troubles; and few men can say as much; few can look a little child in the face and feel that time has not robbed them of the key which can unlock the little creature's heart and make it own them for a playmate in spite of grey hairs and a half century's growth. Father can do this and though in many people's eyes he may seem improvident, selfish and indolent — tho he often does in my own and I wish he were more like other men — yet I begin to see the purpose of his life and love him for the patient persistence with which he has done what he thought right through all opposition and reproach, for that is what few do find."

* * *

The firing on Fort Sumter on Monday, April 15, 1861, ended all doubts and tensions about what was to happen to the country. Lincoln called for 75,000 three-month volunteers. Flags went up in Boston and all over the Union. Volunteers began arriving at Faneuil Hall to join up. Women leaned out of windows to wave and encourage, merchants rushed out onto the streets to wish the men well, and omnibuses and horsecars, with cumbersome politesse, stopped for volunteers to cross the streets. On the afternoon of the seventeenth, the Sixth Massachusetts Regiment left Boston by train. A large crowd gathered at the Boston and Albany railroad station in the South End, near what is now Chinatown. There a clergyman extemporaneously blessed the departing lines of blue-uniformed men. The train was hauled by two locomotives backed into position, and when the commander yelled "Fall into line," the soldiers embarked for war. In Concord a similar scene, on a smaller and more intimate scale, was enacted on the nineteenth. Louisa saw the men off. The day was very emotional, "for in a little town like this we all seem like one family in times like these . . . I've often longed to see a war, and now I have my wish. I long to be a man; but as I can't fight, I will content myself with working for those who can."

Abba's health was intermittently bad that spring, so much work fell on Louisa. Abba was sad to see her illness interfere with Louisa's writing: "It is a real sorrow I find her compelled by circumstances to leave her desk for the kitchen — but life is full of sacrifice for *women,*" she wrote with heavy meaning. Louy had placed herself at May's disposal, a decision that was inevitable — as was the resentment it engendered. In the spring May asked for help with her summer clothes, so Louy found herself sewing and sewing. She worked very hard and felt "very moral" when she did the laundry, picked hops, cleaned house, fixed dinner, and wrote. "May gets exhausted with work, though she walks six miles without a murmur," she remarked bitterly.

Anna was sad to see her sister so overworked and "poor as a rat." John, whom Bronson called a "merchant," worked hard as a clerk in Boston, supporting his wife on a small but steady salary. She was sorry about Louisa's "ragged clothes and shabby things," and decided to put together a bundle of clothes for her. Her tired sister loved the "beautiful surprise," although receiving was never an entirely comfortable experience for her.

Anna recognized that Louisa had a difficult time enjoying herself, that pleasure didn't come naturally to her. She worried about Louy and thought she sounded extremely lonely and homesick for her sisters: *"She tries very hard to do right and be everything to father and mother who suffer very much from this separation from their children, but Louy's ways and modes of thought are peculiar and it is hard work to adapt herself to regular habits."*

In the summer, Louisa spent a month's holiday with her Willis cousins in the White Mountains. She was exhausted "body and soul" and decided to go despite feeling guilty about the indulgence and in defiance of her conviction that "the mountains will fall, all my family die and I shall rue the day I went as long as I live." Anna understood Louisa very well and observed that "she always seems to feel the moment she is having a good time that she is doing wrong and that her duty in this life consists in doing exactly what she doesn't wish to do."

In the fall Louisa and Thoreau both arrived back in Concord, she rested, he very sick. Abba collected herbal remedies to send to Mrs. Thoreau, comforts for the "dear patient." She wished his mother and sister strength and gave "a daily prayerful hope that the brave, just man, may lay aside the corruptible body, for a fuller employment of the incorruptible soul without suffering or strife of spirt."

Louisa was restless and feeling her poverty. Elizabeth Peabody invited her to work in her school at the Alcotts' old home at 20

Pinckney Street. James T. Fields, who had suggested that Louisa stick to education, and his beautiful twenty-eight-year-old wife, Annie, a distant cousin of Louisa's, gave her $45 toward her schoolroom rent and a chamber in their three-story house on Charles Street at the foot of Beacon Hill.

Annie Fields, with a heart-shaped face, huge eyes, and long, thick hair, believed that her mission was to make her house beautiful and entertain and enliven her husband. Their house, which Henry James called a "waterside museum," faced the Charles River and was a beautiful Greek revival effusion. It had wide doorways, long halls, expansive windows, and extensive drapery. The library, upstairs, was the core of the house, a long gracious room with a moss green carpet, matching curtains at windows and door, and one solid wall of books. On the walls hung crayon sketches, oils, a portrait of Dickens, and a proliferation of expensive *objets.* Two white marble fireplaces warmed the room, and a grand piano stood in the middle, presiding over the surrounding throng of busts on pedestals.

Every morning the maids arrived to leave Louisa bottles of hot water and remove the chamber pots under the bed, for the house had no central plumbing. Louisa was dazzled and inwardly gaped at Annie, younger than herself, serenely directing continental dinners, lunches, and breakfasts for Boston's cultivated gentry. Mrs. Fields's style vacillated between the well and the very mannered. On one occasion she was heard to tell her husband that there was a gazelle in the underbrush when she wished him to know that he had a crumb in his beard. But underneath the deadly euphemism lurked a hospitable woman. Louisa wrote to her mother that she had never been in such a worldly paradise.

She didn't like teaching any better than she ever had before, and soon gave up her position with Miss Peabody's kindergarten. In April she was home.

By February, Henry Thoreau had grown too weak to hold a pencil. Bronson visited him often in his small attic room in his mother's yellow house in town. He took cider and apples and sat with the invalid among his collection of arrowheads, bird's nests, and natural artifacts. Henry's books were on shelves made of river driftwood, which his sister Sophia dusted.

Henry worried about the state of his journals and papers and directed his sister to her transcription of his materials. He was talkative and discussed the war and books with Alcott. He never mentioned his tuberculosis or his suffering, nor did he ever appear to wish to remain alive. He retained his ornery charm to the end. When asked if he had made his peace with God he replied, "I did not know we had ever quarrelled." A friend wanted to know what he thought of the world to come and Henry answered, "One world at a time." Henry's sister commented on his dogged refusal to be bowed by, indeed, even to acknowledge, his failing body. "Henry was never affected," she wrote, "never reached by it. I never before saw such a manifestation of the power of spirit over matter. Very often I have heard him tell his visitors that he enjoyed existence as well as ever. He remarked to me that there was much comfort in perfect disease as in perfect health, the mind always conforming to the condition of the body . . ."

In late April Emerson stopped by and read "The Forrester," Alcott's tribute to Henry, who smiled at him and said, "The blue birds and robins are charming my solitary room bringing their music to my dulled senses — but *this* brings light and love, almost revives my life." But Thoreau died on May 6, 1862. Ellery Channing, heartbroken, came to let the Alcotts know of Henry's end. Bronson went to kiss the forehead of his dead friend.

Louisa had lost her source of inspiration for *Moods* and, indeed, for romantic fantasy. Her vision of Thoreau had produced an anxious, pleasurable tension that his death turned to melancholy. The end of their unfulfilled relationship left her empty, dissatisfied, and despondent.

In fulfillment of an old promise to Henry's other admirer, Sophia Foord, Louisa wrote to her former teacher about Thoreau's last few hours. She described his patience and cheer throughout his suffering, and his joke that Nature seemed to be taking a long time at her job but that he was almost finished: "On Tuesday at eight in the morning he asked to be lifted, tried to help do it but was too weak and lying down again passed quietly and painlessly out of the old world into the new." She went on to say that, at Emerson's insistence, Henry was publicly mourned at the church, in defiance of his wishes, "but Emerson said his sorrow was so great he wanted all the world to mourn with him." There were numerous guests at the services, and Emerson read an "address good in itself but not appropriate to the time or place, the last few sentences were these and very true.

" 'In the Tyrol there grows a flower on the most inaccessible peaks of the mountains, called "adelvezia" or "noble purity," it is so much loved by the maidens that their lovers risk their lives in seeking it and are often found dead at the foot of the precipices with the flower in their hands. I think our friend's life was a search for this rare flower, and I know that could we see him now we should find him adorned with profuse garlands of it for none could more fitly wear them."

Louisa told Miss Foord that Channing had written some verses that were sung and that her father had read extracts from Thoreau's writings. There had been many who accused Henry of being irreligious, but his own writings proved them wrong. "If ever a man was a real Christian," Louisa continued, "it was Henry. I think his own wise and pious thoughts read by one who loved him and whose own life was a beautiful example of religious faith, convinced many and touched the hearts of all. It was a lovely day, clear, and calm, and springlike, and as we all walked after Henry's coffin with its pall of flowers, carried by six of his townsmen who had grown up with him, it seemed as if Nature wore her most benignant aspect to welcome her dutiful and loving son to his long sleep in her arms. As we entered the church and birds were singing, early violets blooming in the grass and the pines singing their softest lullaby, and there between his father and his brother we left him, feeling that though his life seemed too short, it would blossom and bear fruit for us long after he was gone, and that perhaps we should know a closer friendship now than even while he lived . . .

"I never can mourn for such men because they never seem lost to me but nearer and dearer for the solemn change . . ." Louisa wrote from a full heart, trying to remember her own distinction between love and self-love. Genuine love meant giving up willingly the physical Henry and retaining her admiration and awe for his memory, desiring nothing for herself. Louisa adjusted gracefully to Henry's death, having never hoped for any real, human love from him. This accommodation to the sad event marked Louisa. She became calmer and more serious, as if she had absorbed some permanent grief.

In June, when John Brown's daughter came to spend the summer at Orchard House, Louisa used her as an excuse for her despondency. The extra work, she said, would keep her from writing. "I think disappointment must be good for me, I get so much of it," she reflected, "and the constant thumping Fate gives me may be a mellowing process; so I shall be a ripe and sweet old pippin before I die." Anna was worried about Louisa, who seemed so forlorn. She could do nothing but feel sympathetic pain: "Her life affords her so little satisfaction, and she lives so for others that it seems too bad."

The news from the war was all bad. Emerson thought that a strong-minded woman should take the Army of the Potomac out of McClellan's unsure hands. Louisa agreed, thinking in October that "a few energetic women could carry on the war better than the men do so far."

She sewed for the men. She made "havelocks," white linen head-pieces named for a British general in India whose troops had used them for protection from the sun. Union soldiers took them south and turned them into nightcaps, bandages, and turbans. That kind of futile gesture did nothing for Louisa's depression. She studied the "lint question" and learned to gather, scrape, and prepare the substance for hospitals. She worked on the shirts that the newly organized United States Sanitary Commission was ordering. But making bandages and clothes was indirect satisfaction at best.

Early in the war Dr. Henry Bellows, a Walpole acquaintance and chairman of the Woman's Central Association of Relief, dispatched a committee to Washington to learn how to help the army. The committee returned with the plans for the U.S. Sanitary Commission and a program to inspect camps, set up soup distribution units, provide transport for the wounded, and put women nurses into hospitals, replacing convalescent soldiers with trained medical aides. It was the last proposal, based on Florence Nightingale's work in 1855 in the Crimea, that stirred Louisa's imagination.

Everywhere she saw signs urging her to action. In Henry's death, in Anna's pregnancy, and in her restlessness and in volatile patriotism. In Boston there was on display in a Washington Street gallery a six-pound iron collar, with three prongs extending out, a rivet in front, and a clasp in back. This hideous slave collar was another sign. Louisa confided in Anna her desire to go, and Anna hoped she would, "as she is a fine nurse and would like it." That November 1862, Louisa made application.

On November 29, 1862, she turned thirty. It was a crucial age,

marking as it surely did the official, public start of her spinsterhood. The Hawthornes sent a package of presents to Lu and her
father and she thanked them with a poem, friendly, grateful, formal, self-mocking, and a little wistful:

> The Hawthorne is a gracious tree,
> From latest twig to parents' root,
> For when all other leafless stand,
> It gayly blossoms and bears fruit
> On certain days a friendly wind,
> Wafts from its spreading boughs a store
> Of canny gifts that flutter in,
> Like snowflakes at a neighbor's door.
>
> The spinster who has just been blessed,
> Finds solemn thirty much improved
> By proofs that such a crabbed soul
> Is still remembered and beloved.
> Kind wishes "Ancient Lu" has stored
> On the "best chamber" of her heart,
> And every gift on fancy's stage,
> Already plays its little part.

14

Hospital Sketches

DOROTHEA DIX HAD BEEN APPOINTED the country's first supervisor of nurses on June 10, 1861. A year later she issued a circular calling for women between thirty-five and fifty, strong, matronly, sober, neat, and industrious. They needed two recommendations attesting to their excellent morals. In return for their services they were offered free transportation to and from their assigned hospital and forty cents a day.

Louisa was young but made up for it in excessive sobriety and matronliness. She had the valuable recommendation of Miss Hannah Stevenson, a well-known Boston reformer who was then in charge of the nurses at the new, well-equipped Armory Square Hospital in Washington. Louisa expected to become a member of Miss Stevenson's staff, but was assigned instead to the Union Hotel Hospital, a converted tavern in Georgetown.

In December 1862, Louisa's orders came through, and her gloom and restlessness were submerged in excitement and anxiety. She worried about leaving her mother alone, but the war seemed to justify it. Bronson observed with pride and insensitivity that he was sending his only son.

Julian Hawthorne and May saw Louisa off at the Concord station. She spent the night in Boston with Annie and John before boarding the complicated series of trains, boats, and horsecars that took her to Washington.

The city of 140,000 was floating with soldiers and runaway slaves, or "contrabands." Louisa saw thousands and thousands of black people, many of them in jobs she had never seen them perform before: as draymen, hack drivers, oystermen, carpenters, even some shopkeepers. Prejudice was even greater in Washington, where citizens were scandalized by the squalid living conditions of the black community. More and more runaways with only plantation skills increased white fears and anger.

The city's grandeur and squalor were equally apparent. The Mall was unkempt, the Ellipse a fetid swamp of sewage from the White House and nearby buildings. Washington's many vacant lots were used for waste, and noisome piles of garbage grew along the dusty streets. It wasn't until 1863 that there was any regular refuse pickup. Stonecutters' tools and huge blocks of marble stood around the unfinished Capitol, its dome draped with scaffolding.

In 1859 an aqueduct had been constructed from Great Falls, ten miles north of Georgetown, but the war had prevented completion of the water system. Much of Washington's water was not fit for drinking and typhoid was a serious problem. Rats, cockroaches, and smallpox were epidemic, as were thievery, prostitution, and vandalism. Culprits were marched through the city wearing signs reading PICKPOCKET or THIEF behind fife and drum players.

Every available building in Washington was commandeered as hospital space, although most of the wounded preferred convalescing anywhere but in a hospital. The close air, rotten straw beds, and haphazard care carried off lives more effectively than Confederate guns. Walt Whitman began visiting Washington hospitals on December 21, 1862, and wrote of the ghastly piles of amputated limbs and corpses left near these institutions. In addition to wounds, the troops were commonly afflicted with chronic diarrhea, typhoid, bronchitis, rheumatism, and pneumonia. There were twice as many sick as there were wounded.

The Union Hotel Hospital was a warren of badly lit, barely ventillated rooms. Florence Nightingale could have had it in mind as a bad example when she stipulated that at least a hospital should not induce disease.

Louisa began her day at 6:00 A.M., running though her ward of ten men, opening all the windows. She endured the complaints of the patients, knowing that the air was stale and foul, "cold, damp, dirty, full of vile odors from wounds, kitchens, wash rooms, and stables." After a nasty fried breakfast, with pale, unpleasant coffee and unsatisfactory half-conversations with the staff, she was back to her ward to "trot and trot." She fed those who couldn't feed themselves, dressed wounds, cleaned, sewed bandages, and oversaw the efforts of her aides, the convalescents. This practice of impressing semihealed patients into menial hospital duties seemed to Louisa and most professionals inhumane and ineffective.

Throughout the morning Louisa ran for bed linens, water, sponges, pillows, and every necessity until she was quite exhausted. When the noon bell sounded, she and her assistants handed around a gummy lunch of meat, soup, potatoes, and bread. After lunch, things were generally quieter, and Louisa often spent an hour or so writing letters for the soldiers before the five o'clock supper. The doctors made a final round after dinner, and the ward settled into quiet talk, card games, and rest until nine, when the gaslights were turned down.

When Louisa arrived at the Union Hotel Hospital, General Burnside had taken command of the Army of the Potomac from McClellan. Thinking to outmaneuver Lee, they marched to Fredericksburg, but Lee surprised him there and the result was a grisly slaughter, the worst carnage of the war, observers said. During that cold, wet December, huge ambulance-wagons drawn by four horses carted men into the hospital in all stages of agony. Wounded men lay waiting, often as long as several days, in the heavy rains before being taken to some receiving station. Louisa was suddenly confronted with maimed and sick men so mudcaked that only repeated washing revealed the extent of their injuries. It was a quick and shocking introduction to male anatomy for the Victorian woman. Louisa doggedly washed filthy body after filthy body.

The doctors administered laxatives like tamarind, cassia, castor oil, and magnesia in large quantities. They dosed with powerful cathartics such as calomel, jalap, and croton oil. Calomel was the most popular, a mercury compound that had been used as an emetic since the sixteenth century. The theory was that the less material in the body, the less chance for disease to feed. Calomel was administered for fevers, bronchitis, dysentery, pneumonia, hepatitis, inflammations, and laryngitis. It was given in enormous, or "heroic," doses with great frequency. Accepted practice was to dose up to the point of salivation, one of the early signs of acute mercury poisoning. At this point patients customarily experienced very sore gums and lost their teeth, their hair, and their voices. Often they could barely swallow, and their tongues swelled to four or five times their normal size and protruded. They extruded a poisonous mucus discharge from their mouths. These were the short-term effects, and if the patient survived them he could look forward to a short, deteriorating life of trembling, anxiety, weakness, rheumaticlike pains, chills, restlessness, delirium, and a host of varied debilities. There was some protest against the use of calomel, but the medical establishment, by and large, swore by it. It was so abused in the army that Surgeon-General William Hammond issued a circular forbidding its issue to the medical corps in May 1863.

Among the casualities of Burnside's disaster was John Sulie, a quiet, handsome Union blacksmith from Virginia whom Louisa rather ignored when he first entered the ward. His strong, bearded face and his impassive demeanor attracted and frightened her, causing her to act aloof. It wasn't until she learned from one of the doctors that he was rapidly dying that she found the courage and freedom to attach herself to him: "Under his plain speech and unpolished manner I seem to see a noble character, a heart as warm and tender as a woman's, a nature fresh and frank as any child's."

John Sulie, who figures largely in *Hospital Sketches,* was Louisa's idea of a hero and a martyr. He was simple, uncomplaining and devoted to his mother, for whose sake he had never married. Louisa's account of his death is as moving a piece of writing as she ever did. His working-class background, rustic speech, gentle manner, and helplessness all made her feel safe with him. His terminal wounds allowed her to feel and express the fullness of her warmth, compassion, and tenderness. She admired and romanticized him, possibly even desired him. In his last days he needed her, and they shared an intimacy that was rewarding and without pain or fear for Louisa. She could be everything to him without censure, sexual consequences, or entanglement.

Shortly after her arrival she was given the night duty, from noon to midnight. She preferred it, and took time in the mornings to explore Georgetown and Washington. She took runs "to keep well, for bad air, food, water, work and watching are getting to be too much for me." She walked in the direction of Washington, seeing the long, mule-drawn convoys of army wagons going toward the front and the loaded ambulances coming back: "That way the fighting lies, and I long to follow." Mending, curing, helping, and consoling didn't satisfy the violent, urgent side of Louisa. Next to fighting, she wanted to be as close to the battlefield as she could. She forced herself to seek out the most grisly operations to get rid of her squeamishness, and she hoped to be transferred to a field hospital.

Louisa made friends with Dr. John Winslow, a sweet, mild Quaker whom she described as "plain, odd, sentimental, but kind hearted as a woman and rather quaint." He replaced a handsome surgeon whose drinking had made his hands shake. Louisa took walks with "Dr. John," who visited her in her dormitory rooms. He invited her to his suite, but she wouldn't go: "Quotes Browning copiously, is given to confidences in the twilight, and altogether is amiably amusing, and exceedingly amusing, and exceedingly *young.*" Louisa, from her vast elderliness, found some safety with men by treating them all as children. Her patients were her "boys" and John Winslow was yet another.

Winslow endured Louisa's condescension and took her to hear a sermon by the Reverend William Henry Channing, the lively nephew of the great Dr. Channing. Louisa found the sermon "flowery" and boring.

In early January, after three weeks' duty, Louisa grew sick, suffering a "sharp pain in the side, cough, fever and dizzyness . . ." She became worse, staying in her room, sewing, writing letters, and fighting her fear and loneliness. On the fourteenth of January the hospital wired the Alcotts and Bronson set out for Washington. Louisa, who had been given the calomel treatment, couldn't sleep without gruesome nightmares. She wondered "if I am to die here as Mrs. Ropes the matron is likely to do. Feel too miserable to care much what becomes of me." The diagnosis was typhoid pneumonia, and the treatment, more calomel. Dr. Winslow came often, bringing wood for the fire, reading matter, good-smelling cologne, "and little messes like a motherly little man as he is. Nurses fussy and anxious, matron dying, and everything very gloomy. They want me to go home but I *won't* yet."

On the sixteenth, Louisa awoke out of a semidelirious dream to see her father sitting by her bed. She was angry with him because it meant she would likely be taken home, but she was also relieved to see a familiar face.

Bronson stayed on for five days to see if Louisa would recover enough to continue her work. He visited with Richard Henry Dana, Jr., who was the United States Attorney for Massachusetts. He had a talk with William Channing and heard him preach, visited with Louisa's patients, and went to the Senate Chamber, where he saw Lincoln. "His behavior was good," Bronson recorded generously. "I wished to have had an interview but am too anxious about Louisa and without time to seek it nor has he time to give."

Mrs. Dana and Dorothea Dix visited Louisa and tried to persuade her to go home. Miss Dix was an uncompromising woman whose demanding nature alienated many supporters. "She is a kind old soul, but very queer, fussy and arbitrary, no one likes her and I don't wonder," wrote Louisa; she later crossed it out. On the twenty-first, Louisa began to feel dangerously strange and agreed to leave. Miss Dix saw her off with a large basket amply stocked with medicines, toilet water, tea, wine, a Bible, a pillow, a fan, and a blanket. Louisa was unhappy to leave "and my boys seemed sorry to have me; quite a flock came to see me off, but I was too sick to have but a dim idea of what was going on."

Father and daughter rode all night on the cars, reaching Boston late on January 22, where they spent the night with the Sewalls. Louisa was very weak and frightened. The next afternoon they took a 4:00 P.M. train to Concord. Una Hawthorne happened to be riding in the coach and Louisa leaned against her shoulder during the trip. The girl was deeply alarmed by Louisa's rolling eyes and morbid pallor.

Louisa arrived home, believing in her delirium that the house had no roof and that no one wanted to see her. She spent two days unconscious and delirious. Sophia Hawthorne wrote to her friend Annie Fields that she was "so changed I think I should not have known her."

For a time no one but the family and Concord's Dr. Bartlett saw her. She was hallucinating and furious much of the time, plagued by scenes from the hospital, the trip, and the conviction that she would not get home. From time to time she would say, "If you will only take that man away, I can bear the rest."

One family member or another was with her constantly. One day when they left her alone for a moment there was a thunderous crash. Abba fell into hysterics, spent from days and nights of worry and wakefulness. May raced into Louisa's room and dragged her sprawling sister up from the floor onto the bed. Louisa yelled, "How could you leave me alone when the room was full of men?"

Abba, Bronson, and May shared nursing duty, sleeping on a couch by Louisa's bed. Abba became exhausted and developed a sympathetic case of Louisa's ailments. When May began to look feverish, Sophia Hawthorne insisted that she eat her meals with them. Lydian Emerson sent the Alcotts her maid.

Anna, who was seven months pregnant, wanted to know how her sister was. The family wanted to keep the worst from her and Bronson wrote her vague, airy letters. But they only made Anna suspicious and she forced the issue. When she saw Louisa with the great hollows around her bloodshot eyes, her swollen tongue, her brownish skin, her ulcerated throat, uncontrollable cough, and her strange demented stare, Anna was appalled. She was sure Louisa would die as Elizabeth had.

Louisa was tortured with strange visions. She imagined a wicked Spanish husband, a grandee in black velvet who said, "Lie still my dear." He startled her by leaping out of closets, in at her from windows, and threatening her night after night. At one point Louisa got out of bed and appealed to the pope in an attempt at Latin. One hallucination took her to heaven, which she found depressingly ordinary and full of people like the Reverend William Henry Channing and Dorothea Dix. She wished she weren't there. In another nightmare she was behind a door that a mob was breaking down. Once she was a witch being burnt, at other times she was being hanged or stoned; "also being tempted to join Dr. Winslow and the two nurses in worshipping the devil. Also tending millions of sick men who never died or got well."

It is impossible to estimate accurately the size of the jolt to her nervous system that the hospital experience gave Louisa. But if the fear released in her delirium is any indication, it must have been enormous. At the hospital her duties collided with her fear of men. She had to repress her terrors and be physically intimate with many males. In her ravings she uncovered hideous fears of rejection and violence. The imagery of Louisa's hallucinations was richly gothic: devilworship, black magic, witch hunts. The Spanish grandee, a character Louisa had used since childhood dramas, was a romantic but fearsome scoundrel, full of vitality and sexuality, who worked his way with women. For a New England woman, Spanish Catholicism, mother of the Inquisition, represented authentic, gaudy sin. Tamed, these fantasies were material for stories. Untamed, they were expressions of Louisa's deepest sexual and emotional horrors.

A Concord housekeeper and mesmerist, Mrs. Bliss, came to consult with Louisa about her pains. She performed her diagnosis by holding Louisa's hands and closing her eyes to "read" the disease. In this posture she magnetized the pains out of her patient. Louisa suddenly felt strong enough to stand up and tried her powers by modeling while Anna fitted a dressing gown to her gaunt frame.

Mrs. Bliss also cured her temporarily of her excruciating back pains. She began coming downstairs in the middle of February: "Found a queer, thin, big eyed face when I looked in the glass; didn't know myself at all . . ." This trip marked the end, as Sophia Hawthorne put it, to "this fierce campaign, one of the fiercest of the war." Sophia was very glad it was over because of her susceptibility to the feelings of others: "So I was the suffering Louisa, and also her weary, distressed father and mother and sisters."

Louisa had lost her yard of beautiful brown hair and covered her bald head with lace hats. Her gums were so painful she could barely eat, and her mouth was covered with sores. Dr. Bartlett continued to come every day, and it is extremely likely that it was at this juncture that she began her intermittent reliance on opium to sleep. She was too tired and weak to enjoy the food, money, and good wishes that friends brought. She "went into caps like a grandma," and tried to adjust to the changes the mercury had made in her body.

By March she was eating more easily and circling around her books, dusting them a little, picking at them, hovering until she was strong enough to begin working. Toward the end of the month she began reading "no end of rubbish with a few good things as ballast."

On March 28, Bronson arrived in Concord with the news that Anna had had a baby boy. Abba left for Chelsea, leaving Louisa for the first time since January. Louisa regretted not being with Anna at her delivery, "a sad disappointment to her as well as me."

Louisa's own near-death had dulled the poignant feelings her sister's motherhood aroused in her. Anna's pregnancy restated her independence from Louisa and the divergent directions the sisters' lives were taking. Anna had chosen the conventional, acceptable female route with its well-documented difficulties and sacrifices. Louisa had opted for a more eccentric course in which there were no rules or by-laws against which she could evaluate herself. Anna could find admirable models everywhere. Louisa's models were strong, "unfeminine" women like Dorothea Dix and Elizabeth Peabody, whose admirable achievements were always undercut by the ridicule of the men and women who would have preferred them to spend their energies cutting a more "female" figure. The responsibilities attached to Anna's choice to marry and to mother weren't necessarily easier than Louisa's, but she didn't have to defend her actions. Louisa had to cope with the implication that she was a misfit as a woman.

* * *

While she was at the Union Hotel Hospital, Louisa got a letter from an editor of *Frank Leslie's Illustrated Newspaper,* saying that her story "Pauline's Passion and Punishment" had won a hundred-dollar prize. This was Louisa's first "lurid," or "blood and thunder," story. She instructed Leslie to publish it under the name A. M. Barnard. For the next five years Louisa wrote for Frank Leslie and other popular Boston papers, keeping the secret from her father and his distinguished friends. Leslie, who had founded his weekly in 1855, specialized in murders, bizarre crimes, fires, executions, and offbeat catastrophes.

Louisa's new secret was both psychologically and financially rewarding. The hundred dollars was a great help, but so was the availability of a market for her least transcendental fantasies and desires. The theme of "Pauline's Passion and Punishment" is revenge for love withdrawn. Pauline is a beauty of great personal strength, self-control, and expressiveness. When wronged, as she is at the opening of the story, she thirsts for retribution. She does not wish to learn forgiveness or to submit to her loss, nor does she believe that the Lord has sent her a trial to help her grow patient and forbearing. Her lover, Gilbert, married another woman and she wants to make him feel lifelong agony.

Pauline is "ardent, dominant, and subtle . . . In the spirited carriage of the head appeared the freedom of an intellect ripened under colder skies, the energy of a nature that could wring strength from suffering, and dare to act where feebler souls would only dare desire." She takes a nineteen-year-old Cuban boy, the lovesick Manuel, as an accomplice in her plot. She tells him she will marry him and learn to love him if he will help her to humiliate Gilbert. Pauline says she will be his wife in name only. He is to woo her very slowly because her passions are still elsewhere. She effectively keeps him a boy.

Louisa reserves to Pauline the emotions that the transcendentalists agreed belonged to men. "I have shed no tears," Pauline explains to Manuel, "uttered no cry, asked no comfort; yet since I read that letter, I have suffered more than many suffer in a lifetime. I am not one to lament long over any hopeless sorrow. A single paroxysm, sharp and short, and it is over. Contempt has killed my love . . ."

To Manuel belong the girlish feelings, the subjection to his lover. He places himself at her disposal, "and very winsome was the glad abandonment of this young lover, half boy, half man, possessing the simplicity of the one, the fervor of the other.

Pauline and Manuel marry and travel to the same resort where Gilbert and his rich new bride Barbara are staying. Pauline parades her handsome Manuel and their sexuality before the unhappily married couple. Pauline and Manuel dance "with slowly increasing speed, in perfect time to the inspiring melody," while Gilbert watches, "fascinated, flushed, and excited as if his heart beat responsive to the rhythmic rise and fall of the booted foot and satin slipper. The music ended with a crash . . ."

Throughout, Pauline is intent on showing Gilbert, and to a lesser extent Manuel, their helplessness. "Have you no power, Gilbert?" she asks.

Pauline's strongest weapon is her distance, her lack of involvement. This was a potent fantasy for Louisa, who felt powerless and angry with her cold, reproachful father. She was no longer afraid of the sixty-two-year-old Bronson Alcott, but the little girl in Louisa, always a dominant part of her, was still confused, hurt, and furious with the strong, arbitrary, unavailable father who loved Anna better than her. The fantasy Louisa has grown so powerful, beautiful, and self-possessed that she can take her father's rejection and turn it back on him, making him as miserable as she was. She will not love men fully. They are permitted to worship her and put themselves at her disposal, but they are not allowed into her life as anything more than ornaments. Manuel becomes her beautiful, rich wife.

Louisa mocks the midcentury pieties, especially the one that tells a woman to love her man into goodness. Gilbert, in a moment of repulsive abjectness, whimpers to his silly wife, who wishes to leave him, "but in executing justice, oh, remember mercy! Remember that I was too early left fatherless, motherless, and I went astray for want of some kind heart to guide and cherish me. There is still time. Be compassionate and save me from myself." The silly wife agrees. But a few pages later Gilbert asks Pauline to perform the same function. She refuses, denying one of the main foundations of womanhood.

In the end Pauline has her "punishment" when Gilbert throws Manuel off a cliff, and Gilbert's wife, who has fallen in love with Manuel's sweet ways, takes a dive after him. Pauline and Gilbert are left staring at each other. The finale is morally efficient, but one thinks that the game wasn't worth the result.

The A. M. Barnard stories read fluently, as easily as they were written. Louisa was tapping veins of emotion that lay very close to her skin. Revenge was a constant leitmotif of her brooding. She wanted desperately not to do what was expected of her, not to deny, sacrifice, or postpone, but to stand up for once and to hand out blame. In her lurid stories she didn't need to be responsible for a morality, an expected metaphysic, or a righteous ending. Her characters could behave with the violence, anger and ruthlessness that she kept tightly locked away. Her women could behave without regard to Concord ethics or Victorian claims of femininity. Pauline denies Gilbert his chance for reform and Manuel his sexuality. In other words, she has renounced her claims of nineteenth-century womanhood.

Louisa's immoral women were the underside of Bronson's ideal female, the inverse of women like Anna. Louisa, by not conforming to the prescribed patterns of womanliness, had nourished her self-loathing for three decades. She identified with Pauline and believed that passionate, sexual women like herself were wicked and grotesque members of her sex. She saw the energetic, ruthless

Pauline as herself let loose. Her understanding of the character is profound and her disapproval is mixed with compassion.

* * *

During her evenings at the Union Hotel Hospital, Louisa had thought of Henry Thoreau, trying to give expression to the inarticulate love she had felt for him for so long. She wrote a poem about her friend and kept it among her papers. Her father found it and read it to the Hawthornes. Sophia was very taken with it and formally asked Louisa if she could send it to Annie Fields to show to her husband James. She sent it to Boston, asking Annie to read it to James: "It is altogether superior in tone to anything I have ever seen of her — so sweet, majestic and calm and serious." Sophia made a mistake in transcription and wrote Annie about her error: " 'Tuned' is so much better that I am afraid I shall be assassinated by some member of the A. family if it be printed 'Turned' through my instrumentality and I *rush* to acquaint you with my error."

Annie and James, who edited the *Atlantic,* had some criticisms, and gently offered them to Louisa despite Sophia's hysterical warnings that Louisa was too proud and stiff to do anything but withdraw her poem. Annie persisted, however, and Louisa, glad to be published in the magazine, accepted the changes gladly, writing to Annie: "Criticism never offends but to me is often more flattering than praise for if any one takes the trouble to criticize it seems to prove that the thing is worth mending." "Thoreau's Flute" appeared in the *Atlantic* in the summer of 1863:

> We sighing said, "Our Pan is dead;
> His pipe hangs mute beside the river;
> Around it wistful sunbeams quiver,
> But Music's airy voice is fled.
> Spring came to us in guise forlorn;
> The bluebird chants a requiem;
> The willow-blossom waits for him; —
> The Genius of the wood is gone.
>
> Then from the flute, untouched by hands,
> There came a low, harmonious breath:
> For such as he there is no death; —

His life the eternal life commands;
Above man's aims his nature rose.
The wisdom of a just content
Made one small spot a continent,
And turned to poetry life's prose.

Haunting the hills, the stream, the wild,
Swallow and aster, lake and pine,
To him grew human or divine, —
Fit mates for this large-hearted child.
Such homage Nature ne'er forgets,
And yearly on the coverlid
'Neath which her darling lieth hid
Will write his name in violets.

To him no vain regrets belong
Whose soul, that finer instrument,
Gave to the world no poor lament,
But wood-notes ever sweet and strong.
O lonely friend! he still will be
A potent presence, though unseen, —
Steadfast, sagacious, and serene;
Seek not for him — he is with thee.

In the late spring Louisa organized and shaped the letters she had written to her family into a three-sectioned reminiscence of her hospital days and gave them to Frank Sanborn to publish in the *Commonwealth,* an abolitionist paper he edited. "Hospital Sketches" began coming out on May 22, 1863, and concluded on June 26. The paper sold out, and soon magazines and newspapers all over the North began reprinting the "Sketches." Publishers approached Louisa with offers to issue them in book form. After some deliberation she chose James Redpath, an abolitionist who had recently put together a memorial volume on John Brown.

At Bronson's suggestion, Louisa dedicated the volume to Hannah Stevenson, who had been responsible for getting Louisa her nursing assignment. Louisa signed a contract providing her with 5 cents from every book sold. Redpath got 10 cents, of which he promised to set aside a nickel for war orphans. The book was priced at 50 cents, which Louisa and her friends thought steep. Later, she blamed the relatively small sales of the volume on its cost.

In August, Redpath sent Louisa bound copies of her book. She wrote, telling him how much she enjoyed seeing "my townsfolk buying, reading, laughing and crying over it wherever I go. One rash youth bought eight copies at a blow . . ." The little hundred-page book, she wrote later, "never made much money, but it showed me my style . . ."

Hospital Sketches is a direct, frank, vigorous narrative about Louisa's patients and the hospital. It has none of the metaphysics of *Moods* or the coyness of *Flower Fables.* It derives its clarity from an abundance of simple detail in each scene: objects, instruments, colors, and smells. The characters are quite flat in the Dickensian sense. They have one predominant trait, either humorous, righteous, or vile. Of psychological insight there is none, but of feeling a great deal. The characters' sentiments fall within the prescribed Victorian perimeters, which forces a meaning from every anecdote. Justice and love bring happiness in heaven if not on earth. It is satisfying, uncomplicated nonfiction.

Louisa, writing as Nurse Periwinkle, aired her wry humor for the first time publicly, having previously reserved it for the family. She drew caricatures, parodied rustic speech, and mocked vices. She introduced the no-nonsense, slightly self-mocking, undeniably preachy tone in later works. Underneath the tone lie the familiar relentless morality, the criticism of vice, and the ever-present pathos. The *Sketches* feature correct sentiments if not entirely complete or truthful ones. Of Dorothea Dix, Louisa wrote: "Long may she wave! Whatever others may think or say, Nurse Periwinkle is forever grateful . . ."

The book's reception was gratifying. Henry James, Sr., wrote to her after reading the articles in the *Commonwealth* in June: "It would be tedious to you to hear how much pleasure an old man like me has taken in your charming pictures and how refreshing he found the personal revelation there incidentally made of so much that is dearest and most worshipful in a woman . . . I have the greatest desire to enroll myself among your friends, having long been your father's friend . . ." Abba's thirty-five years with one of the nineteenth century's most chaotic philosophers must have eroded her analytic faculties to the extent that she didn't recognize James as a contender in the confused-thought sweepstakes. She added a note to his letter: "This is a most distinguished remark of respect, coming from one of the most logical minds of the age."

Louisa's parents loved her success. Bronson saw "nothing in the way of a good appreciation of Louisa's merit as a woman and a writer. Nothing could be more surprising to her or agreeable to us." Abba thought her achievement would encourage her to "greater effort." Never quite satisfied, she thought Louisa was destined to "some deeper surprise than we have yet had — and I predict that she does not fail to establish a respectable position among authorships — it may take years, but she will have no mean rank assigned her now — She is in the vestibule of the Temple. But the high altar is not far off." Abba was a budding stage mother. She looked forward to Louisa's continuing achievements, and thought that if her health held up, "she will earn an honorable independence for herself — and much comfort for us — ."

As for Louisa, she thought "the world must be coming to an end and all my dreams getting fulfilled in a most amazing way." She had seen three publishers vie for her work after fifteen years of struggle and much disappointment. All that time, she thought, must be paying off "and I may yet 'pay all the debts, fix the house, send May to Italy and keep the old folks cosy,' as I've said I would so long yet so hopelessly."

The habits of hard work and self-denial had become permanent with Louisa. She saw May off on vacation and read her sister's letters of parties, sailing, swimming, dancing, and picnicking. She had the chance to spend August on the North Shore, in Gloucester, Massachusetts, but turned it down, "being too busy and too bashful to be made a lion of even in a small way." She stayed home and tried to work between bouts of exhaustion and dizziness. When Bronson's mother died, she sent $5 for the funeral costs. Louisa wrote that May, who was enjoying herself, was "coldhearted," and then she scratched it out.

In July, Sanborn persuaded her to refurbish her letters home from the White Mountains the summer before. She agreed and the series began in the *Commonwealth,* but Louisa discontinued them in the middle. She was "heartily ashamed of them," thinking them "rowdy" rather than funny. "I'm glad of the lesson and hope it will do me good," she wrote.

Louisa continued to work on *Moods* and *Work* that fall, being careful with her unstable health. *Hospital Sketches* brought in enough to ease immediate money anxieties, outfit May for a Boston art course, and have the house shingled.

Abba sorely missed her oldest daughter and grandson. She wasn't sure if she could do without them: "His little coos and smile is a perfect sunbeam — ." Bronson noted in the fall that Abba hardly visited anymore and "would be glad to have mother and son where she might see them daily." He too desired to have Anna around: "Home is a tender word with her, and she, even more than any of her sisters living, carries the substance in her heart of all that renders it lovely and fair." Anna was melancholy and homesick and planned to move back with John and the baby Frederick to Orchard House. But she fell sick instead, and Abba moved to Chelsea to stay with her.

Anna was deeply unhappy and Bronson wrote to Abba that "if anything more than another can aid in raising her health and spirits, 'tis the prospect of coming *home:* for that word is life and happiness, as it ever has been to her. How much she has suffered from being no longer one of the circle in the same sense she was once — more than we knew; and then it was so like her to be silent so long about it. She must come and you with her as soon as she is able, and fair days have come." John, who had been exempted from military duty, and Anna moved into the front upstairs bedroom across from Louisa's in March 1864.

They found Concord quiet. The Hawthornes had withdrawn abruptly from any contact with their neighbors. Abba's oratorical extremes and hysterical family devotion had assaulted Sophia's delicate nerves. One day she wrote to Annie Fields that she couldn't come to Boston the following week: "I was so cut to the heart by the rather ferocious and sudden announcement of Mrs. Alcott on Monday morning 'That General Banks' army was entirely destroyed' and that the rebels were hurrying to Washington and that the governor had ordered off every man capable of bearing arms — and so on — that though feeling very well beforehand, I became as it were a dead woman — and I have accomplished nothing this week. And that terrible news was merely all an exaggeration and I suffered for nothing. Mrs. Alcott is the most appalling sensationalist. She frightens me out of my five senses from time to time with telling me one thing and another and suggesting blood curdling possibilities."

Nathaniel Hawthorne was very sick with what may have been a form of cancer. He sometimes sat in his dressing gown for two or three weeks without doing anything. His illness and Sophia's violent dislike of Abba effectively put an end to communication between the two houses.

On a Sunday in January 1864, Bronson visited Hawthorne and asked if there was any problem between the families. Hawthorne, who, with his wife, considered Bronson "one of the most excellent of men — he could never quarrel with anyone — told him that it was impossible to get along with his wife: "She is a person who prides herself much on her family, is busied in the desire to outshine her neighbors, is totally devoid of the power to tell the truth and occupies herself much with circulating unworthy reports; she seems to possess an oblique vision to which nothing presents itself as it is." Bronson acknowledged that this was so. "Indeed," said Hawthorne, "who should know it better?" Hawthorne assured him that in times of emergency they would be faithful neighbors. Bronson, he said, took it all "like a saint."

Bronson visited the Fields, who expressed admiration for Louisa's book. Her father told them that she had never been "content to wait but so soon as she became content then good fortune came as she always does." Bronson told Fields that Louisa was considering the possibility of going to Beaufort, South Carolina, to teach freedmen at a special school. Fields was interested in publishing the "Plantation Sketches" that he assumed would result. She discarded the idea, but Fields continued to be interested in her work and was eager to see *Moods.*

* * *

Louisa's short service in the war tragically changed her life. She was never well again, and although she had months when she had strength and energy, the poison in her nervous system curtailed these periods until, by the end, she was always sick and exhausted. Louisa was constitutionally very strong and semi-invalidism was unnatural and an anathema to her. Her behavior had always been marked by highs and lows, but her previous vitality had helped her out of her frequent depressions. Before the war, many of her enemies had been in her mind, but afterward she had to confront an incurable malady in her body. She struggled hard against her illness, whose changeable character made it impossible to treat or even locate. But the fight absorbed most of her power, and what was left over she spent on work. Louisa had been trying with some success to confront and exorcise her emotional and social problems before the war. In nursing she was expressing her own fierce humanity in a courageous alternative to marriage and motherhood. It is inevitable that she could have continued experimenting with other demonstrations of her active humanitarianism if the mercury poisoning had not begun its hideous deterioration of her body and nerves.

15

Moods

LOUISA WAS PROUD OF HAVING EARNED close to $600 for 1863 "by writing alone." She was also taken with the facts that she had spent $70 on May and less than one hundred on herself. The rest had gone for family necessities, leaving Louisa satisfied with her triumph over self-indulgence. James Redpath, the abolitionist publisher of *Hospital Sketches,* had been inquiring regularly about the status of *Moods,* and in the winter of 1864 she wrote to say that it was ready. He was worried that success had spoiled her, and the vision of circling publisher-buzzards ready to take his promising writer away troubled him. Louisa wrote reassuringly: "I think the literary laws *are* just and shall abide by them, hoping that your 'faith in my ability' may be rewarded, and future books may prove a good investment for us both." She warned him that *Moods* was very long and "odd, sentimental, and tragical." She had written it for her own amusement and, although her family loved it, she had no way of judging its value. She had been too frightened to take Mr. Emerson up on his offer to read it. She begged Redpath not to talk to her about "genius," having given up on that idea after fifteen years of "rubbishing." "The inspiration of necessity is all I've had and it is a safer help than any other." Louisa was always quick to discourage any discussion of her talents.

"Genius" was a popular Victorian word that Bronson discussed often. To Louisa it meant a kind of godly inspiration that she associated with men like her father. She always downplayed her talent and refused to give herself credit for anything other than a drudgelike capacity for labor. Genius was a luxury men like Bronson could afford, men who didn't respond to necessity. Louisa was half-proud and half-defensive about her writing, and *Moods,* the book closest to her heart, heightened both these attitudes. It was, ironically, the only novel she wrote in which she demonstrated her "genius."

Redpath came on February 4, 1864, to collect the manuscript. He read it overnight and telegraphed Louisa to come to Boston the next day. When she arrived he told her that the novel would have to be published in two volumes at its present length, which he considered a very bad idea. He asked her to cut it in half. She refused and took it back. James T. Fields evaded the length question by saying that it was a good book but he couldn't publish it just then. Louisa returned to Concord very dispirited.

The news from the Hawthornes was bad. Nathaniel was growing grayer and weaker by the minute. In the winter he had taken a trip with Fields's partner, the somber William Ticknor. Ticknor's health deteriorated rapidly before Hawthorne's uncomprehending eyes. He suddenly died on April 10 in Philadelphia. Hawthorne was in an anxious, excitable state. For many months he had been afraid he was losing his mind, and Ticknor's death was a fearful blow. He came home again only to set off for Vermont with his old friend Franklin Pierce. On May 19, Hawthorne died.

Pierce brought Hawthorne's body to Concord. Julian came home from Harvard and heard Lydian Emerson refer to him several times as the "young head" of the house. It rained all that week. Julian, a pudgy adolescent, suggested that the family not look at the body. So they avoided the coffin while friends and neighbors came to view the corpse.

The morning after she heard the news, Louisa climbed the hill behind the houses to gather a bunch of violets from the ground Hawthorne loved to walk. She left them with Sophia, who wrote her a note of thanks. Louisa wrote, "We did all we could to heal the breach between the families but they held off, so we let things rest." Louisa helped decorate the church for the funeral. Many of Boston's most distinguished intellectuals came to see Hawthorne buried along with half of his unfinished manuscript. Louisa thought the whole proceeding extremely peculiar.

After the funeral, Louisa and her father went to Boston to a festival sponsored by the Twenty-Eighth Congregational Society.

Boston was greatly changed by the war. The Common, which was used for a recruiting center, was also the mustering-out spot and was always thronged with blue-uniformed men. There were gun salutes whenever the news was good, after Shiloh in April 1862, after Gettysburg and Vicksburg in 1863. Stores closed and spontaneous processions took place. At musterings-out, the Common malls were covered with tables of food and women waiting for their husbands, brothers, and sons. When the draft had gone into effect the previous year, women had begun rioting in the North End, and the violence spilled into the market area.

Louisa had a fine time at the Fraternity Festival, was complimented, "set up among the great ones, stared at, waited upon . . . I liked it but think a small dose quite as much as is good for me, for after sitting in a corner, and grubbing à la Cinderella it rather turns one's head to be taken out and treated like a princess all of a sudden." Bronson was proud of her and reported to his wife that one woman came up to them and said, "Mr. Alcott is a great man, but his daughter Miss Louisa is greater." "Indeed," continued Bronson, "every where I am coming into importance in these old years, through that rising young lady: people here speaking with enthusiasm of her Genius. — 'The Father of Miss Alcott' honored as never before." All of this both tickled and horrified Louisa. She had no judgment about her own worth, alternatively thinking she was the lowest form of life or the greatest martyr. The only terms she used were moral and characterological, which left her with no neutral vocabulary. She couldn't estimate her talents objectively. Nor did her abilities in any way alter her concept of herself as a bad woman. She was less interested in her skill than in what it produced. She wanted to be loved like Anna, and anything other than that seemed irrelevant, if not idle and worthless flattery.

May had found a patron in Bronson's friend Mrs. Mary Stearns of Medford, Massachusetts. She sent May flowers and offered to pay for her to study art with the German artist and anatomist Dr. Rimmer, in Boston. Louisa lamented: "She is a fortunate girl and always finds someone to help her as she wants to be helped. Wish I could do the same, but suppose as I never do that it is best for me to work and wait and do all for myself." Sanborn had observed that of all the girls, May was the most like her father in having "the

talent for society, and the taste for it which her sisters lacked
..." May was the least influenced by Abba's suspicions and discontents. She took advantage of what people offered and liked them for their generosity. Louisa could only see dependence and misery in the gifts of others.

In July, Louisa nursed a dying Sewall cousin, but managed to leave in August for Gloucester with May. There were dances, picnics, and charades, which she was well and relaxed enough to enjoy: "One mild moonlit night a party of ours camped out . . . and had a splendid time lying on the rocks singing, talking, sleeping and rioting up and down. We had a fine time and took coffee at all hours. The moon rose and set beautifully, and the sunrise was a picture I shall never forget."

In September, Caroline Dall, Abba's friend and patroness of all charities, showed *Moods* to her friend, the sanctimonious publisher A. K. Loring. He liked it very much, but wanted considerable cutting done. He wrote Louisa an evangelical letter, a form of holy pep talk, in which he confessed to being "no scholar" but possessed of some strong feelings about the story. He advised her that concision was important, and that interesting as conversation and description were, they were often skipped over, "and it is folly to write what will be skipped." Loring wanted a story that would build interest until the end, leaving the reader "spell bound, enchanted and exhausted with the intensity with which it was written." To this end he urged her to throw herself completely into the book, which, he thought, suffered from too much head and not enough heart. *"It is in you, you have great powers,"* he told her; she could write "a *live burning* book. . . . 'There is no such word as fail' and you can do it," he concluded. Louisa was oppressed by his fiery enthusiasm and put the book away, grieved, planning to "never touch it again."

Instead, she sat down to write an A. M. Barnard thriller, "V.V., or Plots and Counterplots." The story was published in April of the following year by *The Flag of Our Union,* a Washington Street paper very similar to Frank Leslie's. Virginie Varens, a beautiful, petite, blonde dancer, "mercenary, vain and hollow hearted," had no feelings and tortured the many men who loved her. "I care nothing for lovers; they are false and vain, they annoy me, waste my time . . ." She keeps her chastity, not out of scruple, but to keep her men in their cages.

Virginie marries a nobleman, but is immediately widowed when her cousin-lover-guardian, jealous Victor, kills the young man. When next she surfaces, she is on the trail of her husband's cousin, a noble Scot, already engaged to another woman. Virginie courts his title and fortune.

The A. M. Barnard disguise allowed Louisa to indulge in her private passion for finery. No gray poplins and demure black silk for Virginie: "Her dress was of that vivid silvery green which is so ruinous to any but the purest complexion, so ravishing when worn by one whose bloom defies all hues. The skirt swept long behind her, and the Pompadour waist with its flowing sleeves, displayed a neck and arms of dazzling fairness, half concealed by a film of costly lace. No jewels but an antique opal ring, attached by a slender chain to a singular bracelet, or wide band of chased gold. A single deep-hued flower glowed on her bosom, and in that wonderful hair of hers a chaplet of delicate ferns seemed to gather back the cloud of curls, and encircle coil upon coil of glossy hair, that looked as if it burdened her small head." In Louisa's acknowledged stories her characters frequently deliver mincing little sermons on the vanity of dress, or the righteous joy of turning an old navy muslin apron into a becoming little shirtwaist.

Like Pauline, Virginie's power lies in not loving. She lets Victor fall all over her, "quite unmoved by the tender names showered upon her, the almost fierce affection that glowed in her companion's face. 'You are so cold, so treacherous,' he tells her. 'I have no faith in you, though I adore you, and shall until I die.'"

Virginie's punishment comes in allowing herself to love: "It was impossible to conceal it for when great passion for the first time possessed her heart, all her art was powerless against the touch of nature, and no timid girl could have been more harassed by the alternations of hope and fear, and the effort to hide her passion." She beguiles the Scot away from his fiancée. She almost ensnares him, but his fiancée kills herself and the lord finds out about Virginie's involvement with his cousin's murder. In the end, Virginie is offered a life of captivity in a lonely castle, but prefers to take poison from a ring with a secret chamber, knowing that "submission and repentance" were "not in her nature to give."

Defiant to the last, Louisa's fantasy woman goes unchastened to her death. Unlike Pauline, Virginie's evil has no immediate cause. She is callous and deceitful by caprice. Death pains her less than the denial of her love. The strength of this feeling, once aroused, is Virginie's undoing. Louisa's concept of love was that it needed repression or its furious magnitude would sweep its helpless victim away. Virginie survived only as long as she kept herself from loving. When Louisa had finished "V.V.," she suddenly solved the problem with *Moods.* Virginie's downfall from her own grand passion and the retribution she suffers for loving wickedly reappear in the more acceptable form in the novel: "The whole plan laid itself smoothly out before me and I slept no more that night but worked as busily as if mind and body had nothing to do with one another. Up early and began to write it all over again. The fit was on strong and for a fortnight I hardly ate, slept, or stirred but wrote like a thinking machine in full operation." She cut the book by ten chapters, and although she removed several of her favorite sections, she thought she'd made it a more compact, stronger story.

She sent it off to Loring, who thought she'd done nobly. He objected to a reference to a character reading *Leaves of Grass,* which he thought "a vulgar disgusting conglomeration of words" that appealed to "those of depraved and licentious tastes." Otherwise he wanted it as it was. The family had a celebration.

Louisa executed Loring's desires as quickly as she could despite toothache, pains, and depression, Loring read proof with Mrs. Dall. He offered Louisa a royalty of 10 cents and printed the book so fast that she was able to give Abba a copy on October 8, 1864, her sixty-fourth birthday. "To Mother," wrote Louisa, "my earliest patron, kindest critic, dearest reader I gratefully and appreciatively inscribe my first romance."

And romance it certainly is. *Moods* is an adult fiction about misunderstanding, misplaced love, disappointment, and redemption. It is Louisa's only serious attempt to deal with relations between men and women. It is unquestionably her most evocative and poignant story. Written out of a desire to express and explain herself, it had all the strengths and weaknesses of genuine passion and none of the written-to-order limitations and predictability of her juvenile stories. *Moods* is a flawed novel demonstrating remarkable insight, not just a facility for narration.

The opening inscription is Emerson's: "Life is a train of moods like a string of beads; and as we pass through them they prove to be many colored lenses, which paint the world their own hue, and each shows us only what lies in its own focus." Sylvia Yule, a young girl like Louisa in all respects, is the main character, a girl dominated by her moods. She is odd, a tomboy, frank, natural, sprightly, bright, sometimes rude, disappointed with herself and others for not being better. She tells her father despairingly: "I cannot be like others, and their friendships would not satisfy me. I don't try to be odd; I long to be quiet and satisfied, but I cannot; and when I do . . . wild things, it is not because I am thoughtless or idle, but because I am trying to be good and happy. The old ways fail, so I attempt new ones, hoping they will succeed; but they don't, and I still go looking and longing for happiness, yet always failing to find it, sometimes think I am a born disappointment."

Louisa attempts to explain Sylvia's difficulties by the moods that control her. These, in turn, are caused by her parents' unhappy marriage. From her mother she inherits "passion, imagination, and the fateful melancholy" of a woman who is not loved." Sylvia's mother died when the girl was very young, and Louisa muses on what benefits the girl might have had from a good mother who would have "divined the nameless needs, answered her vague desires, and through the medium of the most omnipotent affection given to humanity, have made her what she might have been." Instead, Sylvia got only a "ceaseless craving for affection . . ." By killing off Sylvia's mother, Louisa protected Abba from the need to read herself into the book. On the other hand, the message is that Abba might as well have died for all the good it did Louisa.

All family troubles derive from the conflict between mother and father. Sylvia's brother Mark is a disappointment as an artist, his conviction and strength sacrificed to family strife: "He loved art and gave himself to it; but though studying all forms of beauty he never reached its soul, and every effort tantalized him with fresh glimpses of the fair ideal which he could not reach." The family always said that May and Louisa had talents but no genius. As for Sylvia's older sister, Prudence, a fussy, nervous, unimaginative woman, she was nothing but her father's "practical tact and talent . . . She seemed the living representative of the years spent in strife for profit, power, and place; the petty cares that fret the soul, the mercenary schemes that waste a life, the worldly formalities, frivolities and fears that so belittle character." Prudence was an "overactive, overanxious, affectionate but most prosaic child."

Anna was worried and dull, a "humdrum" by her own description.

According to Louisa's metaphysic, Sylvia's unstable behavior stemmed from the poisonous seepage from a loveless marriage: "As if indignant Nature rebelled against the outrage done her holiest ties, adverse temperaments gifted the child with the good and ill of each." The unhappy blend of mother and father causes all ensuing troubles. Louisa's psychological insight sometimes surpassed her artistic reach. Knowing the roots of Sylvia's troubles, she tries to use the girl's moods as a leitmotif. In fact, Sylvia demonstrates great stability while talking about her moods. She doesn't act capricious or bedeviled. Her moods aren't arbitrary, but comprehensible responses to her upbringing and environment. Louisa's emphasis on moods seems a twofold effort to let her parents off the hook and to assign arbitrariness to complex behavior.

The story opens in earnest when Mark introduces Sylvia to first one and then another of his friends. Geoffrey Moor is a gentle, sweet man, "womanly," kind and good-tempered. Sylvia intrigues him and he enjoys spending time with her. She responds to his warmth and interest, likes him very well, and wishes to be his friend. Mark then introduces her to his dear friend Adam Warwick. He "was a head taller than his tall friend, broad shouldered, strong limbed, and bronzed by wind and weather. A massive head covered with rings of ruddy brown hair, gray eyes, that seemed to pierce through all disguises, an imminent nose . . . Power, intellect, and courage were stamped on face and figure, making him the manliest man that Sylvia had ever seen." The description is of Thoreau. Sylvia asks her brother about his exciting friend's character. "Violently virtuous," replies Mark. "He is a masterful soul, bent on living out his beliefs and aspirations at any cost. Much given to denunciation of wrong-doing everywhere, and eager to execute justice upon all offenders high or low. Yet he possesses great nobility of character, great audacity of mind, and leads a life of the sternest integrity." Mark tells her that Warwick's profession is studying the world, "as we do books; dives into everything, analyzes character and builds up his own with materials which will last. If that's not genius it's something better."

Sylvia conceives a grand passion for Adam. He represents principled greatness and love of a higher order than she feels for

Geoffrey. She considers Adam a being "with much alloy and many flaws; but beneath all defects the Master's eye saw the grand lines that were to serve as models for the perfect man." He is obsessed with his interior progress, a restless spirit for whom people "are but animated facts or ideas; he seizes, searches, uses them, and when they have no more for him, drops them like the husk, whose kernel he has secured."

Sylvia does not immediately understand the differences between love and friendship. Geoffrey begins to love her, and while she wants him for a friend, she yearns romantically for Adam, who has gone away. She hears news that leads her to believe that Adam has married, despite her half-conviction that he loves her. After several months of loneliness and sorrow, she convinces herself that what she feels for Geoffrey is love and agrees to marry him. Her fondness for Geoffrey makes her believe she can make him happy. His devotion to her is so seductive that she gives in to her great need for love without understanding herself fully: "Sylvia had not learned to reason yet; she could only feel, because, owing to the unusual development of her divided nature, her heart grew faster than the intellect. Instinct was her surest guide, and when she followed it unblinded by a passion, unthwarted by a mood, she prospered. But now she was so blinded and so thwarted, and now her great temptation came. Ambition, man's idol, had tempted the father; love, woman's God, tempted the daughter . . ." Sylvia likes Geoffrey, but she does not love him. It is a grave sin to marry without feeling complete, profound, and overwhelming passion. Her perfidy, the result of her confusion, does great damage to both Geoffrey and herself.

It is not a coincidence that Louisa began working on *Moods* shortly after Anna married John Pratt. John has much in common with Geoffrey, his "womanliness," his unexceptional character, his quiet devotion, his lack of distinction. Louisa herself made cryptic journal entries about her own suitors in this period, who must have fallen into the John Pratt category. Louisa considered the kind of marriage Anna made a crime against nature, and although she immortalized boring young love in Meg's cottage in *Little Women*, such a life was not for her.

Love for Louisa was too engulfing to be experienced. It was complete, blinding, and consuming. It held the promise of perfect blending, the end of struggle and separateness, total peace, and, finally, oblivion. Her needs, identical to Sylvia's, came from disappointments and cravings too great to be filled except in dreams. Rugged, angry, hungry Henry Thoreau's unapproachableness fueled Louisa's longings. Henry's idealistic misogyny was paralleled by Louisa's idealistic disappointment in men. Like Emerson and her father, Henry offered principles without affection, morals without involvement or warmth. And he was sexually attractive to her, stirring up in her buried feelings, doubts, and yearnings. The self-doubt he engendered in her stirred up her earliest childhood disappointments, and she called this unfulfillable grief love.

In the novel, Adam returns to marry Sylvia, only to find her married to his friend. They have a tormented discussion in which Sylvia reveals to herself and him that it is he she loves. She blames her heinous mistake on her unstable temperament, a condition like mumps or shingles that should, she sees, quarantine her from human contact. Her unpredictability and weakness sicken her.

She learns from the powerful feelings Adam's return had produced in her that she must renounce both men. She is doing irreparable wrong to Geoffrey by vainly trying to be his lover. And Adam, she learns, is medicine too strong for her. She discusses him with a friend, who tells her that he "demands and unconsciously absorbs into himself the personality of others, making large returns, but of a kind which only those as strong, sagacious, and steadfast as himself can receive and adapt to their individual uses, without being overcome and possessed. That none of us should be except by the Spirit stronger than man, purer than woman. You feel, though you do not understand this power. You know that his presence excites, yet wearies you; that while you love, you fear him, and even when you long to be all to him, you doubt your ability to make his happiness." This speech is a fascinating insight into Louisa's understanding of passion and its capacity to unfit its victim for moral life. Only God should inspire awe; it has no place in healthy human relations. Sylvia must renounce the all-consuming obsession she feels for Adam, which, if acted upon, would rob her of identity and independence. Louisa saw it as giving up the man in order to quell the feeling. It is arguable that her emotional growth stopped because she couldn't give up her feeling in order to see the man.

Instead of renouncing the fantasy, Louisa renounces the lover and the husband as well. She looks forward to a single life in which she will make herself useful, devote herself to her father, Warwick, who says that "marriage is not the only aim and end of life," supporting her decision. And so Sylvia joins "that sisterhood called disappointed women; a larger class than many deem it to be . . . Unhappy wives, mistaken or forsaken lovers; meek souls, who make life long penance for the sins of others; gifted creatures kindled into fitful brilliance by some inward fire that consumes but cannot warm. These are the women who fly to convents, write bitter books, sing songs full of heartbreak, act splendidly the passion they have lost or never won. Who smile, and try to lead brave uncomplaining lives, but whose tragic eyes betray them, whose voices, however sweet or gay, contain an undertone of hopelessness, whose faces sometimes startle one with an expression which haunts the observer long after it is gone." This unexpectedly poignant passage exposes Louisa's loneliness and her efforts to hide it. It was a permanent condition and underlay the rest of her moods.

Sylvia finds that her renunciation brings her compensation and a graceful departure in a wasting death. She becomes wan but "truly beautiful . . . as the inward change made itself manifest in an indescribable expression of meekness and strength. With suffering came submission, with repentance came regeneration . . ." Sylvia didn't know how to live, but dying came naturally. "Those about her felt and owned the unconscious power, which we call the influence of character, and which is the noblest that gives sovereignty to man or woman."

Sylvia lives with and for her father until, as she is dying, she calls Geoffrey back and offers him her new, purified love. She makes amends for her false love by teaching him how to live with less vulnerability to his feelings. "Genius will be born of grief," she predicts, "and he will put his sorrow into song to touch and teach other hearts more gently than his own has been." Louisa paraphrases Emersonian compensation by inventing the law of the conservation of sacrifices. Sylvia's death gains meaning from the self-denial she has practiced, and this meaning will live on after her. Compensation gives order to what would otherwise be the wanton destruction of young life. Adam dies, too, saving Geoffrey's life. So both lovers atone to the wronged man. Both die for the temerity of loving unwisely.

Much of the poignancy of *Moods* derives from Louisa's all-out effort to thrust her unwilling life, kicking and protesting, into a serene, transcendental schema. Inside the framework of compensation, Sylvia's death becomes a contribution to the battle against moral entropy. The complexity of the characters and the love story rise up in protest against the inflexibility of the ethical structure. And although the characters lie down and take their punishments, submitting to the adolescent simplifications of Victorian black and white, there remains a provocative tension between their rich intricacy and the rigidity of their roles and fates.

This unease makes the novel fascinating and difficult to categorize. Louisa had great courage to write a morally questioning story. But it seemed to have taken her in a direction she couldn't bear to follow. It appears that she grew afraid of what she had attempted and retrenched into works of predictable morality and mechanical observance of transcendental tenets.

Moods registers a quiet complaint against the restraints imposed on active women. Sylvia envies her brother his liberty, longs for the freedom of Adam. These men, like her father and Emerson, preached self-denial and renunciation, submission and patience. But they never had to practice their philosophy. The Alcott women bent to Bronson's will. Louisa struggled to hunch herself up into the meek, undesiring stance of womanhood. It is not surprising that she convinced herself that Thoreau would dominate her as surely as her father. Nor is it surprising that she could not reconcile herself to the further deformity acting on this love would cause her. Thoreau, who was even more frightened than Louisa of the crippling effects he predicted from love, had hidden out years before. Louisa fled deeper into the bushy thicket of her family. Louisa, who misread Thoreau's isolation for overwhelming strength and independence, chose the same defensive-defiant posture. She didn't understand that real independence wasn't shaken by contact with people.

When Louisa saw the proofs of the book she grew afraid that she had attempted too much and failed: "But Emerson says 'that what is true from your own private heart is true for others' so I wrote it from my own life and experience and hope it may suit some and at least do no harm." Later, when fiery feelings of exposure and shame about the book had consumed her rational assessment of and fondness for it, she crossed out "life and experience" and substituted "inner consciousness and observation."

Louisa received ten copies of *Moods* on Christmas Eve and was very pleased with Loring's job. She was excited all week seeing people buying the book, reading it, and talking about it. The praise made her "glad but not proud, I think, for it had always seemed as if *Moods* grew in spite of me, and that I had little to do with it — except to put into words thoughts that would not let me rest until I had. Don't know why."

The first edition sold out in a week. Louisa sent one of her copies to Henry James, Sr., and gave another to her mother on Christmas. Abba was busily clipping Louisa's reviews and advertisements. To her, Louisa wrote: "Now if it makes a little money and opens the way for more I shall be satisfied and you in some measure repaid for all the sympathy, help and love that have done so much for me all these hard years.

"I hope success will sweeten me and make me what I long to become more than a great writer, a good daughter." Louisa continued to feel in a state of becoming with her mother. She was guilty, uneasy, and incomplete in relation to Abba. The role of daughter was her lifelong emotional focus rather than one of many aspects of life. Abba, critic and martyr, held on, nor could Louisa step back from her bullying, badgering, loving, protective mother.

Soon the critical reviews began coming in. She found herself accused of various heresies including free love and spiritualism. She began to think perhaps she had tackled too much, but wrote in her own defense: "Self-abnegation is a noble thing but I think there is a limit to it; and though in a few rare cases it may work well yet half the misery of the world seems to come from unmated pairs trying to live their lives decorously to the end, and bringing children into the world to inherit the unhappiness and discord out of which they were born. There is discipline enough in the most perfect marriage and I don't agree to the doctrine of 'marry in haste and repent at leisure' which seems to prevail. I honor it too much not to want to see it all it should be and to try to help others to prepare for it that they may find it life's best lesson — not its heaviest burden." She did wish she had "done better justice to my own idea."

Young Henry James gave Louisa a condescending review, advising her to write about what she knew. Henry James, Sr., was more enthusiastic, and when he ran into Bronson on the street, he mentioned that his whole family was readings *Dumps*. *"Dumps?"* asked Bronson. "Yes, *Dumps,* your daughter's novel." Louisa dined with the Jameses, by which time they seemed to have learned the title of her book. She was treated, she said "like the Queen of Sheba."

Theodore Parker's widow loved the book: "I felt the truth and beauty of all you said, and wished that all young people would learn from it, what love holy love was, and what an utter desecration of God's most beautiful gift it was, to live long years of married life without the love which really makes the marriage." Mrs. Parker urged Louisa to come and visit the shrine she kept to her husband. She could sit in his chair and look at his shoes. She hoped Louisa would come and think of the man who might have "strengthened you for the hard duties of life, and brought sunshine where else would be darkness."

The reviews continued not good. And the book didn't sell as well as Louisa had hoped. She was hurt and became defensive: "I seem to have been playing with edge tools without knowing it. The relations between Warwick, Moor and Sylvia are pronounced impossible, yet a case of the sort exists in Concord and the woman came and asked me how I knew it . . . It was meant to show a life affected by *mood,* not a discussion of marriage which I know little about except observing that very few are happy ones."

Louisa started writing *Work* but dropped it, feeling burned by her experience with *Moods.* Instead she began on her "rubbishy tales for they pay the best." Her February 1865 effort for the *Flag of Our Union* was a novelette called "A Marble Woman, or The Mysterious Model."

"The Marble Woman" is about an orphan girl whose dying mother sends her to live with a mysterious, bearded artist. Having once loved the girl's mother and been rejected, the handsome recluse decides to keep the girl locked up and emotionless, so she will never feel or suffer. She becomes a marblelike beauty who takes opium to keep her feelings still. She loves her guardian, and they marry, but it is a marriage in name only, made to protect the girl's reputation. Meanwhile, a charming, dying man frequents their house and presumes on his ambiguous relation with the artist. He forms a close attachment with the young bride, who fosters it to make her husband jealous. She succeeds, and in the end their marriage comes to life. The stranger, it turns out, is her father, a reformed convict.

The girl has no mother but two fathers. Motherlessness, a common state in Louisa's stories, gives the girl the chance to love freely not one, but two men. She marries her guardian and her natural father flirts, flatters, and romances her.

The story illustrates the moral, redemptive quality of woman's love. The innocent girl's regard for her guardian gradually warms him up. And the girl's dying father tells her how knowing her love has changed him from a worthless renegade to the tamed man she sees. Woman's love can both purify and generate more love.

At the end of "The Marble Woman," husband and wife wake up emotionally and sexually to each other over the corpse of the girl's father. It seems as if adult love could only occur for Louisa when the family was disposed of.

"The Marble Woman" pounds away again at the theme of an orphan girl retrieving her father's love. The story seems a regression for Louisa, as if the criticism she received about *Moods* sent her back to an earlier stage, demanding reresolution of old conflicts. Once again she works arduously to regain the affection of a cold, distant, older man, thawing him out to reassure herself after discussing her more adult desires publicly in *Moods.*

The story brought Louisa $75, with which she bought firewood, coal, food, and clothing for the family. She took Frank Leslie up on his offer to contribute a column to his paper, entitled "The Chimney Corner," if he agreed to pay on receipt of her work. She was angry with the *Atlantic*'s policy of keeping stories for years without payment.

On April 3, 1865, Richmond fell. Boston celebrated with gun salutes and impromptu parades. The rejoicing and relief only lasted a fortnight, however, before the news of Lincoln's assassination on April 19 put the city into mourning. Bands played dirges, black crepe hung everywhere, and bells tolled. Louisa was glad to have watched the two great events convulse the city: "Saw the great procession and though few colored men were in it one was walking arm in arm with a white gentleman and I exalted thereat."

Louisa kept to herself in Concord that spring. She sewed clothes for Anna's new baby, expected in June. Privacy suddenly became a major concern to her, as visitors began wanting to meet the author. "Admire the books but let the woman alone, if you please, dear public," she wrote in her journal.

Abba went to Anna's in early June, followed by Louisa. Cousin Lucy Sewall acted as midwife and Louisa ran the house. Anna's second boy, John, was born on June 24, 1865, Lizzie's birthday.

While she was keeping house for Anna, Louisa got an offer from Mr. William Weld to accompany his invalid daughter Anna to Europe. On balance, the Welds were more impressed with Louisa's nursing experience than bothered by her lack of foreign languages. Louisa was ecstatic. She had dreamed of going to Europe since childhood and never expected to have the money.

She made quick preparations during the first two weeks in July, leaving Concord on the eighteenth. Bronson wrote that they would miss her "activity and her money, she having contributed largely of her means derived from writing to the payment of family debts, and gladly will more as her ability shall allow. A serving visit will be of great profit to her, and bring spoils for future literary labor."

Europe and *Little Women*

LOUISA SAILED ON THE *China* on July 20, 1865, with Anna Minot Weld and her brother George, a young man on his grand tour. Cunard's first iron-screw steamer, replacing the old paddlers, was a sleek, three-masted ship built on sailing lines, with a smokestack in the middle. It had a top speed of 14 knots and accommodations for 160 first-class passengers at $125 per ticket. Often the ship would take 80 passengers to Europe and crowd almost 800 into steerage on the way back.

Anna Weld was a fretful invalid whose interests were confined to flowers and backgammon. Louisa spent the nine-day crossing bored and uneasy in the stomach, confining herself to the ladies' lounge. She didn't begin to enjoy herself until they had left rainy London to travel through the soft, green English countryside to Dover. There was a hiatus in her pleasure during the crossing to Ostend, when she was very sick. The three traveled to Brussels and on to Cologne, which Louisa found "hot, dirty and evil smelling." She bought some eau de cologne and "very gladly left after three days spent by me nursing both my companions who gave out here."

Louisa and Anna left George behind to take a boat journey down the Rhine. Anna, however, couldn't bear the motion and closeness of the boat, and the women persuaded the captain to let them off. They proceeded overland to Schwabach, a small town between steep hills in Bavaria where Anna arranged to take a water cure. A collection of ancient houses clustered on thin, twisting alleys lay below the springs. The newer resort section, with bathhouses and plush hotels on meticulously tended lawns, surrounded the springs above.

Anna improved with rest and quiet. Louisa found she had little in common with her ward and didn't much like her, judging her frivolous and self-indulgent. Louisa tried to do her job, "but don't think I did so very well, yet many would have done still worse I fancy, for hers is a very hard case to manage and needs the patience and wisdom of an angel." Louisa took drives with Anna and tried to study French with no discernible success. Otherwise she "worried a good deal" about her charge. She spent a restless September, wanting to travel. At night, after Anna was asleep, Louisa would sit in her window looking over the magnificent hills and picturesque village. She let her responsibility toward Anna, and the inferior position she thought it placed her in, so suppress her that she could only steal late-night satisfactions from the new experience.

On the twentieth of September Louisa heard from her family, who were constantly on her mind: "It touched me and pleased me very much to see how they missed me, thought of me, and longed to have me back. Every little thing I ever did for them is now so tenderly and gratefully remembered, and my absence seems to have left so large a gap that I begin to realize how much I am to them in spite of all my faults."

A week later, George Weld arrived to take the women to Vevey in the Swiss Alps. Between Lausanne and Montreux, Vevey is a spectacular spot under the mountains on the north side of clear Lac Leman. After the shock of the glorious scenery dissipated, Louisa grew "very tired of the daily worry which I had to go through with." Nevertheless, Anna did improve and that provided Louisa with some satisfaction.

In November a group of interesting new guests arrived to enliven things at Pension Victoria, where Anna and Louisa were boarding. The women made friends with a Russian couple and a young Polish man. Ladislas Wisniewski, pronounced, Louisa explained, by performing "two hiccoughs and a sneeze," was a tall, thin, delicate eighteen-year-old. He shivered and coughed his way through his first dinner at the pension. Louisa, weak at the knees at so much adolescent suffering, changed places with him to get him out of the draft and next to the stove that had been warming her. In charmingly imperfect English he told Louisa that he had fought in the Polish rebellion against Russian in 1863, for which he had been imprisoned. Many of his friends had been lost. His health and fortune were gone. His parents had forced him to come to Vevey to separate him from a young woman he loved. All this, complete with coughing and peculiar English, was too much for Louisa. She loved the romantic boy with his wild, colorful stories and jumped at the chance to trade French for English lessons.

Louisa got warm letters from Abba, congratulating her on "demonstrating the power of overcoming difficulties by cheerful acquiescence in fate and transmuting evil into good conditions, by preserving industry and wise adaptation of ways to means."

Louisa was finding her conditions less evil with the addition of Ladislas, who had become "Laddie" or "Varjo," which, he confided, his mother called him. He called Louisa a Polish diminutive meaning "little mamma." On her thirty-third birthday, Louisa reflected that she, for a change, although nothing "very pleasant happened . . . was happy and hopeful and enjoyed everything with unusual relish. I feel rather old with my 33 years but have much to keep me young, and hope I shall not grow older in heart as the time goes on." It was a gray, gusty day, with small clouds blowing into squalls and dissolving, like, Louisa thought, her temperament. Laddie played songs for her on the piano and promised her "the notes of the beautiful Polish National Hymn . . ." He wished her "all good and happiness on earth and a high place in Heaven . . ." Despite the distraction offered by the boy, she hoped to be home before another birthday came and went.

Louisa acted as duenna to the romance that grew up between Anna and Laddie. They took walks in the formal gardens and lawns and traded confidences by the lake. In later years Louisa edited her journal references to mask this flirtation. After the publication of *Little Women,* the public thirsted for information about Laurie, who was drawn in part from Ladislas. Louisa may have wished to preserve the illusion that she and Laddie had shared more than a mild friendship. And she probably wished to protect Anna's innocent secret. Biographers have speculated that there was a sexual relation between Louisa and Laddie, but this seems out of the question, given his attraction to Anna and Louisa's character, proclivities, general level of repression, and fear of men. Laddie was lively and young enough to excite and engage her without frightening her. She thought him "very interesting and good" and was quite happy to maintain a relationship based on language lessons and chat.

The women planned to spend the winter in Nice, and on December 6 they left for Geneva to meet George. Laddie accompanied them on the journey around the lake as far as Lausanne, where, tearful, he left them. "Sad times for L. and A.," wrote Louisa, later crossing out the initials and substituting "all."

Louisa took to Nice immediately. Every day she and Anna drove along the half-crescent bay with the lighthouse at either tip, looking at the luxurious hotels along one side and the beautiful flowered walk against the sea. The shops were full of delicate and exotic objects. Up the hills grew towers, castles, and walls in among olive, palm, and orange trees, punctuated with cacti. Louisa watched "monks, priests, soldiers, peasants" and the gaily-colored carriages of rich tourists. Her enthusiasm for the surroundings gave way to homesickness, and she found herself "very tired of doing nothing pleasant or interesting." She tried to teach herself French, but it was a bore without Laddie. Anna's invalidism was making Louisa cramped and grouchy. She longed for her freedom, some money, and friends.

Anna kept Louisa busy with her wishes all day long. She was unwell and worried about and forlorn for Laddie. In a partially scratched out pair of sentences, Louisa wrote that he was in a very "despairing state of mind. I could not advise them to be happy as they desired, so everything went wrong and both worried." On New Year's Day the women gloomily shared a bottle of champagne, drinking the health of everyone they could think of.

Louisa brooded about her situation. She was finding the air "too exciting" to sleep. Her temper was bad. Anna's condition changed very little. Louisa decided to go home in May, although Anna wished her to stay on. "I'm tired of it," she decided, "and as she is not going to travel my time is too valuable to be spent in fussing over cushions and carrying shawls. I'm rather fond of her but she wears upon me and we are best apart. With her sister and a servant she will be as easy as *she* can be anywhere."

By March Louisa was finding Nice "tedious" although it "might have been quite the reverse had I been free to enjoy it my own way." One day Louisa got a wheelchair and lured Anna out of her room to enjoy a roll through a villa swarming with roses. Louisa brought along a picnic lunch, some books, and French lessons. Anna enjoyed herself but made no effort to repeat the performance, and Louisa was tired of playing temptress. She was very glad when Anna's uncle arrived, freeing her to go to Paris.

Laddie met Louisa there and took her to her room on the rue de Rivoli. She indulged in a lighthearted two weeks. She went sightseeing with Laddie and his young Polish friends, who teased Louisa and persuaded her to call Laddie the Polish equivalent of "my darling," assuring her that it meant "my friend."

In the evenings Laddie played the piano for her in his rooming house and told her about his months in Warsaw since leaving Vevey. He made Paris accessible to Louisa through his agile French and spirited enjoyment of the exquisite city. They sat in cafés and went to the theater, Laddie making traveling everything it hadn't been with the headachy, complaining Anna. Louisa parted from her young friend with great sadness, treasuring the bottle of cologne he gave her and the memory of a rare channel of freedom between two continents of obligation.

On May 17, she left for several weeks in London, financed by some money Abba had provided. During her visit she met the romantic, fascinating Mazzini, who discussed the plight of the Poles, by then an immediate, personal concern to her. She met Dickens, who was one of her very favorite, if not her most favorite, novelist. He came as a deep disappointment. She considered him a dandy and disapproved of his diamond stickpin, ring, and studs. She loathed his false teeth and his thin, marcelled hair. She agreed with Richard Henry Dana, Jr., who couldn't stop thinking that the little man with the big eyes was "low-bred." Finally, after a trip to her London publisher, George Routledge and Sons, who gave her five pounds for the right to print *Moods*, on July 5, Louisa sailed on the *Africa*.

The *Africa* was Cunard's last wooden ship, introduced in 1850, an enormous coal-eater that made the trip to Boston in fourteen long, rough days. Louisa was sick the whole time and weak when she got off to greet the waiting John Pratt.

Bronson met her at the Concord station and took her home to Abba, who rushed about in all directions, weeping and giddy with

excitement. Louisa handed out presents : Stirling's *Secret of Hegel*
for her father and an album of pressed flowers from all the spots
she had visited for her mother. Bronson was delighted, noted that
Henry James, Sr., had reviewed the book recently, "an ill natured
if not ignorant critique . . . One can hardly trust him even on
themes he has studied the most."

Louisa heard about Edith Emerson's wedding to William Forbes
at which Mrs. Hawthorne came without mourning clothes and
Waldo wore white gloves, Elizabeth Peabody's Christmas visit
("the same sympathetic serviceable and knowing woman," observed Bronson), and Ellery Channing's calls evening after evening during Bronson's winter absence. The lonely poet sometimes
wrote verse at Bronson's desk and grew very close to Abba. He was
even more solitary since Thoreau's death. Anna, according to
Bronson, "seems to be almost the perfect mother, and her children
patterns of behavior, quiet without restraint and happy . . ." May
was working hard on her pencil drawings. Louisa heard that the
family had just fired a housekeeper, waiting to resume with Louisa
"the former order."

It was a Chekhovian homecoming. Abba was much weaker and
her eyes were failing rapidly. Anna was living in Concord and
wearing an ear trumpet. She wanted the company of her parents.
John, who worked in Boston, came home to his wife and boys on
Sundays. The house needed considerable attention, despite
Louisa's efforts to foresee eventualities. There were many new
debts. It must have seemed to Louisa, as she sat down to start
paying off bills, that a rain forest of obligations had sprung up
around Orchard House, and she had to go out alone again with her
machete to try to hack it back.

After Louisa's hasty decampment, Anna Weld's father was reluctant to pay Louisa's wages. But John was dispatched to extract the
$300 she was owed. "Glad to be done with service of this sort,"
wrote Louisa, sitting down to write "Behind a Mask" for Frank
Leslie. It was done on August 5, 1866, and earned $65.

"Behind a Mask" is a complicated intrigue featuring Jean Muir,
an accomplished actress and schemer who subdues an entire family with her wiles and coolly walks off with the oldest and richest
for her husband. The evening of Jean's arrival as governess in a
wealthy family, she retires to her room, takes off her false braids,

removes a number of teeth, and "slipping off her dress appeared herself indeed, a haggard, worn and moody woman of thirty at least . . ." She pours a stiff drink and remarks that at last she can be herself "if actresses ever are themselves."

The tale is about Louisa's hiding places. At one point Jean says she is "old, ugly, bad and lost." Like Louisa, she parades goodness, talent, sweetness, selflessness, and affection before her public. Inside she is furious, a woman who counts slights and revenges them. Her mode, like that of other A. M. Barnard heroines, is overkill. In a hypersensitive state following her months in service to Anna Weld, Louisa's Jean notices every patronizing smile her position as governess evokes. The falseness of her position taints all her good feelings. She is constantly aware of her hot fury and her clenched jaw. This anger, which she cannot shake, is the reason she considers herself "bad and lost."

Jean Muir knows what she wants and has perfect command of herself and her disguises. She is a heartless seductress who coldly enchants. Jean's relations with men always operate on two planes, what is apparent to them and her real feelings of contempt and power. At one point the young lord asks her if she considers him the master in his house. " 'Yes,' and to the word she gave a sweet, submissive intonation which made it expressive of the respect, regard, and confidence which men find pleasantest when women feel and show it."

Jean plots to make all the men fall in love with her and then run off with the rich, old uncle who will protect her and make few emotional or sexual demands. She reveals this scheme to an actress friend. Together they form an informal vigilante committee to redress men's wrongs against poor women. Jean intends to share her husband's wealth with her friend. Conspiracy is a female trait.

When Jean's letters are found, revealing her perfidy, a young woman remarks, "A woman could not do it." Once again, Louisa created a female so villainous that she has transcended sex.

And again Louisa's artistry and psychology are at odds. Jean is, despite her despicable plans, a very sympathetic character. She is charitable, generous, interesting, intelligent, and human. She acts at times like a sweet Alcott girl, reproving the young lord for laziness: "It was a new experience, and the very novelty added to the effect. He saw his fault, regretted it, and admired the brave sincerity of the girl in telling him of it." And occasionally Louisa allows Jean to relax and forget her wickedness: "For now a soft color glowed in her cheeks, her eyes smiled shyly, and her lips no longer wore the firm look of one who forcibly repressed every emotion. A fresh, gentle, and charming woman she seemed . . ." This Jean is as real as the schemer. Louisa presented the bad Jean as the truth behind the good Jean. She couldn't integrate the two into a complex character and so forced a polarity on them, giving evil the upper hand.

Once more Louisa tried to push characters and feelings into a simple good-evil duality. She denied them their ambiguities, making the distance between right and wrong a dizzying fall rather than a muddy ditch. Even so, "Behind a Mask" is the most mature of Louisa's thrillers, displaying the most complexity of character. The heroine is the most human, her traits, good and bad, plausible and affecting.

The story served as a psychic release for Louisa, just returned from a year of near-freedom. Suddenly she had to slip into her old disguise. She was delighted to see her family, but was immediately caught again in the obligations and pressures that they meant for her. She felt their desire for her to be good Jean, and that demand made the bad Jean well up in her again.

In September, Abba became quite ill. Louisa nursed her day and night, only taking time to write a long story that James R. Elliott at the *Flag of Our Nation* had asked for. He wanted twenty-four chapters, and Louisa turned them out, 185 pages "besides work, sewing, nursing and company" in two weeks. Elliott, unfortunately, turned down "A Modern Mephistopheles," calling it too sensational. It was another fifteen years before it was reworked and published.

Abba continued to be sick all fall. Dr. Bartlett came frequently, and Louisa hired a woman to bathe Abba and give her rubdowns. She had lost all her hair and suddenly looked very old. Bronson thought Abba was worn down by anxiety about Anna, who was unwell. Louisa noted: "Nan and babies a great care, very hard times all round." She was still "very poorly" at the end of October, but could come downstairs for the first time. Louisa never expected to see her strong again, "but thank the Lord, she is still here though pale and weak, quiet and sad." She added: "Life has been so hard for her and she so brave, so glad to spend herself for others. Now we must live for her."

It was Abba's ill health more than any other feature of her homecoming that upset Louisa and made her feel sad, guilty, and jailed. Her mother slipped into senility and the self-absorption of illness, leaving Louisa with all the household and family responsibilities and no appreciation or help. It had been hard enough to try to live for her mother when Abba was a participant in the arrangement, but it was very trying when she was incapacitated and unresponsive.

Anna left in November to be with John in Boston for the winter. This was a relief to Louisa, providing her with more quiet to work. She felt "driven by the prospect of bills which must be paid." She urged herself to turn out two more stories for Frank Leslie. Bronson left for the West "to talk to the young philosophers. Hope they remember to pay the old one," she commented sardonically.

At Christmas she put together a package of presents for the Pratts. Anna and John sent back Longfellow's new book for her. "No one else thought of us," Louisa wrote, adding later: ("Seldom do. Out of sight etc.") Her depression increased with the news that Ticknor and Fields had lost her manuscript of fairy tales that they had engaged to publish. Bronson later secured a promise that the company would pay Louisa, based on the possible sale of 2500 copies of the lost book.

After Christmas Louisa's health gave way. Her exertions had been too great and activated the dormant mercury. She suffered agonizing rheumaticlike pains in her limbs and couldn't sleep. She was so weak and tortured that she couldn't accompany her mother to Boston for the operation she needed to restore her eyesight. Abba returned with half her sight regained, and Louisa began feeling strong enough to manage the house. She fired the housekeeper and tried to keep house and write. But she had underestimated her feebleness and had a frightening relapse. She could only sit in her darkened room and ache and tremble. Her head and eyes hurt. It wasn't until May 2, 1867, that she came down from her corner bedroom for the first time.

By June, Louisa was feeling well enough to write again, but she started slowly. Uncle Sam May came for a visit and gave both

Louisa and May $50 for summer money. Louisa spent $25 of hers on family bills and took the rest with her to Clark's Island for an August vacation.

On her return in September again Louisa faced the debts, which she dreaded "more than the devil." Thomas Niles, a former employee of James T. Fields and at that time a partner at Roberts Brothers Publishing Company, suggested she write a girls' book. She was also offered the job of contributing editor to *Merry's Museum,* a children's magazine that aimed to instruct, specialized in natural wonders, and included poems and stories. To try out her abilities in writing for children, Louisa wrote a story called "Living in an Omnibus" about a poor German family who did just that. The story ran in October and Louisa agreed to begin editing the magazine officially in January, for $500 a year.

Concord's narrowness and predictability oppressed Louisa. Abba's failing eyesight and Bronson's irregular health caused her too much worry to relax. She couldn't write without interruption and couldn't resist working herself to exhaustion over the bottomless hole of family needs. So she packed up her bed and desk and took a room on the top floor of 6 Hayward Place in downtown Boston, not far from the *Merry's Museum* offices on Washington Street.

Boston was showing the effects of growth. The population was close to 200,000, with more than 50,000 Irish. The year before, the legislature had given the city the authority to lay out more streets and widen the existing ones. "Night soil," or sewage, which had been collected in two-wheeled, one-horse carts and carted out to Brighton, was now dumped into the Back Bay from a sewer by the Public Garden. Tipcarts threw ashes and other refuse into the bay from the Mill Dam. The Back Bay, needless to say, was foul-smelling and repugnant. The mud flats adjacent to the Public Garden, extending below what is now Arlington Street, were being filled in and built on to house the city's expanding population. Already along Arlington Street there were fine sandstone houses and, beyond them, dignified brownstones along the newly laid out and landscaped Commonwealth Avenue. The Back Bay was ripe for development and lots sold slowly but steadily through the sixties and seventies, bringing revenue and a new tax base into the city.

In November, May began coming in from Concord to give drawing classes at Louisa's rooms. Louisa completed two mysteries that were so tame that she put her name to them. She also finished a story for *Merry's* about Nan, Lu, Beth, and May giving their breakfasts to poor neighbors. On her thirty-fifth birthday, Louisa considered herself happy, "though no presents for I was well and busy and had sent $140 home this month to make things comfortable."

Niles continued to press her about the girls' story. Bronson wrote to her in February 1868 that the publisher wanted to print both Alcotts. Niles had undertaken to print extracts from Bronson's diaries arranged under the signs of the zodiac. From Louisa, Niles wanted a 200-page story by September. "Now I suppose you will come home soon and write your story," Bronson suggested.

In May, Louisa moved home to begin *Little Women*. She worked at her small writing table, just big enough to fit over her knees, under her bedroom window.

Louisa wrote all day, never rewriting or rethinking a word. She wrote steadily and with concentration but with none of the enthusiasm or exhilaration that had characterized her work on *Moods*. The trees in front of her window grew from pale, translucent green to a rich summer color by the time she had finished on July 15. Niles thought the chapters of the first volume a little dull, and so did Louisa.

She left for a month's rest in Gloucester with May. When she returned she read proof of *Little Women*, worrying that the simple story, the kind of moral biography her father dreamed of, was boring. On September 30 she had copies of her small brown volume with gilt lettering: *Little Women: Meg, Jo, Beth and Amy, The Story of Their Lives. A Girls' Book.* May had illustrated the story, and reviewers complained about the uncertainty of her drawings, but they praised the book. Two thousand copies sold out very rapidly. Pale, verbose Niles was greatly encouraged and urged Louisa to begin the second part.

She rented a room on Brookline Street in the South End, where, on November 1, she started the second volume. She wrote a chapter a day, breaking off to go to Concord in December. Bronson was going west and Abba had decided to move in with Anna for the winter. As Bronson said so perceptively, "The mother and daughter are parts of one another, and cannot be separated long at a time." Louisa closed up the house and took rooms for herself and

May at the Bellevue Hotel on Beacon Street, near the State House.

The Bellevue, run by the Teutonic gymnast Dio Lewis, was a fortress against the pollutions of alcohol and impure food. The kitchen produced a carefully supervised diet and there was a Turkish bath in the basement. There Louisa received a $300 check from Niles and began to be glad that, at his urging, she had retained the copyright to *Little Women* rather than selling it for $1000.

On January 1, 1868, Louisa finished the second volume and took it to Niles. She immediately left the Bellevue for her old rooms on Chauncy Street, where she indulged the fatigue and illness the exertion had cost her. In addition to her usual low-grade discomforts, she had a bad cough and chills. She didn't have time to be sick, she wrote to her mother, adding: "It's clear that Minerva Moody is getting on in spite of many downfalls, and by the time she is a used up old lady of seventy or so she may finish her job, and see her family well off. A little late to enjoy much maybe; but I guess I shall turn in for my last long sleep with more content in spite of the mortal weariness than if I had folded my hands and been supported in elegant idleness, or gone to the devil in fits of despair because things moved too slowly."

On January 22, Louisa heard her father's talk on the historical views of Jesus at the newly formed Radical Club. Afterward there was a reunion of the antislavery forces at their festival: "All the old faces and many new ones. Glad I have lived in the time of this great movement, and known its heroes so well. Wartime suits me as I am a fighting *May*." Her entertainments otherwise were few that winter. She ate lonely squash pie dinners and sewed for Anna and the boys. Her main source of satisfaction was in sending money home, and when her checks didn't come she was bitter.

Despite her fatigue and aching head she took on more work. In the spring she began writing an advice column for young girls called "Happy Women," which included sketches of single women, doctors, teachers, and writers who made their lives models of purpose, self-denial, usefulness, and cheer. She posed spinsterhood as a positive alternative, "for liberty is a better husband than love to many of us." She was lonely, nevertheless, and thought Anna a very happy woman: "I sell *my* children and though they feed me, they don't love me as hers do." Still, she took pleasure in seeing her mother peaceful, sitting in her sunny room without worries, "and that is better than any fame to me."

When she was well enough, she amused herself in going to the theater and keeping track of the extraordinary new fashion, the bustle. Women had suddenly begun transforming their figures with breathlessly tight corsets. And they began walking differently to compensate for the deforming contraption. Over this they wore a horsehair or wire hoop skirt covered with a gored underskirt, which in turn was draped over and tied back tightly in the rear. Whatever kind of drapery went on in the back, the skirts were very tight across the hips. Dresses were usually in crepe, poplin, batiste, piqué, silk, lawn, or voile and had tight bodices with deep square or round necklines trimmed with lace or ruching. The well-dressed woman wore delicate Cromwell boots with front lacing, high heels, and broad square toes worn with fine lisle stockings. Louisa kept extremely well informed on the fashions around her on the theory of "know thy enemy." In subsequent books she took up arms against tight lacing and wobbly little heels.

To balance her guilty interest in clothes, she kept up with the suffrage movement, going to Radical Club meetings whenever possible, listening to Mrs. Julia Ward Howe's conservative feminism and comparing it to that of her father's more radical friends, Mrs. Elizabeth Stanton and Lucy Stone. She knew that at the November 19, 1868, presidential election in Vineland, New Jersey, 172 women, taking advantage of an old statute not specifically excluding them from the vote, cast their ballots. The pending passage of the Fourteenth Amendment caused a great furor among suffragists, some of whom, like Mrs. Stanton, refused to support giving blacks the vote without extending it to include women. Others, like Mrs. Howe, wanted to see blacks vote as quickly as possible and were willing to see the fight for women's suffrage as a much longer one. The ratification of the amendment in July 1868 left a women's movement impressed with the size of the educational task it still had to perform.

Since her nursing experience, Louisa had become deeply interested in women's expanding role in the medical profession. Her cousin Lucy Sewall, who had delivered Anna's second child, had become a doctor. Lucy's father, Samuel E. Sewall, was the director of Boston's Female Medical College from 1850 until 1856 and a trustee from 1856 till 1862. In July 1856, the famous Polish doctor Marie Zakrzewska had visited the Sewalls and excited Lucy's interest in medicine. With the help of men like Sewall and Dr. Henry

Ingersol Bowditch, son of the celebrated astronomer and navigator Nathaniel Bowditch, Boston was relatively more hospitable to women's medical education than most cities. Dr. Zakrzewska was able to found the New England Hospital for Women in Roxbury, and Lucy began her residency there in 1863.

Louisa and Lucy had a strong affection for each other. Each shared an interest in clothes and people and both suffered from chronic bad health. Lucy had a heart condition from which she died, at fifty-four, in 1890, two years after Louisa's death.

In March, Louisa, still unwell, went to Concord to organize her disheveled parents. Abba wished to move back from Anna's and Bronson was home from the West. Louisa opened Orchard House. She was more used up than she had anticipated: "Don't care much for myself, as rest is heavenly even with pain; but the family seems so panic-stricken and helpless when I break down that I try to keep the mill going . . . am afraid to get into a vortex lest I fall ill." To ward off this possibility she decided to take a summer trip with her cousins, Octavius Brooks Frothingham and his family, to their vacation house in Rivière du Loup in Canada. Frothingham was very interested in Louisa's father and his friends, and Louisa enjoyed her talks with him on the sunny galleries of the large house. She would wake up early and stay in bed reading and writing until a maid arrived with milk and crackers. Her room looked out over a croquet field and barn. After breakfast at nine o'clock, Louisa played with the children till dinner at one. After the meal she would take a drive with the Frothinghams in their calache or sit talking on a deck overlooking the lawns. Tea was served at seven o'clock, and the family sat watching the sun set across the busy, ship-filled, twenty-two-mile-wide St. Lawrence. After the children were asleep they lit candles, talking quietly until bedtime. Frothingham had just founded the Free Religious Association, an organization to which Emerson and Alcott belonged, which "proposed to remove all dividing lines and to unite all religious men in bonds of pure spirituality, each one being responsible for his own opinion alone, and in no degree affected in his relations with other associations." Louisa enjoyed her cousin's earnest company and his high-minded conversation.

From Rivière du Loup Louisa traveled south to Mount Desert, Maine, where she learned that Roberts Brothers had sold 23,000 copies of *Little Women*. On August 20, Louisa returned from Maine, a famous woman. Bronson was very pleased with her success: "It is an honor not anticipated for a daughter of mine to have won so wide a celebrity, and a greater honor that she takes these so modestly, unwilling to believe there is not something unreal in it all." Abba, the center shrine around which the little women worship, found the book a "perfect *success.*" She thought it a masterwork: "Power and grace combined — the transition from pathetic to humorous so refreshing — the scenic effect so well sustained."

Bronson began including Louisa among the characters on whom he discoursed during his conversations. Louisa found herself in the company of Margaret Fuller, Longfellow, Emerson, and Hawthorne. Although she protested against this publicity, her father persisted in discussing her: "I find I have a pretty dramatic story to tell of her childhood and youth, gaining in interest as she comes up into womanhood and literary note."

When Louisa returned from her vacation she found her mother very fragile: "I feel as if the decline had begun for her; and each year will add to the change which is going on, as time alters the energetic, enthusiastic home-mother into a gentle, feeble old woman, to be cherished so bravely with her many burdens." Abba knew that her health was not good, and wished she knew a way to arrange things for May and Bronson to leave her "more free." She felt after forty years of "care labor anxiety and poverty cheerfully born [she] deserved rest and competence." In November, taking her health into account, she decided to move to Anna's. "It is only since my impaired health and defective sight that I even considered *myself,*" wrote Abba; "my husband's comfort and the best interests of my family have always had my first consideration." The eerie similarity between Abba's martyred attitudes and Louisa's grew greater as age and illness deprived them more and more of perspective.

After installing her parents with Anna, Louisa took rooms at 43 Pinckney Street on Beacon Hill. On her thirty-seventh birthday she was alone and "writing hard." Her only present was a copy of Bronson's *Tablets*, just published by Roberts Brothers. Louisa's health was poor. Henry Bowditch, a doctor who straddled allopathic and homeopathic medicine, gave Louisa treatments of caustic on her windpipe to restore her voice. She felt ill and coughed and croaked through December. By the New Year she was happy, however, as even Beth's doctor had finally been paid. Roberts Brothers had sent her a royalty check for $8500 on *Little Women.* She was able to wipe out every obligation her family had ever incurred, "thank the Lord! — every penny that money can pay, — and now feel as if I could die in peace. My dream is beginning to come true; and if my head holds out I'll do all I once hoped to do."

Money had become the only motive Louisa would acknowledge. It was neutral — a universally comprehensible necessity, she thought. Going after it was practical, made sense, and betrayed no longings, no dreams. She couldn't be criticized for her writing if it was only a job. She was turning her one channel of self-expression into the chore of a menial. Thoreau's death, the criticism *Moods* had received, her illness, and her mother's decline all strengthened her defensive and melancholic tendencies. She saw her life as a series of installments to be paid against a debt her parents had incurred. She felt that she had fewer and fewer choices, as a woman and as a writer. With popularity, she ceded control over what she wrote. She gave up her pseudonymous gothics as unworthy of the author of *Little Women.* Her audience wanted more little women, and Louisa, rather than expose herself to possible displeasure, gave them what they asked for. Her writing rapidly lost its vitality and expansiveness as it became another extension of her entrapment.

17

Work

MAY AND LOUISA ENJOYED THEIR FREEDOM on Pinckney Street, but Louisa remained extremely sick. Her legs gave her searing pains, her head ached, and it was months before she recovered her voice. She slept only with the aid of opium and was worn thin and pale.

She and May talked of going to Europe. May's friend Alice Bartlett, a tall twenty-four-year-old woman who spoke both French and Italian, was planning a grand tour and wanted May to come along. Thirty-year-old May had dreamed of going to study art. She sketched in pencil and charcoal, decoratively and impressionistically, but without distinction. In Europe she was to find her real talent as a copyist. She made some fine reproductions of Turners and used her imitative skills to develop her own idiom in oils.

Louisa, meanwhile, thinking that if she were valuable enough to earn $2500 at Christmas from *Little Women,* it was inequitable for Roberts Brothers to allow her only a 10 per cent royalty, holding on to 90 per cent of the profits. Her family and friends urged her to take the matter up with Niles. Her publisher had learned his business practices from the sharp James T. Fields, who assured his authors that 10 per cent was the uppermost limit while paying some as much as 25 per cent. Niles, with craft learned from Fields, told Louisa that her estimate of herself as a "second class story teller is just the reason why you ought not to expect more . . . Surely you don't want an additional percentage on a failure," he wrote, suggesting that the about-to-be-published *An Old Fashioned Girl* would be a dismal flop. The book had an advance sale of 12,000 copies and quickly sold more than 30,000, turning Niles's warnings into shoddy stage effects. Niles lied to her flatly when he told her, knowing the contrary, that "no publisher can afford to pay a higher percentage than we now pay you." Other publishers, he went on confusingly, might appeal to her avarice and offer more. "But you, I am quite sure, *without ample reason,* would never desert those who both by their brains and their money have *helped* you to achieve the position you hold today." Louisa agreed to take her 10 per cent on *An Old-Fashioned Girl,* and it wasn't until the publication of *Little Men* that Niles upped the royalty slightly to 18 cents a copy on a $1.50 book — 12 per cent.

An Old-Fashioned Girl was published on April 2, 1870, the day after Louisa's departure for Europe. She recollected ruefully that she'd written it "with left hand aching, one foot up, head aching and no voice . . . as the book is funny, people will say, 'Didn't you enjoy it?' I certainly earn my living by the sweat of my brow."

Polly, the poor heroine of *An Old-Fashioned Girl,* decorated with old-fashioned virtues, comes to live at the house of wealthy friends. They are a discontented lot. The girl is frivolous and lazy, the boy unloved by self-indulgent parents. Polly teaches them all the lessons of love, patience, and cheerful obedience. She gradually changes their relations to one another and shifts the focus of the house to herself. It is a reversal on *Little Women,* yet contains the same simple philosophy and similar fights with selfishness, pride, and willfulness. Polly has to learn to accept poverty, and her adoptive family has to lose their money before their reform is quite carried out. Finally, Polly marries the young brother, who, with Polly's help, has found direction and energy.

As a sop to her mother, who, as she grew older, was more and more concerned with past glories of the May family, Louisa included a story in which the Mays and other relatives, the Hancocks and Quincys, appear to great advantage. She had heard Abba telling her grandsons "that I was the daughter and granddaughter of true patriots — men and women who loved and laboured, and many of them died in the service of their country and for true faithfulness to their principles of freedom and justice — may my dear grandsons never forget the pure nobility of their honored ancestry."

There is a feminist chapter in which a group of Polly's friends meet Kate King, author of a very popular book. Kate, "sick, tired and too early old," tells the women about the risks of popularity and implies that her success has cost her her health. They discuss the emerging woman, and hope she will be "strong-minded, strong-hearted, strong-souled, and strong-bodied . . . Strength and beauty must go together . . . broad shoulders can bear burdens without breaking down . . ." Polly's rich, spoiled friend meets these women and thinks, "Men must respect such girls as these . . . yes, and love them too, for in spite of their independence, they are womanly. I wish I had a talent to live for, if it would do as much for me as it does for them. It is this sort of thing that is improving Polly, that makes her society interesting . . . and her self so dear to everyone. Money can't buy these things for me, and I want them very much."

An Old-Fashioned Girl didn't have the success of *Little Women,* but it did very well. In July, Louisa received $6212, which Samuel Sewall invested immediately in railroad stocks. Bronson did Louisa's financial errands and took out of the interest what he and Abba needed. Sewall, the closest the Alcotts had to what Henry Adams would have called a State Street connection, invested conservatively over the next several years. Louisa's portfolio was a profitable one, heavily favoring railroads.

Bronson was beginning to realize a profit on his western tours. He was well known by now. He would talk for sixty minutes on various subjects, and one of his favorites was "Woman": "I conceive the ideal woman to be a person in whom the sentiments predominate over the intellect: the heart leading the head, the affections the reason; and wherever that combination appears, the type, externally, will be feminine. Every man in whom the affections sway the intellect, by ever so little, impresses us as a woman; is a woman, essentially, in his composition. Every soul in whom the intellect sways the sentiments is masculine, is essentially a man; nor without such discrimination can we comprehend the personality of man or woman." Another of his favorite topics was Louisa, a man according to his scheme. Bronson arrived home just before Louisa's departure: "My wife and Anna are surprised, as were the girls, at my unexpected success. It is something like a miracle for me to bring money and popularity both into my house."

Throughout March, May and Louisa made preparations for their trip. They sewed and packed trunks and on Friday, April 1, John

Pratt helped them on to the train for New York. He saw them aboard the French steamer the *Lafayette*. They cabled home their arrival and settled in.

Louisa stayed below for the ten-day passage, never going up to meals. In addition to seasickness, her head ached and her mind sped along anxiously, giving her no rest. The passage was cold, rainy, and very rough. May came below to share stories with Louisa of her adventures above. She wrote home that she had become the star of the dining salon. Louisa watched May's triumphs and reported that, as usual, everyone loved her, but that there were no flirtations since May wouldn't countenance the only available "fast New York men." The French food disagreed with May, who complained about "horrid soups." For a woman raised on cold water and apples, her digestion had never encountered much of a challenge until it was completely cowed by French cuisine.

Louisa was relieved when the boat docked at Brest. She, Alice, and May found their way east about thirty miles to Morlaix in Brittany, where May raved about every gable and spire. Alice and Louisa, more seasoned, enjoyed the sights at a less breathless pitch.

Louisa was more concerned with her health than with peasants or architecture. While May rushed about sketching everything, Louisa concentrated on the great pain in her legs. She and her companions traveled east slowly in Brittany to Dinan, where they took rooms at a pension run by stout, maternal Madame Coste. Louisa and May were dependent on Alice's French and had little contact with the other boarders. May learned quickly, however, and soon made friends with the concierge's son, Gaston. She and Alice took sightseeing trips on donkeys with him. Louisa stayed in her room before a hot wood fire, taking hot wine potions concocted by Madame. She watched the old town, set in a fruit tree–dotted valley. The buildings approached each other across slender streets. Louisa could smell the fragrances of fresh farm produce from her window and hear Gallic haggling at the open-air stalls of the market. When she felt well enough, she took walks up and down the steep, cobbled alleys, looking at the farmers and nuns and avoiding wagons of vegetables and droves of pigs.

One of Louisa's few satisfactions was in the cheapness of everything. She reveled in the small hotel bills, the gloves she bought for 60 cents, May's sun parasol for 40 cents. Since she eventually paid for everything, she felt justified in getting quite stern with her father for sending a letter with improper postage: "Pa's last letter had only two 2 cent stamps on it, and should have had 16 cents on it in stamps or pay 25 or 39 cents here. Do be smart and have things straight. I don't wish to fuss . . ." She went on fussing, but felt she had to be "as careful as I can, and after this shall send short letters and leave the stories till we come. May's doctor bill will be large I think so I must be careful, but it is necessary, and I gladly pay it." May's eyes gave her recurrent trouble and she had consulted a French doctor.

The Franco-Prussian War caught the travelers that summer and gave Louisa's worries some validity, but her financial concerns were more glandular than circumstantial. She begged her parents to stop sending her newspapers, since the postage was so high and they were a luxury she could do without.

Louisa remained in bed or in her chair while the cold rains of Brittany washed April away. She had plenty of time to brood on the news that Loring was reissuing *Moods*. She wrote home, indignantly telling them that she had asked him not to and that he'd promised he wouldn't: "I won't have it, for it is not *my Book*. I wish Papa would see if it can't be stopped." She wrote to Niles furiously, and with annoying paternalism he replied: "Why what a state of mind you were in to be sure — ." Thinking to tease her down off the ledge of her rage, he went on playfully: "Oh! we publishers, what wretches we are — but aren't you lucky to have *one* publisher who lets you do just as you like and is willing to publish without contracts." Niles explained that Loring thought more highly of the book than Louisa now did, and wished to make some money from what had begun unprofitably.

Bronson visited Niles to see what could be done, and Niles told him nothing. They chatted about June's heavy thundershowers, Concord's abundant strawberries, and how well May and Louisa sounded. Louisa ground her teeth. On June 1 she heard from Loring and wrote to her parents that she was "frothing. The *dreadful* man says that he has the *right to print as many editions as he likes for fourteen years!* What rights has an author, then I beg to know? and where does 'the Courtesy' of a publisher come in. He has sent me a book and if you hear I'm dead, you may know that a sight of the *pictures* slew me, for I expect to have fits when I behold Sylvia with a topknot, Moore with mutton chop whiskers and Adam in the inevitable checked trousers which all modern heroes wear. If the law gives over an author and her works to such slavery . . . I shall write no more books, but take in washing . . ." In June in Blois Louisa received a copy of *Moods;* she was, as she predicted, dismayed with the pictures and claimed to have ripped them out and thrown them into the Loire. The book she hid in the bottom of her trunk: "I couldn't read the story and try to forget that I ever wrote it."

In *Little Women* Louisa said she cut *Moods* to suit everyone but herself. She owned the product as a miserable failure, which she blamed on bad advice from everyone around her. This violent rejection came after the safety she'd found in the simplicity and childishness of *Little Women.* She'd taken no risks, moral or emotional, in her successful book. The ambiguities and revelations in *Moods* made her squirm and sweat, afraid she'd admitted to confusions, feelings, and hopes that she no longer wished to confront. She had stopped being willing to take responsibility for her articulated yearnings for love, her romantic love for Thoreau, and the complexity of her character as a sexual woman. The popularity of *Little Women* did much to convince her that her earlier groping toward complete womanhood was misguided, embarrassing, and even shameful.

As long as the cold weather continued, Louisa felt as sick as she had in Massachusetts. In the middle of May an English doctor, Kane, who had been in India and seen the effects of calomel, or mercury poisoning, before, began dosing her with iodine of potash, which seemed to give her some relief. The "handsome, hearty, grey haired" doctor also prescribed a sleeping draught, and Louisa improved rapidly. May and Alice teased her about the attentive bachelor. Louisa's spirits rose with her restored health and with Kane's kindness and concern. She found him extremely "jolly" and wrote that when he'd discovered she'd been an army nurse "that he should term it an honor to cure me."

With the Kane-induced rally and the warm weather, Louisa began walking again. He discussed mercury poisoning with her: "The bunches on my leg are owing to that, for the mercury lies round in a body and don't do much harm till a weak spot appears when it goes there and makes trouble. I don't know anything about it, only the leg is the curse of my life." Louisa started putting on weight, feeling rested and relaxed. She vigorously refused all offers to write.

She wrote to John Pratt, who was ill, about Kane's theories and medicines. She advised him to drink wine to warm his blood, wear long woolens, and take iodine of potash. John was feeble and lame; he had also taken the calomel cure.

In June the women traveled through Blois to Bex, near Vevey. They settled at the comfortable Hôtel des Bains, where Louisa was well enough to write "The Lay of the Golden Goose," a long verse story about her career as unexpected provider. She took long drives in the lovely Swiss countryside and read novels. May had a more social time, enjoying the other guests. But Louisa felt disapproving of such purposeless entertainment and yearned for "reformers or sages." Passionately American and deeply puritanical, she had no ability to spend time without a moral. She demanded "character and propriety" in her companions.

Without the flattery and distraction of Kane, she fell into a rather somber state. She was irritated to read papers from home in which she found gossip about herself. She knew her parents read her letters to anyone who would listen and reprimanded them, "for I hate to write if Tom, Dick and Harry are to see 'em." As for the anonymous journalists, "I should like to knock their heads off for meddling with what don't concern them old tattletails!"

While the women sat out the Franco-Prussian War in Switzerland, Louisa had a poignant dream, which she related to her mother. She had returned to Concord alone. No one met her at the station, and at home she found, not Orchard House, but "a great gray stone castle with towers and arches and lawns and bridges very fine and antique." She ran into a neighbor who didn't know her. She asked where his house was and he told her that he had sold it to Mr. Alcott, who had built a school. "Where did Mr. Alcott get the means to build this great concern?" asked Louisa. The neighbor told her it was partly his own land and partly the pasture his daughter had left him, "the one that died some ten years ago." "So I am dead, am I?" says I to myself, feeling so queerly. "Government helped build this place and Mr. A. has a fine college here," he went on. Louisa went to a mirror and saw that she was fat, with gray hair and spectacles, looking very much like Elizabeth Palmer Peabody. On the grounds she saw "hundreds of young men and boys in queer flowing dress running about the parks and lawns, and among them was Pa, looking as he looked thirty years ago, with brown hair and a big white neckcloth as in the old times. He looked so plump and pleased and young and happy, I was charmed to see him and nodded, but he didn't know me, and I was so grieved and troubled at being a Rip Van Winkle, I cried and said I had better go away and not disturb anyone, and in the midst of my woe, I woke up . . ." She told her mother that Bronson was welcome to her fortune, "but the daughter who did die ten years ago, is more likely to be the one who helped him build his school of Concord . . ."

The richly suggestive dream has familiar themes of disappointment, feeling overlooked, losing out to her father's boy students. The dream-Louisa sacrifices her life and fortune in return for her father's complete disregard of her. She implies that he preferred the dead Beth. Louisa sadly identifies with Elizabeth Peabody, the strong-minded reformer whom men occasionally admired but never loved. Bronson felt little affection for the eccentric, independent teacher. Louisa saw her as ridiculous and lonely, living vicariously through her married sisters. Bronson's attitude toward Miss Peabody wasn't utterly different from his attitude toward Louisa, to whom he was grateful, but for whom he didn't feel that special warmth that Anna and Beth had evoked. About ten years earlier Beth had died, Anna had married, and Louisa had written *Moods*. Around that time she had renounced her claims for herself, her own emotional needs, and her hope for a husband, and had defined herself as the sole support of her family. She told herself that she was living for them. By sacrificing her own life she had rejuvenated her father, who, in return, had turned his attention elsewhere.

In September the French surrendered and May and Louisa moved on to Italy. Louisa was not very well and felt more like going home than traveling, but she had promised herself a year's trip. After visiting Pisa and Florence, they moved to Rome to an apartment on the Piazza Barberini, overlooking Triton's fountain. Louisa wrote that May was studying water color: "She takes Rome very calmly and has raptures over but few of the famous things.

Her own tastes are so decided that the general opinion affects her very little, and we indulge in our naughty criticism like a pair of Goths and Vandals as we are." Louisa didn't care for Rome and felt oppressed by what she considered the decadence of the culture.

The American portraitist George Healy, who had just painted the pope, asked Louisa to sit for him. She was flattered and agreed. Bronson, always an idealist and never an artist, complained, on seeing the painting in Boston, that Healy had not "painted out the pains and weariness as became his art . . . The flesh is haggard and the features too elongated for a true lifelike likeness."

Word came from home that John Pratt had died on Louisa and Bronson's birthday. His symptoms were enough like Louisa's to suggest that his earlier calomel treatments may have killed him. Anna wrote that his last days were painless, "and not until a few hours before he left us did we realize it was to be so soon." The doctor told him that he was mortally ill and suggested that he make whatever arrangements he needed on Saturday. John's father came over, and John and Anna talked about the children and their home.

On Sunday "he lay calmly looking at the morning sunshine streaming across the room, occasionally turning his eyes upon my face as I sat beside him until at last with a gentle sigh he fell asleep. It was a heavenly deathbed, fitting for the pure and gentle soul that took its flight."

Louisa wrote her sister a revealing and loving letter, saying that John "did more to make me trust and respect men than anyone I know and with him I lose the one young man whom I sincerely honored in my heart." She continued that "no born brother was ever dearer, and each year I loved and respected and admired him more and more. His quiet integrity, his patient spirit, so cheerful and so persistent, his manly love of independence and his brave efforts to earn it for those he loved. Good son, brother, husband, father and friend. I think that record is a noble one for any man and his 37 quiet years are very precious to those who knew him."

Louisa's response to the news was predictable. She began work on *Little Men*, a sequel to *Little Women*, "that John's death may not leave Anna and the dear boys in want." In fact, as Louisa knew, John had saved carefully and provided for his family's comfort. Louisa's sacrifice was financially uncalled for, but her psyche demanded it: "In writing and thinking of the little lads to whom I must be a father now, I found comfort for my sorrow."

She worked steadily throughout the winter, finishing in February, when she decided to go home. The hateful Loring had sent her a check for $700 for the new edition of *Moods,* and she could count on $1000 from Niles against *Little Men.* The money would be enough to leave with May "so she may be happy and free to follow her talent." It had been, she thought, "a very pleasant year, in spite of constant pain, John's death and home anxieties."

In London, Thomas Niles's brother William met her and danced attention on the famous author. Louisa sailed on the *Malta,* leaving May to begin a flirtation with William Niles. Louisa shared her cabin with a woman who came down with smallpox, and she worried throughout the twelve-day crossing whether or not she would be infected.

By a special arrangement, Louisa didn't have to remain on the *Malta* when it anchored in Boston harbor, but instead took a small boat to Long Wharf. There she found Bronson and Thomas Niles carrying a banner reading LITTLE MEN. They all walked past the oyster boats tied along the wharf and took a hack to cousin Lizzie Wells's house on Beacon Hill.

The next day they went to Concord, which was very green and fragrant in May. Louisa thought her mother perilously old and promised herself that she would "never go far away from her again." Her own health continued to be very good and allowed her to enjoy the lovely spring month. Soon, however, she grew tired and ill. She took to her bed in early July, feeling as if the "year of travel was all lost." To add to her overall gloom, Uncle Sam May died suddenly on July 1. Abba was paralyzed with sorrow, and Louisa agreed with Bronson that he was "one of the best of men, who made life sweet wherever he was, and humanity precious." Bronson made the trip to Syracuse and, on July 6, spoke at the services for his brother-in-law, bringing back the account to his mourning wife.

Little Men began selling before publication and hasn't stopped. It is a sweet novel, although tired and mechanical. Like *Little Women,* it is a series of episodes rather than a sustained narrative. It takes place on Plumfield, a school run on Bronson's principles under the direction of Jo and her warm, furry German husband,

Professor Bhaer. The book is Louisa's public vindication of her father, in which she makes him and his theories accessible and famous. "Grandpa March," she wrote, "cultivated the little mind — not tasking it with long hard lessons, parrot-learned, but helping it to unfold as naturally and beautifully as sun and dew help roses bloom." Compared with the other characters, Grandpa March recedes colorlessly into the background. He has none of the funny quirks of the other characters, as if Louisa's affection for him was too untrustworthy to allow her to tease him. She praises him by praising the children he affects. Demi-John, Meg's boy, "was not a perfect child, by any means, but his faults were of the better sort; and being early taught the secret of self-control, he was not left at the mercy of appetites and passions, as some poor little mortals are, and then punished for yielding to the temptations against which they have no armor."

Like Grandpa March, Demi-John is not a lively or interesting character. The problems of good children, or peaceful, good people, didn't interest Louisa much. The affection in the book, of which there is a great deal, is largely directed toward Dan, the wild orphan who shows up, dirty, foul-mouthed, and troublesome. At one point Jo tells her husband that Dan "won't bear sternness nor much restraint, but a soft word and infinite patience will lead him as it used to lead me . . . I seem to know by instinct what he feels, to understand what will win and touch him, and to sympathize with his temptations and faults. I am glad I do, for it will help me to help him; and if I can make a good man of this wild boy, it will be the best work of my life." The headstrong boy appealed to Louisa and she saw herself in his turbulent behavior, his violence, and the anger and energy always just below his surface. She blames his disturbed spirit on having no parents, and gives him Jo as a motherly guide. She also gives him another Thoreau look-alike, a naturalist named Hyde who takes an interest in the boy and helps tame him. She and Thoreau cooperate on this bit of soul reclamation. When Dan gets sent away for almost burning down Plumfield, the scene is deeply affecting, quite a different order of involvement from the cheerful, predictable scenes featuring the good little girls and boys. Louisa understood and communicated youthful misunderstanding, loneliness, and pride.

Jo offers the students the love Louisa always craved: "For love is a flower that grows in any soil, works its sweet miracles undaunted by autumn frost or winter snow, blooming fair and fragrant all the year, and blessing those who give and those who receive."

The girls were of less interest to Louisa. Daisy, Demi's sister, is like Meg, a placid, calm girl who "knew nothing about women's rights; she quietly took all she wanted, and no one denied her claim, because she did not undertake what she could not carry out, but unconsciously used the all-powerful right of her own influence to win from others any privilege for which she had proved her fitness." An Anna-like girl, Daisy is content with her lot and has nothing to learn. Her trials are few because she attempts very little. Her cousin, the beautiful Goldilocks, is even more insipid and boring. She has breathtaking looks and unflawed manners, and sits around being horrified by dirt and activity. Only Nan, a tomboy who wants to be a doctor, gives Louisa and the reader any pleasure. She "attempted all sorts of things, undaunted by direful failures, and clamored fiercely to be allowed to do everything that the boys did. They laughed at her, hustled her out of the way, and protested against her meddling with their affairs. But she would not be quenched and she would be heard, for her will was strong, and she had the spirit of a rampant reformer. Mrs. Bhaer sympathized with her, but tried to curb her frantic desire for entire liberty by showing her that she must wait a little, learn self-control, and be ready to use her freedom before she asked for it."

The publication of *Little Men* seemed like an appropriate time to Niles, Bronson, and Louisa to reissue Alcott's *Record of a School,* on which Louisa said Plumfield was based. Elizabeth Peabody had transcribed the original manuscript and written the introduction, so Bronson had to consult with her about the new edition. She told Alcott that she wanted to write a new preface and "suggests revisions and additions which I rather unwillingly adopt." What she wrote was that she heartily approved of Plumfield, but she had grave doubts about the old Temple School, which was quite a different kind of place.

Louisa suggested that Elizabeth Peabody write a statement saying that the "little women" had been students at the Temple School, thereby interesting Louisa's fans in the *Record.* Elizabeth did not feel she could leave it at that, and insisted on her preface as she had written it. Niles refused to publish an introduction that condemned the school. Louisa thought Elizabeth might take "out the observations and let the book stand simply as a Record of the school without implicating her in the least it would be the best plan." Miss Peabody refused to be parted from her sentiments. Niles, Louisa, and Bronson tried to pressure her, but she remained firm. Alcott finally decided: "We decline having the book published with her qualifying statements." The squabble, settled in Bronson's favor, delayed the reissue until 1874. Louisa's opening statement on *Little Men* had to suffice for the time. "Not only," she wrote, "is it a duty and a pleasure, but there is a certain fitness in making the childish fiction of the daughter play the grateful part of herald to the wise and beautiful truths of the father: truths which for thirty years have been silently, hopefully living in the hearts and memories of the pupils who never have forgotten the influences of that time and teacher."

Louisa spent an invalid's summer. She made a trip to the shore, but the damp air did her no good, and she found no ease. Bronson worried about her, seeing a similarity between her state and Beth's so many years before. She suffered dizzy spells and strange debilitating periods that no one could diagnose or cure. In spite of her pain, she managed to give up the morphine she'd been taking since July.

Toward the end of July Emerson's house caught on fire. He discovered the fire between 5:00 and 6:00 A.M., when he saw flames coming down from the attic. Waldo's library and manuscripts were not destroyed, but his study and the drawing room were badly damaged and he was very upset by the incident. Louisa took some of his papers to Orchard House to dry out, and the family moved to the Old Manse until their home was repaired.

In the late summer, Louisa found two girls to take over the Concord housekeeping, and leaving "plenty of money go to Beacon Street to rest and try to get well that I may work." She moved on September 1, taking rooms at a boarding house near the State House. The family considered moving with Louisa, but she gently dissuaded them. Instead, Bronson wrote to May that she was needed at home.

That fall Niles published a collection, *Aunt Jo's Scrapbag*. *Little Women*'s sales were up to 82,000 and *Little Men* had sold 42,000.

At the end of November, May arrived to run what Louisa called "the machine." She was not overjoyed to be home, but was worried about her mother's health. Her own eyes were troubling her and she was glad to have Louisa's money and care ready at hand. She spent her first night at Louisa's in Boston before the two women went on to Concord.

They celebrated Louisa's birthday in Bronson's study with flowers before a hot fire. Abba sat in a big armchair and watched Louisa fuss over her pretty pile of presents.

Louisa supervised the installation of a furnace in the draughty Orchard House. She wanted "no more rheumatic fevers and colds with picturesque open fires. Mother is to be cosey if money can do it. She seems to be now, and my long cherished dream has come true; for she sits in a pleasant room, with no work, no care, no poverty to worry, but peace and comfort all about her, and children glad and able to stand between trouble and her." By the end of December the furnace was operating, and Bronson wondered "how we endured the last winters."

In January 1872 Louisa's health suddenly improved, and she had several months without her battery of miseries. She had time to work on *Shawl Straps,* a series of travel sketches she was writing for the *Christian Union.*

One contributing factor to her good spirits was the appearance every day for weeks of great bunches of roses from an anonymous source. Her Beacon Street rooms were a fragrant bower and Louisa's curiosity and vanity were piqued.

Another was Harriet Beecher Stowe's letter telling her how glad she was that Louisa was contributing to her brother Henry Ward Beecher's magazine, the *Christian Union:* "In my many fears for my country and in these days when so much seductive and dangerous literature is pushed forward, the success of your domestic works has been to me most comforting. It shows that after all our people are *all right* and that they love the right kind of thing."

Bronson, in the West, noted that it was "very pleasant to be admitted into homes to find a daughter's name a 'household word' — her books better known even than nearer home — her latest preceeding me at every hearthside . . . old and young . . . must needs give three cheers . . . for the author of *Little Women.* Literally, Proud papa is everywhere promoted to the high places and honors on Joe's [sic] account."

Bronson talked to his audiences about Louisa, telling them she had asked him not to. He gave details such as how much the *Christian Union* paid her for the serialization of *Shawl Straps*. He told them about the genesis of Laurie, that he was a combination of four boys; "none of them alone would suit, so Louisa took the best characteristics of each of the boys and out of them constructed the ideal boy . . ." He ventured to say that she should have let Jo marry Laurie and not have disappointed her readers.

In June, Louisa returned to Concord to look after her parents: "Twenty years ago I resolved to make the family independent if I could. At forty that is done. Debts all paid, even the outlawed ones, and we have enough to be comfortable. It has cost me my health, perhaps; but as I still live, there is more to do, I suppose."

Her fame was an annoyance to her, and her father's pleasure in it irritated her. She was enraged to find reporters soliciting her nephews for information and artists trying to sneak sketches of her: "People *must* learn that authors have some rights; I can't entertain a dozen a day, and write the tales they demand also. I'm but a busy worm, and when walked on must turn in self-defence."

Occasionally the Alcotts visited with the Emersons. Lydian discussed her nervous condition, her sleepless nights, and how she hated the sun in the morning for waking her from the little sleep she managed to steal. She was enthusiastic about suffrage and a little miffed that Ellen wasn't more so. But Ellen was completely involved with her father, who whispered confidences to her. Bronson saw less of Waldo and more of Ellery Channing. Emerson, he complained, "does not dissolve like a woman in all moods, his intellect is so exacting and critical. With Channing, it is almost always easy. He is feminine and as magnetic almost as a woman. I call him naturally 'brother' and we flow together. Emerson questions now and demurs."

In the fall Emerson, whose spirits were morbidly low after the fire, set off on an extended trip abroad, with Ellen as guide and translator. The vacation wasn't an unqualified success. Emerson, on the banks of the Nile, said to Ellen, "Could anything argue wilder insanity than leaving a country like ours to see this bareness of mud? — Look! There is some water, and see! there is a crowd of people. They have collected with a purpose of drowning themselves."

In late September 1872, Roberts Brothers brought out Bronson's *Concord Days,* a collection of *pensées,* extracts from his diaries, remarks about his friends and neighbors. He also gave advice. On writing, he prescribed burning "every scrap that stands not the test of all moods of criticism . . . Very little of what is thought admirable at the writing holds good over night . . . never venture a whisper about it to your friend, if he be an author especially. You may read selections to sensible women, — if young the better . . ."

Just after publication he and Louisa made a short pilgrimage to Wolcott. She hadn't been there since she was a girl. For many years she had thought of writing a story about her father, called "The Cost of an Idea," and he suspected the trip was research for her. She never felt easy enough within their relationship, however, to locate a voice in which to discuss Bronson, and she never attempted the story.

On her return she took rooms in Boston, where she expanded *Shawl Straps* for Niles. On November 9, Boston caught on fire and Louisa watched it from her rooms. She found it terrible and splendid, for it appealed to the violence and anarchy in her. "It seemed as if the end of the world had come as we watched block after block melting away like snow. The great granite buildings crumbled and fell so fast that firemen could not venture on the walls, and the light mansard roofs were tinder boxes to catch and spread the flames. Many hundred tons of coal are still burning and at night the sky still glows," she wrote to her father.

She continued: "All the houses between Summer and State Streets are gone, extending back to the water and Fort Hill. It is sad to see the ruined merchants trying to find where their stores once stood for all trace of streets is lost in the burnt region. Roberts Brothers lost nothing though the gun powder explosions in Milk St. broke all their windows. Niles told me that a thousand dollars worth of paper for my book had just been sent to Cambridge . . ." The fire, which burned the newspaper offices of the two major papers, devastated the area from Washington Street, a block away from the Common, all the way to the harbor, speeding up the move westward into the Back Bay. The South End was largely deserted as a residential area, making way for more commercial enterprises.

Louisa came home to celebrate her fortieth and her father's seventy-third birthday on November 29. She spent the day getting

Bronson ready for a conversational trek: "I enjoyed every penny spent, and had a happy time packing his new trunk with warm flannels, real shirts, gloves, etc., and seeing the dear man go off in a new suit, overcoat and all, like a gentleman. We both laughed over the pathetic old times with tears in our eyes, and I reminded him of the 'poor as poverty, but serene as heaven' saying."

After seeing her father off, Louisa returned to Boston to rooms on Allston Street behind the State House, where she wanted to rest and rewrite her old novel *Work*.

The *Christian Union* asked Louisa to write her next novel for them. Louisa agreed, fed up with Niles's cheapness. He bombarded her with frantic letters to reconsider her decision. "I have thought about it overnight and I am quite calm at this moment," he wrote uncalmly. "I hope you will not let the *Christian Union* thieves print 'Work' at any price. They have already attempted to rob me of my hard earned treasure by offering you a bribe in money. Spurn it and thus illustrate in life the principles which 'Jo March' has so beautifully taught in books." Niles knew no shame. But it worked, and Louisa turned down the tempting offer. In return Niles grudgingly gave her a new contract, giving her 12 per cent on the retail price of *Shawl Straps:* "We can't afford to do this, but we are very grateful for your rejection of a recent unprincipled bribe and wish to show that we mean to be liberal."

They haggled out an arrangement to everyone's more or less satisfaction. The *Christian Union* paid Louisa $3000 for serialization rights and Niles would publish the book. Louisa finished four chapters by December 8, writing to her father that she thought it was dull, and it would therefore probably do very well. Louisa, who couldn't use a typewriter, was working on "impression paper," a kind of duplicating paper on which she produced three copies at once — for Roberts Brothers, the *Christian Union,* and her British publisher, Low of London. "This was the cause of the paralysis of my thumb which disabled me for the rest of my life," she wrote later. She taught herself to write with her left hand so her aching right hand wouldn't incapacitate her.

Shawl Straps was selling well. She reported to her father with some amusement that the editor of the Tract Society, a moral-religious publishing concern that had called *Hospital Sketches* "rowdy," now wanted her to write a tract for them. It was, she thought, "a nice little proof that the world does move, even the slowest coaches in it. Ain't I an irreverent huzzy?"

That month, when Louisa received her royalty check, she gave $100 to a needy acquaintance, "a thank-offering for my success. I like to help the class of 'silent poor' to which we belonged for so many years — needy, but respectable, and forgotten because too proud to beg. Work difficult to find for such people, and life made very hard for want of a little money to ease the necessary needs."

In February Anna came down with pneumonia. Louisa rushed to Concord to care for her. For a few days it seemed as if she were not to recover. Anna told Louisa that she must take charge of the boys. Bronson came home from the West almost despairing for his dearest child: "She is a presence chastening and softening every moment and every member of the household." By the time he got to Concord, however, Anna was feeble but unquestionably mending. When she was able to get up, Louisa moved back to Boston.

She was hardly there a month when May gave notice that she wanted to leave. Helen Hunt (later Jackson) invited May to travel with her to California, but instead she decided to return to London to continue her studies. May's health declined in Concord with the claustrophobia and depression that came over her at home. Bronson was sorry to see her go and rhapsodized in his journals about her spring cleaning expertise, her adroit carpet shaking, book dusting, and picture polishing. He wished, not surprisingly, that the women would stay on forever: "It is comforting to have children so competent to discharge the domestic economy, and after some time to furnish the means, in large measure, of living in a style of comfort, honorable to us all. Louisa's income is more than adequate for this . . ." Louisa gave May $1000 and sent her off to London on April 25, 1873.

May's decision caused Louisa to "give up all" her plans. On the last day of April she moved back to Concord. She tried to make arrangements for the fall, desiring to take rooms in the Back Bay or on Beacon Hill, but, she wrote to a friend, "my movements depend so much on others that I can't *promise* anything, but my plan is to have mother with me next winter for Pa goes west early in Oct. and I'm not going to have her or Annie or myself buried up there for another winter."

On May 27, 1873, Emerson and Ellen arrived home. Emerson

had become totally dependent on his daughter. Her attachment to her father was the most fulfilling relation of her life. Like Louisa, she had dedicated herself to her family, but unlike Louisa, she had received considerable respect and love in return. Their house had been repaired, partially at the expense of the town. A cheering crowd greeted father and daughter, and Emerson, confused, turned to Ellen to ask "was it a public day." She was touched and proud, and explained the meaning of the handkerchief-waving throng. Their train pulled in at three-thirty and a barouche collected Waldo and Ellen. A second carriage followed with family and notables, including Sanborn, Louisa, and Bronson. The Concord band and a parade of schoolchildren and adult admirers marched along behind the carriages. The children roared out "Home Sweet Home" when the procession reached the intersection of Main Street and Lexington Road, on the way to Emerson's house. When Waldo reached home he went inside to greet his family and then reappeared to give a little, soft speech of thanks to the townspeople. They responded with three cheers.

The Alcotts visited after the festivities, finding Emerson more forgetful, slower, and without much energy. He was now completely bald and quite fragile-looking. Lydian, on the contrary, was greatly improved, lively, and talkative. Her husband went to bed at eight-thirty and spent his days in silence, while she seemed to have a new source of good spirits.

Louisa took her nephew Johnny to Gloucester the second week in July, but returned almost immediately because of Abba's health. She had developed heart trouble and, for some days, lost her mind. The diagnosis was that her "dropsy affected the brain," and the effect was that she didn't know her family. She rallied slowly and by August 7 could take a short ride, read, and write a letter or two. The three weeks frightened and saddened Louisa: "Marmee slowly came back to herself, but sadly feeble, — never to be our brave, energetic leader any more. She felt it and it was hard to convince her that there was no need for her doing anything but rest." Louisa and her father took her out for rides, brought her flowers, and entertained her with gossip and stories. Louisa read aloud Ellery Channing's new book on Thoreau.

"Work is and always has been my salvation and I thank the Lord for inventing it," wrote Louisa, thinking that but for her intense involvement with her writing life would have been incomparably bleaker. *Work* is the only adult novel Louisa attempted after *Moods*, and it offers more substance than her juvenile fictions. It also reflects the changes Louisa had been through in the long intervening years. The story opens with Christie Devon, a brave twenty-one-year-old orphan, leaving the home of her aunt and uncle. She tells her aunt that "Uncle doesn't love or understand me," and she faces down her gruff, selfish uncle, saying "I know you begrudge me a home, though you call me ungrateful when I'm gone." Christie leaves, defiant and resentful, determined never to be a burden again. These are familiar chords for Louisa to play. She translates her home experience into a bitter consciousness of her dependence on irresponsible parents.

In the city Christie — whose name, by the way, appears in the stock company of the Boston Theater Company in the 1855–1856 season and may have been Louisa's stage name when she tried briefly to be an actress — goes to an "intelligence office" like the one Abba had run. This gives Louisa the opportunity to slur repeatedly the "incapable Irish." The era, she remarks, was before "foreign help had . . . driven farmers' daughters out of the field, and made domestic comfort a lost art."

Christie takes a job as "second girl," waiting on a pretentious family. The work and her employers rankle, and she vows never to go into service again. "She knew very well that she would never live with Irish mates." She falls into an acting job, where her moral if not her physical beauty shines. There are prettier girls all around, but "to a cultivated eye the soul of beauty was often visible in that face of hers, with its intelligent eyes, sensitive mouth, and fine lines about the forehead, making it a far more significant and attractive countenance than that of her friend, possessing only piquant prettiness." The beauty of Christie's nature and its refining effects on people become evident in the theater company. Louisa declares that "fine natures seldom fail to draw out the finer traits of those who approach them . . . Women often possess this gift, and when used worthily find it as powerful as beauty; for if less alluring, it is more lasting and more helpful, since it appeals, not to the sense, but the souls of men."

The opening chapters, in which Christie works as a servant, actress, governess, and companion, are short vignettes with little connective tissue. It isn't until Christie becomes a seamstress and meets Rachel that the story formally opens. Rachel is a poor, timid, scarred woman whom Christie befriends. "Now someone cared for her, and, better still, she could make someone happy, and in the act of lavishing the affection of her generous nature on a creature sadder and more solitary than herself, she found a satisfaction that never lost its charm." Christie begs Rachel to move in with her, but she refuses. One day Christie discovers that Rachel is a fallen women. Christie and Rachel are both fired when the secret comes out. Rachel makes an impassioned speech, saying "that there are kinder hearts among the sinners than among the saints, and no one can live without a bit of love. Your Magdalen Asylums are penitentiaries, not homes: I won't go to any of them. Your piety isn't worth much, for though you read in your Bible how the Lord treated a poor soul like me, yet when I stretch out my hand to you for help, not one of you virtuous Christian women dare take it and keep me from a life worse than hell." Christie reaches out and Rachel tells her that she has saved her: "You have had faith in me, and that will keep me strong and safe when you are gone." This is one of the many testaments to the redemptive power of woman's love.

Rachel disappears into her private purgatory, leaving Christie friendless and miserable. She grows weak and sick, brooding bitterly; Louisa renders her loneliness with affecting force and the strength of real emotion: "Her heart was empty and she could not fill it; her soul was hungry and she could not feed it; life was cold and dark and she could not warm and brighten it, for she knew not where to go . . . she thought sad, bitter, oftentimes rebellious thoughts . . ." She questioned the existence of God, and saw an unendurably lonely life stretching out before her. She thought of suicide. "It is not always want, insanity, or sin that drives women to desperate deaths; often it is a dreadful loneliness of heart, a hunger for home and friends, worse than starvation, a bitter sense of wrong in being denied the tender ties, the pleasant duties, the sweet rewards that can make the humblest life happy; a rebellious protest against God, who, when they cry for bread, seems to offer them a stone."

Christie is about to throw herself into the Back Bay when Rachel turns up. Once again woman's redemptive love saves a soul. Rachel takes Christie to a low-comic Dickensian woman who shelters and feeds her. She introduces Christie to Thomas Power, modeled on Theodore Parker, who inspires Christie with a sermon on working women. Power is "a sturdy man of fifty, with a keen, brave face, penetrating eyes, and a mouth a little grim, but a voice so resonant and sweet it reminded one of silver trumpets, and stirred and won the hearer with irresistible power." Christie is in awe of Power, respects him greatly, and when he introduces her to a Quaker family needing a companion, she takes his advice and the position.

Christie gets on easily with Mrs. Sterling, but her thirty-one-year-old son David, a florist, another version of Thoreau, is harder. Power warns her that he is "rather grave and blunt: with some trouble in his past." Christie, wanting a mysterious romance, is disappointed to find "only a broad shouldered, brown bearded man, with an old hat and coat, trousers tucked into his boots, fresh mould on the hand."

Suddenly the story shifts, and the old, confused, moody, troubled Louisa emerges, called forth by the attractive man: "I never shall outgrow my foolish way of trying to make people other than they are. Gods are gone, heroes hard to find, and one should be contented with goodness, even if they do wear old clothes, lead prosaic lives, and have no accomplishments but gardening, playing the flute, and keeping their temper." This passage is the first we hear of Christie's hero-worshiping tendency. Louisa needed to make a statement about relinquishing her romanticism and abandoning the attitudes expressed in *Moods.* Christie complains to Power that David *won't* be ambitious: "I try to stir him up for he has talents; I've found out: but he won't seem to care for anything but watching over his mother, reading his old books, and making flowers bloom double when they ought to be single." Power tells her not to expect heroes, that "if people don't come up to the mark you are so disappointed that you fail to see the fine reality which remains when the pretty romance ends." Louisa tries to teach herself this lesson, having spent so many years needing giant, imaginary men to make up for the absent father.

The second time around she tries to tame her wild Thoreau. She made him "blunt and honest, domestic and kind; hard to get at, but true as steel when once won . . ." She tells David that "as a general rule, men have been kinder to me than women; and if I wanted a staunch friend I'd choose a man, for they wear better than women, who ask too much, and cannot see that friendship lasts longer if a little respect and reserve go with the love and confidence." In her effort to come to grips with human-sized men, Louisa also recognized that the relations she had with women, especially in her family, were exhausting, draining and strangulating. She envied her father his friendships, yearned for a little of that separation and distance among herself and mother and sisters.

She expresses her moodiness to David. She complains of a lack of steadiness, "so I whiffle about this way and that, and sometimes I think I am a most degenerate creature."

In return he tells her not to be deceived by his look of contentment and cheer: "In reality I am sad, dissatisfied bad and selfish: see if I'm not. I often tire of this quiet life, hate my work, and long to break away, and follow my own wild and wilful impulses, no matter where they lead. Nothing keeps me at such times but my mother and God's patience." Louisa makes David real by opening up his internal troubles for examination. He doesn't indulge in gargantuan, inexplicable, and incomprehensible turmoil as Adam does in *Moods*. He is an understandable man of normal dimensions. Christie suddenly sees David: "His apparent contentment was resignation; his cheerfulness, a manly contempt for complaint; his reserve the modest reticence of one who, having done a hard duty well, desires no praise for it. Like all enthusiastic persons, Christie had a hearty admiration for self-sacrifice and self-control, and while she learned to see David's virtues she also exaggerated them, and could not do enough to show the daily increasing esteem and respect she felt for him, and to atone for the injustice she once did him." Again Louisa sees herself erring on the side of romanticizing quiet struggle and self-sacrifice. She had a rarefied view of suffering, especially the private kind, which she tended to think of as the quickest road to divinity.

In the midst of Christie's growing love for David comes little, flirtatious Kitty, "very pretty, very charming, and at times, most lovable and sweet when all that was best in her shallow little heart was touched. But it was evident to all that her early acquaintance with the hard and sordid side of life had brushed the bloom from her nature, and filled her mind with thoughts and feelings unfitted to her years." This is Abba talking, who believed that worldly contact provided nothing but social diseases. Christie believes

David is falling in love with Kitty and leaves her cosy home to allow the lovers privacy.

She learns a lesson in compensation from her renunciation, "soon perceiving with the swift instinct of a woman, that this was a lesson, hard to learn, but infinitely precious, helpful, and sustaining when once gained. She was not happy, only patient; not hopeful, but trusting; and when life looked dark and barren without it, she went away into that inner world of deep feeling, high thought, and earnest aspiration; which is a never-failing refuge to those whose experience has built within them." Louisa knew much about giving up things, and spoke expertly on the strengthening aspects of self-control.

Eventually David and Christie marry just before David leaves for the Civil War. They have only occasional furloughs together before David is killed, leaving Christie pregnant. Louisa finally came to terms with nonsexual love and respect between men and women, but she couldn't go beyond into speculation on marital relations.

She leaves Christie at forty, a peaceful widow, raising her little girl. She chooses as her life's mission to act as a liaison between working women and rich charitable ladies, a variation on Abba's "intelligence office."

Christie is a less stifled heroine than some of Louisa's earlier women. She has more understanding of men and less fear and contempt for them, allowing her more freedom of action. Louisa's well-chronicled love for Thoreau approached some resolution in *Work.* She effectively made him life-size and stripped him of his disproportionate qualities. She killed him off quickly, but at least her ideal was less tortured and unrealistic.

Bronson praised the book: "Instead of seeking foreign incident and scenery, it deals with home life; matters that concern the multitude . . . It preaches eloquently the gospel of *work* . . . examples drawn from actual experiences of her own — the dignity of labor and sacrifice." Abba, of course, loved it, thought the style "facetious, pathetic, and at times severely true — no compromise with false customs, or weak principles 'good without pretense.' "

The book was well reviewed and Louisa enjoyed writing it, but when the excitement was over, she felt empty and weak. Her mother's illness had given her grave distress. On October 8, she and Anna made an effort to celebrate Abba's seventy-third birthday. They decorated Bronson's study with fall leaves and watched their father give Abba a commonplace book.

Louisa felt unwell and was eager to leave the dampness of Concord. On October 31, 1873, when Abba was well enough to travel, Louisa closed up Orchard House and brought her mother to 26 East Brookline Street in Boston. Louisa was despondent: "When I had youth I had no money; now I have the money I have no time; and when I get the time, if I ever do, I shall have no health to enjoy life. I suppose it's the discipline I need; but it's rather hard to love the things I do, and see them go by because duty chains me to my galley. If I ever come into port with all sails set, that will be my reward perhaps. Life always was a puzzle to me, and gets more mysterious as I go on. I shall find it out by and by, and see that it's all right, if I can only keep brave and patient to the end."

Louisa's life had all the gray hues associated with being an "old maid." She had married what she saw as her duty with its cold obligations rather than attach herself to the fearsome responsibilities of life with a man. In remaining single, Louisa had aligned herself with a group of women who were ridiculed and condescended to. She was tolerated as eccentric, regarded as pitiful and incomplete, probably disagreeable, and as a failed woman, incompetent to attract a man, fit only for the fringes of family and social life. This caricature, not surprisingly, made her sensitive, and she often wrote in defense of the unmarried woman.

Louisa's choice not to marry had many emotional and practical ramifications. Her family supported her morally, but couldn't help approving more wholeheartedly of Anna's life. In society Louisa, who had always been awkward, was by now almost a pariah. The Victorian world regarded spinsters with the same fear and disgust that contemporary society feels for old people. They were hidden away, made to feel ashamed, dressed in gloomy colors, and trotted out only to go to church or baby-sit. Their views were solicited even less frequently than those of married women, and they were regarded as defenseless at a time when women were told they needed all the protection they could get. This obsession with masculine protection was, ironically, the most effective method of keeping women cloistered. Without a male bodyguard, Louisa remained relatively immobile. Her satisfactions grew increasingly scarce because of poor health, family duties, and the suffocating limitations attached to the phrase "old maid."

18

Abba

LOUISA PRESIDED OVER HER MOTHER'S last years, fiercely protective yet at the same time profoundly weary. She had taken over her mother's physical care, but had increasingly withdrawn from her company, which she found more and more oppressive. She substituted, instead, comforts and money. Anna sat around, when she could, and chatted with the old woman. Louisa moved back and forth from Concord to Boston, overseeing the housekeeping arrangements, but retreating from an intimacy to which she couldn't respond. Her withdrawal made her feel intensely guilty, which she tried to cover with harder work and more money. With the exception of one resurrected pseudonymous tale, her stories had lost their vigor. But Louisa cranked them out doggedly long after there was any real financial need. She had accomplished the goals she'd set herself, but in the process she'd become so accustomed to living for and through others that she had little idea of how to live for herself. She took enjoyment in her occasional trips but always curtailed them, pleading, irrationally, the demands of her family. She lived with the fiction of constant Alcott needs guiding her every action. The price for living with this was that when Abba became very sick, Louisa herself almost died, having lived so completely through her mother that her end seemed to call for Louisa's.

At the end of 1873, Louisa established her mother on Franklin Square in the South End, although she didn't like the noise of the large, horse-drawn buses. The square was a pretty spot, a small enclosed park surrounded by large, handsome houses, each on a spacious lot covered with trees. In February, Louisa and her father went to the State House to hear debates on woman suffrage. The cause was slowly gaining ground. Several groups of women had attempted to vote. Susan Anthony had led sixteen women to the Rochester polls in the 1872 presidential election. She was arrested and tried for this action, but the government refrained from fining her. In 1870, Lucy Stone and Henry Blackwell founded the Boston *Woman's Journal.* It was a paper for all women, not just suffragists, and was directed at the sizable conservative constituency of educated women not ready for Susan B. Anthony's more radical the *Revolution.* (The *Woman's Journal* became a stable market for Louisa's thoughts on girls' education, deportment, and dress.)

Abba was invited in March to King's Chapel for the installation of a tablet honoring her father. Louisa hired a carriage and drove the old couple to the services. The occasion rather undid Abba, who sat alone in a pew singing hymns to herself. Louisa introduced her to the sexton. When some ancient parishioners arrived Abba began to cry, remembering her father, vigorous in his "small" clothes, bellowing out his responses every Sunday from his customary seat. After the ceremony Abba said, "This isn't my Boston; all my friends are gone; I never want to see it any more."

Abba never did return. Louisa took her parents home to Concord, where May was home from England. The family gathered at Orchard House to see May's excellent copies of Turner and her original sketches. Anna grew quite gloomy, thinking about Louisa's writing and May's art. She wondered out loud what she had ever done. Bronson, expressing what all the women felt in some degree, pointed to John and Fred, saying, "Here is what you have done; it is more than all the rest."

In June, Louisa got ready for a trip to the White Mountains with Anna and the boys. They spent the summer in Conway, where Louisa wrote *Eight Cousins.* The work brought on her illness again, and by September she was very shaky, once more depending on morphine.

Anna volunteered to move in with Abba and Bronson while Louisa rested in Boston. Bronson thought this an excellent idea: "With this first born and harmonious inmate my house always appears friendly and genial and now, with her boys sharing largely in her personal traits, our apartments become peopled in pleasant associations." Louisa took rooms at the Bellevue and May held a drawing class there once a week. She and Anna shared in the Concord housekeeping. Bronson thought this would be suitable for Abba: "Nothing adds more to my wife's pleasure and comfort I may add, than having Anna . . . for conversation whenever she inclines." Abba, however, felt neglected. Anna had chores "not to be postponed for much gossip with the garrulous old marmee — all right!! . . . I find myself inevitably alone much of the time."

Louisa felt very bad all fall. Even the success of *Eight Cousins* did little to lift her spirits. The novel is an exercise in discussing girls' education. A young, sweet, pretty orphan comes to live with her aunts. They are, by and large, a stiff lot with unhealthy, constricting ideas about raising girls. Uncle Alec, a sensible doctor, saves Rose from the superficial ideas and harmful plans of these women. He makes her exercise and eat properly, prevents her from corseting and becoming neurasthenic and reading suggestive books. He surprises Rose by teaching that housekeeping is an "accomplishment . . . one of the most beautiful as well as useful of all the arts a woman can learn . . . a necessary part of your training." In the chapter entitled "Fashion and Physiology" Louisa gives a clothing sermon. An aunt dresses Rose in an ermine muff, silk, ostrich feathers, and a skirt in two shades of blue with a tight underskirt and an overskirt tied back so tightly that "it was impossible to take a long step, and the under one was so loaded with plaited frills that it 'wobbled' . . . fore and aft . . . A small jacket of the same material was adorned with a high ruff at the back, and laid well open over the breast, to display some lace and a locket. Heavy fringes, bows, puffs, ruffles, and *revers* finished off the dress . . ." The outfit was topped with a "high velvet hat audaciously turned up in front, with a bunch of pink roses and a sweeping plume, was cocked over one ear, and, with her curls braided into a club at the back of her neck, Rose's head looked more like that of a dashing young cavalier than a modest little girl."

Alec is appalled at this version of his Rose and makes her dress in a flannel union suit under a plain brown dress over low-heeled boots. Alec lectures on the evils of corseting and the need to leave the body free to its own shape.

Rose learns through her eight boy cousins, each quite different from the other, that one of her jobs as a girl is to tame and teach boys to be good. Her aunts beg her to use her influence for their improvement. A sensible Aunt Jessie explains that "when girls give up their little vanities and boys their small vices and try to strengthen each other in well-doing, matters are going as they ought. Work away, my dear, and help their mother keep these sons fit friends for an innocent creature like yourself; they will be the manlier men for it, I can assure you."

Rose is a very *good* girl, but not quite perfect. She has her ears pierced, much to Alec's dismay. "I see she is a girl, after all," he remarks gloomily, "and must have her vanities like all the rest of them." Girls are vain and weak, but if they are truly female, they will sacrifice their vanities for the moral improvement of boys. She gives up her earrings so a cousin will give up smoking. "I care more for my cousin than for my earrings," she announces priggishly. Her cousin, however, cannot keep his vow. Exhortation and self-sacrifice having failed, Rose reviles the low sinner: "You are not at all the boy I thought you were, and I don't respect you one bit. I've tried to help you be good, but you won't let me, and I shall not try any more. You talk a great deal about being a gentleman, but you are not, for you've broken your word, and I can never trust you again."

The boys are an opportunity to lecture on materialism, temperance, and bad language. The book is organized as a series of lessons rather than as a story, and although it has some of the sympathy and charm of *Little Women,* it is relentlessly preachy. Louisa makes a touching pitch for maiden aunts, a plea that turns up in most of her works. She confides to the reader that it is her "private opinion that these worthy creatures are a beautiful provision of nature for the cherishing of other people's children."

After a very sickly winter, Louisa was well enough to attend the tenth anniversary of the founding of Vassar in February 1875. She was proud to be among the honored guests, but refused adamantly to make a speech. Instead, she offered to stand and revolve on the speakers' platform so all four hundred girls could see her. Her offer was accepted. Afterward she signed autographs until she couldn't write anymore.

Back in Concord the town was preparing for its centennial celebration. Abba planned an open house and was very excited about the coming festivities. Louisa wished "the whole affair in —

well we'll say Washington, or the next best place to the warm
regions where political rubbish belongs." The work for the occasion devolved on Louisa, which was why she was irritated. Her
mother was feeling a rush of forebears to the head and wanted her
daughter to go to the centennial costume ball as Madame Hancock. For herself, Louisa reported her desire "that a stupendous
new cap shall be evolved from some inspired woman's brain to
deck her aged brow to do honor to the race of May. Hooray."
Louisa was commissioned to get the Hancock punch bowl, a May
Revolutionary relic, to be displayed at their open house.

Abba and Louisa signed the woman suffrage petition, which
stated that, in 1874, 33,961 Massachusetts women were taxed $1,-
927,653.11. This was, of course, taxation without representation.
The centennial celebration, they hoped, would illustrate the irony
of this outrageous injustice.

Louisa was bound and determined to hate the festival and she
was not disappointed. She didn't like the guests trooping in and
out of Orchard House. She was furious that there were no seats set
up for women in the speakers' tent. She grew tired standing
through the speeches, watching with blood in her eye the seated
dignitaries above. When the platform gave way Louisa was delighted, and insisted it was "because they had left out the Women's
Suffrage Plank."

After the centennial she went immediately to Boston, blaming
her collapsed health on the ceremonies: "General *break-down*
owing to an unwise desire to outdo all other towns; too many
people . . ." Louisa wrote an angry account of the evening for the
Woman's Journal, reciting her grievances, slights, rudeness, and bad
organization. Her exaggeratedly aggrieved tone called forth letters of protest from other women, who suggested that a little good
will and patience would have entirely changed the experience for
her.

Louisa spent the summer in Concord while May and Anna went
to Walpole. Abba reminisced with Louisa about the last time the
family was there and about Lizzie's illness and death. Abba looked
back on that period as the end of her activity and the beginning
of her passive acceptance of events: "I said I have done what I
could, Lord help thou mine unbelief save me and mine or slay us
forthwith — straight way the genius of my daughters blossomed

forth — Louisa wrote admirable books, May painted good pictures
— Anna brought a good son among us, and all went well."

Louisa received many visitors that summer. Ellery Channing
called and sat with her and her mother. Mary Livermore, a square-
jawed, determined woman with dark, curly hair and blue eyes came
to the Concord Lyceum to deliver her lecture "What Shall We Do
with Our Daughters?" After her speech, she and Louisa sat up
most of the night talking. Mrs. Livermore had moved to Boston
from Chicago to help edit the *Woman's Journal.* She had been an
army nurse during the war and she and Louisa shared their memories. With Lucy Stone, Mrs. Livermore had been an accredited
delegate to the Massachusetts Republican Convention in 1870.
She recalled being greeted with remarks like: "If a local Republican organization elected a trained monkey as a delegate, would
you feel obliged to accept him?"

One of Mary Livermore's favorite stories was about the time she
and five other girls had gone to see President Josiah Quincy of
Harvard about studying at the university. They demonstrated their
learning for him and he said, "Very smart girls . . . unusually
capable, but can you cook?" They assured him they were expert
domestics. "Highly important," he said. He continually diverted
them from asking their question until finally Mary burst out that
they wanted to go to college with their brothers: "You say we are
sufficiently prepared, is there anything to prevent our admission?"
He told them that the place for girls was at home. "Yes, but Mr.
Quincy, if we are prepared, we would not ask to recite but may we
not attend the recitations and sit silent in the classes?" "No, my
dear, you may not." "Then I wish — " "What do you wish?" "I
wish I were God, for the instant, that I might kill every woman from
Eve down and let you have a masculine world all to yourselves and
see how you would like that!"

In September, Louisa wrote to Samuel Sewall that women
friends, Henrietta Joy and Dr. Rhoda Ashley Lawrence, were trying
to buy a house in Roxbury where they would take in patients as
boarders. They needed three or four thousand dollars, which
Louisa wished to supply. The place, she thought, would be of
inestimable value to worn-out people like herself. The investment,
she was sure, would pay off. She told her uncle that Dr. Lawrence
had been practicing only a year and had earned $1000. The ven-

ture was as much business as charity for Louisa. Dr. Lawrence's establishment, which she helped finance, figured largely in her convalescent periods.

Rhoda Lawrence had just completed her medical training at Boston University, which had absorbed the Female Medical College in 1874. Boston University was a unique school, a training center for homeopaths. The fight between allopaths, the established medical practitioners, and homeopaths had been going on in Boston for many years. Allopaths wouldn't treat patients who had engaged homeopaths, and tried to keep these doctors out of the publicly supported Boston City Hospital, established in 1863. It wasn't until the 1880s that homeopaths were allowed to practice there. There were legitimate criticisms leveled against the theory of homeopathic medicine, based on Samuel Christian Hahneman's theory of the "psora," or itch, which, he believed, shouldn't be suppressed by dosing. But, in general, homeopaths' regard for simple, natural cures and their healthy distrust of "heroic" dosing with potent chemicals made them more humane healers if not the most advanced experimental scientists in medicine. Rhoda Lawrence, born in 1829, was a homeopath, as was Louisa by upbringing and inclination. The two women became close friends, and Dr. Lawrence tenderly looked after her friend's damaged health at her small, homelike infirmary.

At Mary Livermore's suggestion, Louisa went to the October Women's Congress in Syracuse. She made it clear that she was going not as a speaker but as an interested observer. She attended the sessions with her cousin Charlotte Wilkinson, Samuel May's daughter. On the last day they arrived late and had to sit on the stage. A number of dignitaries surprised Louisa by asking for autographs. She later understood that it was a way of identifying her to the large mass of young women who wanted to shake her hand but didn't know who she was. She sat quietly in her black silk through the last speeches and was astonished to be rushed suddenly by girls with autograph albums. She signed as many as her thumb and patience would allow, finally pleading an appointment with her cousin. One asked her to put up her veil. Another wanted to be kissed. Everyone wanted her to write more. "One energetic lady grasped my hand in the crowd, exclaiming, 'If you ever come to Oshkosh, your feet will not be allowed to touch the ground. You will be borne in the arms of the people! Will you come?' 'Never,' responded Miss A., trying to look affable, and trying to laugh as the good soul worked my arm like a pump-handle, and from the gallery generations of girls were looking on. This, this is fame!" Finally Louisa broke into a run through the mob of enthusiastic girls.

After the congress Louisa traveled to New York City, stopping at Niagara Falls along the way. She took rooms at the Bath Hotel, on West Twenty-sixth Street. The hotel was a health institute, like Dio Lewis's Boston temperance hotel, offering all kinds of baths, massages, and a pure diet. The hotel was the most familiar aspect of New York to Louisa. The city itself was rather overwhelming. It had more than a million citizens, with dirty, badly paved streets, unsafe wharves, and an atmosphere of instability and rapid growth. After the war, New York had entered a period of rapid expansion. Grand Central Station opened at Forty-second Street on October 9, 1871, receiving trains on four tracks from the Hudson River Railroad, the New York, New Haven and Hartford, and the New York and Harlem. In 1874 four miles of elevated tracks for local steam-powered trains were completed to complement the omnibuses that ran along the streets. Saint Patrick's Cathedral on Fifth Avenue, the Metropolitan Museum of Art, the Museum of Natural History, and Hunter College were all completed in the 1870s. In 1876, the year of Louisa's visit, New York saw its first bicycle and the completion of Central Park.

One of Louisa's fellow guests, Miss Sally Holley, ran a school for freemen in South Carolina. The two women enjoyed each other greatly and together prepared barrels of food and clothing for the school.

In December, rather to her surprise, Louisa found herself reading Goethe. She reported to her father that she had heard him compared favorably to Plotinus. Away from home, she found the peace of mind and generosity to appreciate her father's achievements and his favorite thinkers. She wrote to Bronson about the discoveries she had made for herself. He was pleased with her offer of philosophic companionship and wrote in his journal: "Philosophy is a growth, it buds and bears its fruits the sooner is not pushed forth . . . Our novelist has taken her time, has not been hindered or provoked but by her own experiences, and now comes the fresh consciousness of personal power — the fruiting of ideas." Louisa made cracks about Concord, the "sacred sandbank," with her fellow guests, but she had learned respect and understanding for her father. Certainly it helped the experience for her to be miles away.

One night Louisa went to a conversation led by her cousin Octavius Brooks Frothingham. An indefatigable organizer, he had formed, in 1869, the "Fraternity Club" for the "entertainment and improvement of its members." There were meetings every two weeks at which members read essays or had a debate or a conversation. There were seventy members who discussed topics such as: "Ought the sexes to be educated apart?," "Does a house burn up or down?," and "Should the matrimonial union be contracted early or late?"

Although she wished to remain silent, Frothingham solicited her views on conformity. Louisa made a statement in favor of noncomformity. She spoke very rapidly and grew red in the face, but managed to talk nevertheless. She found her painful shyness was slightly easier to manage away from home.

New York welcomed the famous writer, and Louisa felt healthy and relaxed enough to enjoy its attentions. Sorosis, a women's club "to promote agreeable and useful relations among women of literary and artistic tastes," invited Louisa to its meetings. Sorosis concerned itself with issues directly related to women, like health and dress reform. In 1873 the club produced a more overtly feminist offspring, the Association for Advancement of Women, whose members included Louisa's friends Julia Ward Howe and Mary Livermore. This group experimented with dropping Miss or Mrs. from women's names to prevent discrimination. One of the Sorosis members, Anne Charlotte Lynch Botta, opened her lovely house at 25 West Thirty-seventh Street to Louisa. Anne Botta was a poet and sculptress who had married an Italian émigré, the philosopher, former parliament member, and Cavour scholar, Vincenzo Botta. Anne Botta entertained the way Annie Fields did, regularly and with the purpose of improving herself and her guests. Whenever he was in New York, Emerson visited the elegant town house, which was always full of fresh flowers and high-minded people.

Louisa wrote home happy letters about parties, visits, and clothes: "New York people strike me as more showy and accomplished than Boston folks, but as intellectual and dignified." At

one party she talked to Bret Harte, Mary Mapes Dodge, Louisa
Chandler Moulton, and a gathering of artists, editors, and writers.
She felt gay and lively all done up in a dove-colored dress with pink
rosebuds and wearing all her jewelry, a lace handkerchief, and long
gloves.

Louisa toured New York, visiting Randall's Island, one hundred
and fifty acres in the East River across from 115th Street, on which
had been built in 1871 the House of Refuge for delinquent boys
and girls. Two brick buildings faced the river, with smaller buildings in the rear. The boys' house was 600 feet long with a chapel,
hospital, bathrooms, and dormitory rooms for the 750 boys. The
girls' house was smaller, designed for only 250 inmates. The whole
structure was enclosed by a 20-foot stone wall separating the boys'
section from the girls'.

On her reformer's tour Louisa also stopped at the notorious
Tombs, at the foot of Manhattan on Center Street, built in 1832
after an Egyptian tomb. The jail had 148 double cells on four tiers.
There the prisoners ate black bread, tea and coffee, a thin soup
that resembled colored water, and occasionally some poisonous,
vile-smelling clam chowder. The first month of Louisa's visit, December 1875, there were three executions in the Tombs.

She was especially interested in a home for newsboys, where for
five cents a day poor boys could get a bed for the night. The shelter
housed 180, who, for another nickel, could buy their meals. One
nine-year-old boy supported himself and his little brother so they
wouldn't be separated.

Louisa wrote home that although she was a social butterfly, she
was a "thrifty" one, and was paying for herself by writing stories.
Abba wrote damply about thrift, calling it "more of a positive
virtue than I was aware of — it gives dignity to life, to economize
the means of living — and what we save from our luxuries, often
enables us to furnish the necessities of life to others — May and I
have chosen this word as our talisman for the year 1876 — " she
wandered on somewhat incoherently. "If I have been improvident
in the past — I have had my reward — If I have been just and loved
my neighbors better than myself my daughters will give me their
care for the short future now left them to work in."

Louisa made a quick trip to Philadelphia to see her cousin the
Reverend Joseph May installed in his new church. She visited her

Germantown birthplace and ran into Elizabeth Lewis, now a woman in her fifties, who had carried on the strange, precocious correspondence with Bronson when she was eight years old.

Louisa's letters from Abba were troubling and gloomy. She wrote, wishing that men would be eaten up, leaving women to rule the world "and bring some order out of chaos — some right out of this complicated mess of wrong — you see a little of it in New York — Boston is waking up to the knowledge of evil, that is devouring its best substance in that doomed city — corruption is in their counsels — crime stalks in their streets unheeded — ." Somberly she wished Louisa all the happiness "you are capable of enjoying." Louisa, who had written happily that she hadn't had an ache or a worry in New York, cut off her vacation and went home in the middle of January.

She had intended to hire a nurse for Abba, but couldn't find one she trusted, so she moved back to Concord. Abba rarely left her room. She quietly read and reread *Moods*. She read it twenty times and thought it Louisa's most remarkable effort. She believed, to Louisa's discomfort, that the novel had "indications of intellectual power hardly discoverable in any of her subsequent lesser writings — her descriptions of scenes, motives, are admirable — I am charmed with it as a piece of fine writing — ."

Abba's health improved enough so that she began coming downstairs in April. But the doctors were not optimistic about her ever recovering completely. Louisa's stomach and legs were troubling her so much that she wrote to her cousin Abby May "on the subject of boots and beer, or legs and lager if you prefer it, or gas and gaiters. I have been told that you, in memory of my honored grandpa, I suppose, wear the latter upon your aristocratic legs . . . therefore the question arises, where does A.W.M. get her noble gaiters. I have asked here and there at stores and the men look as scandalized as if I had demanded the ballot. I mean to have both ballot and gaiters, however, and beginning with the smaller desire of my soul, ask you, man to man, 'Who makes em for you?'

"Likewise having been ordered to drink lager that the intense brilliancy and activity of my brain may be somewhat quenched and a pleasing doziness of my brain produced so that I can sleep and rest my colossal mind, therefore, dearly beloved, I ask you, where does your venerable parent procure *her* lager? I know this was a

deep and awful family-secret — till Leicester burglars revealed it to
an astonished world. But I will keep it and no one can think ill of
aged ladies who need a drop of comfort as we do."

Louisa relaxed over the summer. Anna and the boys were in
Walpole, leaving the house quiet. May and Louisa took staggered
trips to York, Maine, each spelling the other in home chores.
Occasionally Louisa and her father stopped in at the Emersons',
but Waldo could hardly keep up with his old friend. Emerson
complained of old age, that he rarely wrote in his journals anymore. It worried Bronson, who thought it "almost an impiety" to
think his "listener . . . touched with age." But he did find that "the
old themes and the new dragged the more heavily." Emerson was
acutely aware and ashamed of his torpidity and faulty memory.
Bronson, sensitive to his friend's embarrassment, called "less frequently than I should otherwise."

Even Bronson, who prided himself on his eternal youth, was
growing deaf. He found that he was nodding over his journals in
the afternoon: "The blessed mornings remain for continuing the
endless task." He continued to examine his character daily, and
was glad to record that he had an equable disposition: "I have
found a calm temper a friend from my childhood, and have to
thank the happy disposition which my mother gave me. It is not in
my nature to differ with others, but seek agreement."

Louisa welcomed her mother's old friend Lydia Maria Child,
who visited the frail Abba that summer. She and Abba recalled
their adolescent years in Duxbury and their participation in the
abolitionist movement. Mrs. Child liked both May and Louisa,
finding them unaffected and direct. She was impressed with their
dislike of convention and restraint. She was also glad to discover
a talent in Bronson, whom she had always considered fogged in.
At Orchard House she saw that "his architectural taste [is] more
intelligible than his Orphic Saying. He let every old rafter and
beam stay in its place, changed old ovens and ash-holes into Sax-
on-arched alcoves, and added a wash-woman's old shanty to the
rear. The result is a house full of queer nooks and corners and all
manner of juttings in and out. It seems as if the spirit of some old
architect had brought it from the Middle Ages and dropped it
down in Concord . . . The whole house leaves a general impression
of harmony, of a medieval sort, though different parts of the house

seem to have stopped in a dance that became confused because some of the party did not keep time."

Niles had been after Louisa for a sequel to *Eight Cousins*. He had found *Cousins* a little heavy-handed and hoped that "we shall not be able to see the moral in Rose without looking for it hard. If you can write a book without a moral in it which the reader does not see till he gets through and then finds that the author has 'sold' him, such a book will make a hit." Louisa wrote *Rose in Bloom* in the last four weeks of the summer.

Anna and the boys returned from Walpole on September 5, 1876, in time to see May off for Europe four days later. Louisa recognized May's sacrifice in coming home and was generous about her departure: "She has done her distasteful duty faithfully, and deserved a reward. She cannot find the [artistic] help she needs here, and is happy and busy in her world over there."

May's departure upset Abba greatly. She suddenly felt she was dying. In her journal, which she dedicated to May, she detailed her symptoms. She was conscious of having morbidly sensitive nerves, "but reason comes to my aid, and religion adjusts the balance of my faith in the unseen and eternal, and for a while I am patient, and wait, with an almost superhuman courage for the event." Her fears were not grounded, and soon she quit her death watch to begin taking interest in May's lively, gossipy letters. Thirty-six-year-old May wrote about how glad she was to be back studying again. She had made friends with an impressionist painter from Pennsylvania, Mary Cassatt. She wrote to Louisa, her benefactor, that she was "getting on, and feel as if it was not all a mistake; for I have some talent, and will prove it." Louisa and Abba took pleasure in May's gift. "The money I invest in her," wrote Louisa, "pays the sort of interest I like. I am proud to have her show what she can do, and have her depend upon no one but me." Abba talked often about how deeply she missed her youngest, and with what grace she had always done everything.

Louisa called herself "chambermaid and moneymaker" that fall. She nursed her mother while Nan ran the house. "My task gets on slowly," she wrote on her forty-fifth birthday; "but I keep at it, and can be a prop, if not an angel, in the house as Nan is." Bronson remarked on Louisa's patience and sacrifices, calling her his "nobled-hearted child."

On December 2, 1877, ten thousand copies of *Rose in Bloom* were published. Louisa, heeding Niles's warning, prefaced the book with a note saying: "I beg to say that there is no moral to this story. Rose is not designed for a model girl." Saying it, however, does not deny the fact that Rose is a prissy good girl with few of the faults of human beings. She also betrays the haste with which she was written. *Rose in Bloom* is an education in love. Rose gets to select a husband from the gaggle of cousins who have grown up while she has been on her grand tour.

Rose returns from Europe beautiful, elegant, and virtuous. She wants to do something with her life and tells the men that she believes that women have both a right and a duty to a profession. "Would *you* be contented to be told to enjoy yourself for a little while, then marry and do nothing more till you die?" she asks her handsome, unreconstructed cousin Charlie. He has set his cap for Rose and her newly inherited fortune and condescends to her earnest desire to be a philanthropist. He tells her he can't think of "anything more captivating than a sweet girl in a meek little bonnet, going on charitable errands and glorifying poor people's houses with a delightful mixture of beauty and benevolence. Fortunately, the dear souls soon tire of it, but it's heavenly while it lasts."

Charlie woos Rose, and for a while she thinks she may be falling in love. One night, however, he comes home drunk, repelling her utterly. Rose has to give up her hope of love: "The ideal which all women cherish, look for, and too often think they have found when love glorifies a mortal man, is hard to give up, especially when it comes in the likeness of the first lover who touches a young girl's heart." But Rose puts thoughts of loving Charlie behind her. Charlie assumes too much on her affectionate nature and his pretty face. Rose "valued her liberty more than any love offered her." Charlie continues to debauch himself with drink and Rose turns quite away. She is too delicate to bear his degradation: "Only a hint of evil, only an hour's debasement for him, and the innocent heart, just opening to bless and be blessed closed again like a sensitive plant, and shut him out perhaps forever."

Rose induces her circle of men friends to take the temperance pledge. She tells her female friends that she doesn't preach (an untruth), but that she wishes to exert her influence on men for their good. She wants to "try to keep my atmosphere as pure as

I can." Along these lines she attempts to reform Charlie, calling on "the spirit of self-sacrifice, which makes women love to give more than they receive." She urges her handsome cousin to quit his recreations and make a temperate and self-denying pilgrimage to his father in Europe. In return she offers, not her hand, but her promise that she will wait and judge his moral progress on his return. He responds glowingly: "My little saint! I don't deserve one half your goodness to me, but I will, and go away without one complaint to do my best, for your sake." Instead Charlie fails again, gets drunk, and, as a punishment, falls from his horse and dies in a moment of moral overkill.

Rose takes her time, but she slowly finds herself attracted to the studious, outdoorsy, nearsighted Mac, who wants to become a doctor. He is shy and straightforward and reads Thoreau. "A fellow can't spend 'A Week' with Thoreau and not be better for it," he announces. "I'm glad I show it; because in the scramble life is to most of us, even an hour with such a sane, simple, and sagacious soul as his must help one." Mac is aware of his affection for Rose before she returns it. "*I* will be your hero as a mortal man can," he vows, "even though I have to work and wait for years. I'll *make* you love me, and be glad to do it. Don't be frightened. I've not lost my wits; I've just found them. I don't ask anything: I'll never speak of my hope, but it is no use to stop me; I *must* try it, and I *will* succeed." After this lapse into romance Louisa sends Mac away, leaving Rose to realize her love. Mac becomes not only a doctor but an amateur naturalist and a famous poet, outstripping Thoreau in professions. He and Rose, of course, marry.

As a heroine, Rose has none of the energy that anger and frustration give Jo March. She is a Victorian princess with all the literary defects of an overload of virtues. She is never much more than a tedious object lesson in the deadliness of goodness. Nor did Louisa feel much sympathy with her, never having been a good, well-loved, pretty, successful child herself.

In December, Louisa took rooms at the Bellevue. Since the summer Niles had been exhorting her to make a contribution to the Roberts Brothers No Name Series, an edition of novels by popular authors who kept their identities secret. Louisa agreed to produce a fiction and went to work refurbishing an old A. M. Barnard story that Leslie had turned down more than a decade before for being too sensational. Louisa worked on *A Modern Mephistopheles* steadily and with great satisfaction through March: "It has been simmering ever since I read Faust last year. Enjoyed doing it being tired of providing moral pap for the young."

Louisa had finished by March, when she returned home, and, just to keep limber, she fired the cook. She was worried about her mother, who was very frail. Abba's major interest was in May's affectionate weekly letters. Her mother complained about their infrequency but couldn't fault the detail and spirit. May reported that her still life had been chosen to hang in the Salon exhibition in Paris. "Great parents," she teased, "sometimes have great children." She related her successes with the gusto of a woman long under the shadow of her celebrated sister. She told her mother that the selection of her painting was proof that "Lu does not monopolize all the Alcott talent." She warned Louisa that she had plucked only the first feather from her cap "and I shall endeavor to fill mine with so many waving in the breeze that you will be quite ready to lay down your pen and rest on your laurels already won . . ."

Anna had wanted to have her own house for a long time and often asked Louisa for help. Louisa had felt that as long as they had Orchard House there was no need for another establishment. But Anna persisted, and finally, in the early spring of 1877, Louisa agreed to buy the Thoreau house in town. Nan had her dream, Louisa wrote; "when shall I have mine? Ought to be contented with knowing I help both my sisters by my brains. But I'm selfish, and want to go away and rest in Europe. Never shall."

Louisa's *Modern Mephistopheles* came out in April and she enjoyed the curiosity it aroused. Abba told her husband that it "surpasses its predecessors in power and brilliancy — that the author will not easily be recognized by its readers." The style is pure A. M. Barnard, fast-paced, exciting, and sinister. A young poet wishes fame so desperately that he enslaves himself to an older man. His Mephistopheles, Jasper Helwyze, writes brilliant and successful poetry for him in return for control of his life. He introduces the young imposter to a lovely young girl and forces him to marry her. She loves her young, feckless husband, and knows nothing of his bargain. She understands that his relationship with Jasper is unhealthy, and tries to help him untangle it. Eventually he confesses everything, and she vows to help free him from this unnatural alliance by buying their liberty with obedience and good works. In one erotic scene Jasper, who has fallen in love with the innocent wife, gives her hashish. Under the drug's influence she becomes very seductive, expressing her provocative sexuality that she represses in everyday life. She becomes pregnant by her husband and hopes that with a baby the three of them can make new lives for themselves without Jasper's influence. Jasper, meanwhile, confesses his love for her, begging her to redeem him. She agrees only to try to help him be good by observing her self-denying example. She dies in childbirth, leaving both Jasper and her husband to profit from the experience of her unselfish love. Her husband sets out on his reformation and Jasper never forgets her goodness. The ending, obligatorily moral, is less affecting than the unexpectedly sexual elements of the story. The girl's natural sensuality, constantly disguised, shows itself boldy in the drugged tableaux she stages. A beautiful, middle-aged friend of Jasper's openly flirts with Jasper's protégé, adding a level of decadence to the intrigue. The novel has life, completely absent in the Rose sagas. Louisa enjoyed her freedom from the fetters of predictable virtue. She indulged in her taste for romantic corruption, secure in the knowledge that it couldn't be traced to her, the sanctified creator of *Little Women*.

Niles like the story very much, thinking it not so much "sensational as weird and unearthly." He warned her that he didn't think it would be popular: "Nevertheless I like it and to me it is intensely interesting and I think some of your best work is in it. But it seems to me it would be unwise for you to publish it except anonymously, leaving it to be decided in the future whether you would *ever* own it." She never did, unable to acknowledge her own interest in immoral matters. She felt overwhelming pressures on her to be publicly virtuous.

Louisa's health, which had held up throughout the spring, broke down after helping Nan move into her new house. She was laid up for several weeks in an irritable, nervous state. She wanted no visitors and insisted that "the Alcotts are not on exhibition in any way." Anna reported to her father, who had left in September for a short conversational trip, that a woman had told Louisa that her child wished to see her and wanted to know if she was pretty. Louisa told her to tell the little girl that Miss Alcott was old "and very plain." Anna, who had no understanding of Louisa's defensive resistance to fame, wrote to Bronson: "How queer she is about people."

While she was recovering in September, Louisa wrote *Under the Lilacs,* a limp, uninteresting juvenile about a boy and his dog. As if to make up for the fun she had had with *A Modern Mephistopheles,* she bored herself senseless with the new story, recounting the drab adventures of a lost circus boy in search of his father. He finds himself in the bosom of a kindly, stupefyingly dull, rich family that offers him sermons in exchange for his services.

The story's flatness is not surprising, since Louisa wrote it at a time when she knew that her mother was rapidly dying. She took the opportunity to close up the house to all guests, resolved to defend "Marmee's health and home at the point of the bayonet." She received $3000 from Niles for *Under the Lilacs,* to cushion what she anticipated would be an expensive winter. In October she spent some of this advance on a nurse, "fearing that I might give out, and rested a little, so that when the last hard days come I might not fail." Bronson came home and tried to tell his wife about his travels, as was his custom. But she was too tired to listen. She dictated a farewell note to her youngest daughter. May wrote back: "Your little note nearly broke my heart, not to be there with my arms around your neck when you are so ill, and your baby, if no other daughter, should be with you."

Abba told Louisa to stay by her, that she needed her if the suffering should be too great. Louisa sat with her mother while she panted painfully through the fluid in her lungs. When Abba thought the "tide was high" she asked to be moved to Anna's, thinking she might get relief from the change of scene. Suddenly Louisa gave out and spent a week close to death. She thought she might not survive her mother, but managed to rally. On the fourteenth of November, both patients were moved to Anna's house.

As they took Abba upstairs, she said, "The ascension has begun." On a rainy Sunday, the twenty-fifth of November, she was happy all day, believing herself to be a young girl again, surrounded by her parents and sisters. She said her Sunday hymn to Louisa, whom with ironic justice she had begun calling "Mother." She was very cheerful, saying, "A smile is as good as a prayer." Often she waved at May's small picture, crooning, "Good-by little

May, good-by." She repeated to herself quietly, "O, how beautiful it is to die, how happy I am." She told her husband that he was laying "a very soft pillow for me to sleep on." Louisa had feared that she would suffer severely at the end, "but she was spared that and slipped peacefully away. I shall be glad to follow her. I never wish her back, but a great warmth seems gone out of life, and there is no motive to go on now."

Two days later, at sunset, Abba was buried at Sleepy Hollow. Mr. Emerson sat with Bronson and Lydian sat with Louisa and Anna. The Reverend Cyrus Bartol gave the sermon, which Louisa copied painfully with her paralyzed thumb into her ledger. Bartol spoke of the customary sadness of funerals; "but here all is changed, heaven's sunlight shines in upon us, peace reigns, a serene joy fills faces of those who do not mourn . . . only the memory of the imperishable spirit remains to gladden those who came to pay their tribute of love and honor." No one was sad that Abba's long, painful old age was over.

May wrote, grief-stricken and guilty at not having come home: "My only comfort is that perhaps my letters and little triumphs here have given her more pleasure than if I had staid at home with her, for I wasn't the kind and thoughtful daughter that Annie has been to her, and I have so much to reproach myself with that it seems as if I can never forgive myself."

Two days after the funeral, Louisa and her father celebrated their forty-fifth and seventy-eighth birthdays silently, in mourning. Louisa had lost the human closest to her. Her feelings about her mother were powerful, painful, and knotted unintelligibly. Abba's death did nothing to lessen their intensity or confusion. The guilt she inspired lived on in her daughters. In dying she had removed the core of Louisa's emotional life and left her vacant and panicky. "My only comfort is," she wrote, echoing May in self-recrimination, "that I *could* make her last years comfortable, and lift off the burden she had carried so bravely all these years. She was so loyal, tender and true; life was hard for her, and no one understood all she had to bear but we, her children. I think I shall soon follow her, and am quite ready to go now she no longer needs me."

19

Duty's Faithful Child

BRONSON AND LOUISA DREW CLOSER after Abba's death, able to appreciate each other's grief and express through it the halting tenderness they felt for each other. Bronson wrote a sonnet to his daughter, articulating his understanding of her dedicated service to the family. Louisa, who usually felt unappreciated, was touched to receive her father's sympathetic poem:

> When I remember with what buoyant heart,
> Midst war's alarms and woes of civil strife,
> In youthful eagerness thou didst depart,
> At peril of thy safety, peace and life,
> To nurse the wounded soldier, swathe the dead, —
> How piercèd soon by fever's poisoned dart,
> And brought unconscious home, with 'wildered head,
> Thou ever since, mid langor and dull pain,
> To conquer fortune, cherish kindred dear,
> Hast with great studies vexed a sprightly brain,
> In myriad households kindled love and cheer,
> Ne'er from thyself by Fame's loud trump beguiled,
> Sounding in this and the farther hemisphere,
> I press thee to my heart as Duty's faithful child.

Louisa had traveled across the hard years of Abba's sickness to arrive at a deeper, gentler love for her father, whose distance no longer seemed a criticism, but his own eccentric preoccupation with issues that remained unfathomable to her. As an adult, Louisa had found her mother's demanding, even strangling involvement with her a form of intermittently sweet torture. She felt bereft without Abba's intense presence and the intimate, confidential love it embodied, but she found solace in her father's more detached affection.

Bronson and Louisa mourned during the winter of 1877–1878. Together they pored over Abba's papers, thinking to put together a memoir of the woman. The experience intensified their grief. Louisa was fascinated and saddened in reading through records of her mother's "delicate, cherished girlhood through her long, hard, romantic years, old age and death." For Bronson there was the added sorrow that he had contributed to Abba's suffering: "My heart bleeds afresh with the memories of those days . . . of cheerless anxiety and hopeless dependence . . . I copy with tearful admiration these pages and almost repent now of my seeming incompetency, my utter inability to relieve the burdens laid upon her and my children during those years of helplessness. Nor can I with every mitigating apology for this seeming shiftlessness quite excuse myself for not entering upon some impossible feat to extricate us from these streights [sic] of circumstance."

Louisa solicited memoirs and incidents from friends. They came back expressing respect and understanding for Abba's difficult life. Lydia Maria Child remembered when she lived near Abba on Cottage Place in Boston. When Abba was very sick, her friend recalled how moved she was to "hear how her wandering mind was constantly occupied with anxious cares for her children. But careful foresight and unwearied efforts for the welfare of her family never narrowed her sympathies for all her fellow creatures. She was always prompt to help in righting wrongs and alleviating sufferings. These dispositions were, indeed, an inheritance. No one is surprised to find any member of the May family habitually rightminded and kindly, because everybody knows they cannot help it."

Copying sections from her mother's diaries and letters so exhausted and upset Louisa, stirring up in her the familiar feeling that she must make things right, that she fell very ill. Off and on throughout the months after her mother's death she wondered if she were to survive. She described Bronson as restless without his anchor, but she, too, was directionless: "I dawdle about and wait to see if I am to live or die. If I live, it is for some new work. I wonder what?" Without her mother to provide her with an excuse to live, Louisa was at a loss to justify her existence.

Anna kept house for her sister and father, thinking it unlikely that they would ever move back to Orchard House. It was taxing being "house mother and full of cares, everyone coming to me for everything, but it is good to feel so necessary, and I keep up good heart and feel glad my shoulders are so broad and strong for the burden."

Unwittingly, May provided Louisa with a rationale for living. She wrote home about the "tender friend" who consoled her in her grief. Ernest Nieriker, a twenty-two-year-old Swiss banker, played the violin and played chess with May to distract her. As John Pratt had helped Anna through Beth's death by offering sweet, undemanding sympathy, Ernest aided May in the same way. It is a close parallel. Both men were younger — Ernest more than fifteen years younger than May, both were stable, gentle, and responsible providers. They stepped in at moments when the family structure had proved fallible. Only a great breach in the Alcott fortifications allowed outsiders to make any headway into the family. May had helped the process by leaving Concord. Even at that distance she felt home disapproval of her effort to grow beyond the family.

"Your letters," she wrote, "seem almost a reproach to me for being able to forget that dear Marmee has gone from us even during this most happy time of my life." But she was so hopeful and glad that she couldn't pretend to match the doleful mood at home: "My future seems so full of beauty and joy I can think of nothing else. The lonely artistic life that once satisfied me seems the most dreary in the world. Our tastes are so congenial it seems impossible that we shall ever clash, and even were it otherwise I find myself for the first time quite willing to bend to a stronger will and wiser head than my own. Ernest is so gentle yet so firm, and I know he loves me so tenderly that I yield easily, so you see how changed is your wilful, strong-minded sister. She is as gentle and sweet, dear Nanny as yourself."

The couple was married in Paris on March 22, 1878. They took a house in a Parisian suburb, where they lived quietly. May wrote: "I exult in the thought that I need never have a big American establishment to worry me but live in this fine foreign fashion, so independent and delightful." Ernest was a handsome, brown-haired man with a good income and good prospects. May relished their self-sufficiency, "and not a day passes that I do not thank

Heaven I have this good and tender husband to care for me, and must no longer wander over the earth alone." She got messages from Concord implying that her marriage was hasty and her plans selfish and ill-considered. But May was firm and told Louisa that her happiness had not made her "unmindful of her, for it only draws us nearer. But I have laid out my future life and hope not to swerve from my purpose. I do not mean to be hindered by envious people, or anything to divert me from accomplishing my dream." She urged her sister to come and visit, and Louisa looked forward to the idea.

May was very decided about the way she wanted to live. "America seems death to all aspirations of hope and work," she wrote her sister. "Nothing would ever induce me to live in Concord again burdened with cares after this taste of all life can be. If woman wanted a new lease on life let her come here." Certainly Louisa needed a new lease on life. She read her sister's mouthwatering descriptions of her domesticity, and shared the letters with the Emersons. May gave a party for her mother-in-law and covered her table with "fine damask, my pretty silver and plenty of flowers and a green grape-leaf dish piled high with peaches, pears and grapes. Salmon salad, Gervais cheese, cold tongue, nice cake and a *pâté douceurs* such as only the French can make, gave us a charming lunch, finished with wine." May thought if Louisa came and experienced her good life "she will never want to live in stupid America again."

Louisa reflected on the vast differences between her sister's life and her own. They had always been unalike, May pursuing her own life, Louisa pursuing the lives of others. Louisa was lonely and sick while May was "so happy and blest. She always had the cream of things, and deserved it. My time is yet to come somewhere else, when I am ready for it." Throughout the spring May urged Louisa to make the trip. Louisa wanted very much to go, and thought perhaps in the fall, but her health was always problematic: "I doubt if I ever find time to lead my own life, or health to try it."

Louisa spent the spring hiding out from visitors, feeling particularly ill-disposed and unwilling to display herself. One of the reasons she was so fan-shy was that she inevitably was a disappointment. One little girl came away crying from the big, severe, middle-aged woman in black. It was hard to be the source of such

misery and it hurt Louisa. "Why people will think Jo small when
she is described as tall I don't see; and why insist that she must be
young when she is said to be 30 at the end of the book," she wrote
plaintively.

The Reverend Julius Ward, a friend of Bronson's from the West,
came. Louisa stayed in her room throughout his visit. Bronson
asked her to come down but she refused, thinking Ward might
write an article about his visit. "It had hardly occurred to me,"
wrote Bronson, "that our visitor had designs upon us for an article,
for the newspapers, and if it had, his reception by me, had not been
the less hospitable and hearty. Anna's reception was all that could
have been desired . . ." Louisa hated the monster she had created,
a public. Her defensive, bristly nature distrusted attention of any
kind and made extremely bad press. Her father loved flattery and
aggravated her annoyance by encouraging it. She refused to please
him by parading famous in front of his friends. Bronson took to
saving press clippings about Louisa's unsociability and gave her
lectures on it. "Miss Louisa Alcott," read one paper, "is regarded
as rather stiff and unapproachable in society. In Concord, Mass.,
where she lives, it is said that she 'snubs' right and left, in return
for the 'snubs' she received when a poor working girl from those
who perhaps now would fawn upon her."

In the summer of 1878 Bronson's life work had begun in the
shape of the Concord School of Philosophy, a four-week session
of lectures and discussions. The opening lecture was on Plato, of
course, and there followed meetings on ethics, morals, aesthetics,
women, literature, and the gamut of Bronson's interests. Sanborn
acted as treasurer and secretary while Alcott was dean. Bronson
was as happy as he had been in years.

Concord was pleased to find its most unworldly citizen providing them with some commerce, for students came in from all over
needing food and housing. Louisa was glad to see her father in
such good spirits, but felt rather tart about the whole thing. She
would have preferred a conference of philanthropists. She thought
that "speculation seems a waste of time when there is so much real
work to be done. Why discuss the unknowable till our poor are fed
and the wicked saved?"

Anna agreed with her sister and tried to keep out of the way: "I
am like the confectioner who having all the sweets he wishes

chooses plain bread and butter for supper. I have had so much of the so-called philosophy in my life that I care nothing for it, but content myself with what seems to me the true philosophy of every day life. Louisa's motto, 'Do the duty that is nearest thee' seems to me to embrace as much philosophy as most of us need; so few of us are able to do the duty uncomplainingly and bravely."

Part of the sister's disparagement came from the fact that the school demanded a great deal of work and time from them. They opened and decorated Orchard House for seminars and discussions, cleaned, and provided food and tea for the thinkers. Louisa defined a philosopher as "a man up in a balloon, with his family and friends holding the ropes which confine him to earth and trying to haul him down."

Louisa had planned to sail for Europe in September, but Anna fell out of a carriage and broke her leg, a simple but ill-timed fracture. "Louisa takes charge of the housekeeping and all is provided for without inconvenience," wrote Bronson out of his minuscule knowledge of inconvenience. "Always a little chore to be done," wrote Louisa, her jaw clenched. She gave up her plans, fearing that the trip would undo the good that a year's rest had given her: "A great disappointment; but I've learned to wait." For the next two months she kept house while Nan improved "and tried to be content but was not."

In December she moved back to Boston to the Bellevue, where she began work on *Jack and Jill.* She planned to go to Europe in the spring to see May's "ideal life . . . painting, music, love and the world shut out . . . Wise people to enjoy this lovely time as long as they can for it never lasts." Louisa found that she was too weak to do much work and read Mary Wollstonecraft instead.

In January the Papyrus Club honored her at a dinner where the witty Dr. Holmes fussed over her and made her feel special. Young Henry James had warned her to beware of people telling her she was a genius, for she wasn't. It was advice she didn't need, and she enjoyed the dinner without taking the flattery or censure seriously.

The next month, too tired for even limited socializing, she went home to Concord. There she read George Eliot and rested. She didn't enjoy *Daniel Deronda,* finding Eliot "wise but heavy."

She spent as much time as she could with her Concord friend Dr. Laura Whiting Hosmer, who had moved to Concord from Sudbury and married Concord's representative to the Massachusetts General Court, Henry J. Hosmer. Laura, Louisa's "rainy day friend," came to be as close to Louisa as anyone but her mother. They corresponded voluminously, spent vacations together, and formed a strong attachment. Dr. Hosmer looked after Louisa in a motherly way and Louisa relied on her warmth, support, and advice: "She is a great comfort to me with her healthy commonsense and tender patience, aside from skill as a doctor and beauty as a woman. I love her much and she does me good."

On March 16, 1879, Nan's forty-eighth birthday, Louisa reflected on the peculiar relation she had with her sister, so different from herself. She thought Nan "the best woman I know, always reasonable, just, kind and forgiving. A heavenly temper and a tender heart. A good sister to me all these years in spite of the utter unlikeness of our tastes, temperaments and lives. If we did not love one another so well we never could get on at all. As it is I am a trial to her and she to me sometimes, our views are so different . . ."

She was in great pain during the spring, often feeling that life wasn't worth living in such distress: "Long for the old strength when I could do what I liked and never knew I had a body." Because walking was so difficult she bought a phaeton, which her father loved. Unable to work, she took drives and supervised the construction of a fence around Anna's garden. She also put together a box of baby things for the child May was expecting in the fall. "Even lonely old spinsters take an interest in babies," she remarked with the self-pity born of endless pain.

Her disabilities laid wearying siege to her already low spirits. She took rides in the cool, clear June weather only to be reminded of her aches: "Souls are such slaves to bodies it is hard to keep up and out of the slough of despond when nerves jangle and the flesh aches." Laura assured her she was mending, which calmed her fears even if the aches persisted.

She took an outing with her father to the Concord State Reformatory. A carriage called for her and Bronson in the morning and deposited them at the prison at 10:00 A.M., when they found Sunday school in session. Louisa had been asked to give the four hundred inmates a talk. She didn't know if she could combat her fright, but began a moral story drawn from her Georgetown hospital experiences. She grew so interested "in watching the faces of some young men near me, who drank in every word, that I forgot myself, and talked away 'like a mother.' " Bronson told her she had done very well and she was quite proud of herself. After the sermon Bronson gave a talk, and the pair returned home, pleased by the success of their mission.

Laura Hosmer accompanied Louisa on another prison expedition, this time to the Woman's Prison at Sherbourne, where Louisa talked to the resident physician, Dr. Lucy M. Hall, and read the prisoners a story. Louisa noticed the gentler methods employed there and thought they indicated "patience, love and common sense and the belief in salvation for all."

On July 15, the Concord school opened its second session with thirty students. Louisa resented the philosophers "roost[ing] on our steps like hens waiting for corn. Father revels in it so we keep the hotel going and try to look as if we liked it." To rest, Louisa spent a week with Laura and her family on the shore.

In July, Louisa was chosen secretary of the committee to canvas Concord women to register for the school committee elections, in which they were allowed to vote. On Louisa's return from vacation, she became the first woman to register. She told the selectman to put her name on the rolls. He asked for her receipt of the previous year's tax. She hadn't brought it and asked if the current year's receipt would do. He said it would but pointed out that she hadn't paid it yet. She laughed, had the assessor make out her bill, and paid it. "I never did hanker to pay my taxes," wrote Louisa in the *Woman's Journal,* "but now am in a hurry to pay them."

Louisa made rounds in her phaeton, visiting Concord women, but found them "timid and slow." In September she held a meeting to organize the town's first integrated election. The actual work of reform frustrated and exasperated her: "So hard to move people out of the old ruts. I haven't patience enough. If they won't see and work I let 'em alone and steam along my own way." She was a bad politician, self-righteous and convinced of her way with no tolerance for fear or hesitancy.

Her best contributions came from her writing — books, articles, and her many pieces in the *Woman's Journal,* one of the great sources of information on suffrage. Patiently the paper explained to woman that polling places were not as obscene and degraded as rumor had it: "A stream of men of all classes and conditions, coming and going in their every day clothes, but in an orderly and sober manner, with gentlemanly officials and police to see to it that everything is conducted decently, is all that characterizes the polling in Massachusetts cities and towns." The polls, the *Journal* assured women, had "no features more obnoxious to modesty or more offensive to ladies than such as they encounter daily on the streets and in the depots and postoffices."

Louisa settled down to a slow schedule of work that fall. She planned a chapter a day of *Jack and Jill,* with no binges of fourteen hours. "It is so easy to make money now and so pleasant to have it to give," she thought, unwilling to give up her one indulgence.

But her health didn't hold, and she had to slow down, giving up her plan of being with May for her delivery in November: "Give up my hope and long cherished plan with grief. May sadly disappointed. I know I shall wish I had gone. It is my luck."

On October 28th, her mother's birthday, Louisa made a visit to her grave at Sleepy Hollow. She gazed at the small white marker. There were red-leaved blackberry branches trailing across the plot, tangling through the tall grass. On the stone a bird had made a nest.

She took rooms at the Bellevue and worked slowly. On November 8 came the news that May had delivered a healthy girl, Louisa May Nieriker: "Much rejoicing. Nice little lass and May very happy. Ah, if I had only been there! Too much happiness for me."

Louisa gave up her Boston rooms after Lulu's birth, finding it too tiring to be in the city. "Can be sound at home and it's cheaper," she decided. The news from France was not good. May had not recovered from her delivery and continued to weaken. "She was too happy to have it last," predicted Louisa, "and I fear the end is coming. Hope it is my nerves but this peculiar feeling has never misled me before." Reports came that May was too sick to nurse the baby and the little girl didn't like her nurse. "Oh, if I could only be there to see, to help! This is a penance," Louisa continued irrationally, "for all my sins. Such a tugging at my heart to be by poor May alone so far away."

Anna was in Boston and Bronson at the Concord post office looking for letters when Louisa came downstairs on December 31 to find Mr. Emerson holding a telegram and looking at May's portrait. He was wan and red-eyed and handed Louisa a cable, saying, "My child, I wish I could prepare you, but alas, alas." He could not go on. Ernest Nieriker had wired Emerson the news of May's death, thinking he could soften the intensity of the blow. Louisa knew that she wasn't surprised and suddenly felt as if she had known for weeks. She told Emerson that she was prepared: "He was much moved and very tender. I shall remember gratefully the look, the grasp, the tears he gave me, and I am sure that hard moment was made bearable by the presence of this our best and tenderest friend." Waldo tried to find Bronson but missed him, so Louisa had to tell the dreadful story to him and Anna.

Unreasonably, Louisa reproached herself for not being with her sister and punished herself with the tormenting idea that if she had only been there she might have found peace: "I shall never forgive myself for not going even if it put me back. If I had lived to see her and help her die, or save her, I should have been content." There was always a task undone, a job that Louisa could blame herself for not completing. Anna wrote to a friend that she had never seen her sister so "broken; so many hopes are shattered, and so much to which she has looked forward so long has now vanished forever."

May had written that if she died in childbirth not to mourn, for she had had two perfect years. Louisa saw those years, not as a blessing, but as a Faustian bargain whose price was death. It convinced her ever more firmly that happiness was an actionable offense against the natural order of the world. Nevertheless, May's death threw her world out of focus. She had always seen May as the one who defied the course of self-denial, pleased herself, and got what she wanted. Although Louisa disapproved of May's attention to her own life, part of her rejoiced to see someone getting away with pleasure. If it couldn't be her, it should be her little sister. But May's death came as a random, gratuitous act of God's cruelty, which was hard to square with Emerson's tidy transcendental codex.

Ultimately Louisa derived a meaning from Lulu. May had designated Louisa to raise the little girl in the event of her death; "I see now why I lived. To care for May's child and not leave Anna all alone."

Throughout January Louisa mourned. She and her father wrote verses calling up memories of May, and these expressions seemed to ease their pain: "Of all the trials in my life, never felt any so keenly as this, perhaps because I am so feeble in health that I cannot bear it well." She dwelled morbidly on the reports of May's last weeks, when she was often unconscious and feverish, worrying in her delerium about "getting ready for Louy." It was almost impossible for Louisa to accept and absorb the information, to "make it true that our May is dead, lying far away in a strange grave, leaving a husband and child whom we have never seen. It all reads like a pretty romance, now death has set its seal on those two happy years and we shall never know all that she could tell us."

Louisa expected to receive her niece in the spring, but her arrival was postponed till the fall. In March, a trunk with May's intimate articles arrived. It contained the pictures she had painted, the dress and slippers she was wearing when she went into labor, some jewelry, and her workbasket. There was a locket of May's hair tied with a blue ribbon in one of her sepia boxes. Ernest had enclosed a furlined sack, which Louisa put on and felt hugged by her sister. Before her death May had arranged for her diaries to be sent back home, for, like her sisters, family meant Concord, and Ernest never intruded upon the home she carried inside her. The trunk's arrival occasioned renewed grief and Louisa cried piteously over each item.

She tried to sleep, with the help of her laudanum, as much as possible: "Life is so heavy I try to forget it in blessed unconsciousness when I can." She drew nearer to Anna, and had her house repaired and bought her many presents. She was the best sister, wrote Louisa, "God ever made."

Louisa knew that she was to appear in a volume by Mary Clemmer called *Famous Women*. "Don't belong there," she noted, but, knowing that she would be an object of biography, went on one of her frequent letter and diary rampages, destroying whatever seemed unacceptable.

On March 29, the long-awaited Concord school committee elections came up. Louisa wrote up the story for the *Woman's Journal*. Twenty-eight women had registered, but for a variety of reasons only twenty showed up, "all in good spirits and not in the least daunted by the awful deed about to be done." The town meeting proceeded with its customary dullness. Even the novelty of attending didn't counteract the boring aspect of the occasion. She found it like a lyceum lecture, "only rather more tedious." Voting took place late in the meeting. Bronson had asked when and where the women were to vote, and was told that they could vote just as the men did. Bronson suggested that they should come first, "as a proper token of respect and for the credit of the town." The selectmen agreed, and the women dropped their slips of paper into the ballot box first and returned quickly to their seats while the men watched in silence. Suddenly Judge Hoar proposed that the polls close: "The motion was carried before the laugh subsided and the polls were closed without a man's voting; a perfectly fair proceeding *we* thought since we were allowed no voice on any other question." The superintendent of schools protested that the whole town should vote, but was informed that the women voted as the men would have, so it made no difference.

Louisa enjoyed the spectacle of a group of schoolboys watching their mothers, sisters, and aunts making their voting debut. She noticed several husbands and wives enjoying themselves throughout. She hoped that "when the timid or indifferent, several of whom came to look on, see that we still live they will venture to express publicly the opinions they hold or have lately learned to respect and believe."

After the elections Louisa moved back to the Bellevue, feeling sick and unhappy and wanting a change. She made out a will, leaving her father a legacy and dividing the rest between Nan and the boys, with May's paintings and $500 for Lulu. She chased reporters away but was pleased to receive a delegation of thirty girls from Boston University. She told them stories, signed autographs, and enjoyed their considerate attention: "Bright girls, simple in dress, sensible ideas of life, and love of education."

Jack and Jill came out, a story about an impetuous little girl and her friendship with a loyal, steady boy. The girl's willfulness leads the two into a near-fatal sledding accident. The boy is in great pain, but Jill's injury is more serious, and she spends the story on her back, in danger of complete paralysis. Jill is another Louisa-like tomboy who needs the fierce discipline of pain and fear to subdue her lively spirit. The disturbing, violent repression forced on the girl apparently expressed some fear of Louisa's that a natural, spunky little girl had to be flattened or she would cause untold damage. As it is, Jill is responsible for nearly killing herself and Jack.

Her long convalescense, lying month after month on a couch, teaches her to control her exuberant spirits. She learns her duty to train boys in gentleness and mannerliness. She learns obedience and trains to become a saint, "so patient other people were ashamed to complain of their small worries; so cheerful, that her own great new [burden] grew lighter; so industrious, that she made both money and friends by pretty things she worked and sold to her many visitors. And, best of all, so wise and sweet that she seemed to get good out of everything, and make her poor room a sort of chapel where people went for comfort, counsel, and an example of a pious life."

The story is an eerie demonstration that good girls, to Louisa, were emotionally and literally flat on their backs. Learning passivity, even by breaking one's spine, was the only way to become a proper woman. Having learned her part, Jill marries Jack. Her friend Molly, however, never took the cure and "remained a merry spinster all her days, one of the independent, brave and busy creatures of whom there is such need in the world to help take care of other people's wives and children and do the many useful jobs that the married folks have no time for."

That summer Louisa went to York, Maine, leaving Anna to the philosopher hordes. "Philosophy is a bore to outsiders," she concluded. Anna received more than four hundred callers, and when Bronson asked why she didn't attended the sessions, she showed him the list of guests. He said nothing more.

On August 21, Louisa dispatched Mrs. Giles, a capable nurse, to cross the Atlantic to fetch Lulu. Seeing off Mrs. Giles reminded Louisa of May's last departure, "sober and sad, but gay as before. Seemed to feel it might be a longer voyage than we knew." She remembered May wearing her blue cloak, waving. Back in Concord, Louisa found that "grief meets me when I come . . . and the house is full of ghosts."

Louisa went to the docks when Mrs. Giles's boat landed and watched all the debarking children, looking for her own. Finally, the ship's captain approached her carrying a small, yellow-haired, white-wrapped bundle. "I held out my arms to Lulu only being able to say her name. She looked at me for a moment, then came to me saying 'Marmar' in a wistful way and nestling close as if she had found her own people and home at last as she had, thank Heaven!"

She took Lulu back to the house she had rented from her cousin Lizzie Wells at 81 Pinckney Street. It was a four-story brick townhouse facing Louisburg Square. Bronson liked his large, sunny study, but Louisa was unhappy with the condition of the house. Throughout the fall she was distracted by worries over clogged drains, a defective furnace, and, worst of all, rats. In September she got her father outfitted in black for his western tour. "I suppose I am of *'the cloth'* by genesis and genius . . ." he reflected. "Perhaps the doctorate awaits me from authorities yet unnamed."

Lulu was a constant pleasure. She had a pug nose, blue eyes, and a feathering of yellow hair. She was not quite pretty, but well formed, healthy and even tempered. "She always comes to me," wrote Louisa, gratified, "and seems to have decided that I am really 'Marmar.' My heart is full of pride and joy, and the touch of the dear little hands seems to take away the bitterness of grief."

On Lulu's first birthday, November 8, the family celebrated with a small cake, a crown of roses, picture books, toys, flowers, a doll, and a silver mug. During the festivities, they pointed out May's portrait to the little girl, and she took a rose, holding it up to the picture and calling out what her aunts chose to interpret as "Mum! Mum!" while Louisa and Anna cried. Louisa fussed over Lulu and delighted in the girl's first walk: "Had never crept at all, but when ready ran across the room and plumped down, laughing triumphantly at her feat."

The sisters tried to celebrate a cheerful Christmas for the sake of Lulu and the boys, but they were weighed down with thoughts of absent family. The one event that gave Louisa uniquely moral pleasure was the appearance of a young man recently released from the Concord Reformatory. He told Louisa that he had heard her speech and it had done him great good. He had fallen in with some men who were drinking, got drunk himself, and stole something from a doctor's office. After a three-year term he wanted to reform and hearing Louisa had been an inspiration. He left on a geological tour of South American shortly after visiting Louisa. His story allowed her a moment of thinking well of herself: "Glad to have said a word to help the poor boy." The incident appeared, lengthened and embellished, in *Jo's Boys*.

When her health allowed, Louisa contributed to the *Woman's Journal*. She didn't attend a Boston suffrage festival and found herself criticized. Angrily she wrote to the *Journal,* saying that her home obligations had kept her from the fun, but, unlike the others, she had voted. That spring Louisa urged Thomas Niles to publish Mrs. Harriet Janes Robinson's history of suffrage. Mrs. Robinson, a short, firm, and substantial ex-worker from the Lowell mills wrote *Massachusetts in the Woman Suffrage Movement.* Mrs. Robinson noted in her introduction that she was "especially grateful to Louisa M. Alcott and Wendell Phillips for their encouragement, and sympathy with my work . . ." Niles published the book in 1881. He wrote to Louisa that he would "do anything to please" her. He believed in "allowing the ladies, dear creatures, to do just what they have a mind to do, but I believe the bayonet and the ballot go together, and I should hate to see you shouldering a musket."

In March 1881, Louisa visited the new New England Hospital for Women and Children. She wrote the *Journal* a glowing description of the institution and urged its support: "Only women could so perfectly understand the needs of women, and minister to them with such tender skill and sympathy in their time of trial . . . There was laugher and reading aloud in one room where several ladies seemed to be enjoying themselves, with no sign of hospital life but the narrow white beds and uncarpeted floor. A hint to us outsiders to make our own chambers as sweet and wholesome." Louisa approved of women taking over more control of the medical care that affected them. This was the only Boston institution where women could get practical hospital experience as doctors and nurses.

In the spring the family moved back to Concord. Emerson seemed very old, never walking around the village anymore, tilting slightly forward in his black suit. He rarely saw anyone, and wrote to his friend Emma Lazarus that "an old man fears most his best friends. It is not them he is willing to distress with his perpetual forgetfulness of the right word for the name of book or fact or person . . . I have grown silent to my own household under this vexation, and cannot afflict dear friends with my tied tongue . . ." If a visitor would come he would ask Lydian for help: "What was the name of my best friend?" "Henry Thoreau," she would reply. "Oh yes, Henry Thoreau."

Louisa and Bronson dropped over in May for a rare visit, taking Waldo flowers. He took the bouquet and smiled gratefully, hugging the blooms, not speaking. Bronson began talking about his trip out west, and several times Waldo asked if he had met any interesting men, returning to his old theme of the search for American genius. Bronson remarked on the cloud over his friend, which "overshadowed his genius during these later years."

As for himself, Bronson was satisfied to find his friends commending him on his *"youthful presence* and the prospect of future years of activity. They inquire the secret. I were perhaps hardly civil if I answered: 'Keep the commandments.' And yet I know of no other, and am coming to the persuasion that, with the observance of the fine laws of continency and general temperance, a well-born person, might naturally attain to the end of his century and pass onward without most of the infirmities that now afflict old age to shorten his years, and leave their stain on his recollections." He thought his good health rested on a vegetable diet and thinking good thoughts: "It is unquestionable that the ascendency of ideas is favorable to longevity." Emerson, he thought, must have bad genes. As for himself, he complimented himself on his excellent heredity.

After the summer school sessions, Walt Whitman, in Boston to read proofs of his new collection of poems, made a visit to Concord. Louisa was very curious to meet the poet and joined her father and him at tea at Sanborn's. Six-foot-tall Whitman was looking venerable in a wide-collared shirt, carrying a cane and wearing a blue coat. He was interested in Alcott's ideas about Thoreau, Margaret Fuller, Emerson, and Hawthorne, and asked many encouraging questions. He never disparaged anyone and didn't like it when others did. After tea, Sanborn read letters from Thoreau, Horace Greeley, Margaret Fuller, and Ellery Channing.

That fall Louisa took a house on Beacon Hill, building a study for Bronson and a bedroom above it for herself. She was feeling unwell and was restricted to a diet of eggs, milk, and a daily pint of cream. Her only interest was Lulu, whose health obsessed her. The little girl was growing fast and the doctors recommended that she eat meat. Bronson despaired: "They would demonize the little saint, and dim all her beauty, for the sake of adding superfluous muscle and what they call healthful animal life. I wish I may never cease contesting this assault upon her serenity and sweetness of soul."

On the girl's second birthday Louisa showered her with kisses. She brought her downstairs from her bedroom to find a new chair "decked with ribbons and a doll's carriage tied with pink, toys, pictures, flowers and a cake with a red and blue candle burning gaily."

Later that month Louisa and Bronson celebrated their joint birthdays. She was forty-nine and he was eighty-two. She had stitched a cap for him and gave him a book of sonnets.

The little girl worried Louisa. She had minor ills that disquieted her extremely health-conscious aunt. Louisa was forever consulting doctors and giving the girl remedies and elixirs. The girl was also something of a strain for Louisa, tired and ill as she usually was. She found she could calm Lulu down by holding her and telling her stories, but she didn't always have the energy to make up tales with lambs and piggies: "Wish I were stronger so that I might take all the care of her. We seem to understand one another but my nerves make me impatient and noise wears upon me."

In March, Louisa, feeling strong enough for a little reform, helped organize Concord's first temperance society, which she felt was greatly needed. The drinking she observed was being done by native Americans, not the Irish: "Women anxious to do something but find no interest beyond a few. Have meetings and try to learn how to work." By summer twenty-seven young men had signed the pledge.

In the early spring Bronson visited Emerson, telling Louisa how silent and veiled he was. In April he found Emerson in bed. Mrs. Emerson said he had gone out into the cold spring winds without his topcoat and had contracted a mild pneumonia.

On April 26 Bronson was shown into Emerson's sickroom. Waldo put out his hand, saying, "You are quite well?" Bronson said he was but that he was not used to finding his friend in bed. Emerson made some indistinct sounds and Bronson began to leave. Waldo called him back, saying with more clarity, "You have a strong hold on life and maintain it firmly." Then the voice grew unintelligible again and Bronson left, afraid he might not see his good friend again.

On the next day Sanborn called on Emerson, but he couldn't speak. And on the twenty-eighth he died. "Our best and greatest American is gone," wrote Louisa. "The nearest and dearest friend

Father ever had, and the man who has helped me the most by his life, his books, his society. I can never tell all he has been to me, — from the time I sang Mignon's song under his window . . . and wrote letters *a la* Bettine to him, my Goethe, at fifteen, up through the hard years when his essays on Self-Reliance, Character, Compensation, Love and Friendship helped me to understand myself and life, and God and Nature." Louisa had lost a teacher, an idol, and an object of worship who, in his strange, distant way, offered her a practical strength and stability her father lacked.

All of Concord went into mourning, with the library and doorways all draped in black. The flag flew at half-mast, with two long black streamers fluttering below. Louisa decorated the church with pine branches, flowers, and a harp of yellow jonquils. A special train from Boston brought friends like Elizabeth Peabody, President Eliot of Harvard, Charles Eliot Norton, Thomas Wentworth Higginson, Julian Hawthorne, and scores of others. The Reverend James Freeman Clarke gave the funeral sermon for his dear, long-time companion to Emerson's closest friends while hundreds of mourners waited outside the chapel. At Sleepy Hollow, the grandchildren threw flowers onto the grave of his first wife, Ellen, whom he had mourned so long. Throughout the spring and summer Louisa and her father visited Lydian and Ellen, talking of Waldo, bringing their memories of him to the sick widow and heartbroken daughter.

After the summer school Louisa moved to Boston with the newly weaned Lulu. She wanted to look after her health and try to write. On October 22 her father visited John Brown's widow, who was spending a few days at Sanborn's. The next day Bronson wrote about his intention to live to see his hundredth year, and commented again on his robust health. The following day, October 24, 1882, Louisa received a telegram with the news that Bronson had had a paralytic stroke.

Father and Daughter

LOUISA HURRIED HOME TO Concord to find Bronson helpless — partially paralyzed, unable to speak, staring blankly when awake. She was shocked and saddened. She blamed his condition on overexertion. The year before he had written forty sonnets and given fifty lectures at the summer school. His respected homeopathic doctor, Conrad Wesselhoeft, had warned him to slow down, but Bronson had persisted. Louisa blamed Franklin Sanborn for egging him on and tried to limit Sanborn's visits. She saw the stroke as Bronson's punishment for "breaking the laws of health. I have done the same, may I be spared this end."

It looked as if he wouldn't recover and Louisa rather hoped he would die quickly. The doctors gave her no hope for improvement, and the idea of a prolonged convalescence seemed dreary and miserable. She wrote to a friend: "I don't think that he will ever get up again or be himself. He may linger for weeks, but I think he will slowly wear away, his unusual vitality alone keeping him alive so long."

But Bronson had more strength than she thought. In the mornings, his nurse propped him up on a pillow while his bed was aired. He liked to hold on to books although he couldn't read. He made awkward attempts to scratch out letters on a pad. Every day he was bathed and rubbed down. He ate nothing but jelly and milk because swallowing was such a problem.

On the fourteenth of November he began speaking a little, scattered words. Sometimes in his sleep he would articulate a sentence as if he were giving a conversation. "I am taking a predicament," he would say, or, "The devil is never real only truth." When he tried to express something of more than a word or two, he would get frustrated and overexcited and yell or cry.

Louisa, exhausted, sick, and unhappy, took out her misery on the help. She fired nurse after nurse for drinking too much tea, relaxing on the job, having a bad attitude, a cold manner, or a taste for gossip. One drank and another was lazy. Louisa protected her father from company with a zealousness that seems exaggerated. His complete dependence was Louisa's final burden, one for which she had long prepared.

On their birthdays, November 29, Bronson insisted that he was twenty-three and Louisa fifteen. He has resumed his Connecticut nasality, which he had trained himself out of years before. He asked for his mother. The nurse told him she was in heaven and that he would see her there. "Yes," he said, "I think I shall, and she will know me if I *am* eighty-three, and wear a bib when I eat." Louisa could see the remarkable improvement he had made, but wouldn't give it much credence: "The arm swells badly, no use of either limb, no solid food, bowels still torpid, and no desire to leave his bed. I think if the spring finds him here, it will be only a shadow of his former self. I hope that he will be gone to the eternal summer, and leave us only a green mound and a green memory of much virtue, love and beauty."

He was childlike and petulant, demanding and uncontrolled. It was upsetting to Louisa, but she tried to remember compassion when she felt irritation. One day in May when he was worried and fretful she rubbed him with bay rum and told him, "You are a philosopher and must not be upset by small trials."

"Yes, I am, I will do it," he answered and stopped nagging. The nurse walked in and Bronson said, "I was cross, I confess, forgive me, I am so old." He reminded Louisa of Lear, "as he often does at times when the old instincts of a fine and gentle nature show through the weakness and wandering of a troubled brain."

The responsibility of looking after her father, her niece, and herself was so heavy that she began with greater frequency to vibrate between Boston and Concord. In February she tried to rest in Boston and do some work of her own: "This double life is trying and my head will work as well as my hands." She started a book called *Genesis* that she correctly imagined she would never finish.

But she desired a release for her overcharged central nervous system. The anonymity of Boston appealed to her. She felt, with some justification, that Concord was always spying on her. She wrote to a friend about her delight in getting away from pointing fingers and people saying "There's Louisa Alcott. I wonder where she's going, what she has got on, how she does, what she is thinking about and why she does not make *me* her bosom friend."

Louisa was in Concord for the election and registered her disgust that only seven women including Anna and herself had turned out to vote. She got quite stern with displays of irresponsibility and wrote an admonitory letter to the *Woman's Journal* about the slack habits of females. Once a year, she thought, men could have their meals a little late. She criticized "the want of forethought and promptness which shows how much our sex have yet to learn in the way of business habits." She hoped that at another election "they will leave the dishes till they get home, as they do when in a hurry to go to the sewing-society, Bible class or picnic."

Louisa's firm pro-suffrage stand was always at the mercy of her firm pro-housework stand. She maintained a philosophical commitment to the virtue of housekeeping for women, and preached that the domestic arts must be learned and practiced. These arts were broader than just sweeping and cooking and included anything that needed doing: "The home-making, the comfort, the sympathy, the grace and atmosphere that a true woman can provide is the noble part, and embraces all that is helpful for soul as well as body." It was woman's particular "fate to be called upon to lead a quiet self-sacrificing life with peculiar trials, needs and joys, and it seems to me that a very simple one is fitted to us whose hearts are usually more alive than heads, and whose hands are tied in many ways."

Louisa's woman had all the qualities of a man plus a large, biological dose of self-sacrifice. Her life was second to the duties at hand. Because Louisa's sacrifices kept her so occupied, Lucy Stone wrote to her, asking if she had "gone back" on suffrage. Louisa was rather dismayed to be misunderstood and wrote that "I earnestly desire to go forward on that line as far and as fast as the prejudices, selfishness and blindness of the world will let us, and it is a great cross to me that ill health and home duties prevent my devoting heart, pen and time to this most vital question of the age." She aired her reform connections to prove her loyalty: "After a fifty year acquaintance with the noble men and women of the Anti-slavery cause, the sight of the glorious end to their faithful work, I should be a traitor to all I most love, honor and desire to imitate, if I did not covet a place among those who are giving their lives to the emancipation of the white slaves of America." To Susan B. Anthony, who had written asking about Bronson's health, Louisa reexplained herself: "I am very proud of the *good* people with whom I may claim kindred, and wish I could do more to help the noble work they began. But my chore was a private one, and health went in the doing of it, so now I can only look on and say God speed."

Louisa tried to be sure that she had chosen the proper course, and that her duty had been clear. But all she was completely sure of was that she had been sacrificed. "Shall never live my own life," she wrote tersely in her diary. Louisa wrote a young Pennsylvania admirer a long, touching letter about her struggle with her life: "Now when I might enjoy rest, pleasure and travel I am still tied by new duties to my baby, and give up my dreams sure that something better will be given me in time. Freedom was always my longing, but I have never had it, so I am still trying to feel that this is the discipline I need and when I am ready the liberty will come." She had fit her success and her unhappiness into her moral plan, remarking that as a young woman she had believed that "if I *deserved* success it would surely come as long as my ambition was not for selfish ends but for my dear family, and it did come, far more fully than I ever hoped or dreamed in my youth, though health and many hopes went to earn it."

Women, she thought, if they had "hungry minds," must feed them with people and places. She had never liked Concord or found it satisfying and tried to get away as often as possible: "Food, fire and shelter are not *all* that women need, and the noble discontent that asks for more should not be condemned but helped if possible."

Anna didn't understand this about her sister, her desire to move, to learn, to travel. She saw Louisa's restlessness as the pathological component of genius: "This discontent and moody view of life seem inseparable from their gifted natures. So I sometimes thank heaven I am a humdrum, and cannot be gloomy or downhearted long. Though I have many sad hours, something within always bids me hope, and I have a happy faculty for seeing the silver lining to every cloud."

Anna presided, matronlike, over the establishments at Concord, Boston, and Nonquitt, on Buzzard's Bay, south of New Bedford, where Louisa bought a summer house. She looked after Bronson and her sons and consulted with her sister about the help. In June 1884, Louisa sold Orchard House, with Bronson's consent, to William Torrey Harris, a philosopher whom Bronson had met in St. Louis more than twenty years before. Harris eventually became the United States Commissioner of Education and collaborated with Franklin B. Sanborn on a biography of Bronson.

Harris asked Louisa if she would write a memoir of her father. She replied that she didn't know anything about biography, that he and Sanborn should do it to correct Bronson's reputation in the world. As for herself, she remarked that "his philosophy I have never understood . . ."

Louisa worried about her own papers, and spent several sessions reading and destroying documents: "Not wise to keep for curious eyes to read, and gossip-lovers to print by and by." She did a thorough job of weeding out everything that revealed anything but her strict Emersonian view of things. She got rid of most of her diaries and condensed events into snippets and remarks. She would have destroyed the whole works, but had second thoughts, knowing that her life was of interest to her public: "Experiences go very deep with me, and I begin to think it might be well to keep some record of my life if it will help others to read it when I've gone." The material she left conformed to the lessons from Theodore Parker and Emerson that she had spent her life trying to absorb. They had taught that "one can shape life best by trying to build up a strong and noble character though good books, wise people's society, an interest in all reforms that help the world, and a cheerful acceptance of whatever is inevitable. Seeing a beautiful compensation in what often seems a great sacrifice, sorrow or loss, and believing always that a wise, loving and just father cares for us, sees over weakness and is near to help if we call." When the journals did not reflect those lessons, as they rarely did, she destroyed them.

When she had the strength, Louisa devoted herself to Lulu. She was too tired to take care of her all the time, and hired a separate string of nurses: "The ladies are incapable or proud, the girls vulgar or rough, so my poor baby has a hard time with active mind and body . . ."

The little girl had numerous health problems. Louisa, who had been raised to think that the aim of life was the regular movement of the bowels, dosed the girl mercilessly. She even considered using opium, on which she had relied for so long. It is hard to reconcile Louisa's strong homeopathic convictions with her somewhat casual use of narcotics, but like many Victorians she was preoccupied with all aspects of digestion and believed one's health and sanity depended on clocklike evacuation.

The girl was often fretful and hard to manage. Once Louisa decided to spank her. Willfully the child urged her to do it, "and when it is done," Louisa recorded, "is heart broken at the idea of Aunt Wee Wee's giving her pain. Her bewilderment was pathetic and the effect, as I expected, a failure. Love is better, but also endless patience." The stubborn little girl was too much for her aunt, who was forced, for her own health, to leave her with Anna and the nurses.

Bronson appeared to be growing into his second youth. The summer following his stroke he had sprung a new crop of hair on a head that had been bald for decades. He was reading with Louisa's glasses instead of his much stronger ones. His memory and speech were not perfect, but his mind was clear, as was his gaze. Louisa could see improvements but held to her conviction that he was "slowly wearing away it seems to *me* in spite of apparent brightening at time . . . he seems feeble though he eats more and helps get into his chair. He is grown thin and sleepless, does not talk as well as he did some days ago, and both arm and leg swell and are purple even after lying in bed."

In the spring of 1885 Bronson confessed to Louisa that he was tired of living and wanted to "go up." She wrote to a friend that "a little more or a little less light would make him happier; but the still active mind beats against the prison bars, and rebels against the weakness of body that prevents the old independent life. I am afraid the end is not to be peaceful unless it is sudden, as I hope it may be for all our sakes; it is so wearing to see this slow decline, and be able to do little but preach and practice patience."

Louisa's bad health dominated her life: "The hospital experience was a costly one for me. Never well since. Yet it turned the tide and brought success." She suffered all over. The mercury poisoning gave her more severe, rheumaticlike pains, trembling, anxiety, irritability, weakness, and a fluttering pulse. Any extra exertion made her gravely ill and shaky. These symptoms varied in their intensity, but they were always present and increased whenever she made any effort. Her first attempt to write *Jo's Boys* gave her a terrifying attack of vertigo and forced her to stay in bed for a week: "Put away papers and tried to dawdle and go about as other people do."

There was nothing to prescribe for Louisa but rest. Her doctors took the calomel dosing into account, but there was nothing they could do for the barrage of complaints from which she suffered. She tried various paramedical cures herself, including applications of electricity and magnetising.

In January 1885, when her arm was so painful she couldn't write, she tried the "mind cure," a form of mind over body. Louisa made visits to its practitioner, Mrs. Newman, and the two would sit with their eyes closed for fifteen minutes: "I feel very still, then very light, and seem floating over a sea of rest. Once or twice I seemed to have no body, and to come back from another world. I felt as if I trod on air and was very happy and very young for some hours. Yet one does not sleep nor lose consciousness and there is nothing unpleasant about it . . ."

Throughout her life her father had told her that the soul must rule the body, and she was still trying to achieve the restful passivity that she imagined that entailed. She had great difficulty letting go her will and consciousness: "Delicate, gentle people often grasp these things more quickly than the positive ones . . ."

She tried, but her symptoms persisted, and she suffered one cataclysmic dizzy spell that left her "very lurchy when I walk and dizzy when I stoop. Back of headaches, worse in morning and lying down and a general worried state of body."

In March, Louisa tried the cure with a placid assistant of Mrs. Newman, thinking that *two* positive people might be hindering her progress. After thirty sessions, Mrs. Newman insisted that Louisa had it. And Louisa insisted that she didn't, that it had had no greater effect on her than a "moonbeam": "No miracle for me. My ills are not imaginary, so are hard to cure. Vertigo. Ill for ten days."

She was running along the edge of a breakdown all the time: "I think every day the time for a general collapse has come, but I manage to get up and trot along again so I'm not dead yet."

In the fall of 1885, she leased a house for two years on Louisburg Square. She thought the $1650 was very expensive, but moved the whole family in, gratified by a royalty check from Niles for $7591. She knew she would miss her quiet Boston escape, but thought it "best for all so I shall try to bear the friction and the worry many persons always bring me."

She had many ideas for new books, but had been so thoroughly frightened by her first experience with *Jo's Boys* that she postponed working. She wrote to Niles, asking him about bringing out a collection of stories she had told her niece, to be called *Lulu's Library:* "Old ladies come to this twaddle when they can do nothing else."

Louisa's pocket health journal for 1886 was a dismal record of fainting spells, dizzy collapses, vertigo, fatigue, rheumatism, rebellious stomach, and fright. March 27 reads: "Another attack of vertigo. Ill for a week. Sleepless nights. Head worked like a steam engine and would not stop. Planned *Jo's Boys* to the end and longed to get up and write it. Told Dr. W. that he had better let me get the idea out then I could rest." She convinced Dr. Wesselhoeft that she needed to use her energies. He agreed to let her work for thirty minutes a day, and Louisa enjoyed her limited employment, "when I forgot my body and lived in my mind." She continued on through April, writing an hour or two a day and feeling much better for it.

By June, Louisa had finished fifteen chapters and sent them off to Niles, very pleased with her accomplishment after seven years of rest from novels, and she moved the family back to Concord because Bronson and Anna wanted to be there. Louisa was just as glad to leave her experiment in group living behind, finding it expensive and "hard with our mixed family of ten, invalids, nurses, maids, boys and babies." She felt her illness to be a trial to everyone, characteristically seeing her suffering in the context of a burden on the family rather than as an affliction of her own.

She finished *Jo's Boys* in July to everyone's pleasure. Niles planned a first printing of 50,000 copies and the orders literally flooded in. The book is the last of the March family trilogy. It has, not surprisingly, a subdued tone. Louisa makes most of her favorite points: her young women are severely independent, planning careers as doctors, writers, and actresses. The young men learn, through patience and submission, to rule themselves. Louisa's favorite character and alter ego, Dan, from *Little Men,* gets into serious trouble, kills a man out West, and goes to prison for it. In jail he hears a speech, much like the one Louisa gave at the Concord Reformatory, from a woman in middle age dressed in black. Her simple story helps him to learn his lesson and submit to his punishment. On his return he falls in love with Jo's niece, a fairy-like creature of great beauty and sweetness. Dan knows he cannot hope for her, so his last days at Plumfield are spent in vain loving and silent, painful surrender to his lonely fate. The young man, who has become the sympathetic, youthful stand-in for Jo, learns Louisa's lessons of self-denial and going without.

As for Jo, she is older, sadder, and wonders if she should have done differently, remained single, for example. But she returns to the refrain that her duty was clearly to do as she had done. Her spirits are not as high as they had been twenty years before, "for life had never been very easy to her, and even now she had her troubles within and without." Her fame she "never did quite accept," but she was grateful for the money with which she was able to make Marmee's last years agreeable. She thinks of her career with irony, reflecting that the great work and effort that had gone into her first book harvested her little, whereas a hastily written story designed only to make money "came home heavily laden with an unexpected cargo of gold and glory." Despite her great success she considers herself, next to Emerson and John Greenleaf Whittier, "a literary nursery-maid who provides moral pap for the young."

The varieties of pap are several, including lectures of temperance, plain-living, honesty, independence, and self-sacrifice. There is, of course, a speech on the value of spinsters, whose lot has been improved by some who have become famous, proving "that woman isn't a half but a whole human being, and can stand alone." The book closes with many marriages and bright prospects for most, but finally it has a sense of weariness and frustration, and of repressed violence. In the final chapter, called "Positively the Last Appearance," Louisa confesses a temptation "to close the present tale with an earthquake which should engulf Plumfield and its environs so deeply in the bowels of the earth that no youthful Schliemann could ever find a vestige of it." She resists this leaning, but dispatches everyone with great haste and finality, as if the effort to have them all behave so well for so long has become too much for her. This decisive punctuation finishes the trap the March family had come to represent to her. Her groping favorite novel *Moods* brought her no success, but much satisfaction. *Little Women* brought her money, but encased her in a simplistic, morally childish view of the world. Her success identified her so entirely with March family ethics that she could never again stray into more complex thickets or subtler human problems.

After finishing the book, she took her father to the final session of the Concord summer school. She thought, correctly, that it was to be his last time. They listened to Julia Ward Howe discuss the women of Plato's Republic and watched Elizabeth Peabody darting around in her confused way. Louisa was glad she had gone, but soon was very sick again.

It had been such a relief to feel well for July that the renewal of her illnesses discouraged her profoundly. She blamed her relapse on the "everlasting home cares" and thought she would be well but for her duties. She continued extremely sick throughout the fall and winter.

The new year of 1887 began on a "sad lonely day." She had moved into Dr. Rhoda Lawrence's convalescent home in Roxbury for a complete rest: "Feeble and sick, away from home and worn out with the long struggle for health. Have had many hard days, but few harder than this." She had frightful nightmares that kept her from the rest she needed so desperately. She couldn't shut off her brain, which simmered too fast: "Now I know what *fear* is. Never did before. See ghosts, and quake at shadows. Lord help my wits." Her courage was running out. She couldn't eat solid food, and was forced to take myriad nasty remedies for her digestion. She had hot flashes, swollen glands, a bunching of tissue at the neck: "So tired of such a life!" When she was well enough to get up she took short walks. Her state of mind was either gloom or irritation. In her nightmares she saw dead people, saw Lulu killed, found herself in the street naked.

She made little improvement during the spring months and so

had to give up her plans for a summer vacation. Instead, she went with her doctors and the other patients to Mount Wachusett, near Fruitlands. She wrote to a Concord friend of her disappointment: "The patience of Job, the courage of Moses and the faith of all the saints to keep me from swear words and general despair of God and more." She railed against her tiny, bleak world "after so much freedom and strength all these years." Her father was failing, and although not in pain, he had little strength. Louisa saw that any exertion was dangerous to him and she hoped he would "slip very soon."

On September 1, 1887, she made a prophecy: "The end is not far off. The doctors see it and I feel it, Amen." They told her about her enlarged spleen, her sluggish liver, and exhausted brain, her useless stomach and crippled legs, putting clinical words on the awful debility and despair she felt. They warned her that if she didn't eat she would die: "So I eat and suffer. Might as well die." She dismissed Dr. Wesselhoeft, thinking he had given her up. His remedies were too slow and inefficacious, while she felt her life racing away from her: "Suspect he thinks no help possible. So do I, but for A's [Anna's] sake will try anything."

She remained in Roxbury in October without seeing anyone, doing nothing. It was hard work to keep still "after being the hub to the family wheel so long. But it is good for the energetic ones to find that the world can get on without them, and learn to be still, to give up, and wait cheerfully." Once again, she wrestled a meaning, a compensation, out of her protracted suffering. The pain was "part of the discipline I need, doubtless; so I take it as well as I can."

She moved between the solitude of the Roxbury rest home and Concord. Episodes leaving her dizzy, frightened, and with strange neurological sensations took their insidious toll. She moved to Roxbury for the last time in November, where she went on a diet of warm milk and no visits. Her nerves and panics quieted somewhat.

In February she was well enough to make a short visit to Concord, staying long enough to kiss everyone and say hello. She saw that Bronson was rapidly dying. She wrote to a friend: "I don't want to keep him now that life is a burden, and am glad to have him go before it becomes a pain. We shall miss the dear old white head and feeble saint so long our care; but as Anna says, 'He will be with Mother.' So we shall be happy in the hope of that meeting.

"Sunday he seemed very low, and I was allowed to drive in and say 'Good by.' He knew me and smiled and kissed 'Weedy,' as he calls me, and I thought the drowsiness and difficulty of breathing could not last long. But he revived, got up, and seemed so much as usual, I may be able to see him again. It is a great grief that I am not there as I was with Lizzie and Mother, but though much better, the shattered nerves won't bear much yet, and quiet is my only cure."

Her father died on Sunday, March 4, 1888. He was eighty-eight years old and finally willing to relinquish the soul he had studied and nurtured for so long. Louisa wrote: "Shall I ever find time to die?" Two days later, on March 6, she did, sick to death with the ceaseless torture of her poisoned body. There was no reason to fight any longer. She fell asleep at 3:30 A.M. and died with no family nearby. The immediate cause of Louisa's death isn't quite clear. She had taken a carriage ride without a cloak and contracted a fever after the outing. Her body was so depleted that she had no strength to combat the last affliction. And her will had been tested so many times that it was finally slack. She had lived for and through her parents. When Abba died Louisa had almost given up, but in her devotion to her father she had found the determination to continue. With Bronson's death her lifeline snapped. She was left without a conduit into which to pour her dedication, and her existence, built on self-sacrifice, was rendered without meaning.

Anna wrote: "Just how life is to be lived without the dear companion who for more than fifty years has been nearest and dearest to my heart I do not yet see." Unlike Louisa, however, Anna managed to find her own life sufficient reason for living.

Dr. Cyrus Bartol delivered the sermon at the joint funeral: "As the young mother in classic story gave her breast to her famished sire in prison, so this daughter, such a support to her father on earth, was needed by him even in heaven.

"She was her philosophic and unworldly father's counterpart in lucid conception, with an added literary gift. She was that mystic thinker's translation, clear as crystal, into the mother tongue of unquestionable truth. She was his indisputable popularity."

On her father's eighty-sixth birthday Louisa had written him a poem, full of the love and understanding she had come to feel for the old man:

> Dear Pilgrim, waiting patiently,
> The long, long journey nearly done,
> Beside the sacred stream that flows
> Clear shining in the western sun;
> Look backward in the varied road
> Your steadfast feet have trod,
> From youth to age, through weal and woe,
> Climbing forever nearer God.
>
> Mountain and valley lie behind;
> The slough is crossed, the wicket passed;
> Doubt and despair, sorrow and sin,
> Giant and fiend, conquered at last.
> Neglect is changed to honor now;
> The heavy cross may be laid down;
> The white head wins and wears at length
> The prophet's, not the martyr's crown.
>
> Greatheart and Faithful gone before,
> Brave Christiana, Mercy sweet,
> Are Shining Ones who stand and wait
> The weary wanderer to greet.
> Patience and love his handmaids are,
> And till time brings release,
> Christian may rest in that bright room
> Whose windows open to the east.
>
> The staff set by, the sandals off,
> Still pondering the precious scroll,
> Serene and strong, he waits the call
> That frees and wings a happy soul;
> Then, beautiful as when it lured
> The boy's aspiring eyes,
> Before the pilgrim's longing sight
> Shall the Celestial City rise.

Bronson had made a personal as well as a philosophical journey. When Louisa was born and in the fifteen years thereafter, he had been stern, angry, and relentless in pursuit of his own perfection.

His critical, intolerant years marked Louisa with a profound sense of her own worthlessness and depravity. They made her need to exert herself beyond ordinary endurance to prove her right to exist. Out of Bronson's passionate abstraction came Louisa's obsessional practicality, directly proportionate to her feelings of unacceptability. She never entirely lost her feelings of self-disgust, but as she became a success she began to judge herself less harshly and to accept her father. And in resisting her father she learned the strengths of rebellion and self-reliance. Louisa had energy, determination, and an understanding that to succeed often required a long fight, and setbacks would be the rule. As a woman making a career out of writing, Louisa needed all the determination she could muster. She succumbed to some defeats and allowed mild criticism to deter her from pursuing her best fictional instincts. But she never quit writing, and never sacrificed this means of self-expression, even if she allowed it to be limited by what her public wanted.

As she grew older, Louisa came to appreciate her father's more disengaged style, and to feel that men had more understanding than women of the need for some respectful distance between people. As an adult, Louisa had a life larger than her emotions. Her career made her a highly unusual Victorian woman. Paradoxically, she could be more sympathetic to the problems of men because she needed less from them. As a girl she had been scarred by this need, but in reducing it through work she had achieved a stature denied to her mother and sisters, whose worlds consisted in reacting to how they were treated. Louisa had removed herself from the customary Victorian woman's role of passive receiver of hurts and wrongs into an active, contributing member of society. She paid a great price in loneliness. And she never tamed her driving, hungry conscience into letting her enjoy what she had accomplished. Nevertheless, she turned her anxious, unhappy girlhood into financial support and a source of satisfaction and justification to her. To the same degree that she had come to terms with her father, she had made a kind of peace with herself. She never got from him precisely the love that she wanted as a child, but he had given her the motivation and the tools to fashion her own life. Ironically, she achieved the success he always wanted, which constitutes a wry application of Emerson's law of compensation.

Anna lived on in Concord, presiding over her boys and her sister's estate until 1893. At her father's request, Lulu was returned to Europe, where, at this writing, she lives in Germany.

Acknowledgments
and
A Note on Sources

Notes

Bibliography

Acknowledgments

and

A Note on Sources

THE PRIMARY SOURCE for this biography was the copious collection of Alcott papers at Harvard University's Houghton Library. This material includes Bronson Alcott's nearly endless journal, what Louisa allowed to survive of her own and her mother's journals and letters, and miscellaneous papers belonging to other members of the family. I also consulted original documents at the Pierpont Morgan Library in New York City, the New-York Historical Society, the Massachusetts Historical Society, the Berg Collection at the New York Public Library, the Boston Public Library, the Concord Free Library, the Fruitlands Museum, the Schlesinger Library at Radcliffe College, and the Alderman Library at the University of Virginia. I would like to thank the staffs of each of these libraries and institutions for their uniform courtesy and helpfulness.

There have been unusual kindnesses along the way that warrant special mention. Dr. John Haller, Jr., generously sent me an abstract of an article he had written on calomel. The distinguished historian Lyman Butterfield spent valuable time giving me direction on my initial researches. And Winifred Collins, librarian at the Massachusetts Historical Society, went out of her way to be helpful. Richard Wolfe at Harvard's Countway Library of Medicine enthusiastically tracked down uncatalogued records. The entire staff at the Houghton Library, headed by the now-retired Carolyn Jakeman and including Martha Shaw and Deborah Kelley, patiently found material for me for literally months. William Henry Harrison opened the Fruitlands Museum in the middle of winter so I could walk through. My thanks also to Gabriella Eggars for her creative typing of an all but illegible manuscript and to Richard Leibmann-Smith for his careful comments and suggestions. Robert Cowley's and Luise Erdmann's editorial advice was invaluable. And my very special thanks to Susan Moldow for her unflagging interest, kindness, and good cheer.

Specifically cited materials are from manuscript collections; the other quotations are from secondary sources. Both are noted chapter by chapter. For full listings of each secondary source, see the bibliography. Since I have preferred to work and think from primary documents rather than secondary accounts, the judgments and interpretations, for better or worse, are mine.

M.S.
February 20, 1977
New York City

Notes

CHAPTER 1. *Little Women* (*pages 1–17*)

This chapter is the product of more than two years' thinking. Patricia Meyer Spack's literate, compassionate book, *The Female Imagination*, helped crystallize some of my thoughts and suggest a direction to my observations. I have also made use of conversations with E. Rea Paidoussi, whose balanced and humane point of view helped shape my opinions about Louisa's place in her family.

CHAPTER 2. The Lovers (*pages 18–34*)

For Bronson's educational theories, I quoted his *Essays on Education* and his *Observations on the Principles and Methods of Infant Instruction*, I also used David Ripley's "The Educational Ideas, Implementations and Influence of A. Bronson Alcott," and Dorothy McKuskey's *Bronson Alcott, Teacher.* Throughout I have referred to Odell Shepard's biography, *Pedlar's Progress*, but have always returned to Shepard's source, Bronson's own journals. Alcott's cousin William Andrus Alcott left an occasionally useful autobiographical work, *Forty Years in the Wilderness of Pills and Powders.*

The material on Connecticut comes primarily from John Barker's *Connecticut Historical Collections.* I also used Lee W. Storrs's *The Yankee of Connecticut,* the Reverend Samuel Orcutt's *History of the Town of Wolcott, Conn.,* and Sterry and Garrigus's *They Found a Way.*

The May family sources include Nathaniel I. Bowditch's *History of the Massachusetts General Hospital,* Foote's *Annals of King's Chapel,* F. W. P. Greenwood's sermon "A Good Old Age," James Freeman Clarke's *Autobiography, Diary and Correspondence,* and Samuel May's *Memoir of Colonel Joseph May.* Here and many times later I have used Justin Winsor's four-volume *Memorial History of Boston, 1630–1880,* for facts, theory, and color.

The quoted material is from the Houghton Library and is used by permission of the Houghton Library, Harvard University:

"the most diffident man . . ." Amos Bronson Alcott's autobiographical fragment.

"On winter evenings he made . . ." Ibid.

"Her sweet and placid . . ." Ibid.

"A Mother! When is . . ." ABA's journal, September 15, 1828.

"left me shamefaced, ignorant . . ." ABA's autobiographical fragment.

"and soon returned to my . . ." Ibid.

"Sir: In commencing . . ." ABA to William Andrus Alcott, 1824?

"I was permitted to come . . ." ABA's autobiographical fragment.

"a little conspicuous among . . ." Ibid.

"dangerously sick from Feb. 16 . . ." ABA's journal, March 1821.

"Father and mother, how do you think we look . . ." ABA to his parents, January 24, 1820.

"assisting him in his . . ." ABA's autobiographical fragment.

"The Christian religion is the best . . ." ABA's journal, 1828.

"He has listened to the . . ." Ibid., 1827.

"Virtue sleeps confined, benevolence . . ." Ibid., December 6, 1826.

"The common sentiment is not . . ." Ibid., June 25, 1827.

"the interesting woman . . . often portrayed . . ." Ibid., August 1827.

"I should like this winter . . ." Abigail May to her parents, October 10, 1819.

"most striking characteristic was . . ." Abigail May quoted in ABA's journal, September 21, 1828.

"Should you go to Boston . . ." Abigail May to ABA, September 16, 1827.

"Our plans having been . . ." ABA's journal, February 1828.

"I fervently hope your labors . . ." Abigail May to ABA, spring 1828.

"There is a city . . ." ABA's journal, October 26, 1828.

CHAPTER 3. A Victorian Courtship *(pages 35–49)*

The bulk of this chapter comes from Bronson's and Abba's journals at the Houghton Library. I also used Winsor's *Memorial History of Boston*, James Freeman Clarke's *Autobiography*, Foote's *Annals of King's Chapel*, Greenwood's "A Good Old Age," and Samuel May's *Memoir of Colonel Joseph May*.

The Houghton Library references are:

"The circumstances of our . . ." Sam May to Abigail May, July 21, 1828.

"Mr. Alcott was sent for . . ." Abigail May's journal.

"There is no female on earth . . ." ABA's journal, May 30, 1828.

"We are unwilling she should . . ." Ibid., June 1, 1828.

"a world of beings where . . ." Ibid., June 14, 1828.

"we cannot but feel . . ." Ibid., July 15, 1828.

"July 19: But one thing depresses our . . ." Ibid., July 19, 1828.

"We will now wait . . ." Ibid., July 21, 1828.

"The thoughts of your Journal . . ." Abigail May to ABA in ABA's journal, July 22, 1828.

"a mutual disclosure of . . ." ABA's journal, August 2, 1828.

"and particularly at Roxbury . . ." Ibid., August 7, 1828.

"I am engaged to Mr. Alcott . . ." Abigail May to Sam May, August 1828.

"I sometimes wonder what . . ." ABA's journal, October 15, 1828.

"The *female heart* what . . ." Ibid., October 16, 1828.

"I do love this . . ." Ibid., September 1828.

"Nothing but a *total . . .*" Ibid., September 6, 1828.

"I despise fashion and . . ." Abigail May's journal, 1828.

"I doubt my power of reaching . . ." ABA's journal, November 25, 1828.

"I have led her mind . . ." Ibid., December 20, 1828.

"Circumstances suggest the propriety . . ." Ibid., December 29, 1828.

"rather too old-fashioned in his . . ." Ibid., March 20, 1829.

"Not that I can give him any . . ." Abigail May's journal, 1829.

"rather dejected. I burst into tears . . ." Abigail May to ABA, June 10, 1829.

"adopt those measures which promote temperance . . ." Abigail May's journal, 1829.

"I wish the good girl . . ." ABA's journal, November 3, 1829.

"Good girl, I have too . . ." Ibid., December 19, 1829.

"1. Means of becoming acquainted . . ." Ibid., January 17, 1830.

"In a few weeks now . . ." Ibid., April 9, 1830.

"Passed the evening at Col. May's . . ." Ibid., May 23, 1830.

CHAPTER 4. Boston and Bronson *(pages 50–62)*

There is a wealth of material on Boston, but the two most useful sources for my purposes have been Walter Muir Whitehill's marvelous *Boston, A Topographical History* and Winsor's *Memorial History*. I also used Whitehill's *Destroyed Boston Buildings*, Annie Haven Thwing's *Crooked and Narrow Streets of the Town of Boston*, Shackleton's *Book of Boston*, William Rossiter's *Days and Ways in Old Boston*, Mark De Wolfe Howe's *Boston Common*, Isaac Homans's *Sketches of Boston*, the Victorian Society of America's *Victorian Boston Today*, Edward Everett Hale's *New England Boyhood*, Samuel Drake's *Old Landmarks and Historic Personages in Boston*, Charles Damrell's *Half Century of Boston's Buildings*, Abram R. Brown's *Faneuil Hall and Faneuil Hall Market*, Henry Blaney's *Old Boston*, Mary Ayer's *Early Days on Boston Common*, Nathaniel Hawthorne's *Journal* and *American Notebooks*, and *The Education of Henry Adams*.

For Boston's personalities and intellectual climate, sources include Gladys Brooks's *Three Wise Virgins*, Van Wyck Brooks's *Flowering of New England*, Paul F. Boller's *American Transcendentalism*, Kenneth Cameron's *Transcendentalists and Minerva*, Lydia Maria Child's *Letters*, Henry Steele Commager's *Theodore Parker*, Richard Henry Dana, Jr., *Journals*, Octavius Brooks Frothingham's *Recollections and Impressions* and *Transcendentalism in New England*, Henry James's *Bostonians*, Harriet Martineau's *Society in America*, and F. O. Matthiessen's *American Renaissance*. Like everyone who is interested in the nineteenth century, I owe a great debt to the eminent scholarship of Perry Miller, whose anthologies, *The American Transcendentalists* and *The Transcendentalists*, and essays, including *Nature's Nation*, represent the best in American intellectual history. Russell Blaine Nye's *Society and Culture in America* is rich and detailed social history, and his

William Lloyd Garrison and the Humanitarian Reformers is both entertaining and informative. Vernon L. Parrington's *Romantic Revolution* and Arthur Schlesinger's *Age of Jackson* provided background, as did Gilbert Seldes's *Stammering Century*. Louise Hall Tharp's *Peabody Sisters of Salem* was useful here and elsewhere, as was John Weiss's *Life and Correspondence of Theodore Parker*.

Bronson's observations come from his journals at the Houghton Library. I also quote from Samuel Joseph May's *Memoir of Samuel Joseph May*. The remaining quotations come from Bronson's journal at the Houghton Library:

"Amongst the list of divines . . ." June 1828.

"Unitarianism now looks a little . . ." September 1828.

"We need no further proof . . ." May 18, 1828.

"She may perhaps aim at being 'original' . . ." August 9, 1828.

"I have very little confidence . . ." Fall 1828.

"whether *the intercourse of . . .*" October 1, 1828.

CHAPTER 5. A New England Marriage *(pages 63–80)*

On aspects of Victorian marriage and female roles I used *Godey's Ladies' Book,* William Alcott's *Physiology of Marriage* and *Young Husband,* Eleanor Flexner's *Century of Struggle,* John and Robin S. Haller's excellent *Physician and Sexuality in Victorian America,* Harriet Martineau's *Society in America,* Samuel May's *Rights and Condition of Women,* Gail Parker's *Ovenbirds,* Richard H. Shryock's *Medicine and Society in America,* S. C. de Soissons's *Parisian in America,* Mary Higginson's edition of the *Letters and Journals of Thomas Wentworth Higginson,* Commager and Weiss on Theodore Parker, Frothingham's *History of Transcendentalism in New England,* and G. J. Barker-Benfield's interesting but sketchy look at Victorian sexual attitudes, *Horrors of the Half-Known Life.*

On the social and material history of Philadelphia I used Digby Baltzell's *Philadelphia Gentlemen,* Frank Bowers's *Century of Atlantic Travel,* Edward Hocker's *Germantown, 1683–1933,* Clarence P. Hornung's *Wheels Across America,* Charles F. Jenkins's *Guide Book to Historic Germantown,* Dr. Naaman Keyser et al., *History of Old Germantown,* Charles Leland's *Memoirs,* Gerda Lerner's readable and learned *Grimké Sisters from South Carolina,* Thomas and Westcott's *History of Philadelphia,* Tinkcom and Simon's *Historic Germantown,* as well as the Tharp and Brooks biographies of the Peabody sisters.

The family quotations come from Bronson's journals, Abba's letters and journals, and Elizabeth Lewis's letters at the Houghton Library. Bronson's journals concerning his children are there as well.

The Houghton Library citations are:

"love is with us . . ." Abigail Alcott to Lucretia May, June 15, 1830.

"lined with raspberries, currants . . ." Abigail Alcott to Sam May, May 1831.

"There is no living individual . . ." ABA's journal, 1832.

"My friend was the first of my . . ." Ibid., 1873.

"I thought my dear Sam . . ." Abigail Alcott to Sam May, May 22, 1831.

"I read your letter with . . ." Elizabeth Lewis to ABA, 1832.

"But it is not . . ." ABA to Elizabeth Lewis, 1832.

"I think that our letters . . ." Elizabeth Lewis to ABA, 1832.

"His imagination, fed by tales . . ." ABA's journal, April 28, 1834.

"How delightful were the emotions . . ." Ibid., March 16, 1831.

"I am so well and happy . . ." Abigail Alcott to Sam May, March 29, 1831.

"She is blessed with . . ." Abigail Alcott to Colonel Joseph May, May 1831.

"The powerful influence of analogy . . ." ABA's *Observations on the Life of My First Child*, November 24, 1831.

"She seemed impressed by . . ." Ibid., May 24, 1831.

"The motion of the . . ." Ibid., no date.

"it is no more so . . ." Ibid., September 28, 1831.

"She seemed . . . to understand . . ." Ibid., November 24, 1831.

"and has been occupied more . . ." Ibid., no date.

"It is their duty . . ." Ibid., no date.

"I have seen no indication . . ." Ibid., May 24, 1831.

"Infant nature has been . . ." Ibid.

"It is by respecting the will . . ." Ibid., September 28, 1831.

"The Will is becoming . . ." Ibid., October 7, 1831.

"a very fine, fat little . . ." ABA to Anna Alcox, November 29, 1832.

"a most interesting event . . ." ABA's journal, November 29, 1832.

"The young heart is . . ." ABA's *Observations on the Life of My Second Child*, no date.

"That was a beautiful idea . . ." Ibid.

"the character of the subjects . . ." ABA's *Observations on the Life of My First Child During her Second Year*, October–November 1833.

"restored to the discharge of . . ." ABA to Colonel May, November 29, 1832.

"she lives and moves and breathes . . ." ABA to Anna Alcox, November 29, 1832.

"She is generally quite docile . . ." *Observations on the Life of My First Child During her Second Year*, December 1832.

"Father punish." Ibid.

"great faith in the people . . ." ABA's journal, April 1833.

"the noble work upon which . . ." Ibid., April, 1834.

"I felt relieved by . . ." Ibid., May 6, 1834.

"too closely to the *ideal* . . ." Ibid., March 27, 1834.

"During the period of life . . ." Ibid., May 16, 1834.

"keep her mind in a state . . ." Ibid., June 14, 1834.

"brotherly love that I am . . ." Abigail Alcott to Lucretia May, February 20, 1833, and January 19, 1834.

"I cannot smile or engage . . ." Ibid., January 19, 1834.

"much as there is in her . . ." ABA to Col. May, November 29, 1832.

"I live in constant . . ." Abigail Alcott to Lucretia May, June 22, 1833.

"Delightful morning. I have . . ." ABA's journal, June 10, 1834.

"Had she fallen into . . ." Ibid., May 20, 1834.

CHAPTER 6. The Temple School *(pages 81–100)*

In addition to the sources on the city of Boston cited in Chapter Three, I used the Brooks and Tharp biographies of the Peabody sisters, Elizabeth Peabody's edition of the *Record of Mr. Alcott's School,* Shepard's *Pedlar's Progress,* McKuskey's *Bronson Alcott, Teacher,* Alcott's *Conversations on the Gospels,* and Gladden Washington's "Was Bronson Alcott's School a Type of God's Moral Government?" For Margaret Fuller, I used her own *Memoirs,* edited by Emerson, Channing, and Clarke, Julia Ward Howe's edition of the *Love Letters of Margaret Fuller,* Perry Miller's anthology of her writings, *Margaret Fuller, American Romantic,* and Catherine Drinker Bowen's *Yankee from Olympus.* I also referred to Martineau's *Society in America* and Greenwood's "Good Old Age." Here and throughout I have made extensive use of Ednah Dow Cheney's *Louisa May Alcott, Her Life, Letters and Journals,* which supplements the papers at the Houghton Library and includes some material later destroyed. I would like to mention Madeleine Stern's lengthy 1950 biography of Louisa May Alcott, whose bibliography I referred to repeatedly. Stern's exhaustive scholarship is exemplary, and those who are interested in fuller details of Louisa's life should see her book. I have chosen to present only those facts that seemed important in shaping Louisa's emotional and intellectual life. Katherine Anthony's and Bell Moses's biographies of Louisa were without much value for my purposes, and are included in the bibliography as background but not as source material.

The original quotations came primarily from the Houghton Library collection (H), but also from the Henry W. and Albert A. Berg Collection, the New York Public Library, Astor, Lenox, and Tilden foundations, and is used with the library's kind permission (NYPL):

"free from the usual entailment . . ." ABA's journal, September 22, 1834 (H).

"but hopeful and resolute . . ." Abigail Alcott to Lucretia May, April 12, 1835 (H).

"She is more given to free . . ." ABA's journal, January 1837 (H).

"Miss Fuller seems more inclined . . ." Ibid., March 1837 (H).

"redeem infancy from the slavery . . ." Ibid., October 12, 1834 (H).

"I have hitherto perhaps . . ." Ibid., October 26, 1843 (H).

"I believe that I understand . . ." ABA's *Observations,* November 16, 1835 (H).

"disastrous . . . *Without* me, they soon . . ." Ibid.

"from the mere love of action . . ." Ibid., October 30, 1835 (H).

"some discipline will be necessary . . ." Ibid., November 11, 1835 (H).

"The mother does not comprehend Anna's . . ." Ibid., February 4, 1835 (H).

"into the simple wants of . . ." Ibid.,

"With *Louisa* the mother . . ." Ibid.

"Louisa and Anna have separate claims . . ." ABA's *Memoir,* 1836 (H).

"Could I have her under my influence . . ." ABA's journal, November 5, 1834 (H).

"Not so Louisa. There is . . ." Ibid., November 20, 1835 (H).

"Father I love you for punishing me . . ." Ibid., October 29, 1834 (H).

"Early is the sense of good . . ." ABA's journal, no date (H).

"Louisa required authoritative measures in a few . . ." ABA's *Observations,* no date (H).

"refuses and that obstinately . . ." Ibid., November 16, 1834 (H).

"I *punished* Louisa once or twice . . ." Ibid., November 20, 1834 (H).

"Louisa gave signs of impending evil . . ." Ibid., November 10, 1834 (H).

"Anna, should little girls . . ." Ibid., no date, pages 157–159 (H).

"Father I don't love you . . ." Ibid., November 4, 1835 (H).

"No, no — father's — me not take . . ." Ibid., 1835, page 164 (H).

"Do you know what patience is . . ." Abigail Alcott to Mary Peabody Mann, September 2, 1835 (NYPL).

"deliberately, for I am fearful . . ." Colonel May to Abigail Alcott, October 1, 1834 (H).

"And let me add here . . ." Abigail Alcott to Colonel May, October 6, 1834 (H).

"as our virtues susceptibilities . . ." Abigail Alcott to Mary Peabody Mann, September 2, 1835 (NYPL).

"The hour is coming when I shall have . . ." ABA's journal, March 1837 (H).

"I do not know a more exemplary hero . . ." Abigail Alcott to Sam May, ? date (H).

"Amidst the hours of need . . ." ABA's journal, December 1837 (H).

"Mysterious little being!! Oh for the . . ." Abigail Alcott's journal, April 1839 (H).

"I care less for this world than ever . . ." Abigail Alcott to Sam May, April 22, 1839 (H).

"This new attitude in which . . ." Abigail Alcott to Colonel May, February 3, 1839 (H).

"stated my willingness to labour . . ." ABA's journal, June 1839 (H).

"one of those persons . . ." Ibid., March 7, 1839 (H).

"I knew this marketing . . ." Ibid., February 5, 1839 (H).

"living manifestations of my intellect . . ." Ibid., January 21, 1835 (H).

"the better shall I be fitted . . ." Ibid., September 18, 1835 (H).

"Father is the best man in . . ." Anna Alcott's journal, November 1839 (H).

"I make resolutions sometimes . . ." Ibid., December 8 and October 26, 1839 (H).

"Your father knows how much . . ." ABA to Anna Alcott, March 16, 1839 (H).

"dashed off hers with great . . ." ABA's journal, February 3, 1839 (H).

CHAPTER 7. Eccentric Circles *(pages 101–113)*

In addition to Ednah Cheney's *Louisa May Alcott,* sources for this chapter include *Letters of Lydia Maria Child,* John Collis's *Carlyles,* Commager's *Theodore Parker,* Weiss's *Life and Correspondence of Theodore Parker,* Abraham Eisenstadt's *American History, Journals and Miscellaneous Notebooks of Ralph Waldo Emerson, Letters of Ralph Waldo Emerson,* Frothingham's *Transcendentalism in New England, Love Letters of Margaret Fuller, Memoirs of Margaret Fuller Ossoli, Margaret Fuller, American Romantic,* ed. Perry Miller, Lerner's *Grimké Sisters,* Martineau's *Martyr Age in the United States,* Miller's *American Transcendentalists* and *Transcendentalists,* Nye's *William Lloyd Garri-*

son, Rusk's *Life of Ralph Waldo Emerson*, Arthur Schlesinger, Jr., *A Pilgrim's Progress: Orestes Brownson* and *The Age of Jackson*, Seldes's *Stammering Century*, George Tolman's pamphlet, "Mary Moody Emerson," and Winsor's *Memorial History of Boston*. Lyman Butterfield introduced me to Jones Very through a delightful paper he wrote for the Massachusetts Historical Society *Miscellany*, December 1960. This led me to track down Very's demented correspondence with Alcott at the Houghton Library.

The original sources come largely from the Houghton Library (H), but include a letter from the Berg Collection, New York Public Library (NYPL):

"we shall shake hands over . . ." Abigail Alcott to Mary Peabody Mann, September 2, 1835 (NYPL).

"far from catholicism and comprehension . . . ." ABA's journal, no date (H).

"realized my conception of a woman . . ." Ibid., June 1837 (H).

"much impressed by the soul . . ." Ibid., December 1838 (H).

"The heralds are sent forth . . ." Jones Very to ABA, December 8, 1838 (H).

"I find it quite possible . . ." ABA's journal, January 29, 1839 (H).

"He is a psychological phenomenon . . ." Ibid.

"wide polarity between these two . . ." Ibid., June 14, 1839 (H).

"This is criticism," Ibid., 1839 (H).

"the perfect man — a great intellect . . ." Ibid., May 1837 (H).

"I shrink from the eyes . . ." Ibid., June 17, 1839 (H).

"that a purpose like mine . . ." Ibid., 1839 (H).

"constitution is more enfeebled . . ." Abigail Alcott to Sam May, no date (H).

CHAPTER 8. Concordia *(pages 114–133)*

The secondary materials consulted were Cheney's *Louisa May Alcott*, Newton Arvin's *Hawthorne* and his edition of *The Heart of Hawthorne's Journals*, Mary Hosmer Brown's *Memories of Concord*, Bowen's *Yankee from Olympus*, Brooks's *Flowering of New England* and *Life of Emerson*, Canby's *Thoreau*, William Ellery Channing's *Thoreau*, John Christie's *Thoreau as World Traveler*, Meltzer and Harding's *Thoreau Profile*, Franklin B. Sanborn's *Personality of Thoreau*, Collis's *Carlyles*, Emerson's *Letters* and *Journals*, Miller's *Margaret Fuller*, Greenwood's "Good Old Age," Julian Hawthorne's *Memoirs*, Nathaniel Hawthorne's *American Notebooks*, Higginson's *Carlyle's Laugh and Other Surprises*, Hubert Hoeltje's *Sheltering Tree, A Story of the Friendship of Ralph Waldo Emerson and Amos Bronson Alcott*, Miller's *Transcendentalists*, Margaret Fuller's *Memoirs*, Philip Rosenberg's *Seventh Hero, Thomas Carlyle and the Theory of Radical Activism*, Rusk's *Life of Ralph Waldo Emerson*, Sanborn and Harris's *A. Bronson Alcott*, Sanborn's *Bronson Alcott at Alcott House and Fruitlands, New England*, and his *Recollections of Seventy Years of Concord*, Schlesinger's *Age of Jackson*, Shepard's *Pedlar's Progress*, Josephine Swayne's *Story of Concord Told by Concord Writers*, and Warren Austin's *Elder Henry James*.

The original sources for this chapter include Annie Fields's engaging diary at the Massachusetts Historical Society (MHS) and the Houghton Library's Alcott archives (H):

"There is at times . . . ." Abigail Alcott's journal, July 21, 1842 (H).

"Father got breakfast this morning . . ." Anna Alcott's journal, December 23, 1840 (H).

"how people had treated him . . ." Ibid., August 26, 1840 (H).

"the claims of my children . . ." Abigail Alcott to Sam May, August 30, 1840 (H).

"Dear Louisa, I enclose a picture . . ." Abigail Alcott to LMA, March 12, 1843 (H).

"and tho I may adopt some scheme . . ." Abigail Alcott to Sam May, April 4, 1841 (H).

"has left a will, disposing . . ." Abigail Alcott's journal, February 1841 (H).

"half his house and store-room . . ." Abigail Alcott to Sam May, June 24, 1841 (H).

"I cannot offer sympathy . . ." Abigail Alcott's journal, March 18, 1842 (H).

"if his body don't fail his mind will . . ." Abigail Alcott to Sam May, January 18, 1842 (H).

"this is to be the 'test act' . . ." Abigail Alcott to Sam May, April 15, 1841 (H).

"a terrible old bore . . . almost impossible to be rid of him . . ." Annie Fields's diary, July 28, 1864 (MHS).

"impatient . . . interruption, and faithless . . ." ABA's journal, July 1842 (H).

"sped not better than at first . . ." ABA to Abigail Alcott, July 16, August 2, 1842 (H).

"as an incorrigible heretic and infidel." Carlyle to ABA, September 22, 1842 (H).

"My letters are hardly worth . . ." Abigail Alcott's journal, July 21, 1842 (H).

"wife, children, and friends . . ." Ibid., April 1, 1842 (H).

"It is your life which . . ." Ibid., July 21, 1842 (H).

"powers of adaptation to circumstance . . ." Ibid., September 18, 1842 (H).

"My children may not turn out . . ." Ibid., August 28, 1842 (H).

"Oh may my dear daughters . . ." Ibid., May 22, 1842 (H).

"I know it cannot — for my own . . ." Ibid., August 28, 1842 (H).

CHAPTER 9. Fruitlands *(pages 134–152)*

The secondary references include Brown's *Memories of Concord*, Bunyan's *Pilgrim's Progress*, Annie M. L. Clark's *Alcotts in Harvard*, Marianne Dwight's *Letters from Brook Farm, 1844–1847*, Eisenstadt's *American History*, Reverend Walter Elliott's *Life of Father Hecker*, Emerson's *Letters* and *Journals*, Clara Gowing's *Alcotts as I Knew Them*, Hawthorne's *Blithedale Romance*, Meltzer and Harding's *Thoreau Profile*, David P. Edgell's "Bronson Alcott's Autobiographical Index," Nye's *Society and Culture in America*, Harriet E. O'Brien's *Lost Utopias*, Sanborn's *Bronson Alcott at Alcott House and Fruitlands*, Schlesinger's *Age of Jackson*, Clara Endicott Sears's *Bronson Alcott's Fruitlands*, Seldes's *Stammering Century*, Shephard's *Pedlar's Progress*, Lindsay Swift's *Brook Farm*, and Tolman's "Mary Moody Emerson."

Bronson lost his voluminous records of the Fruitlands period on a trip to Upper New York State with Anna. The remaining material includes Abba's journals and family letters at the Houghton Library (H) and letters at the Fruitlands Museum,

Harvard, Massachusetts (F), which has recently acquired a fragment of a diary kept by Louisa. I also used letters from friends of the Alcotts at the Boston Public Library (BPL), by courtesy of the trustees of the Boston Public Library, to supplement information on this period:

"his servants and lovers . . ." Abigail Alcott's journal, October 23, 1842 (H).

"consume that which . . ." Ibid., November 29, 1842 (H).

"almost suffocated in this . . ." Ibid.

"practical Grahamite." William Garrison to George Benson, May 25, 1838 (BPL).

"to try the influence . . ." Ibid., December 24, 1842 (H).

"an unusual quietude — less tenacious . . ." Ibid., January 4, 1834 (H).

"*feelings* and *views* upon the whole . . ." Charles Lane to Abigail Alcott, January 30, 1843 (H).

"puerile and false sympathy . . ." Abigail Alcott's journal, February 6, 1843 (H).

"been aware of the real state . . ." Lane to Abigail Alcott, February 11, 1843 (H).

"His unwillingness to be employed . . ." Abigail Alcott's journal, March 6, 1843 (H).

"A woman may perform the most . . ." Ibid., August 1843 (H).

"O she is very very cross . . ." LMA to Abigail Alcott, Sunday, no date (F).

"come what may I shall . . ." Abigail Alcott to Sam May, November 4, 1843 (H).

"for Mother often says . . ." Ibid., LMA's diary, Saturday, December 23, 1843 (F).

"and when I went to bed . . ." Ibid.

"Christmas is here/Louisa my dear . . ." Abigail Alcott, no date (F).

"restored him, but not made quite . . ." Ibid., no date (H).

CHAPTER 10. Hillside *(pages 153–171)*

The secondary sources include Cheney's *Louisa May Alcott,* Bettina von Arnim's *Goethe's Correspondence with a Child,* Arvin's *Heart of Hawthorne's Journals,* Brown's *Memories of Concord,* Canby's *Thoreau,* Channing's *Thoreau,* Sanborn's *Personality of Thoreau,* Clark's *Alcotts in Harvard,* Emerson's *Letters* and *Journals,* Gowing's *Alcotts as I Knew Them,* Walter Harding's "Thoreau's Feminine Foe," Julian Hawthorne's *Memoirs,* Nathaniel Hawthorne's *American Notebooks,* Hoeltje's *Sheltering Tree,* Hornung's *Wheels Across America,* Meltzer and Harding's *Thoreau Profile,* Miller's *Transcendentalists,* Rusk's *Life of Ralph Waldo Emerson,* Sanborn's *Recollections of Seventy Years in Concord,* Swayne's *Story of Concord,* and Frederick L. H. Willis's *Alcott Memoirs.*

Original materials come from the Houghton Library (H), the Fruitlands Museum (F), and from the A. Bronson Alcott Collection, Clifton Waller Barrett Library, University of Virginia Library (A):

"How thoughtlessly this domestic . . ." Abigail Alcott to Sam May, December 4, 1846 (H).

"some mistake when she was created . . ." Ibid., November 3, 1847 (H).

"to see my husband a little . . ." Abigail Alcott's journal, January 28, 1844 (H).

"a new home established . . ." Ibid., March 22, 1844 (H).

"that the communities are not yet . . ." Ibid., March 31, 1844 (H).

"they *aid*, they *censure* . . ." Ibid., January 28, 1844 (H).

"The family we are now . . ." Ibid., 1844 (H).

"dissatisfied with the whole . . ." Ibid., March 22, 1844 (H).

"a constant almost invariable . . ." Ibid., April 1, 1844 (H).

"O God! How long wilt thou . . ." ABA's journal, 1844 (H).

"to embrace many little charities . . ." Abigail Alcott to Junius Alcott, January 1845 (H).

"Vigilance, punctuality, Perseverance, Prompt . . ." ABA's chart, 1846 (H).

"as a neat disposition for her . . ." ABA to Anna Alcott, March 16, 1845 (H).

"Your dear little head . . ." ABA to Elizabeth Alcott, June 24, 1845 (H).

"they wrote very faithfully," ABA's journal, April 1846 (H).

"Two devils, as yet, I am not . . ." Ibid., March 16, 1846 (H).

"It is a safety valve to her . . ." Abigail Alcott to Sam May, April 18, 1845 (H).

"thrown once more on my . . ." Abigail Alcott's journal, September 5, 1845 (H).

"desultory . . . faulty specimens . . ." Ibid.

"advocates the doctrine of resolute . . ." ABA's journal, February 1848 (H).

"nothing can exceed the strength of her . . ." Abigail Alcott to Sam May, February 29, 1848 (H).

"shanty . . . whirligig . . ." ABA's journal, November 1847 (H).

"that worst affliction of all . . ." Abigail Alcott to Sam May, August 9, 1845 (H).

"has given image and a name . . ." ABA's journal, February 1847 (H).

"clearly, hear distinctly . . . Thus when . . ." Abigail Alcott's journal, September 19, 1848 (H).

"My friends are wearied with . . ." Ibid., December 31, 1846 (H).

"furnish articles for the fancy . . ." Abigail Alcott to Sam May, February 29, 1848 (H).

"but at least I think I shall . . ." Ibid., December 8, 1847 (H).

"will yield to any plan of mine . . ." Ibid., February 13, 1848 (H).

"so disappointed when Father told me . . ." Abby Alcott to her mother, Hillside, no date (H).

"facilitate . . . the emancipation of my children . . ." Abigail Alcott to Sarah Holland (Adams), March 22, 1848 (F).

"labours were incessant, and . . ." Abigail Alcott to Samuel Sewall, July 21, 1848 (H).

"almost frantic," ABA's journal, October 24, 1848 (H).

"If you were here, the spectacle . . ." ABA to LMA, November 29, 1848 (A).

CHAPTER 11. Midcentury *(pages 172–201)*

I used Cheney's *Louisa May Alcott*, Anna Alcott Pratt's *Comic Tragedies*, Louisa Alcott's *Aunt Jo's Scrapbag* and *Flower Fables*. Secondary references include Louis Haselmayer's "Amos Bronson Alcott in Southeast Iowa," Arvin's *Hawthorne* and *Heart of Hawthorne's Journals*, James C. Austin's *Fields of the Atlantic Monthly*, Ayer's *Early Days on Boston Common*, Blackwell's *Lucy Stone*, Blaney's *Old Boston*, Caroline

Bradley's *Western World Costume, Letters of Lydia Maria Child*, Commager's *Theodore Parker*, Damrell's *Half Century of Boston's Buildings, Journal of Richard Henry Dana, Jr.*, Drake's *Old Landmarks and Historic Personages of Boston*, Eisenstadt's *American History*, Emerson's *Letters* and *Journals*, Flexner's *Century of Struggle*, Miller's *Margaret Fuller*, J. C. Furnas's *The Road to Harper's Ferry*, *Godey's Ladies' Book*, Hale's *James Russell Lowell* and *New England Boyhood*, Haller and Haller's *Physician and Sexuality in Victorian America*, Albert Bushnell Hart's *American History Told by Contemporaries*, Hawthorne's *American Notebooks* and *Blithedale Romance*, *Letters and Journals of Thomas Wentworth Higginson* and his *Carlyle's Laugh*, Homans's *Sketches of Boston, Past and Present*, Julia Ward Howe's *Reminiscences*, Mark A. De Wolfe Howe's *Boston Common* and *Memories of a Hostess*, Henry James's *Bostonians*, Charles T. Kennedy's "Commuter Services in the Boston Area," Lerner's *Grimké Sisters*, S. J. May's *Fugitive Slave Law and Its Victims*, and *Rights and Conditions of Women*, Meltzer and Harding's *Thoreau Profile*, Edwin Miller's *Melville*, Mott's *History of American Magazines*, Margaret Fuller Ossoli's *Memoirs*, Rossiter's *Days and Ways in Old Boston*, Rusk's *Life of Ralph Waldo Emerson*, Sanborn's "Reminiscences of Louisa May Alcott," Shackleton's *Book of Boston*, Caroline Ticknor's *May Alcott*, Thwing's *Crooked and Narrow Streets of the Town of Boston*, Eugene Tomkins's *History of the Boston Theatre, 1854–1901*, W. S. Tryon's *Parnassus Corner, A Life of James T. Fields*, Weiss's *Life and Correspondence of Theodore Parker*, Whitehill's *Boston* and *Destroyed Boston Buildings*, and Winsor's *Memorial History*.

The original material comes from the Houghton Library (H) and the Boston Public Library (BPL):

"I cannot always stop to count . . ." Abigail Alcott's journal, January 1, 1849 (H).

"no moral sense or . . ." Ibid., January 23, 1849 (H).

"from the sharks and lust . . ." Ibid., January 24, 1849 (H).

"and rendered me not wholly . . ." ABA's journal, January 27, 1850 (H).

"My efforts hitherto have been . . ." Abigail Alcott's journal, October 9, 1849 (H).

"sympathizing in the details . . ." Ibid., April 4, 1850 (H).

"I stand alone . . ." Ibid., February 25, 1849 (H).

"no rest . . . have been called . . ." Ibid., March 1850 (H).

"but do you realize how important to *me* . . ." Abigail Alcott to Sam May, April 14, 1850 (H).

"we have tried separation . . ." Ibid., April 4, 1850 (H).

"to the thinker's family . . ." ABA's journal, May 6 and 19, 1850 (H).

"begged . . . to clear my existence . . ." Ibid., January 15, 1850 (H).

"some persons . . . take pleasure . . ." Abigail Alcott's journal, May 1, 1850 (H).

"the shammery of what is so . . ." Ibid., July 14, 1850 (H).

"I am sorry if I said anything . . ." Caroline Tappan to Abigail Alcott, summer 1850 (BPL).

"accounted herself nobly . . ." ABA's journal, July 20, 1850 (H).

"Sometimes . . . men are apt to think . . ." Abigail Alcott to Hannah Robie, July 29, 1850 (H).

"She has been more to many women . . ." ABA's journal, July 24, 1850 (H).

"every sentiment of her being . . ." Abigail Alcott to Sam May, February 28, 1851 (H).

"potent persuasions of the parlor . . ." ABA's journal November 23, 1853 (H).

"best of Emerson's intellect . . ." Ibid., January 18, 1850 (H).

"Woman is an allegory . . ." Ibid., January 13, 1850 (H).

"confusing sexes or spheres . . ." Ibid., November 23, 1853 (H).

"the office below stairs . . ." Ibid., February, 1851 (H).

"This diary is taking . . ." Ibid., January 12, 1851 (H).

"with a civil 'nothing'. . ." Ibid., February 2, 1851 (H).

"the active partner of an . . ." Abigail Alcott to ABA, June 28, 1852 (H).

"a respectable position . . ." Abigail Alcott to Sam May, April 2, 1853 (H).

"The girls enjoy it very much . . ." Ibid., January 2, 1853 (H).

"rather higher metal and their . . ." Ibid., September 19, 1853 (H).

"stronger and braver . . . so firm in health . . ." Abigail Alcott to ABA, December 19, 1853 (H).

"a mere tool by which other people can . . ." Ibid., ABA, August 18, 1853 (H).

CHAPTER 12. Beth *(pages 202–217)*

The secondary sources are: George Aldrich's *Walpole as It Was and as It Is,* Emile Barnes's *Narratives, Traditions and Personal Reminiscences . . . of the Village of Walpole, New Hampshire,* Josiah Bellows's "Reminiscences of a Village Life," Bradley's *Western World Costume,* Canby's *Thoreau,* Channing's *Thoreau,* John G. Coffin's's *Discourses on Cold and Warm Bathing,* Commager's *Theodore Parker,* Julia Howe's *Reminiscences,* Mark Howe's *Memories of a Hostess,* Meltzer and Harding's *Thoreau Profile,* Mott's *History of American Magazines,* Nye's *Society and Culture in America* and *William Lloyd Garrison,* Tomkins's *History of the Boston Theatre,* Weiss's *Life and Correspondence of Theodore Parker,* Whitehill's *Boston,* and Winsor's *Memorial History.*

The original documents are from the Houghton Library (H), the Louisa May Alcott Collection, Clifton Waller Barrett Library, University of Virginia Library (L), and the New York Public Library (NYPL):

"1. Late hours . . ." ABA's journal, October 5, 1855 (H).

"the jolly talks over the fire . . ." Anna Alcott to Maria (Holyoke), February 20, 1855 (NYPL).

"I am not a worm . . ." Abigail Alcott to ABA, November 16, 1856 (H).

"revenge and retaliation . . ." Abigail Alcott to Sam May, December 29, 1856 (H).

"Thus I am thrown back . . ." Abigail Alcott's journal, January 1, 1856.

"I think one more incident . . ." Abigail Alcott to LMA, January 8, 1856 (L).

"the Satyr . . ." ABA's journal, October, November 1856 (H).

"twice fifty, three times . . ." ABA to Abigail Alcott, November 13, 1856 (H).

"not quite sure for what she was . . ." Abigail Alcott to ABA, November 2, 1856 (H).

"about town . . . Lizzie is miserably . . ." Anna Alcott to ABA, March 16, 1857 (H).

"$200 or $250 will give us . . ." ABA to Abigail Alcott, April 19, 1857 (H).

"very perceptible ravages . . ." ABA's journal, July 19, 1857 (H).

"is a prolonged guess." Abigail Alcott to ABA, August 1857 (H).

"Boston seems singularly absent . . ." Abigail Alcott's journal, August 6, 1857 (H).

"thinner than ever and . . ." Abigail Alcott to ABA, August 16, 1857 (H).

"I know you miss . . ." Elizabeth Alcott to Alcotts, August 6, 1857 (H).

"for her, communicative . . ." ABA to Alcott girls, August 27, 1857 (H).

"nor do I omit Concord from . . ." ABA to Anna Alcott, August 28, 1857 (H).

"take the reins a little." ABA to Alcott girls, September 9, September 17, 1857 (H).

"and so leave your mother's investments . . ." Ibid., September 9, 1857 (H).

"I watched her with jealous care . . ." Abigail Alcott to Alcott girls, September 29, 1857 (H).

"nothing now but comforts . . ." Abigail Alcott's journal, January 21, 1858 (H).

"now I feel that my darling . . ." Abigail Alcott to ABA, January 1858 (H).

"Yes, nor have I . . ." ABA's journal, January 23, 1858 (H).

"Oh, heavenly air . . ." Abigail Alcott's journal, March 14, 1858 (H).

"she seemed to sleep — her . . ." Ibid., 1858 (H).

"I dare not dwell on the fever . . ." Ibid., March 19, 1859 (H).

CHAPTER 13. "Love and Self-Love" *(pages 218–250)*

The supplementary sources for this chapter were: *The Letters of A. Bronson Alcott*, edited by Richard Herrnstadt, Cheney's *Louisa May Alcott*, and Louisa Alcott's "Love and Self-Love." Additional books include Sanborn's *Recollections of Seventy Years in Concord*, his *A. B. Alcott*, his *Personality of Thoreau*, and "Reminiscences of Louisa May Alcott," Brown's *Memories of Concord*, Julian Hawthorne's *Memoirs*, Swayne's *Story of Concord*, Tolman's "Mary Moody Emerson," Emerson's *Letters and Journals*, Miller's *American Transcendentalists*, Channing's *Thoreau*, Canby's *Thoreau*, Meltzer and Harding's *Thoreau Profile*, Weiss's *Life and Correspondence of Theodore Parker*, Commager's *Theodore Parker*, J. C. Furnas's immensely readable *Road to Harper's Ferry*, Eisenstadt's *American History*, *The Letters of Lydia Maria Child*, Higginson's *Letters and Journals* and *Carlyle's Laugh*, Austin's *Fields of the Atlantic Monthly*, Arvin's *Hawthorne* and *Heart of Hawthorne's Journals*, Stern's *Louisa May Alcott*, Louisa Alcott's *Moods*, Nye's *Society and Culture*, Mary Livermore's *My Story of the War*, Whitehill's *Boston*, Bessie Smith's edition of *Hospital Sketches*, Bowen's *Yankee from Olympus*, Brooks's *Three Wise Virgins*, Tharp's *Peabody Sisters of Salem*, Gowing's *Alcotts as I Knew Them*, Edward Hale, *James Russell Lowell*, Hart's *American History*, and Willis's *Alcott Memoirs*.

The original materials were located at the Massachusetts Historical Society, (MHS), the Houghton Library (H), the Concord Free Public Library (C), and the Pierpont Morgan Library (PML):

" 'Tis a pretty retreat and *ours* . . ." ABA's journal, October 1857 (H).

"a man of most unimpeachable character . . ." Abigail Alcott's journal, April 6, 1857 (?) (H).

"I think well of him and . . ." ABA's journal, April 7, 1858 (H).

"so exclusively we have forgotten . . ." Abigail Alcott's journal, April 6, 1857 (H).

"When I used to build . . ." Anna Alcott's journal, August 1860 (H).

"In a household like my father's . . ." Ibid., no date (H).

"a large *love* nature and her . . ." Abigail Alcott's journal, April 29, 1858 (H).

"He is growing as chatty as any . . ." Anna Alcott to ABA, December 26, 1858 (H).

"Sanborn is very tall . . ." Ibid., December 21, 1857 (H).

"sprightly, entertaining, and a lady of much . . ." ABA's journal, August 29, 1858 (H).

"My dear sir, you have not yet found . . ." Annie Fields's diary, July 28, 1864 (MHS).

"gifts of speech and mode of handling poor James . . ." ABA's journal, November 28, 1858 (H).

"aloof . . . alone without his Eve . . ." ABA to Abigail Alcott, April 7, 1857 (H).

"to conduct so — wanting peace himself . . ." Abigail Alcott to ABA, December 18, 1853 (H).

"mood once claiming to be a man . . ." ABA's journal, March 23, 1859 (H).

"His senses seem double . . ." Ibid., November 5, 1858 (H).

"the greatest blessing and comfort." Anna Alcott to ABA, January 1859 (H).

"lively, wholesome, and American . . ." ABA's journal, December 21, 1859 (H).

"creative as well as her descriptive . . ." Abigail Alcott's journal, January 17, 1860 (H).

"women need protection . . ." Ibid., October 8, 1859 (H).

"The absence of money . . ." Ibid., December 31, 1859 (H).

"Annie are you happy?" Anna Alcott Pratt's journal, May 1860 (H).

"that I shall ever consider myself your Annie . . ." Anna Pratt to Abigail Alcott, May 23, 1860 (H).

"anxious affection . . ." Ibid., no date (H).

"I cannot yet write about it." ABA's journal, May 23, 1860 (H).

"I am sure she is one of the best . . ." Ibid., January 4, 1861 (H).

"I think the family will always . . ." Anna Pratt's journal, no date (H).

"as only Alcotts know how . . ." Ibid.

"though I find it hard to understand . . ." Ibid.

"Her Heart early had . . ." Abigail Alcott's journal, March 1860 (H).

"Nobody gets a chance to speak with him . . ." ABA's journal, February 17, 1861 (H).

"But I can't talk either . . ." Annie Fields's diary, November 1863 (MHS).

"*all* women as authors are feeble . . ." Hawthorne to J. T. Fields, no date (BPL).

"the board obeyed at once . . ." Sophia Hawthorne to Annie Fields, June 1, 1863 (BPL).

"if not born to the act . . ." ABA to Abigail Alcott, October 29, 1860 (H).

"She writes with unusual ease . . ." ABA's journal, February 25, 1861 (H).

"*Dear Lu, I do so love* . . ." Anna Pratt's journal, no date (H).

"much of the beauty of my father's . . ." LMA's journal, March 16, 1861 (H).

"It is a real sorrow . . ." Abigail Alcott's journal, January 1, 1861 (H).

"poor as a rat . . . ragged clothes . . . *She tries* . . . She always seems to feel . . ." Anna Pratt's journal, no date (H).

"dear patient . . . a daily prayerful hope . . ." Abigail Alcott to Mrs. John Thoreau, no date (C).

"The blue birds and robins are . . ." Abigail Alcott to Sam May, April 4, 1862 (H).

"On Tuesday at eight . . ." LMA to Sophia Foord, May 11, 1862 (PML).

"Her life affords her so little . . ." Anna Pratt's journal, no date (H).

"as she is a fine nurse . . ." Ibid.

CHAPTER 14. *Hospital Sketches (pages 251–268)*

Here, I used Cheney's *Louisa May Alcott*, Bessie Smith's edition of *Hospital Sketches*, Constance Green's *Washington, Village and Capital*, Whitman's *Gathering of the Forces* and *Wound Dresser*, Eisenstadt's *American History*, Hart's *American History*, Kaufman's *Homeopathy in America*, William Alcott's *Forty Years in the Wilderness of Pills and Powders*, David Hossack's *Essays on Various Subjects of Medical Science*, Gladys E. Hosmer's "Louisa May Alcott, War Nurse," Kate Hurd-Mead's *Medical Women of America*, William Hudson's "Anti-Calomel Lecture," Livermore's *My Story of the War*, Nye's *Society and Culture*, Shryock's *Medicine and Society in America*, Urdang's "Early Chemical and Pharmaceutical History of Calomel," John Haller's "Samson or the Materia Medica," the *Dictionary of American Biography*, Louisa Alcott's *Behind a Mask*, edited by Madeleine Stern, Tryon's *Parnassus Corner*, and Austin's *James T. Fields*.

The primary sources were found at the Houghton Library (H), the New-York Historical Society (NYHS), the Massachusetts Historical Society (MHS), and the Boston Public Library (BPL):

"cold, damp, dirty . . ." LMA's journal, January 4, 1863 (H).

"Under his plain speech . . ." Ibid., January 1863 (H).

"to keep well for bad air . . ." Ibid.

"plain, odd, sentimental . . ." Ibid.

"Quotes Browning copiously . . ." Ibid.

"sharp pain in the side . . ." Ibid.

"His behavior was good . . ." ABA's journal, January 18, 1863 (H).

"She is a kind old soul," LMA's journal, January 21, 1863 (H).

"and my boys seemed . . ." Ibid.

"so changed I think . . ." Sophia Hawthorne to Annie Fields, February 20, 1863 (BPL).

"If you will only take that man . . ." Ibid.

"How could you leave . . ." Ibid.

"Lie still my dear . . ." LMA's journal, March 1863 (H).

"this fierce campaign . . ." Ibid.

"It is altogether superior in tone . . ." Sophia Hawthorne to Annie Fields, June 14, 1863 (BPL).

" 'Tuned' is so much better . . ." Ibid., June 15, 1863 (BPL).

"my townsfolk buying, reading, laughing . . ." LMA to James Redpath, August 28, 1863 (NYHS).

"It would be tedious . . ." Abigail Alcott's journal, June 10, 1863 (H).

"This is a most distinguished . . ." Ibid.

"nothing in the way of a good . . ." ABA's journal, August 23–26, 1863 (H).

"greater effort . . . some deeper surprise . . ." Abigail Alcott's journal, 1863 (H).

"she will earn an honorable . . ." Ibid., August 25, 1863 (H).

"cold-hearted." LMA's journal, September 1836 (H).

"heartily ashamed . . ." Ibid., July 1863 (H).

"His little coos . . ." Abigail Alcott's journal, no date, 1863 (H).

"would be glad to have mother and son . . ." ABA's journal, October 6–9, 1863 (H).

"Home is a tender word . . ." Ibid., February 17, 1864 (H).

"if anything more than another . . ." ABA to Abigail Alcott, February 19, 1864 (H).

"I was so cut to the heart . . ." Sophia Hawthorne to Annie Fields, May 29, 1862 (BPL).

"one of the most excellent of men . . ." Annie Fields's diary, March 28, 1864 (MHS).

CHAPTER 15. *Moods (pages 269–284)*

Supplementary information came from Cheney's *Louisa May Alcott,* Austin's *James T. Fields* and Tryon's *Parnassus Corner,* Julian Hawthorne's *Memoirs,* Winsor's *Memorial History,* Ayer's *Early Days on Boston Common,* Blaney's *Old Boston,* Drake's *Old Landmarks,* Homans's *Sketches of Boston,* Howe's *Boston Common,* Rossiter's *Days and Ways in Old Boston,* Sanborn's *Memoirs* and *A. B. Alcott,* Louisa Alcott's *Moods* and *Plots and Counterplots,* edited by Madeleine Stern. My special thanks to Jeanie Strouse, an Alice James scholar, for alerting me to the "Dumps" story.

I used material from the Louisa May Alcott Collection, Clifton Waller Barrett Library, University of Virginia Library (L), the New-York Historical Society (NYHS), the Berg Collection at the New York Public Library (NYPL), and, of course, from the Houghton Library (H):

"I think the literary laws . . ." LMA to J. Redpath, no date (NYHS).

"We did all we could . . ." LMA's journal, May 1864 (H).

"set up among the great ones . . ." Ibid., June 1864 (H).

"Indeed, every where I am coming . . ." ABA to Abigail Alcott, June 4, 1864 (H).

"One mild moonlit night . . ." LMA's journal, August 1864 (H).

"no scholar . . . and it is folly . . ." A. K. Loring to LMA, no date (1864) (L).

"a vulgar disgusting conglomeration . . ." Ibid., October 24, 1864 (L).

"But Emerson says 'that what is true . . .' " LMA's journal, November 1864 (H).

"glad but not proud . . ." Ibid., December 1864 (H).

"now if it makes a little money . . ." LMA to Abigail Alcott, January 1, 1865 (L).

"Self-abnegation is a noble thing . . ." LMA to Moncure Conway, February 18, 1865 (NYPL).

"I felt the truth and beauty . . ." L. P. Parker to LMA, February 13, 1865 (L).

"I seem to have been playing . . ." LMA's journal, May 1865 (H).

"Admire the books but let the woman alone . . ." Ibid., June 1865 (H).

"activity and her money, she having . . ." ABA's journal, July 5, 1865 (H).

CHAPTER 16. Europe and *Little Women (pages 285–300)*

Secondary sources included Cheney's *Louisa May Alcott*, Bowen's *Century of Atlantic Travel*, Bradley's *Western World Costume*, *Journal of Richard Henry Dana, Jr.*, Sanborn's *Recollections* and *A. B. Alcott*, Louisa Alcott's *Behind a Mask*, Mott's *History of American Magazines*, Winsor's *Memorial History*, Hale's *New England Boyhood*, Whitehill's *Boston*, Austin's and Tryon's works on James T. Fields, Lerner's *Grimké Sisters*, Blackwell's *Lucy Stone*, Flexner's *Century of Struggle*, Howe's *Reminiscences*, Hurd-Mead's *Medical Women*, Livermore's *My Story of the War*, Harriet Robinson's *Massachusetts in the Woman Suffrage Movement*, Agnes Vietor's *Woman's Quest, The Life of Marie E. Zakrzewska, M.D.*, *Notable American Women*, Mary Oakley's *Elizabeth Cady Stanton*, Frothingham's *Recollections and Impressions*, and, of course, Louisa Alcott's *Little Women*.

Primary materials were at the Houghton Library (H) and the Louisa May Alcott Collection, Clifton Waller Barrett Library, University of Virginia Library (L):

"hot, dirty and evil smelling . . ." LMA's journal, August 1865 (H).

"but don't think I did . . ." Ibid.

"It touched me and pleased me very . . ." Ibid., September 1865.

"very tired of the daily worry . . ." Ibid.

"demonstrating the power . . ." Abigail Alcott to LMA, November 29, 1865 (L).

"very pleasant happened . . ." LMA's journal, November 1865 (H).

"the notes of the beautiful . . ." Ibid.

"Sad times for L. . . ." Ibid., December 1865 (H).

"monks, priests, soldiers, peasants." Ibid., January 1866 (H).

"despairing state of mind. I could . . ." Ibid., December 1865 (H).

"too exciting." Ibid., January 1866 (H).

"I'm tired of it . . ." Ibid., February 1866 (H).

"tedious . . . might have been quite . . ." Ibid., March 1866 (H).

"an ill natured if not ignorant . . ." ABA's journal, January 17, 1866 (H).

"the same sympathetic and serviceable . . ." Ibid., December 24, 1865 (H).

"seems to be almost the perfect mother . . ." Ibid., December 12, 1865 (H).

"Glad to be done with . . ." LMA's journal, July 1866 (H).

"besides work, sewing, nursing . . ." LMA's journal, August 1866 (H).

"Nan and babies a great care . . ." Ibid., October 1866 (H).

"but thank the Lord, she is still . . ." Ibid., November 1866 (H).

"driven by the prospect . . ." Ibid.

"to talk to the young . . ." Ibid.

"No one else thought of . . ." Ibid., December 1866 (H).

"more than the devil." Ibid., September 1867 (H).

"though no presents for I was . . ." Ibid., November 1867 (H).

"Now I suppose you will . . ." ABA to LMA, February 19, 1868

"The mother and daughter are parts . . ." ABA's journal, September 9, 1869 (H).

"I sell *my* children . . ." LMA's journal, January 18, 1868 (H).

"and that is better than any . . ." Ibid., March–May 1868 (H).

"Don't care much for . . ." Ibid., April 1869 (H).

"It is an honor not anticipated . . ." ABA's journal, September 4, 1869 (H).

"a perfect *success* . . . Power and grace combined . . ." Abigail Alcott's journal, April 1869 (H).

"I find I have a pretty . . ." ABA's journal (H).

"more free . . . care labor anxiety . . ." Abigail Alcott's journal, October 22, 1868 (H).

"It is only since my impaired health . . ." Ibid., November 16, 1868 (H).

"thank the Lord! — every penny . . ." LMA's journal, November 1868 (H).

CHAPTER 17. *Work (pages 301–325)*

Secondary references include Cheney's *Louisa May Alcott*, Louisa Alcott's *Old-Fashioned Girl*, *Little Men*, *Aunt Jo's Scrapbag*, and *Work*, Bronson Alcott's *Letters*, edited by Richard Herrnstadt, and *Concord Days*, Ticknor's *May Alcott*, *The Education of Henry Adams*, Rusk's *Emerson*, Emerson's *Journals* and *Letters*, Winsor's *Memorial History*, Whitehill's *Boston*, and Sanborn's *Recollections*.

The original sources are at the Houghton Library (H), the New York Public Library (NYPL), and the Concord Free Public Library (C):

"second class story teller . . ." Thomas Niles to LMA, February 14, 1870 (H).

"with left hand aching . . ." LMA's journal, April 1870 (H)

"that I was the daughter . . ." Abigail Alcott's journal, February 22, 1869 (H).

"My wife and Anna are sprprised . . ." ABA's Journal, January 4, 1870 (H).

"fast New York men." LMA to Alcotts, April 14, 1870 (H).

"horrid soups . . ." May Alcott to Alcotts, April 9, 1870 (H).

"Pa's last letter had only . . ." LMA to Alcotts, September 2, 1870 (H).

"I won't have it, for it . . ." Ibid., April 29, 1870 (H).

"Why what a state . . ." Thomas Niles to LMA, June 21, 1870 (H).

"frothing. The *dreadful* man . . ." LMA to Alcotts, June 1, 1870 (H).

"I couldn't read the story . . ." Ibid., June 24, 1870 (H).

"handsome, hearty . . ." Ibid., May 13, 1870 (H).

"The bunches on my leg . . ." Ibid., May 30, 1870 (H).

"for I hate to write if . . ." Ibid., June 24, 1870 (H).

"I should like to knock . . ." Ibid., July 8, 1870 (H).

"a great gray stone castle . . ." Ibid., August 21, 1870 (H).

"She takes Rome very calmly," Ibid., quoted in ABA's letter to Mrs. Adams, January 7, 1871 (H).

"painted out the pains and weariness . . ." ABA's journal, June 7, 1871 (H).

"and not until a few hours . . ." Anna Pratt to Mrs. Barton, December 17, 1870 (NYPL).

"did more to make me trust . . ." LMA to Anna Pratt, December 1870 (NYPL).
"that John's death . . ." LMA's journal, January 1871 (H).
"so she may be happy and free . . ." Ibid., February 1871 (H).
"a very pleasant year in spite . . ." Ibid., May 1871 (H)
"never go far away from here . . ." Ibid.
"year of travel was all lost." Ibid., July 1871 (H).
"one of the best of men . . ." ABA's journal, July 3, 1871 (II).
"suggests revisions and additions . . ." Ibid., June 1871 (H).
"out the observations and let the . . ." LMA, date? (H).
"We decline having the book . . ." ABA, date? (H).
"plenty of money to go . . ." LMA's journal, October 1871 (H).
"the machine . . . no more rheumatic . . ." Ibid., December 1871 (H).
"In my many fears for . . ." Harriet Beecher Stowe to LMA, quoted in ABA's journal, January 8, 1872 (H).
"very pleasant to be admitted . . ." ABA to Ellen Chandler, December 30, 1872 (C).
"Twenty years ago I . . ." LMA's journal, June 1872 (H).
"People *must* learn that authors . . ." LMA's journal, August 1872 (H).
"does not dissolve . . ." ABA's journal, date? (H).
"It seemed as if the end . . ." LMA to ABA, quoted in his journal, November 20, 1872 (H).
"I enjoyed every penny spent . . ." LMA's journal, November 1872 (H).
"I have thought about it . . ." Thomas Niles to LMA, 1872 (H).
"We can't afford to do this . . ." Ibid., January 2, 1873 (H).
"This was the cause . . ." LMA's journal, April 1873 (H).
"rowdy . . . a nice little proof . . ." LMA to ABA, December 8, 1872 (H).
"a thank-offering for my success . . . LMA's journal, January 1873 (H).
"She is a presence . . ." ABA's journal, November 1872 (H).
"It is comforting . . ." Ibid., May 1872 (H).
"My movements depend so much . . ." LMA to Mrs. Barton, April 22, 1873 (H).
"was it a public day . . ." ABA's journal, May 27, 1873 (H).
"dropsy affected the brain . . ." LMA's journal, July 1873 (H).
"Marmee slowly came back . . ." Ibid., July 1873 (H).
"Instead of seeking foreign . . ." ABA's journal, May 25, 1873 (H).
"facetious, pathetic and . . ." Abigail Alcott's journal, 1873 (H).
"When I had youth . . ." LMA's journal, January 1874 (H).

CHAPTER 18. Abba *(pages 326–344)*

Secondary materials are: Cheney's *Louisa May Alcott*, Whitehill's *Boston*, Flexner's *Century of Struggle*, Blackwell's *Lucy Stone*, Mott's *History of American Magazines*, Lerner's *Grimké Sisters*, Livermore's *My Story of the War*, *Notable American Women*, Kaufman's *Homeopathy in America*, Stokes's *Iconography of Manhattan*, Frothingham's *Recollections and Impressions*, Vietor's *Woman's Quest*, William Kelby's "Unpublished Notes on Randall's Island," John Munro's, *New York Tombs Inside and Out!*, Hurd-Mead's *Medical Women*, Marguerite Winant's *Century of Sorosis, 1868–*

1968, Anne Botta's *Memoirs of Anne C. L. Botta, Letters of Lydia Maria Child,* Ticknor's *May Alcott,* and Louisa Alcott's *Eight Cousins, Rose in Bloom, Modern Mephistopheles,* and *Under the Lilacs.*

Although I didn't quote directly from them, the information on Rhoda Lawrence comes from records at Harvard's Countway Medical Library.

In addition to the sources at the Houghton Library (H), I used letters from the Louisa May Alcott Collection and the Alcott Family Collection, Clifton Waller Barrett Library, University of Virginia Library (L), from the Fruitlands Museum (F), and Louisa's letters in the May-Goddard Collection, Schlesinger Library, Radcliffe College (M-G):

"This isn't my Boston . . ." LMA's journal, March 1874 (H).

"Here is what you have . . ." ABA's journal, no date (H).

"With this first born . . ." Ibid., September 6, 1874 (H).

"Nothing adds more to . . ." Ibid., September 29, 1874 (H).

"not to be postponed . . ." Abigail Alcott's journal, 1875 (H).

"the whole affair in . . ." LMA to "Cousin Fred," April 20, 1875 (H).

"General *break-down* . . ." LMA's journal, April 1875 (H).

"I said I have done . . ." Abigail Alcott's journal, 1875 (H).

"Philosophy is a growth . . ." ABA's journal, December 1875 (H).

"more of a positive virtue than . . ." Abigail Alcott to LMA, December 30, 1875 (L).

"and bring some order out of . . ." Ibid.

"indications of intellectual power . . ." Abigail Alcott's journal, 1875 (H).

"on the subject of boots . . ." LMA to Abby May, September 25, no year (M-G).

"almost an impiety to think . . . Listener . . ." ABA's journal, October 21, 1876 (H).

"The blessed mornings . . ." Ibid., May 7, 1876 (H).

"I have found a calm . . ." Ibid., April 13, 1876 (H).

"we shall not be able to see . . ." Thomas Niles to LMA, August 30, 1876 (H).

"She has done her distasteful duty . . ." LMA's journal, September 1876 (H).

"but reason comes to my aid . . ." Abigail Alcott's journal, September 29, 1876 (H).

"getting on, and feel . . ." LMA's journal, December 1876 (H).

"My task gets on slowly . . ." Ibid., November 1876 (H).

"noble-hearted child." ABA's journal, August 25, 1876 (H).

"It has been simmering . . ." LMA's journal, January–February 1877 (H).

"Lu does not monopolize . . ." May Alcott to ABA, January 14, 1877 (H).

"when shall I have mine? . . ." LMA's journal, April 1877 (H).

"surpasses its predecessors . . ." ABA's journal, 1877 (H).

"sensational as weird and unearthly . . ." Thomas Niles to LMA, February 21, 1877 (H).

"the Alcotts are not on exhibition . . ." LMA to Mrs. Woods (F).

"and very plain . . ." Anna Pratt to ABA, no date (H).

"Marmee's health and home . . ." LMA's journal, 1877 (H).

"fearing that I might . . ." Ibid., October 1877 (H).

"but she was spared that . . ." Ibid., October 27, 1877 (H).

"but here all is changed . . ." LMA's notes on Cyrus Bartol's sermon, October, 1877 (H).
"My only comfort is that . . ." LMA's journal, December 1877 (H).

CHAPTER 19. Duty's Faithful Child *(pages 345–362)*

Here, I used Cheney's *Louisa May Alcott*, Louisa Alcott's articles in the *Woman's Journal, Aunt Jo's Scrapbag*, and *Jack and Jill*, Ticknor's *May Alcott*, Sanborn's *Recollections* and *A. B. Alcott*, Swayne's *Story of Concord*, Julian Hawthorne's *Memoirs*, Hurd-Mead's *Medical Women, Notable American Women*, Robinson's *Massachusetts in the Woman Suffrage Movement*, Vietor's *Woman's Quest*, Kaufman's *Homeopathy in America*, Emerson's *Letters*, and Rusk's *Emerson*.

I made use of Louisa's letters at the Boston Public Library (BPL) and in the Louisa May Alcott Collections, Clifton Waller Barrett Library, University of Virginia Library (L), as well as the documents at the Houghton Library (H):
"When I remember with what buoyant heart . . ." ABA, 1881 (H).
"delicate, cherished girlhood . . ." LMA's journal, 1882 (H).
"My heart bleeds afresh . . ." ABA's journal, June 11–14, 1878 (H).
"hear how her wandering mind . . ." Lydia Maria Child to LMA, June 19, 1878 (L).
"I dawdle about and wait . . ." LMA's journal, April 1878 (H).
"Your letters seem almost . . ." May Alcott to Alcotts, March 15, 1878 (H).
"My future seems so full . . ." Ibid., March 24, 1878 (H).
"I exult in the thought . . ." Ibid., April 1878 (H).
"America seems death . . ." Ibid.
"fine damask, my pretty silver and plenty . . ." Ibid.
"she will never want to live . . ." Ibid.
"so happy and blest . . ." LMA's journal, April 1878 (H).
"I doubt if I ever . . ." Ibid.
"Why people will think Jo . . ." LMA to Lukens sisters, October 2, 1878 (BPL).
"It had hardly occurred to me . . ." ABA's journal, May 22, 1878 (H).
"speculation seems a waste of time . . ." LMA's journal, August 1879 (H).
"a man up in a balloon . . ." Ibid., 1878 (H).
"Louisa takes charge of the housekeeping . . ." ABA's journal, September 11, 1878 (H).
"Always a little chore to be done . . ." LMA's journal, September 1878 (H).
"and tried to be content . . ." Ibid., October and November 1878 (H).
"ideal life . . ." Ibid., April 1878 (H).
"wise but heavy . . ." Ibid., March 1879 (H).
"she is a great comfort to me . . ." Ibid., February 1879 (H).
"the best woman I know . . ." Ibid., March 1879 (H).
"Long for the old strength . . ." Ibid., April 1879 (H).
"Even lonely old spinsters . . ." Ibid., May, June 1879 (H).
"Souls are such slaves to bodies . . ." Ibid., June 1879 (H).
"in watching the faces of some . . ." Ibid., June 1879 (H).
"patience, love and common sense . . ." Ibid., October 1879 (H).

"roost on our steps like hens . . ." Ibid., July 1879 (H).

"timid and slow . . ." Ibid., September 1879 (H).

"It is so easy to make money . . ." Ibid.

"Give up my hope and . . ." Ibid., October 1879 (H).

"Much rejoicing. Nice little . . . Ibid., November 1879 (H).

"Can be sound . . ." Ibid., November 25, 1879 (H).

"She was too happy . . ." Ibid., December 1879 (H).

"Oh, if I could only . . . Ibid.

"My child, I wish . . . Ibid., December 8, 1879 (H).

"He was much moved . . ." Ibid., December 1879 (H).

"I shall never forgive . . ." Ibid.

"I see now why . . ." Ibid.

"Of all the trials . . ." Ibid., January 1880 (H).

"make it true that our May . . ." Ibid., February 1880 (H).

"Life is so heavy . . ." Ibid.

"Don't belong there." Ibid.

"Bright girls, simple in dress . . ." Ibid., May 1880 (H).

"Philosophy is a bore . . ." Ibid., July, August 1880 (H).

"I held out my arms . . ." Ibid., September 19, 1880 (H).

"I suppose I am . . ." ABA's journal, September 21, 1880 (H).

"She always comes to me . . ." LMA's journal, September 19, 1880 (H).

"Had never crept at all . . ." Ibid., December 1880 (H).

"Glad to have said . . ." Ibid.

"do anything to please . . ." Thomas Niles to LMA, February 14, 1881 (H).

"overshadowed his genius . . ." ABA's journal, May 25, 1881 (H).

"*youthful presence* and the prospect . . ." Ibid., June 25, 26, 1878 (H).

"It is unquestionable that the ascendency . . ." Ibid., June 7, 1878 (H).

"They would demonize the little . . ." Ibid., December 9, 1881 (H).

"decked with ribbons and a doll's . . ." LMA's journal, October 1881 (H).

"Wish I were stronger . . ." Ibid., April 1882 (H).

"Women anxious to do . . ." Ibid., March 1882 (H).

"You are quite well . . ." ABA's journal, April 26, 1882 (H).

"Our best and greatest . . ." LMA's journal, April 1882 (H).

CHAPTER 20. Father and Daughter *(pages 363–377)*

The bulk of the material for this chapter was original, including letters at the Fruitlands Museum (F), letters in the Louisa May Alcott Collection, Clifton Waller Barrett Library, University of Virginia, Library (L), letters at the Alma-Lutz Collection, Schlesinger Library, Radcliffe College (A-L), a letter from Louisa to Susan B. Anthony in the Berg Collection of the New York Public Library (NYPL), letters at the Concord Free Public Library (C), letters at the Boston Public Library (BPL), and letters and papers at the Houghton Library (H).

I also referred to Sanborn's *Recollections* and *A.B. Alcott,* Cyrus Bartol's sermon "Amos Bronson Alcott, His Character," Cheney's *Louisa May Alcott* and *Children's Friend,* Louisa's letters to the *Woman's Journal* and *Jo's Boys.*

"breaking the laws of health . . ." LMA's journal, November 1882 (H).

"I don't think that he will ever . . ." LMA to Mrs. Stearns, November 14, 1882 (F).

"I am taking a predicament . . ." LMA's journal, December 1882 (H).

"Yes, I think I shall . . ." LMA to Mrs. Stearns, November 26, 1882 (F).

"The arm swells badly . . ." Ibid., December 30, 1882 (F).

"You are a philosopher . . ." Ibid., May 31, ? (F).

"This double life . . ." LMA's journal, February 1883 (H).

"There's Louisa Alcott . . ." LMA to Laura Hosmer, April 22, ? (L).

"The home-making, the comfort . . ." LMA to the Lukens sisters, February 21, 1885 (BPL).

"gone back . . . I earnestly desire . . ." LMA to Lucy Stone, August 31, 1885 (A-L).

"I am very proud of the *good* . . ." LMA to Susan B. Anthony, no date (NYPL).

"Shall never live . . ." LMA's journal, May 1883 (H).

"Now when I might enjoy rest . . ." LMA to the Lukens sisters, February 5, ? (BPL).

"his philosophy I have never . . ." LMA to William T. Harris, January 7, ? (F).

"Not wise to keep . . ." LMA's journal, August 1885 (H).

"Experiences go very deep . . ." Ibid., August 8, 1885 (H).

"one can shape life best . . ." LMA to the Lukens sisters, Feb 5, no year (BPL).

"The ladies are incapable or proud . . ." LMA's journal, May 1883 (H).

"and when it is done . . ." Ibid., January 1884 (H).

"slowly wearing away it seems . . ." LMA to Laura Hosmer, November 23, no year (L).

"go up . . . A little more . . ." LMA to Mrs. Stearns, May 23, 1885 (F).

"The hospital experience . . ." LMA's journal, April 11, 1884 (H).

"Put away papers and tried . . ." Ibid., October 1884 (H).

"I feel very still, then very light . . ." LMA to Maggie Lukens, March 15, 1885 (BPL).

"Delicate gentle people . . ." Ibid.

"very lurchy when I walk . . ." LMA to Laura Hosmer, March 16, 1885 (L).

"moonbeam . . . No miracle for me . . ." LMA's journal, March 1885 (H).

"Old ladies come to this . . ." LMA to Thomas Niles, July 13, 1885 (H).

"Another attack of vertigo . . ." LMA's journal, March 27, 1886 (H).

"when I forgot my body . . ." Ibid., March 1886 (H).

"hard with our mixed family . . ." Ibid., May 1886 (H).

"sad, lonely day . . . Feeble and sick . . ." Ibid., January 1, 1887 (H).

"Now I know what fear . . ." Ibid., January 7, 1887 (H).

"The patience of Job . . ." LMA to Laura Hosmer, June 1, 1887 (L).

"The end is not far off . . ." LMA's journal, September 1, 1887 (H).

"So I eat and suffer . . ." Ibid., September 3, 1887 (H).

"Suspect he thinks no help . . ." Ibid., September 8, 1887 (H).

"after being the hub to the . . ." LMA to Mrs. Bond, October 16, 1887 (H).

"part of the discipline . . ." Ibid., October 1887 (H).

"I don't want to keep him . . ." Ibid.

"Shall I ever find time . . ." LMA's journal, March 4, 1888 (H).

"Dear Pilgrim, waiting patiently . . ." LMA, 1886 (H).

Bibliography

Adams, Charles Francis. *Richard Henry Dana.* Boston, Houghton Mifflin, 1890.

Adams, Henry. *The Education of Henry Adams.* New York, Random House, Modern Library, 1946.

Alcott, Amos Bronson. *Concord Days.* Boston, Roberts Brothers, 1872.

————. *Essays on Education.* Introduction by Walter Harding. Gainesville, Fla., Scholars Facsimiles and Reprints, 1960.

————. "The Forester." *Atlantic Monthly,* April 1862.

————. *Observations on the Principles and Methods of Infant Instruction.* Boston, Carter and Hendee, 1830.

————. *Ralph Waldo Emerson, Philosopher and Seer.* Boston, Cupples and Hurd, 1882.

————. *Sonnets and Canzonets,* Boston, Roberts Brothers, 1882.

————. *Table Talk,* Boston, Roberts Brothers, 1877.

Alcott, Anna Pratt, *Comic Tragedies,* Boston, Roberts Brothers, 1893.

Alcott, Louisa May. *Aunt Jo's Scrapbag.* Boston, Roberts Brothers, 1872.

————. *Behind a Mask.* Edited by Madeleine Stern. New York, William Morrow, 1975.

————. *Eight Cousins,* Boston, Little, Brown, 1927.

————. *Flower Fables.* Boston, George W. Briggs, 1855.

————. *A Hole in the Wall.* Boston, Roberts Brothers, 1885.

————. *Hospital Sketches.* Edited by Bessie Z. Jones. Cambridge, The Belknap Press of the Harvard University Press, 1960.

————. *Hospital Sketches and Camp and Fireside Stories.* Boston, Roberts Brothers, 1869.

————. *Jack and Jill.* Boston, Little, Brown, 1928.

————. *Jo's Boys.* Boston, Little Brown, 1925, 1953.

————. *Little Men,* Boston, Little, Brown, 1901.

————. *Little Women,* Boston, Little, Brown, 1915.

————. "Love and Self-Love." *Atlantic Monthly,* March 1860.

————. "M.L.," *Journal of Negro History* 14, 1929.

————. *A Modern Mephistopheles.* Boston, Roberts Brothers, 1880.

_____. *Moods.* Boston, Loring, 1865.

_____. *Morning Glories.* New York, Carleton 1871.

_____. *An Old-Fashioned Girl.* Boston, Little, Brown, 1911.

_____. *Plots and Counterplots.* Edited by Madeleine Stern. New York, William Morrow, 1976.

_____.*Rose in Bloom.* Boston, Little, Brown, 1927.

_____. *Silver Pitchers.* Boston, Roberts Brothers, 1876.

_____. "A Sprig of Andromeda." Edited by John Cooley. New York, Pierpont Morgan Library, 1962.

_____. *Under the Lilacs.* Boston, Little, Brown, 1928.

_____. *Work.* Boston, Roberts Brothers, 1873, 1892.

Alcott, William Andrus. *Forty Years in the Wilderness of Pills and Powders.* Boston, John P. Jewett, 1859.

_____. *The Physiology of Marriage.* Boston, John P. Jewett, 1856.

_____. *The Young Husband or Duties of Man in the Marriage Relation.* New York, Arno Press, New York Times, 1972 (Boston, 1839).

Aldrich, George. *Walpole as It Was and Is.* N.H., Claremont Manufacturing Co., 1880.

Anthony, Katherine. *Margaret Fuller, A Psychological Biography.* New York, Harcourt Brace and Howe, 1920.

_____. *Louisa May Alcott.* New York, Knopf, 1938.

von Arnim, Bettina. *Goethe's Correspondence with a Child.* Lowell, Mass., 1841.

Arvin, Newton. *Hawthorne.* Boston, Little, Brown, 1929.

Arvin, Newton, ed. *The Heart of Hawthorne's Journals.* Boston, Houghton Mifflin, 1929.

Austin, James C., *Fields of the Atlantic Monthly.* San Marino, Calif., The Huntington Library, 1953.

Ayer, Mary Farwell. *Early Days on Boston Common.* Boston, privately printed, 1910.

Baltzell, E. Digby. *Philadelphia Gentlemen.* Glencoe, Ill., Free Press, 1958.

Barber, John Warner. *Connecticut Historical Collections.* New Haven, Durrie and Peck, and J.W. Barber, 1836.

Barker-Benfield, G. J. *The Horrors of the Half-Known Life, Male Attitudes Toward Women and Sexuality in Nineteenth-Century America.* New York, Harper & Row, 1976.

Barnes, Emily R. *Narratives, Traditions and Personal Reminiscences . . . of the Village of Walpole, New Hampshire.* Boston, George H. Ellis, 1888.

Bartol, Cyrus Augustus. "Amos Bronson Alcott, His Character, A Sermon." Boston, 1888.

Bellows, Josiah Grahme. "Reminiscences of a Village Life." New York, New-York Historical Society.

Blackwell, Alice Stone. *Lucy Stone, Pioneer of Women's Rights.* Boston, Little, Brown, 1930.

Blaney, Henry R. *Old Boston.* Boston, Lee and Shepard, 1896.

Botta, Anne C. L. *Memoirs of Anne C. L. Botta, Written by Her Friends with Her Letters.* New York, J. Selwin Tait and Sons, 1894.

Bowditch, Nathaniel I. *A History of the Massachusetts General Hospital.* Boston, 1872.

Bowen, Catherine Drinker. *Yankee from Olympus, Justice Holmes and His Family.* Boston, Atlantic Monthly Press, 1943.

Bowen, Frank C. *A Century of Atlantic Travel, 1830–1930.* Boston, Little, Brown, 1930.

Bradley, Caroline. *Western World Costume, An Outline History.* New York, Appleton-Century-Crofts, 1954.

Brooks, Gladys. *Three Wise Virgins.* New York, Dutton, 1957.

Brooks, Van Wyck. *The Flowering of New England.* New York, E. P. Dutton, 1941.

_____. *The Life of Emerson.* New York, E. P. Dutton, 1932.

Brown, Abram English. *Faneuil Hall and Faneuil Hall Market.* Boston, Lee and Shepard, 1900.

Brown, Florence Whiting. "Alcott and the Concord School of Philosophy." Concord, Mass., privately printed, August 1926.

Brown, Mary Hosmer. *Memories of Concord.* Boston, Four Seas Company, 1926.

Boller, Paul F. *American Transcendentalism, 1830–1860.* New York, Capricorn Books, 1974.

Bunyan, John. *The Pilgrim's Progress.* Afterword by F. R. Leavis. New York, Signet, 1964.

Cameron, Kenneth Walter. *The Transcendentalists and Minerva.* Hartford, Transcendental Books, 1958.

Canby, Henry Seidel. *Thoreau.* Boston, Houghton Mifflin, 1939.

"Ceremonies at the Dedication of the Soldiers' Monument in Concord, Mass." Concord, Mass., privately printed, 1867.

Channing, William Ellery. *Thoreau: The Poet Naturalist.* Boston, 1873.

Cheney, Ednah Dow. *Louisa May Alcott, The Children's Friend.* Boston, 1888.

_____. *Louisa May Alcott, Her Life, Letters and Journals.* Boston, Little, Brown, 1928.

Child, Lydia Maria. *Letters of Lydia Maria Child with a Biographical Introduction by John Greenleaf Whittier and an Appendix by Wendell Phillips.* Boston, Houghton Mifflin, 1883.

Christie, John Aldrich. *Thoreau as World Traveler.* New York, Columbia University Press, 1965.

Christy, Arthur E. *The Orient in American Transcendentalism.* New York, Columbia University Press, 1932.

Clark, Annie M. L. *The Alcotts in Harvard.* Harvard, Mass., 1902.

Clarke, James Freeman. *Autobiography, Diary and Correspondence.* Edited by Edward Everett Hale. Boston, 1891.

Coffin, John G. "Discourses on Cold and Warm Bathing." Boston, Cummings, Hilliard, 1826.

Collis, John Stewart. *The Carlyles.* New York, Dodd, Mead, 1971.

Commager, Henry Steele. *Theodore Parker.* Boston, Little, Brown, 1936.

Damrell, Charles S. *A Half Century of Boston's Buildings.* Boston, Louis D. Hager, 1895.

Dana, Richard Henry, Jr. *Journal of Richard Henry Dana, Jr.* Edited by Robert F. Lucid. Cambridge, Harvard University Press, 1968.

Dictionary of American Biography.

Drake, Samuel Adams. *Old Landmarks and Historic Personages of Boston.* Boston, Roberts Brothers, 1895.

Dwight, Marianne. *Letters from Brook Farm, 1844–1847,* Poughkeepsie, N.Y. 1928.

Edgell, David P. "Bronson Alcott's Autobiographical Index." *New England Quarterly* 14.

Eisenstadt, Abraham. *American History, Book I.* New York, Thomas Y. Crowell, 1962.

Elliott, Walter. *The Life of Father Hecker.* New York, Columbus Press, 1894.

Emerson, Ralph Waldo. *The Journals and Miscellaneous Notebooks of Ralph Waldo Emerson,* Vols. 1–10. Edited by William H. Gilman. Cambridge, Harvard University Press, 1961–1975.

––––––. *Journals of Ralph Waldo Emerson.* Edited by Edward Waldo Emerson and Waldo Emerson Forbes. Boston, Houghton Mifflin, 1912.

––––––. *The Letters of Ralph Waldo Emerson.* Edited by Ralph L. Rusk. New York, Columbia University Press, 1939.

Emerson, Ralph Waldo, et al. "Papers Read at the John Brown Memorial Meetings." New York, Pierpont Morgan Library, December 2, 1859.

Flexner, Eleanor. *Century of Struggle.* Cambridge, Harvard University Press, 1959.

Foote, Henry Wilder. *Annals of King's Chapel.* Boston, Little, Brown, 1882.

Frothingham, Octavius Brooks. *Recollections and Impressions, 1822–1890.* New York, Putnam's, 1891.

––––––. *Transcendentalism in New England.* New York, Putnam's, 1876.

Fuller, Margaret. *Love Letters of Margaret Fuller.* Introduction by Julia Ward Howe. New York, 1903.

––––––. *Margaret Fuller, American Romantic.* Edited by Perry Miller. New York, Anchor Books, 1963.

Furnas, J. C. *The Road to Harper's Ferry.* New York, William Sloane Associates, 1959.

Gladden, Washington. "Was Bronson Alcott's School a Type of God's Moral Government?" Boston, Lockwood, Brooks, 1877.

Godey's Ladies' Book. Philadelphia, 1830–.

Gowing, Clara. *The Alcotts as I Knew Them.* Boston, C. M. Clark, 1909.

Green, Constance McLaughlin. *Washington, Village and Capital, 1800–1878.* Princeton, Princeton University Press, 1962.

Greenwood, F. W. P. "A Good Old Age." Boston, S. N. Dickinson, 1841.

Haeffner, George E. *A Critical Estimate of the Educational Theories and Practises of A. Bronson Alcott.* New York, Columbia University Press, 1937; reprinted, Westport, Conn., Greenwood Press, 1970.

Hale, Edward Everett. *James Russell Lowell and His Friends.* Boston, Houghton Mifflin, 1899.

––––––. *A New England Boyhood,* New York, Cassell, 1893.

Haller, John S., Jr. "Samson or the Materia Medica: Medical Theory and the Use and Abuse of Calomel in Nineteenth-Century America." *Pharmacy in History* 13, 1971.

Haller, John S., Jr., and Haller, Robin M. *The Physician and Sexuality in Victorian America.* Urbana, University of Illinois Press, 1974.

Hardington, Walter, "Thoreau's Feminine Foe," *PMLA*, Vol. LXIX, March 1954, No. 1

Harrell, Pauline Chase, and Smith, Margaret Supplee, eds. *Victorian Boston Today.* Boston, New England Chapter, The Victorian Society in America, 1975.

Hart, Albert Bushnell, ed. *American History Told by Contemporaries.* New York, Macmillan, 1901.

Hawthorne, Julian. *The Memoirs of Julian Hawthorne.* New York, Macmillan, 1938.

Hawthorne, Nathaniel. *American Notebooks.* Edited by George Parsons Lathrop. Boston, Houghton Mifflin, 1883.

———. *The Blithdale Romance.* New York, Norton, 1958.

———. *Hawthorne's Short Stories.* Edited and with an introduction by Newton Arvin. New York, Vintage Books, 1946.

Herrnstadt, Richard L., ed. *The Letters of A. Bronson Alcott.* Ames, Iowa State University Press, 1969.

Higginson, Mary Thacher, ed. *Letters and Journals of Thomas Wentworth Higginson.* Boston, Houghton Mifflin, 1921.

Higginson, Thomas Wentworth. *Carlyle's Laugh and Other Surprises.* Boston, Houghton Mifflin, 1909.

Hoeltje, Hubert. *Sheltering Tree, A Story of the Friendship of Ralph Waldo Emerson and Amos Bronson Alcott.* Durham, N.C., Duke University Press, 1943.

Hocker, Edward. *Germantown, 1683–1933.* Germantown, Pa., published by the author, 1933.

Homans, Isaac. *Sketches of Boston, Past & Present.* Boston, Phillips, Sampson & Co., 1851.

Hornung, Clarence P. *Wheels Across America.* New York, Barnes, 1959.

Hosack, David. *Essays on Various Subjects of Medical Science.* New York, 1824.

Hosmer, Gladys E. "Louisa May Alcott, War Nurse." *Trained Nurse Review,* August 1932.

Howe, Julia Ward. *Reminiscences, 1819–1899.* Boston, Houghton Mifflin, 1899.

Howe, Mark A. De Wolfe. *Boston Common, Scenes from Four Centuries.* Boston, Atlantic Monthly Press, 1921.

———. *Holmes of the Breakfast Table.* New York, Oxford University Press, 1939.

———. *Memories of a Hostess.* Boston, Atlantic Monthly Press, 1922.

Hudson, William. "An Anti-Calomel Lecture." Pomeroy, Ohio, May 20, 1854.

Hurd-Mead, Kate Campbell. *Medical Women of America.* New York, Froben Press, 1933.

James, Alice. *The Diary of Alice James.* Edited by Leon Edel. London, Rupert Hart-Davis, 1965.

James, Henry. *The Bostonians.* London, Penguin Books, 1974.

Jenkins, Charles F. *Guide Book to Historic Germantown.* Germantown, Pa., The Site and Relic Society, 1902.

Johnson, Thomas H. *Emily Dickinson, An Interpretive Biography.* Cambridge, Harvard University Press, 1955.

Kaufman, Martin. *Homeopathy in America.* Baltimore, Johns Hopkins University Press, 1971.

Kelby, William. "Unpublished Notes on Randall's Island." New York, New-York Historical Society.

Kennedy, Charles. "Commuter Services in the Boston Area, 1835–1860." *Business History Review* 36, summer 1962.

Keyser, Namaan, et al. *History of Old Germantown.* Germantown, Pa., Horace F. McCann, 1907.

Lee, W. Storrs. *The Yankees of Connecticut.* New York, Holt, 1957.

Leland, Charles Godfrey. *Memoirs.* New York, 1893.

Lerner, Gerda. *The Grimké Sisters from South Carolina.* Boston, Houghton Mifflin, 1967.

Livermore, Mary Ashton. *My Story of the War.* Hartford, Worthington, 1888.

Martineau, Harriet. *The Martyr Age of the United States.* Boston, 1839.

——. *Society in America.* New York, 1837.

Matthiessen, F. O. *American Renaissance.* New York, Oxford University Press, 1941.

May, Samuel J. *The Fugitive Slave Law and Its Victims,* Anti-Slavery Tracts I and II. Westport, Conn., Negro Universities Press, 1856.

——. *The Rights and Condition of Women.* Syracuse, 1846.

——. *Memoir of Colonel Joseph May, 1760–1841.* Portland, Hoyt, Fogg & Donham, 1873.

——. *Memoir of Samuel Joseph May.* Boston, Roberts Brothers, 1873.

McCuskey, Dorothy. *Bronson Alcott, Teacher.* New York, Macmillan, 1940.

Meltzer, Milton, and Harding, Walter. *A Thoreau Profile.* New York, Crowell, 1962.

Miller, Edwin Haviland. *Melville, A Biography.* New York, Braziller, 1975.

Miller, Perry. *The American Transcendentalists, Their Prose and Poetry.* New York, Anchor Books, 1957.

——. *Nature's Nation.* Cambridge, Harvard University Press, 1967.

——. *The Transcendentalists.* Cambridge, Harvard University Press, 1950.

Morrow, Honoré Willsie. *The Father of Little Women.* Boston, Little, Brown, 1927.

Moses, Bell. *Louisa May Alcott, Dreamer and Worker.* New York, Appleton, 1909.

Mott, Frank Luther. *A History of American Magazines.* Cambridge, Harvard University Press, 1957.

Munro, John Josiah. *The New York Tombs Inside and Out!* Brooklyn, printed by the author, 1909.

Notable American Women, 1607–1950. Edited by Edward T. James. Cambridge, Harvard University Press, 1971.

Nye, Russell Blaine. *Society and Culture in America, 1830–1860,* New York, Harper & Row, 1974.

——. *William Lloyd Garrison and the Humanitarian Reformers.* Boston, Little, Brown, 1955.

Oakley, Mary Ann. *Elizabeth Cady Stanton.* Feminist Press, 1972.

O'Brien, Harriet E. *Lost Utopias.* Harvard, Mass., Fruitlands and the Wayside Museum, 1974.

Orcutt, Samuel. *History of the Town of Wolcott (Conn.).* Waterbury, Conn., Press of the American Printing Company, 1874,

Ossoli, Margaret Fuller, *Memoirs of Margaret Fuller Ossoli.* Edited by R. W. Emerson, W. H. Channing, and J. F. Clarke. New York, Burt Franklin, 1972.

Parker, Gail. *The Mind Cure in New England.* Hanover, N.H., University Presses of New England, 1973.

————. *The Ovenbirds.* New York, Anchor Books, 1972.

Parrington, Vernon L. *The Romantic Revolution in America, 1800–1860.* New York, Harvest Books, 1927.

Peabody, Elizabeth. *Record of Mr. Alcott's School.* Boston, Roberts Brothers., 1874.

Ripley, David B. "The Educational Ideas, Implementations and Influence of A. Bronson Alcott," Ph.D. thesis. The College of Education at the University of Iowa, 1971.

Roberts, Josephine. "Elizabeth Peabody and the Temple School." *New England Quarterly* 15.

Robinson, Harriet H. *Massachusetts in the Woman Suffrage Movement.* Boston, Roberts Brothers, 1881.

Rosenberg, Philip. *The Seventh Hero, Thomas Carlyle and the Theory of Radical Activism.* Cambridge, Harvard University Press, 1974.

Rossiter, William S. *Days and Ways in Old Boston.* Boston, R. H. Stearns, 1915.

Rusk, Ralph L. *The Life of Ralph Waldo Emerson.* New York, Scribners, 1949.

Sanborn, Franklin B., and Harris, William T. *A. Bronson Alcott: His Life and Philosophy.* New York, Biblo and Tannen, 1965.

————. *Bronson Alcott at Alcott House, England and Fruitlands, New England (1842–1844).* Cedar Rapids, Torch Press, 1908.

————. *The Personality of Thoreau.* Boston, 1901.

————. *Recollections of Seventy Years of Concord.* Boston, 1909.

————. "Reminiscences of Louisa May Alcott." *Independent* 72, March 7, 1912.

Sayler, Sanford. *Marmee, The Mother of Little Women.* Norman, University of Oklahoma Press, 1949.

Scharf, J. Thomas, and Westcott, Thompson. *History of Philadelphia, 1609–1884.* Philadelphia, L. H. Everts, 1884.

Schlesinger, Arthur M., Jr. *A Pilgrim's Progress: Orestes Brownson.* Boston, Little, Brown, 1939.

————. *The Age of Jackson.* New York, Mentor, 1945.

Sears, Clara Endicott. *Bronson Alcott's Fruitlands.* Boston, Houghton Mifflin, 1915.

Seldes, Gilbert. *The Stammering Century.* New York, John Day, 1928.

Shackleton, Robert. *The Book of Boston.* Philadelphia, Penn Publishing Company, 1916.

Shepard, Odell. *The Journals of Bronson Alcott.* Boston, Little, Brown, 1938.

————. *Pedlar's Progress: The Life of Bronson Alcott.* Boston, Little Brown, 1937.

Shryock, Richard H. *Medicine and Society in America, 1660–1860.* New York, NYU Press, 1960.

de Soissons, S. C. *A Parisian in America.* Boston, 1896.

Spacks, Patricia Meyer. *The Female Imagination.* New York, Knopf, 1975.

Stern, Madeleine B. *Louisa May Alcott.* Norman, University of Oklahoma Press, 1950.

Sterry, Iveagh H., and Garrigus, William H. *They Found a Way, Connecticut's Restless People.* Brattleboro, Vt., Stephen Daye Press, 1938.

Stokes, I. N. Phelps. *The Iconography of Manhattan Island, 1498–1909.* New York, Robert H. Dodd, 1918.

Swayne, Josephine Latham, ed. *The Story of Concord Told by Concord Writers.* Boston, W. B. Clarke, 1905.

Swift, Lindsay. *Brook Farm.* New York, Macmillan, 1900.

Tharp, Louise Hall. *The Peabody Sisters of Salem.* Boston, Little, Brown, 1950.

Thwing, Annie Haven. *Crooked and Narrow Streets of the Town of Boston.* Boston, Marshall Jones, 1920.

Ticknor, Caroline. *May Alcott: A Memoir.* Boston, Little, Brown, 1928.

Tinkcom, Harry M., Tinkcom, Margaret, et al. *Historic Germantown.* Philadelphia, The American Philosophical Society, 1955.

Tolman, George. "Mary Moody Emerson." Concord, Mass., 1902.

Tomkins, Eugene. *The History of the Boston Theatre, 1854–1901.* Boston, Houghton Mifflin, 1908.

Tryon, W. S. *Parnassus Corner, A Life of James T. Fields, Publisher to the Victorians.* Boston, Houghton Mifflin, 1963.

Urdang, George. *The Early Chemical and Pharmaceutical History of Calomel. Chymia:* Annual Studies in the History of Chemistry, Vol. 1. Philadelphia, University of Pennsylvania Press, 1948.

Vietor, Agnes. *A Woman's Quest, The Life of Marie E. Zakrzewska, M.D.* New York, D. Appleton, 1924.

Warren, Austin. *The Elder Henry James.* New York, Macmillan, 1934.

Warren, Henry D., et al. *The History of Waterford, Oxford County, Maine.* Portland, Hoyt, Fogg & Donham, 1879.

Weiss, John. *Life and Correspondence of Theodore Parker.* New York, Appleton, 1864.

Whitehill, Walter M. *Boston, A Topographical History.* Cambridge, Harvard University Press, 1968.

———. *Destroyed Boston Buildings.* Boston, Massachusetts Historical Society, 1965.

Whitman, Walt. *The Gathering Forces.* New York, Putnam's, 1920.

———. *The Wound Dresser.* Edited by Richard M. Bucke, M.D. Boston, Small, Maynard, 1898.

Willis, Frederick L. H. *Alcott Memoirs.* Edited by Edith Willis Linn. Boston, 1915.

Winant, Marguerite D. *A Century of Sorosis, 1868–1968.* New York, 1968.

Winsor, Justin. *The Memorial History of Boston, 1630–1880.* Boston, James R. Osgood, 1881.

Index

Index

Abolitionist movement, 32,
101–3, 190–91, 196–98, 205–6,
221, 226–27, 239–40
Adams, Henry, 303
Addison, Joseph, 30
Africa, 289
Alcott, Abigail May "Abba"
(LMA's mother): birth, 30;
character and personality, 7–8,
32, 46; courtship with Alcott,
33–49; death, 343–44; early life,
30–32; first meeting with
Alcott, 29–34; health problems,
7, 45, 67, 77, 78, 79, 96–98,
170–71, 181, 193, 229, 234,
242, 244, 292–93, 299, 314,
319, 324, 326, 336; marital
relations, 7–8, 63, 66, 75–76,
77, 79, 80, 122–23, 134–35,
137, 139, 148–49, 154, 175;
marriage, 49; relief work in
Boston, 176–77, 179–80, 186;
views of womanhood, 46–48,
66–67, 122–23, 143–44,
153–54, 166, 168, 336
Alcott, Abigail May. *See* Nieriker,
May Alcott
Alcott, Amos Bronson (LMA's

father): attitudes toward
women, 16, 37, 40, 46, 47, 66,
166, 187–88, 303; birth, 18;
character and personality, 3, 7,
29, 122, 197, 243–44; *Concord
Days*, 316; Concord School of
Philosophy, 349, 352;
"Consociate Family, The," 142;
Conversations on the Gospels, 85,
86, 94; courtship with Abigail
May, 33–49; "Days and Works
at Fruitlands," 142; dietary
beliefs and practices, 98,
150–51, 155, 222; early life,
18–29; educational philosophy,
3, 25–27, 33–34, 73–74; family
provider, 7, 67, 80, 120–22,
123, 151, 153–54, 155, 158,
168, 170, 181, 189, 191, 202;
father, 72–75, 151; first
meeting with Abigail, 29–34;
first visit to Boston, 34; on free
love, 62; friendship with
Emerson, 108–12, 168, 188,
359–60; Fruitlands experiment,
134–52; health, 294, 337;
influenced by Garrison, 58–59;
influenced by Quakers, 24, 67;

Alcott, Amos Bronson *(cont.)*
    itinerant lecturer, 123–24, 126,
    194–95, 221; last illness and
    death, 362–74; marital
    relations, 63, 66, 75–76, 77, 79,
    80, 122–23, 134–35, 137, 139,
    148–49, 154, 175; marriage, 49;
    "Observations on the Life," 72;
    "Orphic Sayings," 57, 124,
    125; pedagogue, 70–71, 84–85;
    "Psyche, the Breath of Childhood,"
    110; *Record of a School, The,* 82,
    312–13; relationship with
    daughter, Anna, 72–75, 76,
    88–89, 90–92, 99–100, 120,
    134–35, 171, 327; relations
    with Nathaniel Hawthorne,
    237–38, 267; religious beliefs,
    24, 27, 54–55; schoolmaster in
    Boston, 53, 67, 81–100;
    schoolmaster in Cheshire, 25,
    27–28, 50; schoolmaster in
    Germantown, 67–78; sex
    education and, 84–85;
    superintendent in Concord,
    243; *Tablets,* 299; teaches his
    daughters, 73–74, 84, 89–94;
    Temple School, 81–100, 113,
    116, 122, 125, 137; theories of
    motherhood, 74; tours in West,
    227, 293, 295, 303, 314; visit to
    England, 127–31
Alcott, Anna Bronson. *See* Pratt,
    Anna Alcott
Alcott, Chatfield, 22, 23
Alcott, Elizabeth Peabody (LMA's
    sister): birth, 82; illness and
    death, 208, 212–17, 219, 227
Alcott, Elizabeth Sewall. *See*
    Alcott, Elizabeth Peabody
Alcott, Louisa May: abolitionist
    movement and, 101–3, 191,

198, 206, 230–33, 240;
    adolescence, 164–201; amateur
    acting, 174–75, 200–201, 203;
    attitude toward writing, 3, 8–9,
    147, 195, 230, 270, 300,
    319–20, 353; Barnard, A. M.
    (pseudonym), 259, 261, 272,
    273, 291, 340, 341; birth, 76;
    character and personality, 1, 6,
    7, 9, 11, 77, 85–86, 87, 88,
    89–92, 93, 100, 122, 129, 155,
    165, 175, 179, 188, 204, 210,
    229, 259, 261–62, 271, 279–80,
    315, 323, 324, 325, 349; death,
    374; distrust of men, 8,
    138–39, 143, 154, 177, 220,
    257–58, 287, 376; domestic
    service in Dedham, 193–94;
    early life, 78, 83–84, 87–94,
    114–33, 140–52, 157–71; editor
    of *Merry's Museum,* 294;
    education, 136, 155, 161–63;
    family provider, 206–8, 209,
    220, 227, 228, 269, 284, 290,
    296, 307, 308, 315; feminist,
    206, 222–23, 244, 297, 302,
    327, 330, 331, 332–33, 352–53,
    355–56, 358–59, 365–66; final
    illness and death, 369–74; first
    trip to Europe, 284–89; Flora
    Fairfield (pseudonym), 190,
    198; health of, 1, 253–58,
    267–68, 293, 296, 298,
    299–300, 313, 325, 327–28,
    336, 342, 346, 348, 351, 353;
    Henry David Thoreau and, 8,
    116–19, 155, 164, 226–27, 306;
    last will and testament, 356;
    mercury poisoning, 1, 253–54,
    255–58, 306, 369; at Miss
    Chase's school, 155; in New
    York City, 333–35; nurse in

Georgetown, 9, 249–56, 351; personal appearance, 1, 177, 207; playwright, 200–201, 210; Ralph Waldo Emerson and, 4, 155, 167, 361–62; relationship with family, 9–10, 131–32, 208, 219–20; relationship with father, 6–7, 13–14, 76, 77, 87, 89–93, 124, 137–38, 168, 204–5, 229, 243–44, 260–61, 308, 316, 345–46, 363–65, 375–76; relationship with mother, 8, 65, 80, 87, 89, 93, 121–22, 135, 146, 154, 162–63, 179–80, 281, 326, 338, 344; relationship with sisters, 77–78, 87–89, 135–36, 174, 178, 206–8, 215, 217, 245, 259, 323, 343, 351, 354–55, 366; schoolteacher, 176, 179, 182, 192, 193, 194, 221, 246; second trip to Europe, 303–10; sexual awakening, 154–55, 165–68, 187; suicide attempt, 227–28; use of opium, 258; Vassar College, 329; views on marriage, 220, 236, 325; working habits, 1, 3, 8–9, 240, 242, 274, 295, 317; works of, see Works of Louisa May Alcott
Alcott family, 12, 15, 17, 176–77, 181, 195–96, 220; in Boston, 50–67, 81–115, 171; in Concord, Mass., 114–33, 157–71, 218–367; financial difficulties, 67, 75–78, 80, 93–96, 114, 120–22, 123–24, 132–33, 153, 169, 209; in Germantown, Pa., 68–80; in Harvard, Mass., 140–56; in Walpole, New Hampshire, 202–17

Alcott House, 127, 129, 136, 170
Alcox, Chatfield, 22, 23
Alcox, Junius, 128, 157, 159, 163
Alcox, Thomas, 21, 23
Alcox (Alcott), Anna Bronson (LMA's grandmother), 18–19, 209, 265
Alcox (Alcott), Joseph Chatfield (LMA's grandfather), 18–19
Alcox (Alcott), William Andrus, 19, 20, 21, 22, 23, 24, 25, 63
Amateur Dramatic Company, Walpole, N. H., 203
American Journal of Education, 60, 61
American Museum of Natural History, 333
American Preceptor, The, 19
Andrews, Stephen Pearl, 211–12
Anthony, Susan B., 188–89, 211, 327, 366
Anti-Slavery Convention, Boston (1850), 187
Appeal in Favor of that Class of Americans called Africans (Child), 103
Arnim, Bettina von, 166, 167, 183, 229, 362
Association for Advancement of Women, 334
Atlantic Monthly, 65, 175, 228, 233, 234, 241, 262, 283

Baron, Francis, 114
Barnard, A. M. (LMA's pseudonym), 259, 261, 272, 273, 291, 340, 341
Barry, Thomas, 200, 201
Bartlett, Alice, 301, 304, 306
Bartol, Cyrus, 344, 374
Beecher, Henry Ward, 314
Beecher, Lyman, 20, 58, 59

Bellows, Henry, 249
Benson, Helen, 33
Biddle, Nicholas, 68, 121
Blackwell, Henry, 327
Blake, Harrison, 211
Bloomer, Amelia, 188
Bond, Louisa, 153, 204, 210
Booth, Edwin, 205
Boston, Mass.: in the 1820s and 1830s, 50–54; in the 1850s, 173–74; in the 1860s, 294; fire of 1872, 316; "Water Celebration" (1848), 173
Boston Atlas, 53
Boston City Hospital, 332
Boston Courier, 95
Boston Female Anti-Slavery Society, 102, 103
Boston Female Society for Missionary Purposes, 51
Bostonians, The (James), 60
Boston Maine Insurance Company, 30
Boston Quarterly Review, 106
Boston Recorder and Telegraph, 50
Boston Theater, 200–201, 210, 320
Boston University, 336, 356
Boston Vigilance Committee, 191, 193, 197
Botta, Anne Charlotte Lynch, 334
Botta, Vincenzo, 334
Bowditch, Henry Ingersol, 298, 299–300
Bowditch, Nathaniel, 298
Bower, Samuel, 141, 142, 146
Box a Cox, 203
Bremer, Fredrika, 177, 183
"Brick Ends," 155–56
Briggs, George, 198
Bronson, Tillotson, 19, 20, 21
Brook Farm, 119, 126, 141, 148, 163, 218

Brooklyn, Conn., 28–29, 33, 34, 36, 102
Brown, Antoinette, 187
Brown, John, 227, 230–33, 239, 240, 243, 263, 362
Brownson, Orestes, 106–7, 108
Buckminster, Joseph, 56
Bullfinch, Charles, 51, 52, 54
Burns, Anthony, 197
Burns, Owen, 203
Burnside, Ambrose E., 253

Calvin, John, 33–34
Calvinism, 21, 29, 45, 107, 108, 238
Carlyle, Thomas, 78, 109, 128–29, 130, 183, 205
Cary, Mary Ann. See May, Mary Ann Cary
Cassatt, Mary, 338
Catholicism, 176
Cavour, Camillo Benso di, 334
Celestial Railroad, The (Hawthorne), 57
Channing, Ellen Fuller, 119, 225
Channing, William Ellery, 32, 41, 54, 60, 82, 94, 106, 115, 119, 121, 138–39, 159, 188, 189, 205, 225–26, 238, 247, 248, 255, 256, 290, 315, 319, 331, 360
Channing, William Henry, 257
Chapman, Henry, 103
Chapman, Maria Weston, 103
Chase, Maria, 155
Cheney, Ednah Dow, 123, 124, 125
Cheshire, Conn., 25, 29, 33, 34, 51
Cheshire Academy, Cheshire, Conn., 20
Child, David Lee, 103

Child, Lydia Maria (Francis), 32, 103, 144, 231, 337, 346
China, S.S., 285
Christian Union (periodical), 314, 315, 317
Civil War, American, 9, 10, 190, 239–40, 244, 249
Clarke, James Freeman, 45, 56, 175, 362
Clemmer, Mary, 355
Cogswell, Horatio, 158
Coleridge, Samuel Taylor, 76, 78, 109
Commonwealth (periodical), 263, 264, 265
Concord Academy, 117
Concord Dramatic Union, 221
Concord Lyceum, 331
Concord School of Philosophy, 349, 352
Concord State Reformatory, 351, 358, 371
Confessions of an English Opium Eater (De Quincey), 194
"Connecticut River fever," 23
Coste, Gaston, 304
Craft, William and Ellen, 197

Dall, Caroline, 233–34, 272, 274
Dana, Richard Henry, Jr., 125, 191, 197, 256, 289
Daniel Deronda (Eliot), 350
Davis, James, 51
Davis, Paulina Wright, 187
De Quincey, Thomas, 194
Dial (periodical), 57, 124, 125
Dickens, Charles, 9, 145, 177, 246, 289
Dix, Dorothea Lynde, 60, 82–83, 251, 256, 257, 259, 264
Dodge, Mary Mapes, 335
Douglass, Frederick, 187
"Dove Cote," 117

Dr. Wilbur's Idiot Asylum, Syracuse, N.Y., 203, 241
Drunkard (Smith), 200
Dwight, John, 126

Earle, Sarah H., 187
Edgeworth, Maria, 25
Edward VII, King of England, 241
Edwards, Jonathan, 25
Eliot, Charles William, 362
Eliot, George, 350
Elizabeth, 184
Elliott, James R., 292
Emerson, Charles, 109, 110
Emerson, Edith, 119, 290
Emerson, Ellen, 119, 196, 198, 225, 237, 315, 318–19
Emerson, Ellen Tucker, 109, 362
Emerson, Lydia Jackson, 109, 117, 138, 234, 257, 270, 315, 319, 344, 347, 359, 361, 362
Emerson, Mary Moody, 108, 109, 112, 118, 138, 223, 224
Emerson, Ralph Waldo: attitude toward women, 66, 67, 167, 169, 224; death, 361–62; friendship with Alcott, 103–12, 168, 188, 359–60
Emerson, Waldo, 119, 125, 127
Episcopal Society, 20–21
Erie Canal, 68
Everett, Abraham, 141
Everett, Edward, 52, 56

Fairfield, Flora (LMA's pseudonym), 190
Famous Women (Clemmer), 355
Faneuil Hall, Boston, 50, 52, 103, 244
Federal Street Church, Boston, 32

Female Medical College, Boston, 297, 332

Feminism, 63–67, 101, 143, 185, 187–88, 206, 211–12, 233, 327, 330, 331, 332–33, 334

Fields, Annie, 246, 256, 262, 266, 267, 334

Fields, James T., 183, 194–95, 208, 233, 238, 246, 262, 267, 270, 293, 294, 301

Fitchburg Railroad, 114, 157

Flag of Our Union, The (periodical), 272, 282

Follen, Charles, 60

Folsom, Abby, 104

Foord, Sophia, 159–60, 163, 248

Forbes, William, 290

Forrest, Edwin, 205

Fort Sumter, 244

Foster, Stephen, 156

Fox, George, 24, 109

Francis, Convers, 32, 56

Frank Leslie's Illustrated Newspaper, 259, 272

Fraternity Club, 334

Free Religious Association, 298

Frothingham, Octavius Brooks, 55, 58, 66, 201, 298, 334

Fruitlands, 134–52, 153, 154, 184, 373

Fugitive Slave Law (U.S.), 190, 191, 196, 198

Fugitive Slave Law and Its Victims, The (May), 196

Fuller, Sarah Margaret. See Ossoli, Sarah Margaret Fuller

Gannet, Ezra, 205

Gardner, Walter, 156

Garner, Margaret, 197

Garrison, William Lloyd, 33, 58–60, 102–3, 137, 175, 187, 191

Geist, Christian, 214

George Routledge and Sons, 289

Germantown, Pa., 68, 75, 78, 94, 336

Germantown Academy, Germantown, Pa., 67, 68

Gibbon, Edward, 30

Godey, Louis A., 190

Godey's Lady's Book (periodical), 63–64, 190

Goethe, Johann Wolfgang von, 166, 183, 333, 362

Goethe's Correspondence with a Child (von Arnim), 166

Graham, Sylvester, 98, 101, 137

Greaves, James P., 129, 134, 136, 137

Greele, Louisa May, 32, 41, 42, 43

Greeley, Horace, 121, 184, 360

Greenwood, Francis, 49

Grimké, Angelina, 102, 103–4

Grimké, Sarah, 102, 104

Hahneman, Samuel Christian, 332

Haines, Reuben, 67, 68, 69, 75, 76

Hall, Lucy M., 352

Hammond, William, 254

Harper's Ferry, 230, 231

Harris, William Torrey, 367

Harte, Bret, 335

Harvard, Mass., 140–56

Harvard Divinity School, 55, 56, 189

Harvard University, 31, 105, 108, 117, 186, 232, 331, 362

Hawthorne, Julian, 237, 251, 270, 362

Hawthorne, Nathaniel, 52, 57, 114, 115, 116, 119, 126, 183, 184, 191–92, 214, 237, 241, 242, 266, 267, 299, 360;

attitude toward women, 238;
character and personality, 224,
237–39; death, 270
Hawthorne, Sophia Peabody, 60,
61, 85, 86, 115, 119, 191–92,
214, 237, 238, 239, 241, 246,
256, 257, 258, 262, 266, 267,
270, 290
Hawthorne, Una, 237, 239, 256
Hayne, Robert, 59
Healy, George, 309
Hecker, Isaac, 141–42, 146
Hedge, Frederick Henry, 54, 56,
205
Herbert, George, 243
Higginson, Thomas Wentworth,
65, 69, 175, 197, 225, 233, 362
Hildreth, Richard, 53, 210
"Hillside," 158–71, 191, 214
Holley, Sally, 333
Holmes, Oliver Wendell, 118,
226, 238, 350
Homeopathy, 332
Homer, 211
Hosmer, Cyrus, 119
Hosmer, Edmund, 113, 115, 151,
157
Hosmer, Henry, 119
Hosmer, Henry J., 351
Hosmer, John, 163
Hosmer, Laura Whiting, 350–51,
352
House of Refuge, New York City,
335
Howard Atheneum, 234
Howe, Julia Ward, 206, 230, 297,
334, 372
Howe, Samuel Gridley, 175, 206,
230
Hume, David, 31
Hunt, Harriet, 187

Jackson, Andrew, 68, 101, 121
Jackson, Helen Hunt, 318

James, Henry, 60, 115, 131, 246,
281, 350
James, Henry, Sr., 128, 223–24,
264, 281, 282, 290
Jenkins, Frederick (Shadrach),
191
Jesus Christ, 13, 27, 54, 55, 81,
85, 296
Johnson, Samuel, 31
Journal (Fox), 24, 111
Journal (Woolman), 24
Joy, Henrietta, 331

Kansas-Nebraska Act (1854), 196
Kant, Immanuel, 56, 205
Keys, John, 20–21

Lafayette, Marquis de, 2
Lafayette, S.S., 304
Lane, Charles, 129, 130, 135–36,
137, 138, 139, 140, 141, 142,
143, 145, 146, 147, 148, 151,
160–61, 163
Lane, William, 135, 139, 140,
145, 148
Larned, Samuel, 141, 142
Lawrence, Rhoda Ashley, 331,
332, 372
Lawson, Father, 104
Lazarus, Emma, 359
Leaves of Grass (Whitman), 211,
274
Lee, Robert E., 253
Leland, Charles Godfrey, 71
Leslie, Frank, 283, 290, 293, 340
Lewis, Dio, 241, 296, 333
Lewis, Elizabeth, 70–71, 77, 81,
336
Liberator, The (periodical), 59,
102, 232
Lily (periodical), 188
Lincoln, Abraham, 244, 256, 283
Little, Brown and Company, 4
Little Women, 1, 27, 196, 277,

Little Women (cont.)
    287, 295, 296, 299, 300, 301,
    302, 303, 306, 309, 310, 314,
    372; autobiographical nature
    of, 4–17; characters of, 4–6,
    10–12; father's influence on, 3,
    6, 16; popularity of, 4, 15–16,
    313–14
Livermore, Mary, 331, 332, 334
Loan of a Lover, The, 219
Locke, John, 25, 55, 56, 68
Longfellow, Henry Wadsworth,
    61, 194, 201, 293
Loring,A.K.,272,274,281,305,310
Loring, Ellis Gray, 59
Lovering, Alice, 228, 230
Lowell, James Russell, 174, 175,
    181, 185, 201, 233
Lundy, Benjamin, 58
Lyman, Theodore, 102, 103

Macbeth (Shakespeare), 205
McClellan, George B., 249, 253
McEllis, Charles, 197–98
Malta, S.S., 310
Malthus, Thomas, 31
Mann, Horace, 60, 194
Mann, Horace, Jr., 242
Mann, Mary Peabody, 60, 70, 85,
    94, 103, 115
Marble Faun, The (Hawthorne),
    238
Martineau, Harriet, 58, 63,
    65–66, 95, 103
Massachusetts General Hospital,
    30
*Massachusetts in the Woman Suffrage
    Movement* (Robinson), 359
May, Abbie, 336
May, Dorothy Sewall (LMA's
    grandmother), 30, 32–33
May, Joseph, 335

May, Joseph (LMA's grandfather),
    30–31, 41, 44, 45, 49, 53, 80,
    93–94, 97–98, 122, 181
May, Louisa. *See* Greele, Louisa
    May
May, Lucretia, 29, 33, 67, 72, 80,
    96, 104
May, Mary Ann Cary, 33, 41, 97
May, Samuel, 177, 178, 182, 185
May, Samuel Joseph (LMA's
    uncle), 34, 35, 59, 124, 189,
    197, 235; Abba's letters to, 52,
    67, 68, 72, 95–96, 121–22, 127,
    128, 147, 150, 167, 170, 181,
    192, 196, 201, 240; as
    abolitionist, 102, 187, 196; and
    Bronson Alcott's introduction
    to Abba, 28–33; death of, 310;
    death of son, 42; and financial
    aid to Alcotts, 139–40, 148,
    182, 214, 293–94; and Grimké
    sisters, 104; visits to, 44, 45,
    157, 193–94
May family, 2, 30, 35, 302, 346
Mazzini, Giuseppe, 184, 289
Melville, Herman, 238
Merry's Museum (periodical), 294,
    295
Metropolitan Museum of Art,
    333
Mexican War, 190
Milton, John, 81, 112, 183
Minot, George, 186
Missouri Compromise, 196
Montaigne, Michel E., 40
Moral Tales (Edgeworth), 25
Mott, Lucretia, 79, 187, 211
Moulton, Chandler, 335

National Philanthropist (periodical),
    58
National Women's Rights

Convention, Worcester, Mass. (1850), 187
Nature (Emerson), 119
New England Hospital for Women and Children, 298, 359
New Harmony, Indiana, 29, 61
Newton, Isaac, 68
New York City, 144, 211, 333–35, 336
New York Tribune, 184
Nieriker, Ernest, 347–48, 354, 355
Nieriker, Louisa May (LMA's niece), 353, 356, 357–58, 360–61, 362, 367–68
Nieriker, May Alcott (LMA's sister): birth, 122; death, 354; marriage, 347
Nightingale, Florence, 249, 252
Niles, Thomas, 294, 295, 296, 301, 302, 305, 310, 312, 313, 316, 317, 338, 339, 340, 342, 359, 370
Niles, William, 310
No Cross, No Crown (Penn), 24
Norton, Andrews, 56
Norton, Charles Eliot, 362

Old Manse, 119, 313
Old South Church, Boston, 30, 45, 194
Orchard House, Concord, Mass., 1–2, 3, 218, 237, 266, 290, 298, 307, 313, 314, 325, 327, 330, 337, 341, 346, 350, 367
Ossoli, Sarah Margaret Fuller, 57, 86–87, 95, 108, 111, 115, 124, 125, 126, 166, 169, 299, 360; death, 184–85
Otis, Harrison Gray, 59, 81
Owen, Robert Dale, 29, 61, 106

Palmer, Joseph, 140–41, 146, 150, 151
Papyrus Club, 350
Paradise Lost (Milton), 93
Parker, Lydia, 193, 205, 228, 282
Parker, Peter, 173
Parker, Theodore, 56, 66, 123, 175, 187, 192–93, 197, 205, 206, 209, 228, 230, 367
Parrish, Alexander, 52
Pattison, Edward and William, 21–22
Peabody, Elizabeth Palmer, 60–61, 70, 81, 82–83, 84–86, 87, 105, 108, 109, 115, 124, 169, 171, 173, 223, 231, 233, 234, 239, 245, 259, 290, 308, 312–13, 362, 372
Peabody, Nathaniel, 214
Penn, William, 24
Pestalozzi, Henry, 78
Peterson's Magazine, 190
Philadelphia, Pa., 67, 68, 70, 78, 94, 121, 335; first railroad, 75
Philadelphia Female Anti-Slavery Society, 79, 102
Phillips, John, 50
Phillips, Wendell, 187, 191, 236, 359
Pierce, Franklin, 198, 239, 270
Pilgrim's Progress, The (Bunyan), 5, 24, 25, 57, 99, 150, 182, 243
Pillsbury, Parker, 105, 146
"Pine Place," 68
Plato, 3, 58, 76, 78, 81, 162, 197, 349
Plotinus, 333
Poe, Edgar Allan, 225
Pope, Alexander, 30
Pythagoras, 3, 197
Pratt, Anna Alcott (LMA's sister): birth, 72; engagement and

Pratt *(cont.)*
  marriage, 219–20, 234–35
Pratt, John, 217, 218–19, 221,
  229, 234, 236, 245, 251, 266,
  277, 289, 290, 293, 303–4, 307,
  309–10, 347
Pratt, John Frederick, 266, 319
Pratt, Minot, 218, 309
Protestantism, 107
Pythagoras, 3

Quakers, 24
Quincy, Dorothy Sewall, 2
Quincy, Josiah, 50, 52, 186, 331
Quincy, Josiah, Jr., 174

Radical Club, Boston, 296, 297
Redpath, James, 263, 264, 269,
  270
Richardson, James, 186, 187
Riordan, Johnny, 118
Ripley, George, 57, 119, 126, 230
Rivals (Sheridan), 203
Roberts Brothers Publishing
  Company, 294, 298, 299, 300,
  301, 315, 316, 317, 340
Robie, Hannah, 176
Robinson, Harriet Janes, 359
Robinson, Susan, 112
Rosalind, 128
Rough Diamond, 203
Roxbury, Mass., 38
Russell, William, 60, 69–70

Saint Patrick's Cathedral, N.Y.,
  333
Sanborn, Franklin B., 192, 217,
  221, 222, 225, 230, 234,
  239–40, 241, 242, 263, 265,
  271, 319, 349, 360, 363, 367
Sanitary Commission, U.S., 249
Saturday Evening Gazette, 198, 200,
  203, 228

Scarlet Letter, The (Hawthorne),
  183, 194
Schiller, Johann Christoph
  Friedrich von, 183
Seth Thomas Clock factory,
  Plymouth, Conn., 21
Sewall, Deacon, 30
Sewall, Dorothy, 2
Sewall, Edmund, 117
Sewall, Ellen, 117
Sewall, Lucy, 284, 297, 298
Sewall, Samuel, 59, 171, 181,
  209, 297, 298, 303, 331
Shakers, Society of, 144, 151
Shakespeare, William, 81, 205
Shepard, Odell, 23, 137
Sheridan, Richard Brinsley,
  203
Slavery, 10, 32, 60, 101, 141,
  146, 168, 190, 206, 239;
  Underground Railroad, 168,
  191, 226
Smith, Adam, 25
Smith, William Henry, 200
Society in America (Martineau),
  95
Society of Calvinists, 28
Socrates, 27, 81
Sorosis, 334
Spindle Hill, Wolcott, Conn., 18,
  21, 23, 24, 163, 191, 204
Staël, Madame de, 183
Stanton, Elizabeth Cady, 188–89,
  297
Stearns, Eliza, 169, 170
Stearns, Mary, 271
Stevenson, Hannah, 251, 263
Still River Village, Harvard,
  Mass., 151, 155, 157
Stone, Lucy, 187, 211, 297, 327,
  331, 365
Stowe, Harriet Beecher, 183, 200,
  314

Sulie, John, 254
Sumner, Charles, 205–6, 241
Swedenborg, Emmanuel, 124
Syracuse, N.Y., 157, 203, 208, 241, 332

Temple School, Boston, 81–100, 113, 116, 122, 125, 137, 192, 218, 312; birthday celebration at, 93; decline of, 114–15
Thompson, George, 102
Thoreau, John, 116–17
Thoreau, Sophia, 117
Three Sisters, 21
Ticknor, Howard, 208
Ticknor, William D., 183, 270, 293
Town and Country Club, Boston, Mass., 175, 188
Tract Society, 317
Thoreau, Henry David: character and personality, 116–17; death, 246–49
Transcendentalism, 55, 56–58, 107, 128; women and, 66, 188, 220
Tubman, Harriet, 240
Turgenev, Ivan S., 115
Turner, Joseph M. W., 327
Turner, Nat, 102
Twenty-Eighth Congregational Society, 270

Union Hotel Hospital, Georgetown, 251, 252–53, 259, 262
Unitarianism, 54–56, 106, 107

Vaux, Roberts, 67, 78
Very, Jones, 104–6, 108, 175
Vicar of Wakefield, The (Goldsmith), 145

Virgil, 205
Voltaire, 55

Walden Pond, 7, 114, 164, 165, 226
Walpole, N.H., 170, 201, 202–17, 330, 337, 338
Ward, Julius, 349
Washington, D.C. 251–52
Waterbury, Conn., 21
Webster, Daniel, 51–52, 190, 191
Webster's Spelling Book, 19
Week on the Concord and Merrimac Rivers, A (Thoreau), 164
Weld, Anna Minot, 285, 286, 287, 288, 289, 290, 291
Weld, George, 286, 288
Weld, William, 284
Wells, Elizabeth, 170, 201, 203, 207, 310, 358
Wesselhoeft, Conrad, 363, 370, 373
Whitman, Alfred, 221–22
Whitman, Walt, 61, 252; character and personality, 211; personal appearance, 211, 360
Whittier, John Greenleaf, 102, 371
Wilkinson, Charlotte May, 332
Williams, Henry, 191
Willis, Benjamin, 200, 203, 209
Willis, Elizabeth, 200
Willis, Hamilton, 200, 201, 205, 210
Willis, Llewellyn, 156, 159, 189
Windship, Charles, 200, 210, 234
Windship, Warren, 38
Winslow, John, 255, 257
Wisniewski, Ladislas, 286–87, 288, 289
Wolcott, Conn., 18, 25, 201, 316
Wollstonecraft, Mary, 350

Woman in the Nineteenth Century (Fuller), 185

Woman's Central Association of Relief, 249

Woman's Congress, Syracuse, N.Y. (1876), 332–33

Woman's Journal, 327, 330, 331, 352, 355, 358, 359, 365

Women: dress of, 188–89, 297; education of, 29; status of, 7, 64–67. *See also* Feminism

Wood, Abram, 141, 146

Woodhull and Claflin's Weekly, 211

Woodnotes (Emerson), 198

Woolman, John 24

Wordsworth, William, 25, 109, 111

Workingmen's party, 106

Works of Louisa May Alcott: *Aunt Jo's Scrapbook,* 313; "Behind a Mask," 290–92; "Bianca," 174; "Captive of Castile, The," 174; "Chimney Corner, The," 283; *Christmas Elves, The,* 203, 210; *Eight Cousins,* 327, 328–29, 338; *Flower Fables,* 198–200, 229, 264; *Genesis,* 364; "Greek Slave, The," 174; "Happy Women," 296; *Hospital Sketches,* 254, 263–65, 269, 317; "How I Went Out to Service," 187; *Jack and Jill,* 350, 353, 356–57; *Jo's Boys,* 358, 369, 370–72; "Lay of the Golden Goose, The," 307; *Little Men,* 302–3, 309, 310–12, 313, 370; "Living in an Omnibus," 294; "Love and Self-Love," 228–29, 233, 234;

Lulu's Library, 370; "Marble Woman, or The Mysterious Model, A," 282–83; "Modern Cinderella, A," 234, 241; "Modern Mephistopheles, A," 292, 341–42, 343; *Moods,* 8, 16, 240, 242–43, 247, 264, 265, 269, 270, 272, 274–81, 289, 295, 300, 305–6, 308, 310, 320, 322, 323, 336, 372; *Nat Bachelor's Pleasure Trip,* 200, 234; "Norna; or The Witches Curse," 174; *Old Fashioned Girl, An,* 301–2, 303; "Olive Leaf, The," 178; "Pauline's Passion and Punishment," 259–61; poems, 119–20, 145, 147, 149–50, 156, 162, 164, 190, 232, 250, 262–63, 375; *"Rival Prima Donnas, The,"* 198, 200, 210; *Rose in Bloom,* 185, 338, 339–40; *Shawl Straps,* 314, 315, 316, 317; *Success,* 242; "Sunlight," 190; "Thoreau's Flute," 262–63; "To the First Robin," 121–22; *Under the Lilies,* 343; "Unloved Wife, The," 174; "V. V., or Plots and Counterplots," 272–74; *Work,* 193, 240, 265, 282, 317, 320–24. *See also Little Women*

Wright, Frances, 61–62

Wright, Henry, 129, 130, 136

Yale University, 19, 21

Zakrzewska, Marie, 298